THE ANGOLA HORROR

━━ The ━━

ANGOLA HORROR

THE 1867 TRAIN WRECK

THAT SHOCKED THE NATION

AND TRANSFORMED

AMERICAN RAILROADS

CHARITY VOGEL

CORNELL UNIVERSITY PRESS · ITHACA AND LONDON

First published 2013 by Cornell University Press
Printed in the United States of America

Design by Kate Nichols

Library of Congress Cataloging-in-Publication Data

Vogel, Charity Ann, author.
    The Angola Horror : the 1867 train wreck that shocked the nation and transformed American railroads / Charity Vogel.
        pages cm
    Includes bibliographical references and index.
    ISBN 978-0-8014-4908-6 (cloth : alk. paper)
    1. Railroad accidents—New York (State)—Angola. I. Title.
    HE1781.A54V64   2013
    363.12'20974796—dc23   2013002291

Cornell University Press strives to use environmentally responsible suppliers and materials to the fullest extent possible in the publishing of its books. Such materials include vegetable-based, low-VOC inks and acid-free papers that are recycled, totally chlorine-free, or partly composed of nonwood fibers. For further information, visit our website at www.cornellpress.cornell.edu.

Cloth printing   10 9 8 7 6 5 4 3 2 1

TO MY PARENTS,

Michael and Stasia, who love words and ideas.

TO MY DAUGHTERS,

Mercy and Annabel, who love good stories.

AND, MOST OF ALL, TO MY HUSBAND,

Todd Joseph, who always knew, and who makes me better.

Ad majorem Dei gloriam

Contents

Cast of Characters

IN ANGOLA

Henry Bundy—Owner of Angola's chief wood and flour mill, located on Big Sister Creek

Dr. Romaine J. Curtiss—Angola's charismatic young doctor who had served as an assistant ship's surgeon during the Civil War

Frank E. Griffith—Civil War veteran and family man who lived near Big Sister Creek

Thankful Griffith—Wife of Frank E. Griffith

James Mahar—Switchman for the Buffalo and Erie Railroad in Angola

John Martin—Owner of Angola's tin shop

J. M. Newton—Angola's station agent for the Buffalo and Erie Railroad

Huldah Southwick—Wife of Josiah Southwick and mistress of a brick home situated near Big Sister Creek

Josiah Southwick—Prosperous and well-respected Quaker farmer who served as justice of the peace in Angola

Alanson Wilcox—Angola wood dealer and brother of Cyrus Wilcox

Cyrus Wilcox—Owner of a boot shop in Angola's business district and brother of Alanson Wilcox

ON THE TRAIN—CREW

Charles Carscadin—Longtime railroad man and engineer on the New York Express

Charles Newton—Greenhorn fireman on the New York Express

Benjamin F. Sherman—Conductor of the New York Express and a veteran trainman with fourteen years' experience on the railroads of New York State

Gilbert W. Smith—Forward brakeman on the New York Express

John Vanderburg—Rear brakeman on the New York Express

James A. Woods—Baggage man on the New York Express

ON THE TRAIN—PASSENGERS

In the last car

Benjamin C. Aikin—Husband and father from Hydetown, Pennsylvania, traveling to visit one of his grown children

John W. Chapman—Successful attorney from Massachusetts about to marry Clara Green, a woman connected to an infamous murder case

Eliakim B. Forbush—Patent attorney returning home to Buffalo after winning a case in Cincinnati

Eunice Bellows Fuller—Former teacher and wife of Jasper Fuller of Spartansburg, Pennsylvania, accompanying her husband to Buffalo

Jasper L. Fuller—Resident of Spartansburg, Pennsylvania, on his way to Buffalo to buy goods for a store

Zachariah Hubbard—Canadian carpenter traveling from Westfield, New York, toward his home in Ontario to join his family

Morgan Kedzie—Eighteen-year-old son of a Rochester, New York, family returning home for Christmas after a trip to Iowa

Abbie Gustie Kent—Bride from Grand Island, New York, on a honeymoon trip

Granger D. Kent—Groom from Grand Island, New York, on a honeymoon trip

Joseph Stocking Lewis—Twenty-three-year-old graduate of Williams College headed toward his family in Batavia, New York

Charles Lobdell—Newspaper editor traveling from La Crosse, Wisconsin, to his Christmas Day wedding in Connecticut

J. Alexander Marten—Assistant city engineer in Erie, Pennsylvania, traveling with his friends for pleasure and to visit his ailing mother in Vermont for the holidays

Isadore Mayer—Traveling agent of the famous dramatic actress Adelaide Ristori

Edward T. Metcalf—Railroad clerk from Erie, Pennsylvania, taking a holiday pleasure trip with friends

Arila Nichols—Wife of Norman Nichols and mother of a young daughter, traveling east with her husband for work

Norman Nichols—Resident of Ashtabula County, Ohio, traveling east with his wife, Arila, to find work

Elam Porter—Lawyer traveling from Cincinnati, Ohio, toward his wedding in Massachusetts

Ammon H. Spier—Young husband and father from North East, Pennsylvania

Stephen W. Steward—President of a bank in Corry, Pennsylvania, and director of a small railroad in rural New York and Pennsylvania

Amos H. Thomas—Coal dealer from Utica, New York, on his way home with his wife, Mary

Mary Thomas—Wife of Amos H. Thomas of Utica, traveling home with her husband

William W. Towner—Surveyor from Erie, Pennsylvania, taking a holiday pleasure trip with friends

In the second-to-last car

Ira Babcock—Resident of Syracuse, New York, traveling with his wife, Lydia

Lydia Babcock—Woman from Syracuse, New York, traveling with her husband, Ira

Anna Chadeayne—Thirteen-year-old daughter of Mary and Daniel Chadeayne

Carry Chadeayne—Three-year-old daughter of Mary and Daniel Chadeayne

Mary Chadeayne—Mother traveling with two daughters, Anna and Carry; her husband, Daniel, was in Titusville, Pennsylvania

Robert J. Dickson—Buffalo resident and son of a prosperous Lake Erie ship captain who was traveling with a friend and colleague, J. Frank Walker

Alexander E. Fisher—Minnesota resident and owner of a stoneworks on his way to be married in Madrid, New York, over the Christmas holiday

Emma Hurlburt Fisher—Minnesota mother accompanying her brother-in-law Alexander to his Christmas wedding in New York State

Minnie Fisher—Baby of less than a year old carried in the arms of her mother, Emma Hurlburt Fisher of Minnesota

Frances M. Gale—Daughter of Lydia M. Strong, recently widowed by the death of her physician husband; traveling with her child back to Buffalo

Josiah P. Hayward—Twenty-four-year-old station agent for the Buffalo and Erie Railroad in State Line on the Pennsylvania–New York border; husband of Anna Shaw Hayward

Christiana Gates Lang—Widow traveling from Minnesota to Vermont to begin a new life with her two surviving children

James Lang—Twelve-year-old son of Christiana Lang

Mary Lang—Ten-year-old daughter of Christiana Lang

William H. Ross—Civil War veteran from North East, Pennsylvania

Lydia M. Strong—Wife of a Buffalo jeweler and sister-in-law of Dr. Orin C. Payne of Fredonia, New York; traveling with her daughter, Frances M. Gale, back to Buffalo following the funeral of Frances's husband

Lizzie D. Thompson—Sister of Simeon Thompson of Worcester, Massachusetts

Simeon Thompson—News dealer from Worcester, Massachusetts, planning to relocate with his sister Lizzie to the West

J. Frank Walker—Son of a prominent Buffalo jeweler traveling with his friend and colleague Robert J. Dickson

Elsewhere on the train

Benjamin F. Betts—Wood dealer from Tonawanda, New York, returning home to his family

Dr. Frederick F. Hoyer—Physician from Tonawanda, New York, and neighbor of Benjamin F. Betts

IN BUFFALO

Robert N. Brown—Superintendent of the Buffalo and Erie Railroad

John Desmond—Assistant superintendent of the Buffalo and Erie Railroad

Peter Emslie—Chief engineer of the Buffalo and Erie Railroad

William G. Fargo—Founder of the Wells, Fargo and American Express companies in Buffalo, New York, and codirector with Stephen W. Steward of a small upstate New York–Pennsylvania railroad

Levi Jerome—Baggage master for the Buffalo and Erie Railroad in the Exchange Street depot

Rev. John Chase Lord—Pastor of one of the city's largest and most prominent churches, Central Presbyterian

J. Harrison Mills—Civil War veteran and budding artist interested in newspaper journalism

John Nicholson—Captain with the Niagara Frontier Police

Dr. J. I. Richards—City coroner

Julius Walker—Well-to-do city businessman and father of J. Frank Walker

William Williams—President of the Buffalo and Erie Railroad

IN CLEVELAND

John Davison Rockefeller—Twenty-eight-year-old businessman with offices in New York City and Cleveland and a modest home on Cheshire Street in Cleveland

Laura Celestia Spelman Rockefeller—Wife of John D. Rockefeller

ELSEWHERE

Zuleann P. Aikin—Wife of Benjamin C. Aikin of Hydetown, Pennsylvania

Daniel Chadeayne—Family man in Titusville, Pennsylvania, whose wife and daughters were on board the New York Express

Clara Green—Fiancée of John W. Chapman in Massachusetts and former wife of the infamous Malden murderer Edward W. Green

William Green—Seventeen-year-old youth who claimed to have narrowly missed boarding the New York Express in Dunkirk

Andrew Fisher—Husband of Emma Fisher and father of Minnie Fisher in Owatonna, Minnesota

Anna Shaw Hayward—Young wife of Josiah P. Hayward, Buffalo and Erie station agent in State Line, Pennsylvania

Ellen McAndrews Hubbard—Wife of Canadian carpenter Zachariah Hubbard and mother of three children

Marcus "Brick" Pomeroy—Editor at the La Crosse, Wisconsin, newspaper with Charles Lobdell

George Westinghouse Jr.—Twenty-one-year-old mechanic and Civil War veteran living in Schenectady, New York

THE ANGOLA HORROR

America on the Rails

You can not tell what may happen when you go traveling
on a train. It is not like starting out all together in a wagon.

LAURA INGALLS WILDER,
By the Shores of Silver Lake

NGOLA SHOOK the nation.

The derailment of an express train on December 18, 1867, in the little
upstate New York village, an event in which about fifty people died—the
number would never be known for certain—was so grisly a scene that it became branded in the national imagination as "the Horror." No other words
were necessary.

Nearly ten years later, the Angola wreck retained its powerful place in
the American mind. When a train careened off a bridge in Ashtabula, Ohio,
in 1876, the engineer of the Pacific Express was said to have summoned up
the previous disaster as the only way to understand the new incident. Thrown
out of the window of his locomotive, the Columbia, as it tumbled into the
Ashtabula River, the engineer was reported by his fellow trainmen to have
muttered three words as he was pulled from a snow bank in a badly injured
state: "Another Angola Horror."[1]

That might have happened. Then again, perhaps those words were a dramatic twist inserted by a newspaper reporter or editor in 1876. The newspaper industry—like journalism itself—was still taking shape in the era of the
Angola wreck and developing into the form we know today. Raw, direct-from-
the-scene coverage of news, and especially of tragedy, was prized enough that
editors might take liberties with sequences of events, with the precise wording
of quotations, with death tolls, so as to deliver to readers that unforgetta-
ble first-person experience. The dispatches and illustrations from Angola and

Buffalo in December 1867, which would appear in the nation's newspapers and magazines in the days and weeks to come, were maximized to provide a visceral sense of the devastating accident. Some audiences would learn of the wreck right away. Others would take weeks to hear of it. Mistakes would be made in the reporting of the wreck, and corrected—or not. In all cases, the brutality of Angola would be laid bare before the eyes of thousands of people, in gritty news accounts and illustrations. "Slaughter," the headlines would read. "Horror," they called it. One popular magazine with a national circulation ran a sketch of the dead victims of Angola, charred, mostly legless and armless, in a large-size picture on its front page.

That was one important reason the memory of Angola haunted the nation a decade later. The day's newspapers, and its oft-sensationalistic journalists, played a significant role in turning the scenes at Angola into indelible images and phrases. Extensive coverage was devoted to the wreck's grisliest details. Lengthy stories filled local newspapers and magazines from coast to coast for weeks in December 1867 and January 1868, and illustrations of scenes of the wreck—sparing no detail—appeared in such widely read national publications as *Frank Leslie's Illustrated Newspaper* and *Harper's* and *Kelley's* magazines. The wreck was described in newspapers in cities as far away as London. "There have been as many persons killed in a Railway Accident before," the *Times* of London observed shortly after the disaster, "but seldom have so many ghastly and appalling incidents been crowded into a catastrophe of the kind as at Angola."[2]

But newspapers could not manufacture the level of interest that Angola commanded. The timing of the wreck at Big Sister Creek, not far from Lake Erie, caught many Americans at a moment in which they were especially attuned to disaster, and keenly aware of the fragility of life. Angola happened just two and a half years after the end of the Civil War—a time in which people were readjusting to peacetime and civilian life, imagining themselves once again secure. Major railroad accidents of the postwar period shattered this uncertain, nascent sense of security. The Angola wreck showed that the threat of unexpected, large-scale slaughter was powerful, pervasive, and perhaps unmanageable. The fact that so many of the victims' corpses could not be identified—nineteen, according to the railroad, although the actual number was likely higher—added an ugly twist to this sense of vulnerability, and surely reawakened for many painful memories of the decimation of war. Two years after the conclusion of the Civil War, it was hardly as if Americans needed the reminder. The war, lasting from 1861 to 1865, had taken the lives of some 750,000 soldiers—or about one in ten white men of military age in 1860.[3] The war came as a tidal crest of death in a century brimming with it. Infant mortality was high, many children died of illnesses and injuries, old people died of sicknesses and complaints that today can be cured with a trip to the drugstore. To read a newspaper from the mid-nineteenth century is to be plunged into a world where sudden death was commonplace. Scalding, scarlet fever, horse kicks, childbirth, buggy accidents, seizures, falls, drowning, smallpox—notices of such deaths cluster thickly in the pages of newspapers, and many more were so routine as to go unmentioned.

Set into this culture rife with mortality, the anticipation of—and the witnessing to—horrific railroad wrecks gave Americans in the late 1860s another reason to feel less than safe. This sense of insecurity was magnified by the fact that rail travel was becoming increasingly common for men and women across the country.

Rail lines had been in operation for more than thirty years by the time of the Angola disaster. People from all over the country had traveled on railroads and become used to the experience. Railroads had reached into many of the settled areas of the country: by 1860, the nation's 30,626 miles of track had pushed into thirty-one states and had extended almost as far as the edge of the westward frontier.[4] A glimpse at the number and variety of Angola's victims bears this fact out: adding the injured to the killed, the disaster affected 100 or more individuals, hailing from thirteen states and two countries, and representing a wide variety of social classes and professions—from bank presidents and lawyers, to shopkeepers and clerks, to housewives and the unemployed. It was a time in which passenger trains had become "culturally and psychically assimilated," as historian Wolfgang Schivelbusch has put it, by most of the public.[5] As for that train-riding public, it now included many women, children, and elderly people, in addition to the groups of youthful male travelers who had predominantly used the lines before the Civil War. Railroad accidents, when they occurred, now increasingly struck at populations Victorian-era society considered the most vulnerable. Increased mobility meant increased exposure to injury and death on the part of women, children, and elderly citizens who, whether at home or on the road, were supposed to be protected by *somebody:* if not a male family member, then an institution, a community, or a railroad company. A wreck in which a baby or virginal young woman was injured or killed was more than a shame; it was a breach of social trust. That happened at Angola, and many of those people who witnessed it— rescuers, other passengers, onlookers—were never the same afterward.

These accidents not only hurt vulnerable classes of people, but did so in ways that were unseemly by being thoroughly public. To die or be badly injured in a railway wreck in the post–Civil War period was to have your name and identity exposed in the nation's press—not once, but over and over again. People read of the corpses at Angola and learned that the clothes—indeed, all the clues to gender and station in life—of some of the victims had been burned wholly away. For women, especially, this was a sensation of exposure and violation that was frightening and new. The death of a young woman in a railroad accident—away from home, perhaps alone, at times in gruesome circumstances that often left the remains difficult to recognize—was about as far as it was possible to get from the sort of "good death" in the confines of the household that was valued in the decades both before and right after the Civil War. For women and children this public nature of death on the rails was a shocking new reality, and a troubling sign of what modernity might mean for them. "A torn glove there!" ran one poem, written after the crash, about a maidenly young woman supposedly killed in the Angola accident. "In it still lingers, the shape of the fingers; / That some one has pressed, may be, and caressed, / So slender and fair."[6] Daniel Chadeayne, whose wife and daughters were on the train that wrecked at Angola, wrote grimly from the scene of the accident to friends in Titusville, Pennsylvania, that he was particularly thankful that his female relations had "escaped so well out of such a general slaughter."[7]

The Angola Horror also commanded enormous public attention because the wreck spoke directly to the ways in which Americans of the period viewed the railroads. Since the 1830s, men and women across the country had been dazzled by the success and expansion of the nation's network of railways. At the same time, there was a realization that the railroads meant some aspect of danger, along with the mobility, opportunity, and excitement that the rail lines surely provided. As trains became more useful they ceased to be the light, slow-moving, insubstantial carriages that they had been in the early days of railroading in the country—a time in which a typical journey might be a pleasure excursion lasting only a few miles. Passengers were now traveling faster, over hundreds of miles of track, and in bigger groups on larger cars pulled by more massive locomotives. By the middle of the century, the reach and power of these new sorts of railroads affected people beyond those who were riding as passengers. Railroads were shaping the communities, small and large, that they passed through along their routes. Many of these ripple effects were positive; but there were negative ones, as well. There was, for instance, a dawning realization that the railroads could be vectors that allowed for the faster spread of contagious illness and disease, such as yellow fever, among other social ills.[8] Still, most of the risk of the railroads fell to those riding the trains. The degree to which railroad travel had become more convenient and popular coincided with the extent to which, under hazardous conditions or with poor operation, these faster and heavier trains could be vehicles for brutal accidents. In the late 1860s, the realization of that fact was growing, and this created a potent combination of allure and fear where the fledgling railroads were concerned. When railway accidents happened, they "reawaken[ed] the memory of the forgotten danger and the potential violence" that the trains represented.[9] Just so, in the wreck at Big Sister Creek in Angola, a truss bridge adjacent to the Angola railroad station some twenty miles southwest of Buffalo, Americans glimpsed with frightful clarity just what could happen when the technological and human frailties of this system of bigger, faster, heavier trains came to light.

Much had changed about the railroads, over the years. But some important factors had not. Decades after those first historic, short-duration rides for passengers, many railroad trips still entailed anxiety-provoking sensations and experiences. And those anxieties were well founded. Wax candles and kerosene lamps for illumination, coal- and wood-burning stoves for heating cars, unreliable signaling mechanisms, flawed and unpredictable iron rails and switches, outdated link-and-pin couplers—all of these were in everyday use on railroads in the United States in the 1860s, and most would remain so for years. George Westinghouse Jr., a young man of twenty-one living in Schenectady, New York, in 1867, had not yet invented the air brake that would revolutionize the production of locomotives and cars by making them capable of safe and efficient stops controlled from the front of the train. Rudimentary hand brakes, operated by brakemen laboring in difficult conditions on the tops and end platforms of cars, still were uniformly used.

There was more. Trainmen typically had to meet no physical or intellectual criteria for employment. There were generally no tests, not even for hearing or the ability to discern one color from another (two fitness tests that would be phased in for the first time on American railroads in the 1870s and 1880s).[10] Bridges on the railway routes, often poorly built and infrequently maintained, were so nerve-wracking in some cases that they were, in the words of Charles Dickens, "most agreeable when passed."[11] Passenger cars had little in the way of shock absorbers, and jolted and rattled along the rails so jarringly that doctors warned passengers about the damage they might do themselves with "railway spine." As for car couplers, Ezra Miller had patented an automatic device in 1863 to replace the primitive link-and-pin system in use at the time, but many railroads did not take it up until the 1870s. Even then, many railroads opted for their own coupling systems, which led to an unsafe situation lasting for decades in which no coupler uniformity existed, meaning that connections between cars could be too loose, too tight, or otherwise faulty and unreliable.[12] As a result, the death toll for employees as well as passengers was high. "All through my employment as a switchman," wrote one railroader who worked coupling trains in this period, "[my sister] kept one clean sheet for the express purpose of wrapping up my mangled remains."[13]

In addition to this risky hodgepodge of faulty technology and poor regulation, American trains operated under a fractured system of local times, without the structure and reliability of a national railroad standard time. Trains often passed through regions with multiple differing local times, especially as railroad networks matured and routes grew longer. This led to problems for people trying to track trains or plan their own travel. And because these discrepancies occurred over routes on which trains often still shared single-track lines and limited turnouts and sidings, miscommunications and misunderstandings about the timing of arrivals and departures could lead to missed connections or much worse—including head-on collisions, called "meets," as well as the deadly telescoping of trains by other trains.

Reading about the events at Angola and seeing artists' renderings of the scenes in Big Sister Creek both inspired and validated the public's fears about how wrecks on the roads could play out for unsuspecting men, women, and children. Their anxieties ranged from the still-felt general uneasiness instilled by four years of war to the specific concern for the well-being of family members who boarded trains for business trips or family visits. In the popular art and literature of the period, their nervous anticipations were distilled, often to stunning effect. One such illustration, "The Horrors of Travel," appeared in *Harper's Weekly* magazine in September 1865, two years before the wreck at Angola. It depicted an onrushing locomotive bearing down upon fleeing passengers—men,

In illustrations published in popular periodicals, Americans in the mid-1800s were warned of the dangers inherent in railway travel. This illustration, called "The Horrors of Travel," appeared in *Harper's Weekly* magazine just months after the end of the Civil War. It depicted a specter-like figure of Death, riding a locomotive, chasing down innocent men and women. From *Harper's Weekly*, September 23, 1865.

young women, babies—while carrying a frightful figure, a ghoul-like specter of death, garbed in tattered robes, brandishing a sharpened scythe.[14]

Such images were both a cause of and a response to the prevailing cultural climate of uncertainty about rail travel. Accompanying this image in *Harper's,* an editorial summed up the national mood. "During the present year Death appears to have set his mark upon the traveler," it stated. "There has come to be a general feeling of insecurity and distrust, and every man or woman who steps out of a railway car or steamboat at the termination of their journey unhurt does so with a feeling of sensible relief."[15] By the 1870s, Walt Whitman would link the thrill and the nerve-wracking power of railroads together in poetry, writing of the locomotive's "black cylindric body, golden brass and silvery steel" but also the "dense and murky clouds out-belching from thy smoke-stack."[16] Whitman made it clear that the locomotive had irrevocably changed the American landscape, in ways that were still being seen, felt, and measured. In this vein, in 1866, Louisa May Alcott turned the devastation of a train wreck into a plot device in *Behind a Mask,* a novella of deception and mistaken identity. In Alcott's story, the protagonist, Jean Muir, receives news that a man important to her has been killed in a railroad smash-up. "The poor young gentleman is so wet, and crushed, and torn, no one would know him," she is informed, "except for the uniform, and the white hand with the ring on it."[17] In an echo of the fiction, words such as these spoken by a messenger to Muir would appear in newspapers across the country after Angola, as readers absorbed bulletins from Buffalo and Big Sister Creek in which descriptions of artifacts were published in an effort to match victims with their identities. The *Buffalo Post* of December 23, 1867, listed dozens of such items, from the lofty to the mundane, found among the ashes and wreckage in the creek bed after the disaster. Examples included a pair of silver ice-skates, a small gold ladies' watch "without any inscription," the metal end-cap of a surveyor's staff that had been carried aboard the train by a young engineer from Buffalo, and a bunch of keys, melted to a lump, but yet intact enough to see that "several of the keys [were] numbered 24."[18] Each of the items in the newspaper listings was a portrait of a life stopped abruptly. Each struck chords in the hearts of men and women who read such accounts with emotions of concern and fear, looking for answers.

And so, for decades after 1867, Angola served as a watchword that conveyed to men and women the danger and unpredictability that came with the purchase of every train ticket.

BY THE CLOSE of the nineteenth century, the Angola derailment ranked with a small handful of others—Ashtabula (1876), Camp Hill (1856), Chatsworth

(1887)—as one of the worst railroad wrecks the nation had seen. That assessment has been corroborated in more recent times. Robert C. Reed, a railroad disaster historian of the mid-twentieth century, ranked Angola and Ashtabula as the two "most notorious railroad disasters" in the country's history.[19] Robert B. Shaw, another historian of train wrecks in America, wondered at the peculiar hold Angola exerted over the nation's collective consciousness. "For some reasons not entirely clear," Shaw wrote, "this accident secured a particularly strong hold upon the public imagination of that generation."[20] This was true despite the fact that Angola, deadly as it was, had claimed fewer total victims than other major wrecks.[21]

The generation of Americans that witnessed the Horror—embarking on the work of Reconstruction; only dimly anticipating the struggles between capital and labor and between industrial growth and regulation that would transpire in and through the Gilded Age and Progressive Era—bequeathed the facts of Angola, but not the vibrancy of its memory. The story faded in the late nineteenth century and first decades of the twentieth. While the journal and newspaper accounts endured, the oral history of the wreck fell out of currency, not just in the nation but in the region of western New York where the wreck had happened.

Now, in some ways, the incident at Big Sister Creek feels remote from our modern world. Technology, a fact of modern life with which people in the nineteenth century were just becoming acquainted, surrounds us in our daily lives in the twenty-first. Details of the story might make it seem antique: the Victorian-era clothes the women wore, the car stoves at which the children warmed their hands, the jobs the men, just getting over the trauma of the Civil War, were looking forward to filling. A survey of these features could suggest a period drama, glimpsed vaguely through one of the tiny peephole windows that served as viewing stations on early trains. These elements can combine to create a sense that the narrative of Angola is a story of time gone by.

But that conclusion deserves reconsideration. We know that, in witnessing the Angola Horror, men and women in the nineteenth century found themselves moved, in profound and telling ways. The force of the experience of Angola—whether that of a rescuer looking for survivors on the evening of the wreck or a reader of newspapers in a distant city—was strong, and, as noted earlier, that strength was not by any means the simple result of sensational journalism. People of the 1860s knew what fear and powerlessness felt like, and Angola became for them a talisman of the uneasy tension they lived with. We may be more used to the experience of high-speed transportation than the men and women aboard the New York Express, but we know some of their uneasiness. We know what it feels like to ponder the meaning of an individual life in the face of larger social, technological, and economic changes—changes that can seem to be out of the control of any individual or community.

In this way, the heated, sometimes sensationalistic journalists of the Angola period did us more of a favor than we might have imagined. They brought characters to life—real people that we can relate to, and empathize with, today. Reading the news accounts of the wreck and studying the illustrations that appeared on full pages in the magazines that circulated around the country, we meet the men and women that were swept up in the events of December 18, 1867. Among the passengers, heroes, victims, and onlookers were Dr. Romaine J. Curtiss, the brilliant and troubled military surgeon, returned too soon to scenes of carnage and death; conductor Benjamin F. Sherman, an experienced railroader who did his best to fulfill his duties in dire circumstances; the young Westinghouse, pondering the mysteries inherent in stopping thousands of pounds of racing metal on a thin iron track; bright men like Elam Porter and Joseph Stocking Lewis, college graduates embarking on promising careers; average women like Christiana Gates Lang and Emma Hurlburt Fisher, who would have remained anonymous all their lives, perhaps, had they not been caught up in this terrible event. Angola is their story. By considering first-person perspectives on the events of 1867, we are given the chance to engage with the worries, fears, hopes, and ambitions that average Americans felt and thought about so soon after the nation's epic war. The two hundred or so passengers riding the train that cold December day did not consider themselves to be representative—yet the life stories that brought them to that point offer striking insights into the time and place in which they lived. By looking at the Angola Horror, unquestionably a pivotal moment in American railroad history, from the perspectives of these people, we can explore the important legacies of this wreck from the standpoint of the history of the post–Civil War period.

Angola also speaks to us directly as a story of average people caught up in a terrific and unstoppable event. It offers insight into what it is like for everyday people to become victims of the technologies with which they live—technologies they may not fully understand or know how to control. And this narrative addresses how the media both expresses and creates our experience, be it firsthand or as an observer at a distance. Further, the story of the Angola Horror calls attention to how and what individuals and communities remember and memorialize, and what they come to forget.

For some 140 years, the victims of the Angola wreck never received a monument or memorial. That fact alone, set alongside the importance of the wreck in its own time, is worth thinking about.

"ANOTHER ANGOLA," the engineer at Ashtabula had mourned. But Ashtabula wasn't another Angola—it was a tragedy of its own. What follows is the story of the wreck that took place near the shores of Lake Erie, where the Buffalo and Erie Railroad passed through the small community of Angola, New York, on December 18, 1867.

There had been carnage on the rails between Camp Hill and Fort Washington, Pennsylvania, and in time disaster would strike the roads at Ashtabula, Ohio, and Chatsworth, Illinois. The stories of those events have been told, and surely will be told again. This book is the first recounting of what happened that day, and the days that followed, at Angola.

CHAPTER 1

Troubled Sleep

THEY WERE DREAMING.

The train moved along, a spot of color in the dull, snow-blanketed landscape of mid-December, a rush of sound in the silent womb of winter in western New York. As it swayed forward, rumbling at speeds approaching thirty miles an hour over the ice-crusted tracks toward the city more than twenty miles away, the heads of its two hundred passengers were likely filled with memories of what they had left behind, and visions of what they were journeying toward. Some surely dreamed of love. Some, of business. Some perhaps let their thoughts stray to the holiday season, Christmas and New Year's, that lay just a week in the future. Many of them were traveling long distances—the railroads let them do that now, even women and children, in ways that hadn't been possible a generation or two before. They were pioneers, hesitant and ambivalent ones in some ways, but pioneers nonetheless.

One of them wished he could leave his dreams behind.

Sitting in his upholstered seat in the second-to-last car of the train, Josiah P. Hayward no doubt felt apprehensive, as did other passengers around him. Unlike those passengers, however, some of whom might still be relatively new to the experience of train journeying, Hayward was used to railroad travel; it was part of his job. But he was more tense than usual this weekday afternoon—and, as a result, he had taken a few unaccustomed precautions.

Hayward's fears had originated in a nightmare he had suffered six months earlier. The twenty-four-year-old Pennsylvanian, who worked as a station agent for the Buffalo and Erie Railroad in State Line, a village on the New York–Pennsylvania border, had been asleep in bed next to his wife of two years, Anna Shaw Hayward, that night in June. As he slept, his mind filled with fearsome images.[1] In his dream, Hayward saw himself standing in an unfamiliar place—a desert. Just as he began to examine his surroundings, Hayward heard a tremendous noise behind him: a "terrific crash," as if the gates of hell themselves had been unlocked. He turned to look, and found himself confronted with a piercingly bright light, so strong that it seemed "to reach to the very heavens."[2] What Hayward heard next was worse: screams. Dozens of them, mounting to the skies, pleading for relief—a wave of sound that was heartbreaking in its hopelessness. Hayward felt terrified; he then looked around and saw, to his surprise, a man standing nearby who was dressed as a monk.

"Where do the screams come from?" Hayward, in his dream, heard himself ask.

"From Hell," the monk answered.

"What does it mean?" he persisted.

"It means," the monk responded, "you must instantly die."[3]

Struggling awake, Hayward found himself bartering with the dream-monk in his state of semiconsciousness. More time, he begged. The monk considered, then told him he might have six months more before the dream would come to pass. At that moment, Hayward was shaken awake by Anna, who told him he had been thrashing wildly in his sleep. The death dream made a strong impression on both husband and wife.[4] Hayward found himself returning to the episode often in conversation with friends and family, not just for days or weeks, but for months afterward. It would later become a tidbit seized upon by the day's sensation-seeking journalists.

It wasn't like Josiah Hayward to feel so uncertain. He was the son of a farming family in the small community of North East, Pennsylvania, which had done well on the land; the Haywards had owned $3,200 in real estate and property by the Civil War. Young Josiah had been raised in an environment of practicality and common sense. As an employee of the Buffalo and Erie Railroad, he had been placed in a position of trust and responsibility.

After the Civil War ended, Hayward had chosen the railroads for a career because he had seen their potential. Thousands of young men his age had done the same thing, looking to the railroads as a means to achieve success and status—far more attractive than the family farm for a good livelihood. The post–Civil War period had, in fact, been something of a soot-scented gold rush; by 1870, more American men would be working for the country's railroads than in any other occupation.[5] By 1900, railroads and industries supporting their operation, from locomotive manufacturers to producers of wooden ties, would employ "at least one-tenth of the adult population of [the] country."[6] Hayward, working for the Buffalo and Erie Railroad in that winter of 1867, was on the leading edge of that economic and cultural development.

A responsible employee, Hayward tried to shake the effects of his vision, sticking to his daily routine and focusing on his job. When early on a mid-December afternoon it became clear that he would need to take a quick trip to Buffalo by train, he boarded the chuffing cars that stood waiting in the State Line station. But Hayward did not climb aboard the Buffalo and Erie's New York Express without lingering trepidation.

Perhaps in grim irony, perhaps in search of a good-luck token with which to counteract any bad fortune that awaited him—or perhaps just thinking of Anna, and the future—Hayward made a brief stop before mounting the iron steps to the second-last of the train's passenger coaches. At the station window, he reached into his pocket and pulled out a few coins—fifty cents' worth. He plunked them down on the counter and took a small slip of paper from the agent in return.

When he climbed into the car, Hayward had a $3,000 insurance policy ticket tucked inside his coat. It was the biggest one he could buy.

HAYWARD'S JITTERS may have had as much to do with the time of year as with his nightmare. For winter, as railroad travelers in the 1860s liked to joke, was widely known to be "smash-up season."

Whether it was the icy and hazardous conditions, the dim light and shorter days, or the increased traffic due to the holiday season, no one knew for sure, but many travelers felt that more severe wrecks happened on the rails in the cold-weather months than at other times of year. Their own observations attested to the fact, which seemed to be borne out by the tallies of accidents and deaths that were reported in the pages of many newspapers and periodicals. It wasn't just inexperienced passengers who held this opinion; educated types, including newspaper and magazine editors, shared this view. Railroads were considered newsy items to the era's editors and reporters all year round, of course, but in the wintertime, such accounts seemed to crowd especially thickly onto the news pages in local papers. "The suicide, fire, railroad and steamboat accident term is upon us, and we shall be glad when it subsides," the *Boston Herald* stated in an editorial published in December 1867. "We truly are having a sup of horrors that taxes not only the full-face type of newspaper offices, but strains also to its utmost tension the nervous systems of the strongest-hearted among us."[7]

There was a lot of railroad track on which to fix these concerns. By 1840, the nation had laid 3,000 miles of track, far more than the 1,818 miles in operation in Europe. Between 1850 and 1860, track mileage across the country had shot up at a rate four times that of the previous decade.[8] Much of it lay in places in the country, like Pennsylvania and New York, where freezing weather, snow, and ice were factors for a good portion of the year. And so, in this same unforgiving winter of 1867–68, none other than *Scientific American* magazine called attention to "the fact noticed by journalists and observing newspaper readers, that certain months of the year are particularly prolific of railroad casualties."[9] The magazine continued:

> The periodic return of this smash-up season ... is even predicted by enterprising journalists, and it must, so they affirm, like the dog days, run through a certain course before it finally dies out. If, for causes beyond our ken, certain months of the year are peculiarly favored in this respect, it is evident that such a season is now upon us, for the record of the past few months shows a long list of railway casualties of all kinds and of all degrees of horror.[10]

Old superstitions, combined with questionable inductive reasoning, may have led some people to connect railroad crashes with a particular season. If so, that was hardly surprising, given that railroads had long been linked with superstitious beliefs and practices in the United States—from the way passengers and trainmen avoided trains bearing the number 13, to the ghost stories connected with dangerous places along the rails, to the way crew members marked the trackside graves of railroaders killed in the line of duty (the symbol of a broken wheel was often used to signify a trainman's place of burial). Passengers may not always have voiced these ideas explicitly, but the way they spoke of and acted around the railroads, as well as the way they incorporated the imagery and culture of trains into their lives, revealed the uneasy mixture of their feelings. By 1867, many American men and women had ridden on trains. They had had enough contact with the railroads that they were beginning to feel capable of using them for their own various purposes, from work to visiting relations to traveling to school. But that did not mean that these men and women felt comfortable and at ease about the railroads on which they rode. To the contrary, Victorian railroads and their machines, which did not seem to obey the laws of nature in certain ways, were viewed by many men and women of the period as foreign, threatening—even slightly otherworldly.[11] The public response to them—part fascination and embrace, part fear and rejection—found expression in such manners of thinking as the "smash-up season." It found expression, at times, in black humor.

This may explain why the Victorians frequently gave their locomotives colorful names, often borrowing them from mythology, literature, warfare, or the animal kingdom, or using them to sum up aims and ambitions.[12] One midwestern railroad hopefully dubbed an early locomotive the "Pioneer." The Buffalo and Erie Railroad and its predecessor line, the Buffalo & State Line, offered riders the chance to settle in for journeys behind locomotives called Vixen, Vampire, Hecla, and Vulcan; newspapers of the day did not name the locomotive pulling the New York Express. (Later on in the decade, some railroad company executives, perhaps realizing more fully the power of public relations, began naming locomotives more sedately, with modest titles like the Charles H. Lee and the Dean Richmond.)[13] Of course, if naming the beast didn't work as a way of taming it, then there was always humor to fall back on. And so, in Mark Twain's *The Innocents Abroad,* published in 1869, the author had his narrator refer to railway accidents in an offhanded way that was nonetheless carefully pitched to the pressing concerns of the age. "No, they have no railroad accidents to speak of in France," the narrator states in Twain's novel. "But why? Because when one occurs, *somebody* has to hang for it!"[14]

THE JOURNEY of the New York Express came a week before Christmas. A time to be home, or to think of returning there, if one had been unlucky or unwise enough to stray. Outside, temperatures across upstate New York and in northwestern Pennsylvania were frigid, and hadn't risen above the freezing mark in nearly two weeks.[15] In the city of Buffalo, much to the satisfaction of young men and women, sleighing had begun a little over a week earlier, on December 10, with the arrival of steady, thick snow. "Sleighing begins," noted William Ives, the librarian for the city's Young Men's Association, in his weather journal.[16] Area newspapers marveled that the sudden cold snap extended deep into the middle of the United States. "Good sleighing in Washington and Louisville, three hundred miles south of this latitude," noted one, the *Hamilton (Ont.) Evening Times.*[17] It had begun to feel like winter, and like Christmas.

On board the four passenger coaches of the eastbound New York Express that Wednesday afternoon rode many men, women, and children who were on their way to visit family members and friends for the holidays. This in itself was a sign of the times: a generation or two before, the train might not have been so full of young women traveling toward reunions with family, of babies, of older people making journeys to visit grown children, of newlyweds. Railroads had made such trips—many of them all-day affairs—possible, and affordable, and, for the most part, safe. The express train as a result was stuffed to groaning with trousseaus and wedding gifts, as well as all manner of Christmas surprises: pen wipers, sachets, volumes of Tennyson and Dickens.[18] In the baggage cars and in the coach cars as well, trunks and traveling cases contained gaily wrapped presents—some bearing the name of Cleveland businessman John D. Rockefeller—while others were stuffed into the valises clutched by passengers. There was little room to move about, as each car contained a full complement of fifty or so people; travelers crammed their belongings beneath their seats, or shoved them into overhead racks, hoping for the best.

The Christmas holiday always had meaning, of course, but this year was special. Though the war between North and South had ended a little more than two years before, an undeniably wartime feeling still hung in the air, especially where holidays and family celebrations were concerned. So many men had served, and so many died: about 750,000 soldiers in all, from both sides of the conflict, and each of those deaths had torn a gaping hole in homes, families, and communities.[19] Two years later, those wounds still ached. All over the country, people struggled to pick up the pieces of lives shattered by the war, to cope with the "debris and debris of all the slain soldiers of the war," in the words of poet Walt Whitman, who voiced a realization many families knew all too well, that the slain soldiers were able to find rest, in the soil of their early graves, long before their bereft loved ones could. "They themselves were fully at rest, they suffer'd not," Whitman had written. "The living remain'd and suffer'd."[20]

In the winter of 1867, however, that lingering sense of sorrow and loss was coupled with a new sensibility. It was one that suggested that perhaps the best and most productive way to celebrate Christmas was to do so as a unified nation, bonding together over a shared experience of hope. *Godey's Lady's Book*, in its issue that December 1867—a periodical some passengers on the New York Express may well have been reading—had argued for just this kind of transformative Christmas, a season that would bring citizens from all parts of the country together in a spirit of brotherhood and emotional unity.[21] Christmas could become a moment that was more important, and perhaps more uniquely American, than even the Fourth of July. The magazine stated it this way: "To us—Americans—Christmas should be the glorious holiday of the year."[22]

Despite these calls for unity and peace, the winter of 1867–1868 seemed to many to possess an odd, unsettled feeling. The nation, emerging from a bitter war that had made its citizens examine the first principles of their democracy, was entering a new phase of its history. No one knew what that phase would look like. Bracing change was coupled with a contemplative, backward-gazing attitude befitting a country that had just survived horrific conflict. In Christmastide editorials, newspapers including the *Baltimore Sun* urged readers to look not just to the future but to the past as well, as a way of understanding what the nation needed. "To the American people there is a reflection suggested by this festival which should admonish them of the duties they owe to each other," an editorial in the Maryland newspaper stated. "The war ... teaches still more eloquently the lessons of mercy and forgiveness."[23]

For regular folk, this unsettled atmosphere expressed itself as a feeling that time was passing ever more quickly. Many other aspects of life—the railroads and communication through telegraphy, to take two examples—were also speeding up. As a result, time itself was proving trickier to handle. The railroads, opening up faster routes between distant points, had revealed problems with the country's geography-based time measurement system. Under this system, individual towns and cities set their own local times without regard for their neighbors, or for travelers or businesses that communicated among various locales. The time dilemma added to the public's feelings of dislocation and disorientation. Although an association of railroad superintendents had called for a standardized time system in the United States as early as 1849, by 1867 the development of such a system had still not happened.[24] In Buffalo, the city's main railroad depot erred on the safe side, offering travelers three separate clocks, each showing a different time. Two clocks provided the times used by the railroad lines serving the station; the third showed the city's own "Buffalo time."[25] Helpful, perhaps—but far from perfect. Passengers on board the New York Express could hardly be blamed for keeping their own time that Wednesday afternoon, and many of them did. J. Frank Walker, the son of a prosperous Buffalo jeweler and watch purveyor, wore an elegant gold watch and chain on his vest.[26]

As if in agreement with these feelings of disturbance and displacement, the natural world in that cold-weather season seemed unsettled as well. Residents in outlying towns in the rural Southern Tier of New York reported spotting a panther near their homes and businesses several times that fall; it appeared to slink between various communities, now popping up in one, now showing its face in another. That was strange, for this area of the state, so long an unexplored wilderness, had stopped feeling like one years ago. The panther was a reminder that some element of the untamed remained. And there were other hints. The week before, on December 12, a strong easterly wind had kicked up along the Niagara River, escalating by midday to such strength that it pushed the water backward, lowering the surface of the river so that the riverbed lay exposed, confounding humans and fish alike. "Great was the consternation among the finny tribes," one newspaper correspondent joked.[27] Newspapers as far away as Philadelphia marveled over the "miraculous" occurrence, which grounded boats and drew spectators to the scene. "In Buffalo Creek," one paper reported, "all the vessels moored there were grounded, and the stream of water, in ordinary times pouring an immense volume over the rocks, one hundred and sixty-four feet high [at Niagara Falls], was reduced so low as to enable the bold adventurer to cross dry shod from the American side to Goat Island, a distance of eleven hundred feet."[28] Caused by a seiche, this event was an anomaly; it had happened one other time in the century, in 1848, and that was a springtime drying-up due to ice jams at the outlet of Lake Erie.[29] The disappearance of the river in December was nearly unheard of.

Even more troublingly, at 3 a.m. that Wednesday—twelve hours and ten minutes before the New York Express would pass through Angola—residents of the region were startled awake by the sensation of a small but unmistakable earthquake.[30] The "distinct shock," widely felt throughout Buffalo and as far away as Syracuse, passed after about "a minute and a half," the *Jamestown (N.Y.) Journal* reported. But it left many residents feeling nervous and wary. Some people saw the earthquake as a sign from Providence, warning of death, judgment, heaven, or hell. "Verily, what are we coming to?" wondered the *Buffalo Post*.[31] Another paper saw the temblor as a glimpse of the "awful grandeur" of an avenging God. "Very many fervently pious people supposed that the Judgment Day had actually arrived, and remained in a state of almost suspended animation for several seconds, expecting to hear 'the last trumpet sound.' … A dancing party suddenly broke up and departed for home and places to pray."[32] Ill at ease, even when the shaking stopped, people reached for their guns, their children, their spouses, and wondered.

ICY WINDS swept across the frozen fields of upstate New York and buffeted the varnished walls of the passenger coaches of the New York Express as the 410-foot-long train glided through the colorless landscape.[33] Ahead lay the station of Angola, and beyond the village a fifty-foot-high truss bridge over Big Sister Creek, a waterway that had frozen over for winter. Angola was a through-point on this day's schedule, not a station stop. Then there would be Buffalo, a little more than twenty miles beyond, with its Exchange Street depot near the city's harbor—the station of the three clocks. Buffalo offered the bustle of city life and an array of connections to points east: Rochester, Syracuse, Albany, New York City, the New England states.

In addition to physical geography, the express train was surrounded as it moved through the winter scenery by an invisible terrain rich in American and railroading history. A year and a half before, the black-draped funeral train of Abraham Lincoln had passed along these tracks, following a thirteen-day route from Washington, D.C., to Springfield, Illinois. The trip included a day's stop in Buffalo, where crowds turned out to view the president's body; then, on April 27, 1865, Lincoln's coffin had been loaded onto a catafalque car and transported by the Buffalo and Erie Railroad between Buffalo and Erie, Pennsylvania. The funeral train had passed through Angola at about 11:13 p.m., ten minutes behind a pilot engine that checked the track for obstructions.[34] "This Pilot Engine and Funeral Train will have Exclusive Right to the Track over all other Trains upon the line," directors of the Buffalo and Erie had warned the public and railway crews.[35] People from the rural areas around the community of Angola had clustered near the tracks to see the body of the president make its slow journey home.

During the four years before that moment, the same railroad tracks had delivered thousands of the sons of New York's upstate regions to the front lines of combat in the Civil War, often with patriotic sendoffs at the area's railway stations. "Marched down Main St to Church, where a Flag was raised on first-Church," wrote James Husted, a recruit who left Buffalo for the Union army's Fort Runyon in northern Virginia in May 1861. "Street and buildings crowded with citizens, stores trimmed with Streamers of Red, White & Blue and Flags, marched to Depot followed by the immense concorse [sic]. Great time amongst the boys bidding their Friends goodbye which are repeated over and over again. ... The last farewell is said and last kiss given and the Train moves slowly off leaving many a Sad Heart and moistened eye."[36]

The history of the region wasn't all grim. The city of Dunkirk, on the Buffalo and Erie's route along Lake Erie southwest of Buffalo, was becoming a center of rail-related business activity. Soon the city would be home to the Brooks Locomotive Company. George Pullman, inventor of the sleeper car and founder of the Pullman Palace Car Company, had been born in nearby Brocton. The route of the express also passed through the hometowns of national leaders including William H. Seward, the current secretary of state, and Ely Parker, the Native American aide to General Ulysses S. Grant who helped the Union commander draft the documents of surrender at Appomattox.

One of those on board the New York Express likely more aware of this historical backdrop to the day's route was Benjamin F. Sherman, the train's conductor. A bearded man with a receding hairline, thick eyebrows, and a kindly if beleaguered face, Sherman was making his routine rounds as the train headed toward the Angola station. He was in the last car of the train, talking to passengers, greeting friends, and answering questions. Just two months past his fortieth birthday, Sherman, a native of White Creek in Washington County, had made his career on the railroads of upstate New York since the early days of passenger service in 1851. When the Buffalo & State Line Railroad,

Benjamin Franklin Sherman of the Buffalo and Erie Railroad, the conductor of the New York Express on December 18, 1867, was a veteran railroad man in upstate New York. He was known as genial, kindly, and experienced. From the *Buffalo Times*, 1901. In the collection of the Buffalo History Museum, Buffalo, New York.

predecessor to the Buffalo and Erie, had opened for business, Sherman was given the honor of conducting the first—or at least one of the first—trains to run out of Buffalo on the new line. By the time the Civil War was over, Sherman was one of the best-known conductors on the road.[37]

When he boarded the train midway through its route earlier that afternoon in Erie, Sherman had loaded his pockets with the tools of his trade: his timetable, orders for the day's travel for his section of the route, and a copy of the conductors' "bible," the slim book of rules and regulations governing his duties and responsibilities toward the train and its passengers. He also took his pocket watch, an important possession, since some of the local railroads could be single-track affairs, and preventing accidents by keeping to a correct schedule was as much his job as the engineer's.

Now, Sherman worked his way through the cars of the train, talking to the people around him and keeping one eye on the ticking away of time. The journey had reached the stage every long railroad trip eventually did: that of dullness and discomfort. Backs ached, heads pounded. Hands and faces felt grimy and soiled. Children—at least seven in the last two cars of the train alone—grew restless, then bad-tempered. The lucky ones slept; everyone else endured.

About two hundred men, women, and children had boarded the express train that day. Many of these travelers had climbed into the cars at daybreak in Cleveland. Others had shivered while waiting at small local stops along the line in the cold morning air. By afternoon, they sat stolidly in the dim, watery light that filled the swaying coaches. Every now and then, those passengers sitting near the sides of the cars would crane their necks to gaze out of the frost-tinged "peephole" windows. There was not much to look at—mostly "panel, veneer, and daub," as some travelers of the time had noted wryly. "All of the exhilarating effect of buggy riding is lost in these cages," one traveler had complained.[38] And so they rode, and dreamed, and waited. In the second-last car of the train, a thirteen-year-old girl helped her mother care for her three-year-old sister. Nearby, one of the smallest passengers in the last two cars, an infant named Minnie, snuggled in the arms of her mother, a young woman from Minnesota. In the train's last car, a young couple from Grand Island, the Kents, no doubt sat close together, the shiny, unmarred gold bands on their left hands—if not their private glances and smiles—giving them away as the newest of newlyweds. Her ring bore two intertwined initials: "GDK to AFG."[39] In the same car, an eighteen-year-old from Rochester, Morgan Kedzie, would have looked forward to the reunion with family that waited for him at the end of a trip to visit an uncle in Iowa.[40] Not far away, two attorneys—one from Boston, the other Cincinnati—surely fingered the wedding bands they each carried with them in anticipation of the nuptial ceremonies that awaited them on Christmas Day. A Wisconsin newspaper editor was also on his way toward an East Coast wedding.

And then there was Joseph Stocking Lewis, a passenger who likely would have been a shade cynical about all this romance aboard the New York Express. A bright and witty graduate of Williams College, at twenty-three years of age Lewis, who had spent the previous year running a tannery business in Pennsylvania, had only recently reported to his chums that his heart was still safely untethered to any young woman. This was due, joked the sandy-haired bachelor with the mischievous eyes and full lips, to his "not having as yet met with any of the 'female persuasion' whose attractions were strong enough to excite my breast [with] those emotions or intentions which would lead to anything ultimate."[41] But it was Christmastime; anything could happen. So perhaps even Lewis held out hope, hedging his phrase with those telling

Joseph Stocking Lewis, seen here in an 1864 class photo from Williams College, was a carefree young professional traveling on the New York Express to see his parents. At twenty-three years old in 1867 he alleged that his heart still remained unattached to any young woman. Courtesy of Williams College Archives and Special Collections, Williamstown, Massachusetts.

words, "as yet." He was on his way home to Batavia, New York, for Christmas, to visit his parents—and perhaps meet someone new, even someone of that "female persuasion."

CONDUCTOR SHERMAN finished collecting tickets as the train approached Angola. He walked to the forward part of the last car and stood near the glass-paned door and potbellied stove, which glowed with white-hot heat. He probably allowed himself to relax, in these seconds, by chatting a bit with John Vanderburg, the rear brakeman, who was pulling on his gloves and fastening his coat in preparation for heading out onto the platforms of the rear car and the second-last car. Around them, passengers dozed and shifted.

As they did, something else was taking place underneath the last car of the train.

For some distance, a single wheel on the train's last truck—the framework that held the sets of wheels together—had been rolling along the tracks unevenly. To the casual observer, nothing might have been noticeable. But something in the wheel was flawed; and behind it, in the axle that held together the rear wheels, a bend or curvature had formed. As the back wheels of the train moved over the rails—set four feet, ten inches apart, the Buffalo and Erie's standard gauge—they did so in a way that didn't precisely match the movements of the train's other wheels. The rear wheels shuttled back and forth as they spun. The vibration could be measured in fractions of an inch—not enough to be felt, even, by anyone sitting in the cars above. The irregular wheel and axle had been enough to throw the truck of the last car off kilter as the train traveled the miles between Erie and Angola. Because the wheel did not roll over anything unusual at its moments of shuttle-like movement, it eventually shunted back into position.

At 3:10 p.m., that changed. The wheel rolled through Angola, past the village's station house, and over a frog, or juncture in the tracks, located about two hundred yards beyond the depot. As it passed over the frog, the flaw in the wheel struck the place where the two strands of track separated. It jarred.

Above, young Frank Walker's gold watch ticked off the seconds. The Kents spoke in low tones. Babies fussed. Josiah Hayward pushed back the foul memory of his nightmare, over and over, as it stirred in the corners of his consciousness. Below them, the momentum of the wheel might have kept the circle of spinning metal on the track; it didn't. With a jerking movement, the wheel rose and then fell off the track, thudding onto the wooden ties beneath. Passengers felt the lurch in their stomachs. There was now the thudding noise of iron wheels clattering along wooden ties. Ahead lay the Big Sister bridge, a low, brownish-gray smear against the horizon. The train moved toward it, still running at close to its thirty-mile-an-hour speed.

Suddenly, in the air around them, they could hear the shriek of a whistle calling for "down brakes."

The train flew out onto the bridge. For one moment, all hung in midair. The coal stoves crackled merrily, suspended for the briefest glimmer of time along with everything else in the cold December sky.

CHAPTER 2

Angola at Dawn

I **N ANGOLA,** a rural settlement some twenty miles southwest of Buffalo in western New York state, people had become so accustomed to the trains by 1867 that they noticed them only when something went amiss: when a train was held up by bad weather, for instance, or running far behind schedule.

Since the early 1850s, trains had been the backdrop to their lives. Even for those residents who didn't work for the railroad or ship goods by train, the rail lines were of central importance. They had made the village what it was; they defined its day-to-day existence. Every Angolan knew what it was like to halt a conversation in mid-sentence to wait for the shriek of a train to fade away. Many residents knew the movement of the Buffalo and Erie's trains through the community, as well as those of other railroads, by the whistles alone; they could judge the speed of a passing train by its sound. "I am so accustomed to hear whistles," said one Angolan employed by the railroads, "that I pay no attention to them unless I have some special business with the train."[1]

That morning, as their clocks crept toward 7 a.m., there had been no reason to pay any special notice. In the village, residents were waking up within the walls of homes that had recently been framed out with native yellow pine, oak, and maple, cut down near the Big Sister ravine, hauled through the streets to Mill Street, and then shaped into boards in Henry Bundy's Angola Steam and Water Power Mill.[2] They shrugged into coats for farm chores, kindled fires in the stoves in their kitchens. Angola was still mostly agricultural, though the railroad depot and the village's commercial center were hubs of activity. In the

Angola Hotel and boardinghouse, on Commercial Street adjacent to the rail-road tracks, a few sleepy guests opened their eyes and began to stir. The hotel had recently been purchased by S. P. Imus, a former stagecoach driver for the Ohio Stage Company, who no doubt often told of how he had driven the last stagecoach passengers through the Angola area on February 22, 1852.[3]

Residents of Angola had chosen the area, a place along Lake Erie in the town of Evans that originally had been called "Evans Station," because the location seemed pretty and relatively well-situated. Inland, yet close enough to Lake Erie to be out of the path of the worst of the lake's winter storms, which tended to pass over the area, the village—which would be officially in-corporated in 1873—offered points of connection to the larger world beyond. As railroads were becoming increasingly common as modes of travel for aver-age Americans, they were also tying these citizens' hometowns—places like Angola—to an ever-broadening network of rail lines that had extended over much of the countryside by 1867. Railroads tied Angola to places both east and west—to Buffalo and Niagara Falls in one direction, Dunkirk, Erie, and Cleveland in another—and made its residents feel connected to the country's past in the East, as well as with its blossoming westward future. As a sign of the urge for connectedness possessed by these men and women, lore had it that the village had chosen its name after the country in Africa—a place none of them would ever see, but one they could imagine.

Angola had potential. It offered, if not excitement, then capability. People in the village had learned to grab the circumstances handed them in life and make the most out of them—to take what came along and make it better. And in the Angola rail yard, two employees of the Buffalo and Erie Railroad were trying to do just that.

J. M. Newton, station agent for the village, and James Mahar, a switch-man for the railroad, were discussing a problem with the tracks that had cropped up during the night. Mahar had noticed it at dawn, when he had made his first rounds of the day on the railroad property, a narrow strip of land be-tween Commercial and Railroad streets in the village. A piece of rail not far from the station had snapped in two. Maybe it had been the cold; maybe the rail had just worn out. Though a process for turning pig iron into steel had been invented more than a decade before by Henry Bessemer, for most railroads in the 1860s—including the Buffalo and Erie—steel rails were still largely a curiosity. The new rails' quality was uneven; they were expensive, to boot. As a result, as with many innovations involving railroads, even in these decades of steady expansion and the increasing familiarity of the public, the adop-tion of new technology lagged behind the invention process. Some railroads figured they would wait to see the new innovations thoroughly tested, and all the kinks worked out, before they implemented changes on their own routes. Others were just interested in the cheapest alternative—usually the older technology—in a day and age when the public's susceptibility to the allure and glamour of the rails could often temporarily outweigh their anxiety and demands for safe practices. Thus, though steel rails were touted as "one of the most important inventions of the age," by 1867 just 2,550 tons of these rails, at a costly $120 per ton, were being produced for railroads in the United States on an annual basis.[4]

Iron, however, they knew. Men like James Mahar, a native of Ireland who had spent years working for the railroads, had accumulated expertise in handling the temperamental qualities of iron rails: their deterioration under daily wear and tear, their inability to handle the heavier trains that were becoming more common, and their finicky behavior in very hot or cold temperatures. Repairs on broken and bent rails and other iron pieces—wheels, axles—were common in the winter, because "such failures were always greatest in cold weather."[5] This Wednesday morning, the problem of the broken rail was made more pressing by the fact that the village's traffic was about to pick up for the day. The first freight of the morning was due within the hour—a through train to Toledo.

Mahar, thirty-one years old and a family man who lived in Angola with a wife and three children, had already had a difficult morning. He had not had an easy time kindling blazing fires in the stoves inside the wood-frame station house and freight house. That was another part of his duties, in addition to inspecting the rails and rail beds for flaws and blockages. It was necessary to light fires early so that the buildings would be heated for employees and passengers well before the sun came up.[6] Now there was the rail problem to deal with. Mahar knew it was up to him to get the track in working order before the Toledo freight came through.

The broken length of metal needed to be ripped out, and a new length driven in. Then the whole section of the track would need to be checked to make sure it was properly gauged. Railroad gauge, to within fractions of an inch, was of utmost importance. Most railroads set their own gauges—the Buffalo and Erie did, as did its neighboring lines—just as they set their own standard times. The wheels of incoming trains needed to be able to roll over the width of track that the railroads promised to provide: if a four-foot, ten-inch gauge was advertised, that's what the railroad needed to maintain, or else safety could be compromised. Any alterations in the distance between the iron rails, whether by defective equipment or slipshod gauge calibration, could be enough to cause a derailment. Many railroad men of Mahar's generation had seen such things happen, and nobody wanted to see a derailment or crash happen on his watch. The men in the Angola station knew that there was a chance the chief engineer of the Buffalo and Erie Railroad, Peter Emslie, would pass over the line that morning as part of his regular duties for the railroad. Emslie, a railroad veteran who had ridden the same length of track two years before during a test run for a locally built engine that had covered forty-two miles in a dazzling ninety-five minutes, had a keen eye for problems with the route he oversaw.[7]

Angola's railroad employees were used to this task, because iron rails wore out fast, generally needing to be replaced every four to six months.[8] But doing this repair in the midst of regular daytime traffic could pose a challenge. And, to make matters worse, the broken rail wasn't on a straightaway, but at a frog in the track—a juncture where one rail curved in to join another—some six hundred feet past the depot building. Mahar and Newton talked about the repair that needed to be done. Then Mahar went to get his tools. Meanwhile, Newton walked into the depot, which was now starting to warm up.

Twenty years old in 1867, the man who was likely the J. M. Newton later described in accident inquests was the son of a well-to-do Angola farmer who was one of the village's more prominent citizens. He was young to be doing the job of station agent, but not strikingly so, at a time when some railroads were hiring telegraph operators as young as fourteen or fifteen.[9] Already, Newton had shown the sort of eye for meticulous detail that the railroads embraced. In his office in the village's station, just a few blocks down Main Street from his home on Pleasant Street, Newton scrupulously kept a log book into which he jotted his notes and observations on every train that passed through the village, whether it stopped in Angola or not. This sort of careful attention to detail was part of the reason Newton was good at his job. It was also one of the reasons this Wednesday morning was trying for him. There was the broken rail to worry about, and then there was also the problem that had cropped up with his station clock.

The timepiece had bedeviled him for a week. Each day, Newton would wind the clock and check it against the Buffalo and Erie Railroad's standard time. Each day, Newton's clock lost a little. Not much: perhaps half a minute a day, or three-quarters of a minute. In any other setting, Newton wouldn't have minded much about the discrepancy. But, as he and Mahar and the others working in the village for the Buffalo and Erie knew, the railroads succeeded and failed by accurate timekeeping. It was the image of dependability they sold the public, their way of maintaining safety standards, a ticket to profit and success.

Newton couldn't be blamed if he felt a twinge of pressure. He knew he needed to make his clock work correctly, so that he could keep proper time throughout the long day to come. He began "regulating" the mechanism, checking it against the official time reports from Buffalo, and tinkering with the works.[10] With any luck, he would get it fixed. And with a little more luck, this would be the most trying problem he had to deal with all day.

ANGOLA WAS MEANT TO BE a jewel in the crown of the Empire State— a successful railroad village along the shores of Lake Erie, a stopping point on the business and travel routes between New York City and Cleveland. And, early on, that seemed possible. The village lay in a prime location in the town of Evans, a sprawling rural region along the Lake Erie shoreline some twenty miles southwest of Buffalo. Evans possessed a striking beauty. Its allure centered on the intersection of earth and water: numerous sandy beaches offered easy access to the lake; wide creeks, including Eighteen Mile and Big Sister, wound through the uplands and let their fish-filled waters out into the lake in gentle bays. Along some areas of the shoreline, ancient bluffs filled with rich deposits of fossils towered eighty feet into the air, offering peerless views of the Canadian coast across the water, Buffalo to the east, and Dunkirk to the west. Evans and Angola had been blessed with resources from the start.

And people hurried to make the most of them. Though Evans was not carved out as a separate municipality until 1821, the area had been settled as early as 1804 by an innkeeper named Joel Harvey, who had crossed Eighteen Mile Creek—in these pre-railroad days, likely with boats and wagons—with an eye toward land to its west. Several families followed closely on Harvey's heels. The first birth in the town happened in 1811; the first marriage occurred on June 28, 1815, when Persis Taylor wed Whiting Cash.[11] Whiting Cash himself would die that December, in 1867, a seventy-five-year-old patriarch in the community, "one of our oldest citizens…who has been more or less identified with its entire history."[12] As the region grew in population, the geographic area of Angola—which would later be mapped out as about 1.4 square miles of territory set slightly back from the Lake Erie shoreline, 686 feet in elevation, and abutting Big Sister Creek—drew much of its settlement. The village, which took the name Angola for its official title in the 1850s, soon became a center of population in the broad swath of land southwest of Buffalo. By 1860, the area around the creek was home to about forty-five families, some living in the commercial district abutting the railroad tracks, others in homes spread out in outlying sections that were still largely forested or open fields. Although many of its qualities and characteristics made it unique, Angola offered, in this period of its history, a glimpse into the sorts of rugged little communities that were being used as through or stopping points by the burgeoning railroads, all over the country—and transformed in the process.

Big Sister Creek gave the village its early identity, and an important reason for existence. Together with its companion stream, Little Sister Creek, the creek formed half of the "Two Sisters" pair of waterways that helped irrigate parts of southern Erie County. The name of the larger body of water was deceptive: this "creek" was wide and could be deep and even dangerous, depending on the season. In the 1860s, Big Sister was located a quarter-mile or less from the Angola business district. It was described as "a shallow stream, at the ordinary level, bordered on the eastern side by a low flat, thirty or forty rods wide, while its western bank rises with considerable abruptness to the level of the surrounding country."[13] The temperamental freshet ran high and wild in the spring and after rainstorms, iced over in the winter, and sometimes nearly dried out in summer. Drownings in its waters had been known to happen, especially in the spring and fall. From the time of the earliest settlements along its banks, Big Sister Creek had given mothers in the Angola area reason to worry.

But while some settlers grumbled that nobody would ever settle in Angola for the farmland—which tended to be sandy loam or clay-pocked soil—others spoke rapturously about the beauty of Big Sister's wooded banks, clear waters, and picturesque views. Joseph Bennett, who moved to Angola as a young man during this period, wrote in his journal that "no one would ever have settled here, as farmers—if the Western Prairies had been in market."[14] But Bennett, later a leader in shaping this area of southern Erie County in business, agricultural, educational, and spiritual concerns, also wrote about his delight in strapping on his ice skates and exploring the Big Sister waterway, where he found "about half a mile up...a bend around a *beautiful* flat."[15] Bennett recorded his reaction to this pleasant natural scene: "Thought I never saw a more beautiful spot."[16] He was looking at roughly the place where Henry Bundy and later his three sons would operate a tool manufacturing concern and mills, which would produce both lumber and flour; where a truss bridge would be erected over the waters of the creek, to connect Angola with the east. He was looking at the eventual route of the Buffalo and Erie's 1867 New York Express.

Though the creek helped draw settlement to Angola, ultimately it was the railroad that spurred the village's steady growth from the late 1840s onward. Early settlers had been lured to the village first by the planned route, then by the construction, of the Buffalo & State Line Railroad, which began taking shape in 1849. Among some Seneca populations of upstate New York, Angola became known as "Dyo-a-his-tah," or "place of the depot."[17] Milling and the production of lumber for the growing urban areas of Buffalo became a profitable business in Angola—which could ship material to Buffalo and other eastward points quickly and cheaply. The area's natural resources suddenly were of value far beyond its borders. Demand created more business in the village, more development of its commercial areas, and brought in more residents. The railroads were reshaping Angola, and its people, as they reshaped everything they touched.

The railroads brought in numbers of men and women from surrounding areas—at least during the warmer months—who sought out Angola because of its sandy beaches and swimming coves. During the 1870s, observers would remark on the seasonal hubbub in the village, consisting of crowds of travelers arriving, trunks and valises in tow, for summer vacations in cottages and cabins along the lake. "Yes, sometimes when the afternoon train arrives," local witnesses noted, "there is such a large crowd at the depot, that a person has to edge his way through."[18]

People liked Angola, and many stayed. The community grew steadily throughout the Civil War, reaching about 320 residents by the early part of the 1860s and continuing to grow to more than 600 people by the early 1870s.[19] Though it didn't yet have a newspaper, Angola boasted a lively commercial strip along a broad Main Street. By 1867, Angola residents could visit, all within a few blocks, the First Congregational Church, the Angola Hotel (located to the rear of the station house next to the train tracks), the Big Sister–powered milling operations of resident Henry Bundy and his sons, S. L. Beckwith's harness shop for leather goods, Mrs. I. S. Thompson's shop for millinery and dresses, a saloon or two, a Masonic Hall, Cyrus Wilcox's storefront business for boots and shoes, and Martin & Tifft's tin shop. There were also two dry goods stores, including one, Lyman Oatman and Sons, where Lyman, David, and Leroy Oatman swore that they provided only the "latest and most elegant designs" to Angolans, all at "Buffalo prices."[20]

Because of all this energy and activity, by the 1860s people in Angola felt that they mattered. Many railroad communities in the Civil War period and afterward shared this feeling, the sense that because the railroad tied them to the larger world, they had a special importance and value not shared by other towns and villages that had been left off the railroad routes. The glamour and appeal of the nation's railroads—linked to danger, it is true, but tantalizing nonetheless—rubbed off on even modest little places like Angola, touched by routes like the New York Express, which by its very name suggested that Angola was connected not just to familiar places like Buffalo, Erie, and Cleveland, but to faraway and imagined ones such as New York City. Likewise, places not linked to railroads became somewhat isolated during this time, as historians including Michael Freeman have shown, able only to observe the "useless spectacle" of the railroad, without participating in it.[21]

In the United States, railroads were often laid out along meandering pathways that did not look much like the ruler-straight roads typically found in

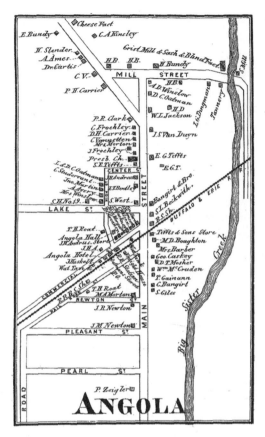

Angola, shown in this map from the 1860s, had a thriving business district and a number of substantial family homes. The Buffalo and Erie Railroad tracks bisected the village's center on a diagonal, also cutting across Big Sister Creek.

Europe, particularly in England. American railroads generally curved their way through the landscape, diverting around obstacles, following natural changes and features in the terrain, and accommodating stops in many smaller settlements.[22] This "natural" approach was one that early railroad companies debated with some difficulty.[23] Should they make the railroads as simple and straightforward as possible—or should they make them less direct routes that took their time getting from place to place, but perhaps brought more communities into connection with the larger commercial and social world? Part of the decision-making process was often the political and economic pressure placed on railroaders to make sure that the lines traveled through—and thus opened up for development—certain areas of the landscape. In this sense, it was not surprising that Angola, which was already a settled area connected

to water and stagecoach routes, became a stopping point on the Buffalo and
Erie's route. Figuring out these knotty logistical problems contributed to the
delays that kept many smaller railroads from opening in the time frames originally scheduled. In the end, each railroad made its own decision. The Buffalo and Erie, which sliced through Angola at a forty-five-degree angle on its
Buffalo-to-Pennsylvania path, was more direct than many.

At Angola, as at every point along these routes, the arrival of the railroad
had important effects. Finding themselves station stops or through-points,
people in countless places like Angola arranged their daily lives and schedules
around the trains. For those who had come to Angola on the railroads in the
period after the late 1840s and 1850s, it was perhaps an easy transition to
make. Many Angolans, whether they were longtime citizens or new arrivals,
no doubt felt optimism about the presence of the railroads. They also knew
that things were changing, and would go on doing so. And no one had any
idea where those changes would end.

WAKING UP THAT MORNING inside his farmhouse on Main Street, with
its floor-to-ceiling front windows offering views out over Big Sister Creek, was
an intense-looking man with a high, domed forehead and dark brown hair.
Dr. Romaine J. Curtiss, twenty-seven years old, a Civil War veteran and a bachelor, was still relatively new to Angola, but he was already the focus of much of
the village's interest and attention. Two years before, shortly after the end of the
war, Curtiss had arrived in the area. A native of Huron County in Ohio, he was
on largely unfamiliar ground in Evans and Angola, which had gotten its first
resident doctor less than a decade before, in 1858.[24] Before that moment, Curtiss's experience in upstate New York had centered mostly on Buffalo, where he
had attended medical college for a short time before enlisting in the army with
the commencement of the war. He was twenty-two at the time.

During his military service, Curtiss spent some three years standing over
stretchers and operating tables for both the Union army and navy. He had
served as a medical cadet on a hospital ship for the army and then later served
as an assistant surgeon for the navy on board a ship on active duty, the gunboat
USS *General Burnside*.[25] In both settings, he had cared for men suffering from
the wounds of war, contagious diseases, attacks of panic, venereal disease, and
nerves. Curtiss's military service seemed to have burned off many of the illusions and ideals with which he had set out upon his medical studies—indeed,
many of his illusions about humanity itself. "Life is too short for most men to
learn how to live," Romaine Curtiss would later write, introspectively, "or get
ready to die."[26] The experience affected him in powerful ways.

Romaine J. Curtiss, shown here in later life, was Angola's charismatic young doctor in 1867. He had been an assistant ship's surgeon in the Civil War and was looking for respite in the postwar period. His methods caused quite a stir in the small rural railroad village. Courtesy of the Joliet Area Historical Museum, Joliet, Illinois.

By 1867, Curtiss had been ready for a new sphere of practice, and Angola must have seemed just the ticket. Taller than most men of his generation, at more than six feet, with fair skin and flashing dark blue eyes that belied his Spanish bloodlines, Curtiss had a face and physique that commanded attention—and did so at once, upon his arrival in the railroad community by the shores of Lake Erie. Curtiss surely observed the village of Angola with care; then he decided to hang his shingle as a medical practitioner of a general nature suited to the surrounding area, a place for treating the complaints of farm families, birthing babies, looking over ailing children, and the like. The doctor purchased the house on Main Street, a wood-frame affair positioned at the top of Mill Street—so named for Bundy's business—and set up his medical practice in an office in the home. From his rooms, you could gaze out over the gentle downward slope of Mill Street, all the way to the Big Sister.

It had seemed such a propitious start. And for a time, things went as well as Curtiss might have hoped. But it soon became clear that Curtiss and the village were something of an ill-suited match. The reasons for that were complicated. The young doctor carved out a special practice, soon after his arrival, in handling the gynecological and obstetrical problems of area women.[27] In a Victorian era "in which doctors normally didn't go within arm's length of a woman's reproductive zone," and female patients were typically asked to point out to doctors their problems on a dummy model rather than submit to an actual exam, Curtiss's forthright, comparatively modern approach to treating Angola's women was viewed as little short of revolutionary.[28] His methods were varied: he would examine a patient's body, use electrical shock or other therapies if they seemed warranted, do surgeries and internal manipulations. Whether from his treatment or for other reasons, many of his clients bore children, or recovered from chronic problems with bleeding, discharges, or infertility. But in some ways, Curtiss's approaches were fodder for talk. He became a figure both sought out and, in some quarters, either disliked or dismissed. An outsider in upstate New York in other not unimportant ways, owing to his Roman Catholic faith and his Spanish heritage, young Dr. Curtiss was nothing if not controversial.

But Curtiss was not only a man who had a talent for medicine; he also possessed a broad-minded outlook—a quality that was only slightly less prominent than his stubborn streak. At times, Curtiss would take up an unpopular idea—germ theory and the need for sanitation in public drinking water were two of his favorite causes, long before many doctors paid any attention to them—and trumpet his beliefs to the public at large.[29] He would go so far as to lecture the millionaire industrialist Andrew Carnegie, in letters printed in newspapers, that Carnegie should part with a chunk of his fortune to establish a school for the study of curing disease and improving longevity for all Americans.[30] "I think Carnegie would give his name to an era of the world's development were he to create and found a university in Chicago to teach hygiene, which is truly the science of all sciences," Curtiss wrote, near the close of the century.[31] As a result, some would eventually claim that Curtiss owned "one of the most brilliant minds in the west."[32] Others criticized him, and even labeled him a quack. It didn't matter either way to Curtiss, who felt he had a moral obligation to share his ideas of right and wrong with others. "Throughout the country," the doctor wrote, later in his life, "there is one man in every six hundred, whose business and profession it is to know the things which people must know, in order to live long and well."[33] Because he knew these things, Curtiss's thinking went, he had a duty to serve—and to set an example by his words and work.

In Angola and its environs, in the post–Civil War period, many doctors were far more conservative than Curtiss, even at this early stage of his career. Perhaps inevitably, the young doctor's theories struck sparks in some quarters. One day, in a local parlor, Curtiss got into a heated discussion with two older physicians from the area, about pneumonia. The illness was rampant in the village, taking the lives of residents every month. Curtiss listened to the two men debate whether bleeding should be used to treat the sickest cases. One doctor "advised his friend not to bleed so much," Curtiss recalled. "'I find,' said he, 'since the cholera epidemics, that people can't stand bleeding as they used to.'"[34] Curtiss, as he later recalled, reacted to this mind-set with barely concealed impatience. He couldn't stand what he saw as the "old heroic inquisitional torments" of medicine.[35] Modern medicine, he felt, should be able to handle whatever situations a doctor faced.

After all, Curtiss surely reflected to himself, he had already seen the worst conditions a doctor could face, on the decks of a hospital ship during wartime. Nothing could be more terrible than that.

IN THE OFFICE where he kept his log book and the station's telegraph instrument, J. M. Newton heard in the distance the echo of the whistle of the inbound Toledo freight. Outside the depot, switchman James Mahar also heard it. He realized with a start that ripping out the broken rail would have to wait. The freight would be there before they could finish the repair. Because the break was on part of the frog, and not a straight section, Mahar knew the freight could get over the bad portion of track safely, given a little guidance. He grabbed a few signal flags and ran down the track toward the creek. Waving frantically, Mahar managed to get the oncoming freight to slacken speed enough so that it was able to pass over the damaged section of track safely. As it disappeared into the horizon, heading west, Mahar and a few others got to work tearing out the broken section of rail and replacing it with a new piece.

Afterward, Mahar wanted to be sure things were done right. He trotted up and down the length of track containing the frog and switch—not once, but several times. "I saw that it was in its position and properly spiked," Mahar said. "I passed up and down three times....It was in its proper position every time I passed. I am sure the rail was all right then."[36] It was better to be over-cautious about safety, than not careful enough.

Some 175 miles away, on a route that aimed straight at the village of Angola, the New York Express was on its way, building steam.

CHAPTER 3

Getting Under Way

T WAS EARLY IN CLEVELAND, but already John Davison Rockefeller's day had gotten off on the wrong foot. Bad timing, in itself unusual for Rockefeller, had been at the root of it. It wasn't like the twenty-eight-year-old businessman to deviate from his schedule, especially where work was concerned. Most mornings, Rockefeller conducted his affairs with precision. His daily agenda moved along in as neat and orderly a fashion as the columns Rockefeller totted up in the brown-backed ledger books he used to record notations on every sum he spent, down to the 52 cents he had recently paid for repairing a pair of shoes.[1] Punctuality was part of Rockefeller's character, much like correct manners, Sunday church attendance, and fastidiousness about drinking and the theater. Being on time for appointments was a standard to live by for the young husband and father, who had been raised in a Baptist home and practiced his faith devoutly as an adult. Moreover, the practical-minded side of Rockefeller believed in personal responsibility. One took care of oneself, in his view, and took care of business—and not always in that order.

That Wednesday, Rockefeller had risen at daybreak. He had planned to get ready for a train trip to New York City, where he wanted to squeeze some business into the week remaining before Christmas. He was headed to the East Coast office of his oil refining firm, where William Rockefeller, his younger brother, oversaw operations. By making the trip so close to the holidays, Rockefeller could also visit William and William's wife, Mira, and young children.

John Davison Rockefeller was an up-and-coming young businessman from Cleveland, traveling to New York City on December 18, 1867, for the purpose of visiting his company's offices in the city and distributing Christmas gifts among his relatives. Timing, that day, was on his side. Courtesy of the Rockefeller Archive Center.

It was a plan that combined business with pleasure, and still got Rockefeller back home to his own wife and baby daughter in time for Christmas.

To get to New York in a timely fashion, Rockefeller knew he needed to leave Cleveland on that Wednesday's early express. The Cleveland-to-Erie train would connect him to the Buffalo and Erie's New York Express in Erie later that day. He would be in Buffalo late in the afternoon. The eastbound train was scheduled to leave Union Station in Cleveland at 6:40 in the morning. It was a route Rockefeller had taken many times before. As president of the firm Rockefeller, Andrews & Flagler, John D. Rockefeller, like many American men of his generation and socioeconomic class, had become accustomed to using the railroads for business travel. In fact, Rockefeller now took the trains almost as frequently as the horses he personally preferred for transportation purposes. The approach worked, for by harnessing the rails to bring in business, Rockefeller's prospects in the region had grown. "I undertook to visit every person in our part of the country who was in any way connected with the kind of business that we were engaged in, and went pretty well over the states of Ohio and Indiana," Rockefeller later said, of this time in his career. "To our great surprise, business came in upon us so fast that we hardly knew how to take care of it."[2]

It didn't hurt that the railroads were pushing forward into these territories as fast as materials could be shipped to construct them. Nearly forty-eight hundred miles of railroad line had been laid in Ohio, Michigan, and Indiana during the 1850s, and by 1860 Ohio offered more railway miles than any other state in the union.[3] People were making use of the new railroad lines in record numbers, including many groups of people—women, families, children—who hadn't felt comfortable on the trains even a decade or two before. Rockefeller's timing here, as usual, was fortuitous. By the time he got his career well under way, the Clevelander had become so familiar with the railways that he used them for pleasure-oriented, social ends as well as business ones. In 1864, following his marriage to Laura Celestia Spelman, Rockefeller had spent $490 on a wedding trip that took the couple by train to Buffalo, Niagara Falls, Montreal, Quebec, Boston, Worcester, New York City, and Albany.[4] More recently, in the summer of 1867, Rockefeller had taken his family—daughter Elizabeth, or "Bessie," had been born in 1866—on a sojourn to New York City that had cost more than $300.[5] Though he was young, Rockefeller, like many men across the country and even a good number of women, was by any measure a practiced passenger of the rails. "In these early days," he later said, "I was a good deal of a traveler."[6]

Following through on his plans, Rockefeller packed his valise on the morning of December 18, 1867, in the couple's home at 29 Cheshire Street with items he felt necessary for his trip: clothes, his slippers, the family's good umbrella. He also stuffed into the bag the Christmas gifts he planned to give William's family.

It was to be an elegant Christmas for the whole Rockefeller family, despite the fact that a downturn in the oil market earlier that year had sent prices of refined oil rocketing down till they were below that of crude. Many refineries were still suffering that autumn and early winter.[7] But Rockefeller had held on to his place as head of the top oil refining concern in Cleveland, a vibrant company that had grown to include thirty-seven employees and $200,000 in capital.[8] The Christmas presents purchased by Rockefeller and Laura, known to her family as "Cettie," that holiday season reflected the guardedly optimistic way the couple viewed their prospects, as well as their upwardly mobile status. (They spent $60 on holiday giving in 1867, a time when the average worker was earning less than $1.50 a day.)[9] The Rockefellers' Christmas budget had included "ear-drops" for John's sister Mary Ann, stacks of handkerchiefs worth $23, assorted scarves, a brooch costing $4.25 for Laura's mother, and a

Laura Rockefeller, a young wife in 1867, bid goodbye to her husband, John, on that fateful morning, as he left their Cheshire Street home in Cleveland for a trip to New York City. Here she is pictured with a baby that may be Bessie, the couple's first child. Courtesy of the Rockefeller Archive Center.

set of fancy buttons for John's father, the colorful and erratic William Avery Rockefeller. The buttons cost the couple $6.50—the most they spent on any one individual that season.[10]

Perhaps Rockefeller was thinking of Christmastime on that Wednesday morning, as he headed from his modest home on Cheshire Street—the first home he and Laura had owned as newlyweds—to Cleveland's Union Station. Or perhaps he was feeling the pressure of the bad oil market, and focusing his thoughts on business matters. Whatever his thoughts and emotions, Rockefeller arrived at the city's central station, a waterfront complex that had been built the previous year, and purchased a ticket for the eastbound express. The ticket—which likely cost him about $2.46—guaranteed his passage through to Erie, then on to Buffalo, where he could connect with the New York Central's overnight express in that city's Exchange Street depot.[11] If he made his connections as planned, Rockefeller would be in Manhattan by 7 a.m. the following day—well in time to meet his business partners.

Ticket at the ready, Rockefeller no doubt strode through Union Station and walked briskly up to the waiting express. He approached the last passenger coach of the train and loaded his valise onto it. He picked out a seat, then sat down to wait for the shriek of the whistle that would announce his departure.

Six-forty came and went on the clock. Rockefeller realized, as the minutes ticked by, that the train was not leaving on time. He decided to investigate the situation. He climbed down from the car, leaving his valise behind at his seat to hold his place.

Poking his head into the station's waiting room, Rockefeller saw an acquaintance and struck up a conversation to pass the time. After some minutes had passed, Rockefeller saw how late it had gotten. He went to inquire about the express and was told it had just pulled out—without him.

Rockefeller, gazing after his departing train, decided to run for it.

DAWN THAT DAY in the villages and cities that lined the route of the New York Express brought frigid temperatures and the heavy, immersed sensation that came with the arrival of snow: snow that had just fallen, snow that steadily approached.

Men and women—Josiah P. Hayward, John D. Rockefeller, and some two hundred others who were planning to board the train that day—rose from their beds in homes and hotels to find themselves surrounded by the hallmarks of a Lake Erie winter: frosted windowpanes, icy bedroom floors, chilly dining rooms, stiffened clothing. Hurriedly, they splashed water on their faces and dressed. Men fumbled with the buttons of wide-legged trousers and shrugged into low-collared shirts and shawl-style vests. Women slipped on their undergarments—chemises, corsets, petticoats, crinolines, more petticoats—thankful for the flannel from which some of the garments were made.[12] Dressing could be a challenge at this time of year, especially for women, whose outfits often weighed several pounds; the luckier ones, like Laura Rockefeller, had some household help to make the task easier. War widows donned plainly cut dresses in tones of black, gray, or violet; they were still in the midst of mourning periods that could range from two and a half to three years.[13]

Those citizens living in rural areas along the Cleveland-to-Buffalo route scuttled hastily outside into the seventeen-degree temperatures and northwest winds to do chores, then rushed back inside to warm themselves at hearths and stoves. The winter had arrived, abruptly and without warning. After a warm early December—one that had almost fooled some in Buffalo into believing

Christmas might be balmy; the thermometer had hit forty-one degrees on December 6—the weather had changed course in the preemptory fashion of the upstate snowbelt. Temperatures had dropped precipitously, and the first significant snowfalls of the year covered the ground. By the end of the month, residents in upstate New York would remark over a mean temperature for the month that was fully four and a half degrees colder than December readings for the past decade.[14] Now, a week before the Christmas holiday, lawns and fields were blanketed with soft folds of snow, and the runners of sleighs left deep creases in the drifted streets and byways.

But there was also an uglier side to the season. On the Erie Canal, 539 boats had come to a halt, frozen in by ice build-ups; their decks and holds strained with 43,746 barrels of flour, 1,484,358 bushels of wheat, 3,700 sides of leather, cargoes of peas and pig iron and petroleum, and seemingly countless tons of cheese. All this was going to waste in the icescape of the stilled canal.[15] The *Buffalo Express* carried reports of a New England man who had been found frozen to death in a snowbank.[16] Another newspaper observed grimly that the death toll on the Great Lakes had been particularly bad during the sailing and shipping season that was just coming to a close: 211 lives had been lost, almost double the total of the year before.[17]

AS ROCKEFELLER DASHED after the departing train, passengers aboard its swaying coaches settled into the thickly upholstered cushions of their iron-framed seats and took up conversations or reading material—books, newspapers, magazines like *Harper's Weekly* and *Godey's Lady's Book*—or else sank into thought. Underneath them, the wheels of the train rumbled as they picked up speed; the couplers moved against one another with clanking noises, iron against iron. Inside the cars of the train, the men, women, and children who filled the seats gave a glimpse of the wide variety of passengers that railroads in America now attracted as a routine course of business. Ex-soldiers, ladies, clerks, lawyers, shopkeepers, engineers, schoolteachers, children, company presidents—the train contained all these and more, and was in certain telling ways a window onto the traveling public on the nation's railways in the late 1860s.

Some of these varied passengers on board the New York Express likely let their thoughts wander to pleasant topics, in this early morning hour—topics such as love and marriage. Elam Porter was no doubt one of these. Like many other passengers on board the train that day, Porter had begun his life in one part of the country yet was currently living in another, Ohio. His movements around the country had been shaped by needs both career-related and personal, and they had been made possible by the railroads. Porter, like other passengers on the New York Express that morning, offered a glimpse of the tapestry that made up the country's population, and its expanding mobility. They had come from all over the nation, and they were heading to all sorts of different points, for all sorts of reasons. They were leaving old homes, going to new ones, returning after time away. They were marrying, conducting business, seeking fresh starts. Together, the stories of their lives extended from Texas to Canada, from Minnesota to Connecticut, from Wisconsin to Tennessee. They came from everywhere, and were heading everywhere. Their journeys were important to people all over the country.

Sitting in the last car of the express, near where Rockefeller had intended to ride, Porter, the pudgy, boyish-looking attorney from Ohio, surely let his mind drift to Mary Melcher, the young woman in Stoughton, Massachusetts, who waited for him at the end of his trip. Porter and Melcher, a "very beautiful and accomplished" teacher, intended to be married in Massachusetts within the week.[18] Afterward, the couple planned to travel back to Cincinnati, where Porter had been living for the past few years.

The thirty-year-old lawyer had come to law as a second career. His first, after graduating from Tufts College in 1860, had been as principal of a New England high school. Porter had worked hard in the law in the midwestern city to build a rosy future for himself and his fiancée. In leaving Cincinnati for the East, Porter had put it bluntly to a friend: "I'm going to begin," he said with emphasis, "to really *live*."[19]

He surely wasn't the only one aboard the passenger car thinking that way. As the outline of Cleveland's Union Station fell away behind the steaming express, Charles Lobdell, a solitary traveler sitting not far from Elam Porter in the last car, also nursed a special joy—the kind of happiness that came only rarely, with nuptials, the birth of children, and perhaps a few other times in one's life, with any luck. This week, Lobdell, like Porter, would have called himself lucky. Ambitious and talented, the young editor had been working at a newspaper in Wisconsin for the past two years. After much drudgery, his writing, especially the opinion pieces he penned on political topics of national and local interest, had begun to attract attention in Wisconsin and around the country. Lobdell's boss, the controversial editor Marcus "Brick" Pomeroy, had noticed this success and responded to it: he had recently promoted Lobdell to be his second-in-command at the *La Crosse Democrat*, largely on the strength of the written work he had done at the paper.

Now, the thirty-four-year-old journalist was on his way home to Connecticut to see his family for Christmas. The Lobdells, as a clan, had ink in their blood. Charles's father, Jerome, had reputedly been the first man in the

Elam Porter, shown in an 1860 photograph, was a promising young lawyer in the Cincinnati area in December 1867 and was on his way to wed his betrothed, who waited for him in Massachusetts. "I'm going to begin to really *live*," he had told friends, when starting his trip east. Courtesy of the Digital Collections and Archives, Tufts University, Medford, Massachusetts.

state to make a living as a printer; his brother John was a compositor. For these reasons, the other men had understood Lobdell's reasons for heading west to take the editorship in Wisconsin.[20] Though it was far from his New England roots, the *Democrat*, a Copperhead newspaper read all over the country, had been just too good an opportunity for Lobdell to pass up. But as the express headed east from Cleveland, Lobdell wasn't just looking forward to a reunion with his father and brother. He, like Elam Porter, had wedding plans. His trip was centered on a Christmas Day ceremony in Bridgeport, after which Lobdell and his wife would travel to La Crosse to start a new life together.

Sitting in the last car of the train, Norman and Arila Nichols of rural Ashtabula County in Ohio had their dreams as well—in this case, of better job prospects. The couple had left their young daughter, Philinda, at home with relatives, and were traveling east to see if they could find a new place for the family to settle and find work. After they did, they planned to return to fetch their daughter, so the family could be reunited.

John William Chapman, thirty-four, a well-regarded Boston attorney, also rode the train with what could only have been an uneasy mixture of hope and concern in his heart. A native of Ipswich, Massachusetts, Chapman had left home at age twelve to earn his living and had worked for a time as a feather and bedding salesman before turning to the study of law. Married in his early twenties to Agnes Allen, a Nova Scotia native who became the mother of his two children, Chapman had advanced in his profession and in the esteem of his peers. Yet Agnes had died, leaving Chapman with two small sons, Walter and Willie, to raise. Now, the attorney was hurtling toward a new life—and the glare of a limelight that the nation's journalists had turned upon him.

Engaged to be married for the second time on Christmas Day, Chapman was planning to wed a woman, Clara Green, who had previously been married to a man at the center of an infamous New England murder case, the Malden murder. In 1863, Clara's then-husband, Edward W. Green, a postmaster in the bucolic town of Malden, Massachusetts, had become the first American citizen to rob a bank and kill someone in the course of the crime.[21] The murder had been covered in scintillating detail in the country's newspapers. Clara Green, just twenty-three at the time, had been nine months' pregnant when the murder had taken place. Green had been hanged for his crime in 1866, despite Clara's vigorous defenses of him to the nation's voracious press. "Sir, if his heart was so wicked as some may believe, would not my heart turn against him? Sir, I have been brought up to abhor wickedness and crime in its gentlest phases. Could I, then, so love him," she asked, in a plaintive letter that was published in Boston newspapers, "if his heart was so wicked?"[22] Clara Green happened to be Agnes Chapman's sister. After Agnes died, Chapman and Clara fell in love, and Chapman, a respectable sort who was partner in the law firm Manning, Glover & Co., as well as superintendent of the local Sunday school, had asked Clara to marry him. The approach of the wedding day was made delicate by the fact that Clara Green was now a household name, thanks to the sensationalistic coverage in newspapers of the day, and one linked to her former husband. "Wife of the Malden murderer," the newspapers called her, when mentioning her engagement to Chapman.[23] Chapman would have known, as he rode toward Buffalo, that he himself was about to become, by extension, a public figure.

Emma Hurlburt Fisher of Owatonna, Minnesota, was the opposite of John W. Chapman and Clara Green: a very private person. Sitting in the second-last car of the train as it began its journey east, Fisher was accompanying her brother-in-law Alexander E. Fisher to his wedding, which was to be held in Madrid in northern New York State over the Christmas holidays. Emma would have cuddled her baby daughter, Minnie, in her arms as the train moved along, building steam.[24] Before the war, the Fisher family had lived in Madrid;

Minnie Fisher, a baby of less than one year in 1867, was one of the train's youngest passengers when it derailed at Angola. Fisher, shown here later in life, may have been the child who became a symbol of hope in the midst of the wreck's grief and shock. Courtesy of Wendy K. Bolinger.

subsequently Emma, her husband, Andrew E. Fisher, and Alexander Fisher had moved west to Minnesota to find fresh opportunities. Now Andrew had stayed behind in Owatonna, to keep an eye on the successful business that he and Alexander had created, a stone-carving outfit that specialized in decorative works, including gravestones.

Of the three attorneys on board the last two cars of the train, the eldest and most well-established was Eliakim B. Forbush, and he was also enjoying a moment of professional success. A noted patent lawyer in Buffalo, Forbush had just won a big case in a Cincinnati courtroom and was returning home to share his good news. His wife, Emily, and son, W. H. Forbush, who was a partner in his father's law firm, waited for him at the end of his trip. "All business...done promptly and correctly," newspaper advertisements for Forbush's law firm promised.[25] He had delivered on that this week.

Sitting in the end car of the train, not far from Elam Porter and Charles Lobdell, Forbush could now at last relax and think about the upcoming holiday. It would be an especially happy Christmas, for at least some of those on board the New York Express that morning. All signs pointed to it.

JOHN D. ROCKEFELLER, running after the departing train down the platform of Cleveland's Union Station that Wednesday morning, was hardly unique. Flustered passengers who had been "too late to the train" had become so commonplace by the 1860s that they had become figures of public comment—and collective mirth. A Cleveland newspaper reported that one railroad in the city mounded up, in one year alone, "almost one hundred pieces of unclaimed baggage" just like Rockefeller's—each piece "properly checked and marked," lacking only an exasperated owner to claim it.[26] In the literature and art of the day, descriptions and drawings pictured the plight of such hapless travelers in humorous terms. "The man who lets himself loose to pursue a train is a public benefactor," wrote satirist Benjamin F. Taylor. "Everybody is pleased with the performance—but the performer. The loungers on the platform at the station encourage him with shouts that put 'spurs in the sides of his intent.' The engineer leans out at his window and lets the engine whistle for him, and sometimes slackens a little, just by way of delusive encouragement."[27] An illustration labeled "A Little Late!" showed a man running behind a train, waving his umbrella and losing his hat to the wind, while onlookers guffawed. The smoke coming out of the train's stack puffed the words, "I've Got Your Trunk, I've Got Your Trunk, I've Got Your Trunk."[28]

And so Rockefeller's dash down the platform may have provoked smiles, if not outright chuckles, among the early morning crowds hurrying through

Cleveland's railway station. The express train rolled over the tracks, slowly at first, but inexorably picking up speed as it headed toward the east—Buffalo and points beyond. Rockefeller's bags were on board; there was no way to call them back, once the train started, or stop the retreating cars.

Rockefeller gave up. He stopped running. He had been left behind by the train—and was "not a little vexed" about the situation, reported the *Cleveland Herald*.[29] His day, which had already seemed taxing, had just gotten a good deal longer and more difficult.

In a moment, Rockefeller would begin to plan how he could catch up with his belongings and get his day's journey back on track. For now, though, he was nothing more than a frustrated young businessman, standing on the railway platform, watching his train disappear into the distance.

CHAPTER 4

En Route

AS THE SNOWY LANDSCAPE of rural Ohio slid past the ice-crusted windows of the New York Express, so did the minutes and hours. By mid-morning, nearly two hours and sixty miles out of Cleveland, the train cruised through the village of Ashtabula. Slackening slightly, the express rocked out onto an iron expanse across the Ashtabula River: an imposing truss structure, 165 feet from end to end, suspended seventy-six feet above the surface of the frozen river.[1] The bridge appeared hulking, almost ominous, in the pale morning light.

People had said many things about Ashtabula's bridge since it had opened two years before, but they hadn't called it beautiful. One Ashtabulan wrote of the discomfiture of newcomers—such as those passengers on board the express train—who spied the ungainly metal frame for the first time. "Travelers by the wagon road, at a distance up the river a mile away, would stop and look at this structure, apparently built high in air, and watch the cars as they passed in bold relief against the sky, almost as if a spectre train were traversing the blue vault above," wrote Stephen D. Peet, a local minister. "It was a dizzy height. There was something almost fearful in the sight. The recklessness of danger impressed the observer."[2]

Despite its ugliness, or perhaps because of it, the bridge was the talk of Ashtabula. It had been the cherished project of the Cleveland, Painesville, and Ashtabula Railroad, which had spent $75,000—enough for seven new locomotives—on its construction. Moreover, the design of the bridge was the work of Amasa Stone Jr., the president of the Ohio railroad, who considered the structure to be the pinnacle achievement of his career.³ The railroad had opened the bridge as an "experimental" structure, meant to gauge how well iron would do as a replacement for wood in railroad bridges.⁴ The structure included two massive trusses made of the metal, which supported a double-track line not from above, but from below.

Etched in black tracery against the winter sky, Ashtabula's modern-looking bridge couldn't have been more different from the bridge that awaited the express farther down the line, at Big Sister Creek in Angola. That structure was a wood and stonework Howe truss, simple and unfussy, with tin plating nailed to parts of it for an added dollop of homeliness. The two bridges making possible the journey of the New York Express that day formed a study in contrasts, like one of the era's new rifles—long-range, breech-loading—next to an old-fashioned flintlock musket.⁵ The contrasting bridges spoke of the railroads, too, which seemed such modern and progressive systems, but which still in many ways had one foot planted firmly in an older and potentially more dangerous era of technology. One structure gestured toward the future; one spoke of the past. It was clear to anybody who gazed on them which bridge was which.

In late December 1876, the iron trusses of Ashtabula's bridge would collapse to the bottom of the Ohio riverbed under the weight of the inbound Pacific Express, killing some eighty travelers, many of them making Christmas journeys. Six years afterward, Amasa Stone Jr. would shoot himself through the heart in the bathroom of his opulent Victorian mansion on Cleveland's Euclid Avenue—not far from where John D. Rockefeller and his family lived—having become a "harassed and tragic figure" in the wake of the Ashtabula bridge disaster.⁶

Bridge accidents could do that to a person, a community, a railroad. They could be impossible to live down—or to leave behind.

TWO YOUNG MOTHERS aboard the New York Express likely watched the Ashtabula bridge flash by through the frost-rimmed windows of the train. Emma Fisher and Christiana Lang would then have turned back to the tasks that had absorbed much of their time that morning: soothing restless children and checking timetables. Both women, average female citizens of their class and generation, fixed their sights on the ends of their journeys, which were intended to carry them to happier places. Fisher and Lang exemplified the increasing commonness of railroad travel for women in 1867; on a typical day, trains carried many women like them, private people who were making journeys—for a wedding; to relocate a family—that their mothers and grandmothers might not have undertaken. Both had far to go, and more challenging days ahead of them than most of the passengers on board the train, as each was traveling with children—yet without a spouse or parent to help her manage the trip.

Emma Hurlburt Fisher, the Minnesotan from Owatonna, sat in a rearward car of the train and rocked her bundled baby in her arms. Fisher, twenty-four years old, was traveling with what may well have been one of the express train's youngest passengers, her daughter Minnie, an infant just nine months old. Not far away sat Christiana Gates Lang next to her own two children. The thirty-five-year-old mother, who had left Minnesota earlier in the week, was heading east with her son James, twelve, and daughter Mary, ten. Lang's plan was to try to establish a new home for the threesome in New England, in Vermont, the place she had been raised. The two mothers no doubt exchanged sympathetic glances, if not hands-on help, as the minutes ticked away and the express coasted along through Ohio farmland and toward the Pennsylvania border. Traveling with babies or children over long distances in harsh winter conditions had never been easy, but the conditions of the wooden train cars made it especially difficult. The cars were cramped and crowded, their lighting dim and unreliable. Delays were frequent, good meals few and far between. Luggage could easily be lost, possessions scattered. If the rocking motion on occasion did help soothe the babies on board, it was counterbalanced by the station stops, which tended to be jerky. Each time the doors opened and shut, blasts of freezing air entered the compartments.

Fisher was luckier than Lang in one respect, however. At least she had a traveling companion for this part of her journey. Her brother-in-law, twenty-three-year-old Alexander E. Fisher of Minnesota, rode next to her on the train. Alexander was the younger brother of Emma's husband, Andrew. The two brothers were close, and had thrown in their fortunes together following the Civil War. After Andrew Fisher fought for two years as an infantryman—and been discharged because of injury in 1863—he and Alexander had moved from their hometown of Madrid, a hamlet in St. Lawrence County in New York State, to the west. The pair had settled in a town not far from Rochester, Minnesota, and opened the Owatonna Marble Works. Their business, which specialized in stonecutting and carving, had done well. By 1867, the outfit of "Fisher and Bro." was known in that region of Minnesota as "General Dealers in Foreign and Domestic Marble of All Kinds," as well as "Manufacturers of Monuments, Tombs, Head-Stones & Furniture Marble." "Call and examine our stock," an advertisement for the firm read. "It will cost you nothing, and may benefit you." Their gravestones, the Fisher brothers claimed, were of such quality that they "cannot be surpassed in the West."[7]

Now Alexander was headed back to Madrid, to marry a girl from his old hometown. The marble works had done well enough to allow for the purchase of an extra railway ticket for the journey. Andrew needed to stay home to mind the shop; his wife, however, could be spared. Emma Fisher, taking Minnie with her, accompanied her brother-in-law to his Christmas wedding.

Like most women travelers of the period, Emma Fisher was free to go to her brother-in-law's wedding—but not so free that she could leave her baby, or society's expectations, behind. Fisher and the other women on board the New York Express that morning coped with these expectations in grittily practical ways along the route.[8] At stops in communities big enough to have anything larger than the most bare-bones of depots, Emma Fisher, Christiana Lang, and other female travelers disembarking from the New York Express's coach cars found waiting rooms, dressing rooms, bathrooms, and drinking fountains for women passengers that were generally separate and isolated from the male facilities. This separation of the sexes was part of the effort of Victorian-era railroads to both accommodate the prevailing idea of "separate spheres" for men and women, and to promote it as an invention of their own. Rail companies knew that women would travel more readily if railroad-going was perceived as seemly and respectable. Yet the questions raised by female train travel—including that of how women's modesty could be preserved when they were forced to eat, sleep, and use washrooms in public—were endlessly challenging for railroads in the period. Companies patched together solutions as best they could. Train cars were typically open to all, except for most smoking cars; waiting rooms could be segregated or open, depending on the size of the station; washrooms were usually discrete.

Emma and Alexander Fisher thus sat together while the train coasted along through the landscape of Ohio and Pennsylvania. During station stops, Alexander could often accompany Emma into waiting areas, as he was her escort for the trip, and thus was allowed by railroad rules to stay near her; but at other moments they traveled apart. Emma did the best she could, swaddling Minnie in blankets and surely relying on the kindnesses of other women travelers—like Mrs. Lang, with her own two children in tow—in certain parts of the station.

It was just as well Minnie Fisher was too small to know what was happening around her. The daughter of Emma and Andrew Fisher had been born less than nine months earlier, on March 28, 1867, potent day of the last quarter moon.[9] No doubt about it, from the first Minnie was a Thursday's child; as the children's rhyme then in vogue had it, it was a fate that meant she had "far to go." Later in life, Minnie Fisher Brown Ahlstrom would reflect in this way about her birth year of 1867: "I am born. To what purpose I have yet to learn....I am one of those unfortunates a saulty nature pitched turned too high, by suffering brought yes—and to start life cross eyed is a hardship difficult to overcome and you are about beat before you begin."[10] All that wondering, all that ruefulness over a "cross-eyed" start in the world was, for Minnie, yet to come. Right now, she was nothing but a bundle wrapped in blankets, snuggled securely in her young mother's arms.

AT LEAST EMMA and Minnie Fisher had a relative along with them on the cross-country journey. Christiana Gates Lang did not—and she needed the help, situated as she was in the middle portion of a lengthy trip back to the East and to her childhood home. Longing for more than Vermont's wooded scenery, Lang no doubt hoped for the New York Express to ferry her to a fresh start and a new life.

She had started her travels the previous day in Minnesota, her home for a short interval. A little more than a year before, in October 1866, the former Christiana Gates had packed up her belongings and her three small children in Boston. She was headed westward. Her decision had been prompted both by grief and practicality: three and a half years before, her husband, Robert Lang, a thirty-three-year-old Scottish-born American who had built up a promising career as a bookkeeper in Boston, had unexpectedly died. His passing left his widow as the sole support of the family, consisting of James Beattie, who was eight; six-year-old Mary; and little Annie, the baby, who had been just three years old at the time.[11] Since then, Christiana Lang had been alone, and it hadn't been easy. Uprooting children never was, though lots of young widows—some of them, unlike her, bereaved by the recent war—were doing so at the same time. These young women formed part of the changing demographics of the people on board train cars in the late 1860s and afterward. For people like Lang, railroad travel was becoming increasingly common in a way it had not been for previous generations of female citizens. Formerly the bastions of men, and primarily young men, railroad coaches in the postwar culture were dotted with women just like her, often accompanied by children. The western part of the country was particularly tempting to Lang and other families because it represented a fresh field of opportunity. With railroads springing up in these far-flung territories as quickly as ties could be laid, the West was more accessible—including for women and children without men to care for and support them—than it had ever been.

Soon after settling into their new home, however, the Lang family had found themselves struck by a second tragedy. Annie, the youngest child, sickened and died. Heartbroken and surely seeking a measure of peace, Christiana Lang decided to relocate her brood yet again.[12] This time, they were headed back to New England—not to Boston, but to the familiar countryside of Christiana's own childhood.

Now, sitting in the clattering passenger coach of the New York Express, at least another half-day's travel ahead of her, Lang certainly began to feel the full effects of her journey.

Like others on the train, including dozens of women, her face and hands were covered with a sticky film—a mix of soot, smoke, grease, and sweat—that hours of railroad travel had slicked on her body. Her lungs breathed in and out the stale, uncirculated air of the car, which was largely uncushioned from the jolts, jars, and sharp curves of the roadbed. Even her clothes had been affected; the hems of Lang's full skirts, like those of other women on board the express that morning, were smeared with ugly yellow-brown stains—souvenirs of the gobs of runny tobacco juice that covered the walls and floors of the coach cars.[13] Rubbing at the marks was futile, as nothing would expunge the amber-hued stains.

Male passengers weren't supposed to spit tobacco in the cars, but they did, and the overworked train crew had enough to do without taking time to find and punish the offenders. No matter the route or area of the country, floorboards on most passenger train cars of the day were infamous for their vileness—and the New York Express was no different. "There is no room to deposit any small article under one's feet and even if there was they would be spit on to a certainty," complained one traveler of the time. "Indeed, even in the event of dropping money on the floor no decent person could venture to pick it up unless he put on an old glove."[14] Thus, by the second day of travel, as Christiana Lang and other women on board the express knew, even the most ladylike and fashionable of women just gave up. Looking worse for the wear on the railways was taken for granted; it could even, when approached with the right spirit, become a badge of honor—a totem of miles covered, distance spanned, obstacles surmounted. One gritted one's teeth and endured the rough conditions, from the tobacco spit and piercing cold to the bad food and backache-inducing seats. The last thing many women travelers wanted was to become a caricature of fussiness—like the young woman in the joke making the rounds that winter, who had boarded a train car, sniffed her nose at the gobs of tobacco juice on the floor, and then hitched her skirts up and edged over to sit in an empty seat next to a young bachelor. "Do you chew tobacco?" the prim miss asked the stranger. "No ma'am," came the reply, "but I can get you a chaw if you like."[15]

Christiana Lang may have enjoyed the anecdote—or, indeed, any reason to smile—that winter morning. But it had been two days now; she would have felt herself nearing the limits of her endurance. James and Mary were old enough to sit without clinging to her, but it was hard to make the hours pass quickly for children who were cold, uncomfortable, and hungry. They still had many miles to go before they would be home. Lang, like the other women passengers riding with her, no doubt looked around her, then tweaked her voluminous skirts, trying as every woman did to find the elusive position in which she would remain both modestly tucked in and clear of the sopping floor.

At least they were moving. When it came to railroads and wintertime travel plans, you learned to be thankful for the small things.

AHEAD OF THE EXPRESS lay the winter-bleached fields of Pennsylvania, stark and sparkling in the late-morning light. Beyond waited the city of Erie: bustling outpost on the Great Lakes, western Pennsylvania's port on the world, and already infamous for its colorful railroading history.

The train was running behind schedule, but there was nothing passengers like Emma Fisher and Christiana Gates Lang could do about it. Indeed, there was little the train's own crew members could do. Though the route from Cleveland through Erie to Buffalo was billed by the railroads as an express run, that didn't mean it was fast. Average speeds ranged upward of thirty miles an hour, but not by much. And express trains were subject to disruptions and delays, just like the regular-service trains with which they shared the region's still partly single-track lines. The label "express" typically meant that a route's station stops were somewhat more limited than on other runs—no more, no less.

With stops factored in, each of which required the time-consuming application of manual brakes, even a quick passenger train of the period was only going to make about twenty-two miles an hour on most trips.[16] Samuel Clemens, or Mark Twain, was among the many travelers of the day who discovered this fact the hard way. Trying to get from New York City to Elmira aboard a slow-moving express mail optimistically dubbed the "Cannon Ball," Twain became so frustrated at the train's lack of speed that he fired off a telegram to his destination at one of the many station stops along the way. "TRAIN STOPS EVERY FIFTEEN MINUTES AND STAYS THREE QUARTERS OF AN HOUR," Twain wrote to his friends. "FIGURE OUT WHEN IT WILL ARRIVE AND MEET ME."[17]

Without question, train travel of the day was taxing and exhausting for passengers, men as well as women. It was hard to believe that people had once dressed up for outings on the trains—like going to church or to a party. But they had. In fact, in the not-too-distant past, many women and men had donned their Sunday-best outfits for rides aboard the cars. In the early heyday of the 1830s and 1840s, when wooden railway coaches wore coats of brightly colored paint and bore ambitious names like "Pioneer" and "Columbus," carriages had rustled with pale silks and delicate velvets, lace gloves, fine veils, and bristled with gold-topped canes and fancy feathers.

But travelers had soon learned that dressing in such a way was not a good idea, unless one wanted these clothes ruined by sparks, smoke, oil splashes, and grease spots. Nowadays, even the most unpracticed riders knew what to wear on board a train like the New York run: ruggedly built, dark-colored dresses in fabrics like wool and worsted, sturdy leather boots, and warm cloaks and capes. The fashion authority *Godey's Lady's Book* in December of

1867 was offering a "traveling dress" that tended toward the conservative: "We recommend the twilled winseys trimmed with mohair braids and fanciful bands of silk," the magazine's editors wrote.[18] And though for regular wear the popular colors that winter were cheery ones—purple, green, blue, or "sunny Bismarck"—the magazine recommended that traveling ladies stick to the basics: black, brown, and gray. Some women and men even opted for dusters, floor-sweeping overcoats designed to keep the grime of railroad travel entirely off their persons.[19]

Getting into the proper gear and clambering onto the platform of a railroad car was usually just the beginning of most passengers' struggles with discomfort. Seat selection was a fraught business. Some riders—many of them men who had traveled the rails and considered themselves expert on such matters—insisted that the safest seats in the event of a crash were the rearmost ones in each car, and tended to monopolize those places when boarding. Others thought the middle seats were safer, and pushed their way to those. Debates like these were familiar on American railroads, where passengers had long argued over where one should sit in order to walk away unharmed from derailments and wrecks. On one 1855 journey, a British traveler in the United States was nonplussed to find himself being advised by another passenger on what to do to survive a "smash": "He proceeded with a coolness deserving a better cause to instruct us how to place ourselves, laying great stress on the importance of sitting diagonally in order not to receive the shock directly on the knees," Charles Weld noted. "He strengthened his advice by assuring that he was experienced in railway accidents and…it would be prudent to change our seats at the next station."[20]

Other passengers, including many women, had a different tactic when selecting seats. They wanted to be warm aboard the cars, first and foremost. Thus they entered the coaches like flagships sailing into battle, heading for the potbellied stoves that stood at the ends, or sometimes at the middle on the left or right side, of the cars. There was an art to picking seats near the stoves, as there was a certain range of space where travel was most comfortable—not too close to the fires, where passengers would sweat and broil, but not too far away, where it grew so frosty in cold weather that you had to stamp your feet on the floorboards to keep feeling in them. The smartest travelers knew enough to pick a seat a few rows away from the stoves, but facing toward them, and out of the range of any ventilation paths that would send soot flying into their faces and clothes. One passenger of the period described finding a "tumult" on board a passenger car, which turned out to be a scuffle over precisely these desirable rows of seats. "Men [were] jostling each other and rushing in at every available aperture…like so many maniacs," the traveler marveled. "It appears that in Winter there is a choice of seats, the preferable ones being such as are not too near or too far from the stove and the race was for these seats."[21]

Once settled into their seats inside a carriage, men and women found the cars dim and stuffy, like cabinets left unopened too long. The smell was one you grew used to, on board the cars, but never fond of: smoke from the heat stoves blended with the acrid sweetness of tobacco juice in the brass cuspidors and on the floors, walls, and windows, a "pestiferous decoction" that merged with the scent—sometimes overpowering, especially in winter—of fifty or sixty human beings, enclosed in tight quarters in sweaty heat or teeth-chattering cold.[22] Personal hygiene could never be taken for granted, and many passengers had been traveling for days without the opportunity to thoroughly wash. Passengers often carried with them their own snacks and meals, because timetables could not be trusted when it came to the frequency, duration, or location of meals. And so, on top of these primal scents was layered the occasional top-note of hard-boiled egg, cold chicken, sauerkraut, pumpernickel bread, or ripe cheese.

Railroads had begun to pay attention to these conditions on board their passenger cars. Starting in 1862, in response to loud complaints, many railroads shifted toward the use of a "clerestory" roof in cars, in an effort to increase ventilation for passengers. The older style of cars, as one observer put it, forced "foul air into your lungs" owing to its low-ceilinged construction; as a result, travelers sat "placidly breathing typhus and death."[23] Clerestory roofs, on the other hand, offered a raised center panel that allowed for small windows and air vents, both for light and air to pass through and for smells and smoke to escape. By 1867, this type of roof was downright fashionable in railroading circles, and many passengers were convinced it helped them breathe better—they now demanded it, for just that reason, on the routes they traveled.[24] The New York Express offered passengers this new style of coach car, and the men and women sitting on board the train's cars on that Wednesday morning doubtless felt thankful about the fact, as they whiffed at whatever extra light and oxygen the roof vents allowed in.[25]

The improved roofs represented the most recent in a line of attempts by mid-nineteenth-century railroad companies to make passenger coaches somewhat more bearable for travelers. This had been an ongoing struggle. Railroads were still uncomfortable and downright dangerous, which passengers dealt with—or chose not to think about—at their preference. Because the railroads were the most modern form of transportation available, and because of their undeniable glamour, most railroad companies were having no trouble selling tickets, despite the discomforts they forced on passengers. Their efforts to incorporate change were sometimes genuine, often half-hearted, and usually governed by questions of money. So the story of changes in railroad passenger car quality had been an uneven one.

It was also, in many ways, a story marked by more failures than successes. Lighting and warmth were particularly sticky issues. In the earliest wooden cars, illumination had come from wax candles—two of them, typically, one at each end of a car. But the candles weren't safe, nor were they effective, especially as cars lengthened to accommodate more people. Railroads responded by installing glass-chambered kerosene lamps to handle the job of lighting, but the lamps had their own flaws. They smoked and guttered, stank up the cars, and at times even fell into the laps of unsuspecting passengers.

Some passengers feared the lamps on board railway cars, and considered candles a marginally safer alternative. "Thousands of families in the country have been bereaved by the breaking and explosion of kerosene oil lamps....Why not return to the old and much safer practice of using candles?" one worried passenger begged in a letter to *Railway Times* in 1868. "It will cost but little more to light the cars, and there will be no violation of the 'rule of safety.'"[26] But by 1870, most railroads had shifted to kerosene.[27] Other passengers were not sure the change improved comfort and safety in the cars. One traveler of the period described the "dim religious light" that filled American passenger coaches: "The atmosphere resembled that of a limekiln, dry and baking, the effect of a large stove at each end, aggravated by all the windows being closely shut. The car had no division from end to end, a length of some fifty feet, while to light this large apartment the Pennsylvania Railway had generously provided two candles swung in glass globes as in the stateroom of a steamer."[28] The effect of the dimness was to make one want to go to sleep, even during the middle of the day. "But 6 p.m. was rather early for a car full of people to seek repose," the traveler noted. "As if in playful irony, a newsman appeared offering papers and magazines for sale."[29]

Though some newer methods of heating railroad cars were being tested by a few American railroads—cars between New York and New Haven and some in Boston were operating in the winter of 1867–68 with heating systems of twelve gallons of warm water running through a pipe under the floors of each car—the Buffalo and Erie and other railroads in its class were not showing any signs of abandoning the practice of using potbellied stoves for warmth.[30] Perhaps these railroads felt that heating passenger cars was a challenge to which there was yet no effective answer. And because some trains became stuck in the winter during snowstorms, especially in the West and Northeast, passengers and crewmen often preferred to see stoves in the cars— which they could keep going with wood or coal—rather than hot-water pipes, which could freeze. "A system which secures the heating of the cars with certainty during the intense cold of one of our northern snow storms with the train possibly snowed up, and one which at the same time is not open to the objections to stoves in case of collision or the upsetting of a car is a pretty difficult thing to devise," one editorial stated. "The inventor who solves the problem will be a great public benefactor, while at the same time he will insure himself a fortune."[31]

Ticket-buying passengers boarding the New York Express found that the cars used for the Erie-to-Buffalo portion of the journey—despite the kerosene lamp fixtures installed in the cars—would be lit the old-fashioned way, with candles. Wax tapers stood at the ready, should they be needed; when lit, they cast a glow onto the plush seats, the full-skirted dresses of the ladies, and the dark walls of the carriages, covered in thick coats of varnish.

WHEREVER THEY SAT in the coaches of the New York Express, the men, women, and children on board had tucked into their pockets and purses the items most precious to them: keepsakes for the journey ahead, reminders of what they held dear, or items that they couldn't be separated from, even for a few hours. The possessions spoke to their needs and desires, to what they considered too important to pack away to the baggage car.

Emma Fisher had her jewelry. Charles Lobdell, the Wisconsin newspaperman, had with him the large ring that was the token of his membership in the Freemasons; he likely valued it almost as much as the wedding ring he was hoping soon to don. James McLean, a Harlem resident who worked at a steam-fitting company in New York City, carried with him some tools of his plumbing trade and his own watch.

Other men—including, eventually, Benjamin Aikin of Hydetown, who still waited to board the train at a station down the line—also carried firearms tucked into their vests or coat pockets. These armed riders were far from atypical: in the rude conditions of the period's travel, many journeying American men took with them loaded weapons for their own protection. Having a gun on hand helped in case of disturbance on the train—unruliness, train robbery, pickpockets—and also gave passengers a feeling of security when they were stranded in strange cities in between legs of their journeys. One traveler summed up the prevailing attitude when informing an English visitor on a Mississippi railway in 1867 that "it was quite possible that [he] was the only man unarmed on the train."[32]

Tucked into valises and hand-trunks, the possessions on board the New York Express that morning were no different from those one would find on any other passenger train of the period. Rings, books, souvenirs, weapons: what was important to people didn't change, and it usually broke down into categories that were familiar to everybody—love, money, faith, and fear.

CHAPTER 5

Delays

CONDUCTOR Benjamin F. Sherman's voice, carrying through the crisp air, would have echoed off the brick walls of Erie's cavernous Union Depot. "All aboard! Express to Buffalo—New York Express—all aboard!"[1]

It was a practiced voice, but today it no doubt contained a note of tension. Passengers clustered in the waiting rooms of the station would have heard it, and wondered. Some surely gazed out the windows of the depot at the weather and guessed at the reasons for Sherman's strained tone. The station clock was ticking down the minutes to 1 p.m., the sullen, leaden-gray sky threatened snow, and the Buffalo-bound express train was just now readying to leave. The train had been scheduled to pull out of Erie at 10:20 a.m., but the minutes had passed, turning into hours, and then the passengers had been advised to take their dinners in the depot. The train was now two hours and twenty-four minutes late, with the potential for even more tardiness down the line.[2]

The problem, as Sherman had learned, had been caused by a mechanical breakdown with another train along the route. With still partly single-track lines owned by several different railroad companies stretching between Cleveland and Buffalo, and frequent breakdowns in rails and equipment, such delays were common. Still, everything was now up in the air: arrivals at other stations, wood and water stops, connections in Buffalo, fuel and heating supplies, and passengers' tempers. As a result, the genial face of the forty-year-old conductor—who preferred to be called "Frank," a shortened version of his middle name, rather than by his given name or title—bore a harried look, rather than its usual expression of humor, as he walked through the waiting areas of the Erie station, calling out for boarders.[3] Delays upset the day's schedule and left one—whether a rider traveling for two days or a crew member on his thousandth trip—enervated and exhausted. They took all the momentum out of a journey, and made it drudgery.

Though Sherman was only beginning his work for the day—his job was to supervise the train on the Erie-to-Buffalo leg of its journey, a roughly eighty-mile stretch of road—he could already feel his patience being tested. The rule for conductors on the timeliness of trains was clear: conductors of passenger trains "must use every endeavor to keep their trains punctually *on time*."[4] Sherman, who had lots of experience under his belt, and was already well on his way to a reputation as "one of the pioneer railroad men of the East," knew his duty was to bring the now severely behind-time express train into its final destination in Buffalo by 6 p.m., in enough time to meet all connecting trains waiting to depart for the East—in questionable weather.[5] It was a daunting task.

In the ladies' waiting room, Sherman would have made his call for boarders again. "Express to Buffalo, all aboard!" As he did so, he likely took note of some of the passengers clustered there. A woman with two children and a pile of bags at her feet; she looked like she was traveling a long way, perhaps making a one-way journey. Another woman, quite young, rocked an infant in her arms. Sherman's gaze would have roved over the tidy and luxurious room, with its upholstered armchairs and drinking fountain. The "beautiful apartment" of the ladies' parlor of the Erie depot—at forty-six by forty-two feet, a space noticeably bigger than the same rest area provided for gentlemen passengers, with the exception of a few who were allowed to accompany ladies into the female quarters as traveling companions—usually had a matron on duty, to help women travelers with using the washroom, which offered private toilets, mirrors, and wash basins with deep sinks.[6] Use of this amenity was free of charge, too: a welcome touch, after all the expense of traveling. Sherman may have nodded to the women passengers gathered there, and they in turn would have acknowledged him with their eyes, or with flutters of their hands. Christiana Gates Lang and Emma Hurlburt Fisher, along with the other women in the room, most if not all of them holding first-class tickets, would have risen from their seats, in these moments, and begun to adjust their belongings. The room surely sprang to life: Sherman would have heard the scrape of boots on carpet, the snap of suitcases being shut, tinkling laughter, a scolding tone or two. As a group, the women would have shaken out their long cloaks, tied on their

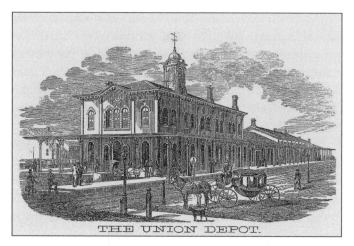

THE UNION DEPOT.

The new Union Depot in Erie, seen in an 1867 drawing, was an impressive, architecturally elegant building the Pennsylvania city was proud of. In this city, conductor Benjamin Franklin Sherman took charge of the train for the leg of its journey to Buffalo. Courtesy of the Erie County Historical Society, Erie, Pennsylvania.

hoods, and fastened their veils. They were ready to resume their day's journey, tiring as it had been, or in some cases begin their travels.

Across the room, Arila Nichols, twenty-seven years old and in mourning for the baby son she had lost three months before, gathered up her possessions; she would sit with her husband, Norman, on board the train.[7] Lizzie D. Thompson, a twenty-six-year-old woman from Massachusetts, also prepared to climb on board, where she would take seats with her brother, Simeon. The Thompson siblings were on their way home from a trip to the West to look for employment prospects for the young man. Simeon E. Thompson, a newspaper dealer who was widely known and well-liked in their hometown of Worcester, was ready for a change. The young man of "upright character" was planning to take on a new challenge—the management of a large farm in one of the western territories—before long, and his sister was planning to help him.[8]

Conductor Sherman continued down the hallway, past the shaving stations where time-pressed male passengers could get a lather, steam-towel, and shave inside of thirty minutes, and walked into the men's waiting room.

He had a few more minutes to collect passengers. Outside the station, the New York Express stood huffing on the track, the black hulk of its locomotive gleaming. Eight train cars stretched behind the engine, waiting. Four of the carriages were baggage cars; four were passenger coaches. As the express throbbed in preparation for departure, the men jokingly called "car knockers" made their usual rounds.[9] They were company men from the Buffalo and

Erie Railroad, charged with inspecting the underparts of the train at each major stop along its path. The knockers now crawled alongside the engine and cars of the express, looking over its wheels and axles. They bent down to peer under the carriages, and tested the soundness of the iron parts with a quick knock—*thunk THUNK*, it went, the sound of their work giving them their sobriquet.[10] Some of the car inspectors were more thorough than others, Sherman knew. It all depended, as with so much in railroading, on who was in what spot at a particular time.

Not that Sherman anticipated any real problems with the wheels or axles today. No, this afternoon it seemed like tardiness and bad weather would be the main problems he had to deal with. Such difficulties didn't make his job in handling the traveling public any easier. Today, as on any typical day for someone in his position, some passengers treated Sherman with respect verging on awe; they called him "captain," even "skipper," and lowered their eyes when speaking to him, in deference.[11] This was the reaction Laura Ingalls Wilder would have, on seeing a railroad conductor for the first time: "Oh Mary!" she said to her sister. "So many shining brass buttons on his coat, and it says CONDUCTOR right across the front of his cap!"[12] But others fretted and complained to Sherman, and seemed to hold him personally responsible for the fact that the train was behind schedule. Even in the progressive period for railroads that the late 1860s represented, Sherman knew, some travelers still held conductors in low regard—seeing them as sneaky, self-serving, and dishonest. The bifurcated public image was an old stereotype, but a persistent one. It dated back to the earliest days of passenger rail service in the nation, when conductors, as a novel breed, were viewed as both remote gods and shady figures hell-bent on losing one's luggage or causing one to miss a train's departure. "A conductor, if dishonest, is not a rogue because he is a conductor, or a conductor because he is a rogue," wrote Benjamin F. Taylor, in one of his travelogues. "As a class, conductors are as honorable as lawyers, physicians, bankers."[13] The fact he had to write it proved not everyone thought it true.

Sherman also knew that the public didn't see all the work that went into his job. His role was to keep the trains running on time, to look out for the public welfare—and to make it all look effortless. Of course, one of the most serious duties of his job was to keep the train and its passengers safe from harm. Conductors like Benjamin F. Sherman—a man who was described by observers as "intelligent, watchful, painstaking"—were charged by their superiors with heavy responsibility.[14] Their mission on the railroads was to "in all places and circumstances, regard the safety of the train as of the first importance, and leave nothing undone which w[ould] secure safety."[15] All this, at a time when many railroad conductors earned a rate of $2.10 per trip, no matter how long or arduous, with no overtime pay. No wonder sentiment in the profession was already fomenting that would lead, within a matter of months, to the 1868 founding at Amboy, Illinois, of the nation's first conductors' union.[16]

Now, stepping into the gentlemen's waiting area, Sherman would have made his cry for boarders once more. He had no manifest to check passengers' names against—most railroads didn't use such lists, as ships often did. But his job did require him to round up as many travelers as he could, and get them into their seats in time.

"All aboard! Express to Buffalo."

His words were certainly met with jubilation from a small group of young men who had been sitting together, waiting for the train, in the men's waiting parlor. They would have jumped to their feet and begun to pick up their satchels and struggle into their overcoats. The three men, all Erie residents, no doubt joked and bantered with the easy conviviality of good friends. They were remarkably alike in some ways. Each was a professional who was carving out a bright career in the city. Each was active in church and community. The three had decided together to take a pleasure trip just before Christmas—to enjoy a respite from work, and a chance to visit family and friends in New York City and other places on the East Coast.

Taken together, Edward T. Metcalf, William Warworth Towner, and J. Alexander Marten could be counted as among the "most promising young men" in the Pennsylvania city.[17] Towner, twenty-five years old and a surveyor, came from a well-to-do family in Erie. His father, Jehiel, had made money as a contractor and business proprietor, and by 1867 was living the life of a gentleman of the city in the family's home on French Street. Metcalf, twenty-four years old, was a railroad clerk. He had lived as a boarder in a house a few doors down the street from Towner, and knew both Towner and Marten through their mutual membership in the city's First Presbyterian Church.[18] Marten, a young man of about the same age, already held the distinguished position of assistant city engineer in Erie.[19] Now he was traveling to Vermont to visit his mother for the holidays; she hadn't been feeling well, and he wanted to see her.

As Sherman gazed around the gentlemen's parlor and called one final time for boarders, J. A. Marten straightened his baggage and picked up his book. Then, along with his friends, he walked out of the room and onto the waiting train. Into his book, Marten, ever the practical type, had slipped $50 in cash—for safekeeping.[20] You just never knew, on the trains.

THE DELAYS Conductor Sherman found himself coping with had given passengers from the New York Express time to drink in the sights in Erie's central railway station—a facility that had been completed just the year before and was considered a jewel of the city's architecture.

The building, a private project that had been built and paid for by several of the railroads serving the city in order to fill their need for a central terminal, had cost the eyebrow-raising price of $100,000.[21] Citizens of Erie took pride in the sight of the lofty 480-foot-long depot, which had been built in the Romanesque style, with a towering cupola and appointments to the exterior window and door casings of sandstone that was imitation, but which bore, locals bragged, "every appearance of the regular article."[22] Indeed, the structure had been designed to compete with depots popping up across the country, in the wake of the railroads' rapid progress westward. Its stately, grandly scaled architecture offered a hint at the self-conception of an industry that saw itself as nationally, if not internationally, significant. Erie's Union Depot, city officials boasted, would outdo in elegance and comfort any railway depot "in the whole West."[23] (And, railroad circles being relatively small, it was perhaps not surprising that the man who oversaw the building's construction was Cleveland's Amasa Stone Jr.)

Railroad officials, including those of the Buffalo and Erie, thinking ambitiously, had used the new depot as a chance to make a statement—to show that they knew what luxury was, even if they couldn't always provide it aboard their cramped and chilly passenger coaches. In an important sense, they couldn't have picked a more suitable city in which to make such a display. Erie was a community already rich in railroading lore—including one of the more colorful chapters in the industry's history. In the early 1850s, Erie had been the site of the "Erie Railroad War," also known as the "Gauge War," a heated struggle for control of local railroad lines that highlighted an issue that had been one of the most controversial faced by the railroads to that point: gauge width.

The problem was simple but bitterly divisive. Early railroads installed tracks at widths of their directors' choice; examples in the United States in the 1840s and 1850s ranged from four feet, eight and a half inches, a standard British width, to five and six feet, and in the 1870s some railroads would experiment with narrow-gauge roads of between three and four feet.[24] The incompatibility in track widths caused delays and difficulties with the transportation of goods across state lines and through different regions within states. It also endangered and inconvenienced passengers, who were forced to deal with the train changing, baggage carting, and station switching that such differences made necessary in places that encompassed more than one gauge. That had been the situation along Lake Erie in the early 1850s. The principal railroad serving the Erie area used a gauge that measured six feet, which was as much as fourteen inches different from other roads in the region. Passengers hoping to travel from Buffalo to Cleveland—a common trip, some 183 miles in length—had to stop midway, disembark from their cars at North East in Pennsylvania, ride the wide-gauged line to Erie, disembark and change trains again, and resume their journey westward. "Within a reach of but twenty miles of track," one observer noted, "two transfers of passengers and freight were inevitable, a vexatious and expensive condition of affairs."[25] Among the prime beneficiaries of the lack of standardization, many observers pointed out, were the peanut vendors, popcorn sellers, and pie men of the city of Erie—hence the conflict's other, more derogatory title, the "Peanut War."[26]

Bad in summer, in winter the conditions became downright untenable, endangering both life and property. The situation continued until, "like a fishbone in one's gullet," the whole matter became so intolerable it forced a conclusion.[27] That conclusion was the Gauge War, which began on December 7, 1853, when residents responded to the railroad's efforts to change local track widths by gathering in the snow outside the Erie city courthouse to form an impromptu defensive force. The two sides—a goodly portion of Erie's residents, opposed by the railroad companies—were intractable. Citizens and merchants didn't want the gauge to change, because the delays caused by the disjunctions in track size meant passengers through the region often had to stay hours, if not overnight, in the city. On the other side of the debate stood the railroad companies, most particularly the Erie and North East, which saw the value in a uniform gauge. Work crews for the railroad went out to alter the gauge, repeatedly, and were beaten back by angry mobs. The city council waded into the fracas, ordering the railroad not to change its gauge and threatening a $500-per-day fine if it did.[28] Property was destroyed, after the protestors sawed through area bridges; another mob attacked railroad employees at the nearby township of Harborcreek. Horace Greeley, the editor of the *New York Tribune*, attempting to travel through Erie on his way to a speaking engagement, was seriously delayed and missed his speech.[29] In the pages of his newspaper, he described the delays and called the Erie citizens "rioters," their hometown the "inhospitable northern neck of Pennsylvania."[30]

By 1854, the Commonwealth of Pennsylvania had to step in to help quell the situation. Local militia aided in calming the populace—at least long enough for the rails to be re-laid at the new width. On February 1, the first train passed from Buffalo through Erie to Cleveland on the uniform gauge.[31] The conclusion of the Erie Gauge War was an important moment in railroading, both locally and nationally, in that it sent the message that nothing, and no one, would be allowed to stand in the way of railroad progress.

By June 1867, in calmer circumstances, the railroads that served Erie achieved another important milestone. In that month, officials of the Erie and North East and the Buffalo & State Line railroads approved a merger of the two companies that created a single entity: the Buffalo and Erie Railroad. "Yesterday," the *Buffalo Courier* reported that month, "the stockholders of the Erie and Northeast Railway Company met at Erie, Pa., and ratified the articles of agreement entered into several weeks since, by the Directors of the Company and those of the Buffalo and State Line Company."[32] The other half of the deal played out at eleven o'clock on the morning of June 25, 1867, when the stockholders of the Buffalo & State Line approved the deal. In prescient words, the *Courier*'s editors asserted that the merger was an important development for both cities. "This consolidation derives additional importance," the paper stated, "from the probability that it will prove the initial step of the union of all the railways between Buffalo and Toledo, and, possibly the connection may eventually extend further East and West."[33]

That was a shining goal for the future; in the meantime, the merger just made sense. The Buffalo & State Line ran for sixty-eight miles from Buffalo to a small hamlet on the state's border with Pennsylvania—the place where Josiah P. Hayward manned the station office. The Erie and North East covered twenty miles of territory between Erie and the community of North East, on the state's border with New York. Neither railroad on its own could offer passengers and shippers uninterrupted transit between the cities of Buffalo and Erie; together, however, they could.[34]

Typical of the period in founding and formation, the two railroad lines initially shared many similarities—they had even opened for business in the same year, 1852—and a few big differences, including gauge size and track miles. The Erie and North East had been organized first, in Erie in 1846. The road had gotten off to a promising start, after which work on its construction sat idle for a few years—a common occurrence. The line was conceived as a twenty-mile span linking Erie with the state's eastern border. Company president Charles M. Reed set the gauge for the railroad at six feet, and the railroad opened for business on January 19, 1852, with a celebration that included an excursion train carrying President Millard Fillmore, Secretary of State Daniel Webster, and members of Congress.[35] The railroad owned six passenger cars and two locomotives.

Meantime, the Buffalo & State Line had been organized in 1848 in Fredonia, New York, and envisioned as a sixty-eight-mile road from Buffalo westward to the New York–Pennsylvania border. Leaders in planning for the road were Dean Richmond, a Buffalonian who had made money in lake shipping and grain elevators, and James S. Wadsworth, a wealthy Geneseo resident who ended up in the Union army and died in the battle of the Wilderness.[36] At first, the idea for the new road was a tough sell in the lakeside communities through which it would pass. In Fredonia and Dunkirk, so convinced were residents that a railroad competing with steamships on Lake Erie would be a "miserable failure" that it took a full year of "teasing and drumming" by proponents before the $68,000 seed money for the road—$1,000 a mile—could be raised. Even then, investors gave over their cash grudgingly, mainly to escape the "persistent, troublesome committee" that had been canvassing them.[37]

But by February 22, 1852, the line had opened for passengers and freight—at a gauge of four feet, ten inches, the Ohio standard gauge. It was also a gauge close to the four feet, eight and a half inches of the powerful New York Central, which covered 297 miles.[38] The gauge offered a telling glimpse at both the self-image and the ambitions of the Buffalo railway: it hinted that road builders saw the route's future—even in a canal-tied, lake-centered city such as Buffalo—connected as much to the fortunes of the western territories as to the old trade routes with Albany and New York. It showed, too, that the railroad considered itself in a class with the biggest and best roads in operation.

At last, the cities of Buffalo and Erie were connected by rail. Financially, the gamble in building the roads between the two cities seemed to pay off. In its first two years of operation, the Erie and North East saw company earnings double, from $62,380 to $126,600; the Buffalo & State Line saw a similar doubling in this period, from $202,713 to $451,371, in one year's time.[39] A state report showed that the railroad operated eighty-eight miles of road, along with another forty miles of doubled track and sidings.

Of course, not everything went smoothly—before or after the merger. Animals were killed on the tracks frequently, resulting in annoyed farmers demanding cash settlements, which were paid out at the end of every month. One farmer had sixteen sheep killed by Buffalo & State Line trains in a single month; another farmer received twenty dollars from the road for two heifers killed in 1856.[40] The railroads also paid out settlements to people whose baggage had been lost. (In one case, the Buffalo & State Line managed to temporarily lose the trunks of an entire operatic troupe, which cost them $500 to remedy.)[41] Other problems were more serious. In August 1856, one of the Buffalo & State Line's locomotives, the Vulcan, exploded with "terrific violence" when an iron plate covering a portion of the firebox broke and released with pressure, throwing the fifty-four-thousand-pound engine twenty-five feet from the track into a ditch.[42] Upon inspection, railroad officials found that the Vulcan's iron plate had a twenty-four-inch flaw running through it, a problem labeled a "congenital defect" in the machine.[43]

The lesson was a troubling one: when a piece of railroad equipment, even one as visible and well tended as a locomotive, possessed such a hidden flaw, it could operate for miles—and months—without incident, only to explode dangerously and without warning.[44] A railroader at the time summarized the meaning of the Vulcan explosion this way: "Local defects, whether original or produced, may exist for a long time before the actual failure of the defective parts....Corrosion sometimes goes on entirely unsuspected."[45] It was a lesson that had unsettling implications for other sorts of railroad equipment: rails, switches, wheels, axles, couplers, frogs. Something could look all right to the naked eye—to a practiced eye, even—and not be all right at all.

IN HIS YEARS in the business, Sherman and other conductors of his generation had learned that they were like sea captains or presidents of small countries: responsible not only for the members of the public entrusted to their care, but also for the performance of their trainmen. Many of them, veterans like Sherman especially, chose to handpick their crew. Trains the size of the New York Express typically ran with five or six men—two brakemen, a fireman, an engineer and the conductor, sometimes a baggage man—and so every member counted for a good deal. On a day like this, when schedules were upset and weather unpredictable, it was as important for Sherman to have colleagues beside him that he could trust as it was to have his watch in working order and his timetable ready to hand.

Still, a conductor's choices were limited to the men available—the ones the company had hired. Smaller roads like the Buffalo and Erie suffered from high employee turnover, because qualified labor was scarce in the late 1860s. Potential employees were so much in demand in some quarters that they were asked to pass no basic measures of fitness—such as the ability to hear well or a lack of color-blindness.[46] On today's run, Sherman's crew included locomotive engineer Charles Carscadin, an employee of Buffalo-area roads since 1852; rear brakeman John Vanderburg of Buffalo; front brakeman Gilbert W. Smith of Irving; fireman Charles Newton, a greenhorn; and James A. Woods, a baggage man, also of Buffalo.

Sherman knew them all well, but Carscadin he knew best. The two veterans went back together fourteen years on the railroad. "I think he is a first-class engineer," Sherman later said of Carscadin. "I never saw him drink liquor but once while on duty, and he did not drink so much then that he could not attend to his duty perfectly."[47] As for Gilbert W. Smith, he would have been typical of the waves of new recruits that the railroads had absorbed in the wake of the war's end. These men were simply educated, many of them from farming backgrounds; they had been burnished into hard workers and impervious employees by years spent in the theater of war. Contrary to the legends that would grow up around railroad crewmen—particularly brakemen, who had the reputation of being cowboys—Smith would have been the sort of employee that many railroad workers resembled.

The Gilbert W. Smith riding the train that day as forward brakeman was likely a young man who had grown up in humble surroundings in Irving, a small rural community in upstate New York, not far from Angola. Shortly after turning eighteen, in November 1861, the slight youth with the gray-blue eyes and brown hair had enlisted in Company D of the Seventy-Eighth Infantry then forming in the state. Smith joined the army on impulse—and without his father's permission. (He was hardly alone. At the other end of the state, in Schenectady, a fifteen-year-old boy named George Westinghouse Jr. would do the same thing and be returned to his parents when the Union army initially refused to take him. Westinghouse ultimately served in both army and navy.)[48] Later in life, when asked about his occupation upon enlistment, Smith would scrawl "school-boy."[49] As if to bear out his words, military records show Gilbert Smith was not done growing when he enlisted; five foot eight and a half inches in 1861, he grew another inch and a half over the next few years.

Once in uniform, Smith saw action for nearly a year. He was captured near Charleston, West Virginia, on October 4, 1862. Paroled two days later and sent back to Union lines near Harpers Ferry, Smith must have felt overwhelmed. Around November 1, 1862, he left the Union army without leave—"deserted," in the words of government paperwork, although federal officials noted that he did not desert a military duty but merely left without permission. (Again Smith was far from alone: by 1862, desertion had become such a problem for the Union army that President Lincoln wrote to General McClellan that forty-five thousand men of the Army of the Potomac were "still alive and not with it." "How can they be got to you," Lincoln asked, "and how can they be prevented from getting away in such numbers in the future?")[50] Smith, for his part, had gone home. After a two-month hiatus, in January 1863, he rejoined the army, then was discharged. Military and civil judgments would clear Smith of any wrongdoing, though his federal pension would be docked for the time he had been away. In later years, Smith would put the matter simply. "I was taken prisoner and paroled," he stated, "and my father took me away."[51]

By 1867, as a brakeman for the Buffalo and Erie, Gilbert Smith had a good job and was earning a steady wage. He got to see a lot of the countryside of New York and Pennsylvania—in nice weather, the brakeman's chief treat. His future looked bright. But train crew members like Smith knew their jobs for the violent and unforgiving roles they were. Mistakes cost you in serious ways, and even without mistakes, every trip meant a chance for injury. Brakemen, engineers, firemen, and conductors—the ones who physically made the trains run—were, by some calculations, representative of about 20 percent of the railroads' workforce at this time, but accounted for 60 percent of all fatalities in the industry and 56 percent of all injuries.[52]

No one had promised these men an easy job. The dangers of railroad work were understood, even taken for granted—especially by men who had so recently fought a bloody war. It was in the air; it was, like soot, part of the atmosphere.

SHERMAN'S TRAIN SNAKED along the Lake Erie shoreline, grinding every now and then to a stop to admit blasts of cold air when the platform doors clattered open, along with clusters of frigid passengers.

In North East, two young men stepped up to the train. William H. Ross, twenty-four years old, and twenty-six-year-old Ammon H. Spier were brothers-in-law who lived in the rural community. They looked over the crowded coaches and were forced to choose seats in different cars. Ross, a veteran of the war, found a seat in the second-last car. Spier, a husband and the father of two small children, squeezed into the rear coach. A few miles down the track, the train crossed from Pennsylvania into New York and jolted to a stop in State Line. The hamlet's wood-framed depot stood a half mile down the road from the modest farmhouse where Josiah P. Hayward had roused his wife Anna with his terrible dream. Now, as Hayward climbed aboard the train's second-last car, he could feel the $3,000 insurance policy he had just purchased, tucked within his coat.

The express cruised along, still about two hours behind schedule. It consisted of four passenger coaches, three first-class cars and one second-class, and four baggage cars. However, only half the train's rolling stock—and none of the train's last three cars—belonged to the Buffalo and Erie Railroad, railroad crew members would later confirm. The train's last three cars, according to testimony Benjamin F. Sherman would later give in court, belonged to the Cleveland and Toledo and Cleveland and Erie railroads; the second-class coach on the train that day was a Buffalo and Erie car.[53] Such mixed lots of cars on train runs, known as "mixed consists" in the industry, were common in the late 1860s among railroad trains, especially on shorter-line roads that moved passengers along segments of a longer route.[54]

Sherman planned to make the train's scheduled stops as advertised. But he wasn't planning to dawdle in any of the stations, and he surely wasn't considering any unscheduled stops. By early afternoon, the conductor would have been in no mood for any further changes to his agenda. "I gave the engineer no order as to running the train," Sherman said.[55] That meant the train was going to stick to the basics and try to make time.

As the minutes ticked past 1:30 p.m., the train steamed toward its next goal, Westfield, a bucolic village midway between State Line and Brocton. There, a forty-one-year-old carpenter named Zachariah Hubbard stood on the station platform, no doubt jangling the keys on his large iron key ring with impatience. He was waiting, and the temperature was dropping. A thermometer about ten miles away in Mayville would register six degrees below zero by the following morning, and Hubbard could feel it in the wind on his face and fingers.[56] He longed for the steamy heat from the coal stoves aboard the train. It couldn't come fast enough.

In the meantime, there was nothing to do *but* wait. Hubbard, a Canadian, was on his way home to the Port Dalhousie area of St. Catharines, Ontario, to see his wife, Ellen McAndrews Hubbard, thirty-seven, and their children William, fifteen, Martha, twelve, and Margaret, six. Like most passengers, Hubbard would have known the trains to be unpredictable beasts. You coped the best you could, and that is what Hubbard did as he waited for the shriek of a whistle in the distance. The woodworker had been living in Westfield temporarily while working for a man in the village, but now he was done. The Hubbard family certainly looked forward to being together again, especially with Christmas coming. Ellen Hubbard would have been particularly eager for Zachariah's homecoming. A practical Presbyterian who had been born in Scotland, Ellen Hubbard was strong and resourceful, but she was looking forward to having her husband home again.

At 1:46 p.m., Zachariah Hubbard climbed aboard the New York Express and settled into his seat on the last car of the train. He relaxed, and began to warm up. The train moved forward, again, toward the east.

CHAPTER 6

Approach

———◆———

THE WOOD DEALER Benjamin F. Betts hastened down the platform of the Brocton station, coat flapping behind him, wooden floorboards clattering under his feet. People pushed past to his left and right, intent on hellos and goodbyes, reunions and removals, but Betts's eyes would have remained focused straight ahead. He didn't rattle easily; a man in his business couldn't. But today had been a test of his patience, and he surely wouldn't have wanted anything more to go awry.

As the Tonawanda businessman hurried along the platform, snow slid from the folds of his overcoat, and gray slush squeaked beneath the thick soles of his boots. It was somewhere around 2 p.m.; in his haste, it was no surprise that even Betts had lost track of the exact time.[1] From the railway station outdoors to the dining room, then back outdoors again, now through the snow to the train—it all did a number on one's shoes and clothing, not to mention one's mood. Earlier in the day, the express inbound to Brocton from Erie had been delayed longer than anyone expected, by two full hours. Betts and the other passengers waiting in the depot—among them Jasper and Eunice Fuller, a couple from Spartansburg, Pennsylvania, as well as Benjamin Aikin of Hydetown, plus others who had climbed down from the Corry Cross-Cut's connector train that afternoon—had been advised to see about getting their dinners in town. Betts took the suggestion to heart, and got his meal. The American Hotel would have been suggested: perhaps oysters, a house specialty, were on the day's menu.

But getting to any restaurants hadn't been easy, partly because the station was a stiff hike and a small hill away from the center of Brocton, but also because in weather like this no one wanted to get too deeply involved in a plate of food and miss the train—there wouldn't be another for hours. The situation wore upon the nerves; one had to keep getting up and down, checking for the black hulk of the locomotive. Betts and the other passengers would surely have pitied Mary Chadeayne, a wife and mother whose husband had been in Titusville, Pennsylvania, who was shepherding her daughters Anna, thirteen, and Carry, three, throughout the afternoon on her own.[2] Betts himself, at thirty-nine hardly an old man, on days like this no doubt thought longingly of the desk in his comfortable office, the cozy hearth in his home.

The train's whistle shrieked, abruptly, like a teakettle snatched from a blistering stove. A few snowflakes floated down from the sky, disappearing as they neared earth into the clouds of smoke and steam from the train. It would snow before nightfall, a real snow. Hustling along, Betts fixed his gaze on the engine and the row of eight cars glistening in the mid-afternoon light. The doors were closed; the train appeared about to pull away. Unbelievable, that he could come close to missing his ride after all that time spent waiting: time lost, work lost, money lost.

Betts had come to Brocton, as he went most places, for the wood. The agricultural community had started life as "Salem Cross Roads"—a name picked out of a hat by a settler one winter's night—but had grown because of its location on Lake Erie and the fact that its fields grew good grapes, fruit that made for some of the best wine in New York.[3] By the Civil War, Brocton and the surrounding town of Portland had become a prosperous place, home to 373 families.[4] George Pullman had been a member of one of them; born in 1831, he lived in Salem until he was seventeen. (By 1867, Pullman had incorporated the Pullman Palace Car Company and unveiled the first "hotel car," "The President," which offered in-suite sleeping and dining on Canada's Great Western Railway.)[5] As a sign of the area's success, residents in the 1850s decided to change the settlement's name to "Brocton" by combining the surnames of two hotel owners, J. H. Minton and a Mr. Brockway.[6] By the late 1860s, Brocton boasted restaurants and hotels, wine shops, socials, and dances; by 1910, the village would attract three railroads providing sixteen passenger runs a day.[7] Passengers on some trains delayed in Brocton would report on fancy dinners arranged for them at the American Hotel, along with sleigh rides and wine tastings.[8] There were worse places to be stuck while waiting for a train.

Betts, however, would have had no eyes for any of it, as he dashed for the New York Express. Ahead of him, clouds of smoke and soot rose into the cold air. His stomach full of the dinner he had just consumed, Betts bounded for the train's last coach as he heard the conductor bellow a final call. "Express to Buffalo! New York Express!"

Betts jumped, reaching out a hand for the iron railing of the rear platform. He caught it and began to haul himself aboard. Just then, the glass-windowed door at the end of the coach opened, letting out a puff of sour-smelling air. A man stepped out, followed in a moment by a well-dressed lady.

"Full, it's full!" they called to Betts, waving him away with gloved hands.

"Full!" echoed Betts, stepping back from the coach, his face no doubt revealing his disbelief. In front of him, the train clanked and hissed, each link and pin straining to move, as the car gave up the weary groan of metal forced into motion.

It was the way things had gone all day. The one consolation to his problems of the day had been friendship—of the unexpected sort. Forced to kill time, Betts had struck up conversations with the people clustered near him in the waiting room and restaurant. The Fullers, on their way to buy supplies for their store; W. C. Patterson, a passenger who had boarded in Hydetown with Benjamin Aikin; Aikin himself, bound for Wyoming County to visit one of his five grown children.[9] Betts had liked one man in particular: a Pennsylvanian in his mid-fifties, reserved of manner, with a squared jaw and penetrating gaze. Stephen W. Steward, a substantial-looking man with dark eyes, neatly combed brown hair, and deeply carved lines around his mouth—in the right light, he looked not unlike Abraham Lincoln—was president of the First National Bank in Corry. He was also involved in the area's railroads, as a director—along with William G. Fargo, founder of the Wells Fargo company—of the Buffalo, Corry and Pittsburg Railroad, a 36.7-mile span of track connecting Brocton in New York with State Line, and at the time operating five locomotives along with a complement of twenty-six cars.[10] Both of these concerns appealed to Benjamin Betts, who had a creative mind and saw the raw potential in the wood he purchased and sold: the possibility of beautiful structures, designed for both form and function.[11] Steward was certainly a good man to know. Betts had shared his dinner table with the banker, and thought of him as a new friend.

Now Betts looked up at the train and saw, through the glass window, his friend Steward settling into the last seat on the coach car.[12] There was truly no other room. Full, even overfull, the train was about to leave.

The wood dealer realized he had one last chance, and he bolted to seize it. His coat flapping around him, Betts dashed out from behind the rear car and ran along the side of the end coach, its varnished walls bearing letters that spelled out the name of the Cleveland and Toledo Railroad, and the car's number—No. 21.[13] The elegant script blurred beside Betts as he sped toward the front of the car, then past it, and up to the rear platform of the

The most important person on board the train that day, in business terms, Stephen W. Steward was the president of a bank in Corry, Pennsylvania. He was also a husband and father. Courtesy of the Chautauqua County Historical Society, Westfield, New York.

second-last coach. It was a Cleveland & Erie car that had been in use by the Buffalo and Erie Railroad, and it, too, was No. 21. Heaving himself onto the carriage's platform, Betts surely gasped for breath. A jolt would have rocked his body backward and then forward again, as the car below him was put in motion.

He had made it. He had caught the ride he needed: the ride that would take him into Buffalo, where he would connect with a short-line route that would take him to his own home city a few miles to the north, and to his wife, Mary, and their four boys.[14] The youngest, Edward, was only nine years old. Surely he would still be awake, listening for Betts's tread on the step, his turn of the latch.

❧

JUST AFTER 2 P.M., according to later witness testimony, as the express train steamed away from Brocton, station agent and telegraph operator J. M. Newton picked up a piece of paper in his office in the Angola depot. It was an order, and it affected the inbound passenger train. With Sherman's engine running two hours behind, road officials were scrambling things around to keep traffic moving.

"Conductor and engineer of Freight No. 6," the telegram read. "Run ahead of New York Express to Buffalo." The order bore the name of John Desmond, an assistant superintendent of the Buffalo and Erie Railroad, who was coordinating the flow of traffic that day from his offices in Buffalo.[15]

Newton at this moment would have looked up and out the window, to where the No. 6 freight train rested on a sidetrack. It had been there perhaps fifteen minutes—not long. So far, seven trains had passed through the village between the first freight of the morning at 7 a.m. and the eastbound No. 6. Angola station hands, including Newton, had also noted that Peter Emslie, the chief civil engineer of the Buffalo and Erie Railroad, had passed through on one of the westbound trains, headed toward some work he was doing for the railroad farther down the line. (Emslie would pass through Angola aboard local trains twice that morning, in fact, noting as he did so that all seemed to be "in perfect order" along the track.)[16] Now, crew members of the latest freight had just finished attaching another car to its lengthy consist, or make-up of cars. The freight's original order had been to remain in Angola until the express rolled through, before heading off for Buffalo behind the faster passenger train. But that order had changed.

Newton would have felt some degree of resignation as he shrugged on his heavy coat and pulled open his office door, braving the winter chill once more. On days like this, one had to deal with circumstances as they arose. Adjustments were constantly being made in railroad schedules; despite their perceived strictness, the day's orders were actually quite fluid. Telegraphed commands, like the one in Newton's hand from Desmond, ruled the day. Though there was some chatter that a new method of controlling trains had recently been devised—the so-called block signaling system, designed to keep trains a safe distance apart by dividing the route into "blocks" or intervals, and in use for two years on the Camden and Amboy road—it was still a rudimentary manual technique, one that wouldn't be improved upon by electricity until the 1870s.[17] There was, in the meantime, the telegraph machine—itself a relatively novel device—and plenty of young men like Newton, hired to trot messages back and forth. (That there were so many young men at the controls of the telegraphs was occasionally made clear in embarrassing ways. Earlier that year, a few telegraph operators in Buffalo had been caught using the wires to send a joke to Cleveland. "To Haman Deggs, Cleveland," the gag ran. "Sallie will die, just come quick. A Hungryman." The prank made the newspapers—where news editors evidently got a charge out of the sophomoric humor—in both cities as well as in Chicago.)[18]

Outside the depot, Newton flagged down James Mahar, the switchman, and told him about the change. Then the two men trudged over to the waiting freight and talked to the train's crew. As the small knot of men conversed, their breath would have turned to tendrils of vapor that rose like smoke in the frigid air. Then, within minutes, the No. 6 freight was watered, fueled, and ready. It lumbered over the repaired frog juncture and wing rail east of the Angola station, the place where Mahar and the others had labored that morning to hammer a new rail into place. Back on the main line, the freight picked up speed and rumbled off into the distance.

Newton watched it go, then surely headed back to his office. He had much to do, to get ready for the approach of Sherman's express. Mahar, meanwhile, locked the switch back into place in the wake of the No. 6. Mahar was the only one in Angola allowed to work the device, and he took his role seriously. Then he walked off down the track to inspect the frog and rail. He had to make sure everything was all right, if only for his own peace of mind. In Mahar's words, such diligence in patrolling the rails and switches was nothing less than his job. "I consider it a portion of my duty," he would later say, in his plainspoken fashion.[19]

And so, just as he had numerous times that day, the vigilant switchman now bent down and scrutinized the place where the broken rail had snapped. It seemed fine. Even to his experienced eye, nothing looked amiss. "It was then as it had been all day," Mahar stated. "I am sure the rail was all right, then."[20]

Satisfied, he tramped through the snowdrifts back to the freight house.

ACROSS THE STREET from where James Mahar had studied the snow-crusted rail, another man stood shivering in a storefront doorway, his restless eyes scanning the landscape. Cyrus Wilcox, owner of a boot shop in Angola's business district, had seen his brother Alanson walking down the tracks toward the bridge and the open country on the other side of the creek. He wondered what Alanson, a wood dealer, was up to. Perhaps his brother had some business on the other side of Big Sister Creek, or meant to pay a call on a neighbor. From his spot in the doorway of his shop, it would have been impossible for Cyrus to tell.

Alanson Wilcox wasn't the only one out and about that afternoon. Angola was alive and humming, the small strip of businesses across Commercial Street from the railroad tracks a center of activity. To the left of Wilcox's shoe shop, Sely Blackney was surely bustling about in his grocery store, sacking flour and bagging sugar for customers doing their Christmas baking; to his right, the bell on the door to Mrs. I. S. Thompson's dress and millinery shop would have tinkled frequently with the comings and goings of stylish women, each eager to have the most fashionable holiday hat. As Cyrus Wilcox—his name, which referenced an ancient Persian king, an odd juxtaposition to his job as a shopkeeper—watched his brother climb the hill on the other side of the Big Sister, he couldn't help but wonder. Alanson must be headed toward the home of Josiah Southwick, the area's justice of the peace. On that side of the creek, there was really not much in the way of destinations, other than Southwick's brick home with its Italianate styling and gracefully arched windows, one of the loveliest structures in Angola. What could Alanson be up to?

Wilcox turned back into the interior of his shop. He would have realized that there was no more time to waste wondering. He no doubt made sure the door was fastened; the wind was sharp as a knife. There were shoes to clean and repair, lasts to tend to, customers to mind. And yet, as Cyrus Wilcox resumed his tasks, his mind returned to his brother. He would keep one eye on the window, he decided. And when he saw Alanson pass back along the tracks, he would flag him down and find out what was going on.

JOSIAH SOUTHWICK'S was the sort of front door that was forever being knocked upon. Farmer, father, justice, statesman: Southwick was all those things, and a devout Quaker, too. This meant he had the habit of listening with kindly interest when his neighbors brought him their problems and prides, their questions and quarrels. He was a patient man, and a wise one, and he knew the value of a helping hand.

The morning and early afternoon of December 18, 1867, had been no different. Southwick would have risen early in his home on the outskirts of Angola, across Big Sister Creek from the business district and within close range of the tracks and truss bridge. Old habits died hard, and even now, at thirty-nine, when he could claim a place as one of the region's most successful men—the owner of many acres of farmland, a community leader—Southwick still went about his life according to the patterns ingrained in him by decades of farming. He and his family lived in rhythm with nature and the passage of each season; they planned for the future, but took each new day as it came.

The early morning hours would have passed quietly, as was usual, in the Southwick home on Mill Street. The property had cost $1,500 when Josiah and Huldah Hawley Southwick, who had married in 1850, bought it in 1853. The house had come with more than five acres of farmland, which the couple had added to over time. For Southwick, the acreage meant a chance to expand his farm operations, which were already well on their way to becoming recognized as among the most productive in the state. (In 1855, a report by Congress on domestic animals included a table showing the annual

Josiah and Huldah Southwick, shown here in later years surrounded by family, turned their stately brick home near Big Sister Creek into a temporary hospital for the care of the wreck's wounded. Josiah Southwick, a Quaker, was a justice of the peace in Angola at the time. Courtesy of Diana M. Crippen and the descendants of Ulric Southwick.

production of six of Josiah's top-performing cows, one of which approached the three-thousand-quart mark.)[21] To a couple like Josiah and Huldah Southwick, the brick home in Angola—big enough for four bedrooms and two staircases, one for household help—would have represented success. Set on a slight hill, and rising two full stories, the house gave the effect of remoteness; it could appear, to the fanciful, to be peering from a lofty perch at the little village. The structure had been built in the 1840s with walls nearly two feet thick and an exterior of locally made brick in a distinctive orange color stippled with black.[22] Three chimneys kept the house warm, supplying heat to almost every room. By 1867, Josiah and Huldah, thirty-four, had filled the house with four children—three boys, Richard, John Jay, and Wilfred, and a girl, Lillian, who was just three years old.[23]

Best of all was the view. The front windows of the home offered a thrilling landscape: the sloping hillside and Big Sister ravine, the railroad bridge, and beyond that the businesses of the commercial district. From their parlor windows, the Southwicks could see the trains pass every day, in daylight and dark. The sound of the trains, their clanks and whistles, had become the background cadence to their lives. In the spring of 1865, when Abraham Lincoln's funeral train passed through Angola, draped in mourning and bedecked with a portrait of the slain president, Josiah and Huldah would have been able to watch it pass without ever leaving the rocking chairs on their front porch.

Now, Josiah Southwick prepared for a weekday afternoon that—thanks to the season—would lean more heavily not toward farming duties, but toward social calls and business ones.

AT DUNKIRK, the train's last major stop before Buffalo, the New York Express slowed to a halt on a sidetrack. Material needed to be offloaded, and the express was to drop one of its four baggage and cargo cars at this stop, reducing the total number of the train's cars to seven. A small handful of travelers, among them Dr. Orin C. Payne, a fifty-one-year-old physician and clergyman from Fredonia who was headed to Angola for the afternoon, used the opportunity to climb on board. Most of the new boarders chose to sit in the forward carriages—they were slightly less crowded than those in the rear of the train.[24] If Orin Payne had opted for a rear car, he might have noticed that his sister-in-law, Mrs. Lydia M. Strong, was also on board the train. Strong was sitting with her daughter, Frances, and grandchild in the second-last car. But Dr. Payne did not.

While the new passengers settled in, another express, this one headed west to Cleveland, sped by on the main line, sending a shower of sparks and soot over the stilled train. Sherman would have watched the other train stream past, checking his watch as the minutes ticked by. It was coming up on 2:30 p.m.—well over two hours past the express's timetable departure time of 12:05 p.m. from Dunkirk.[25] On the heels of the New York Express now pressed the Buffalo and Erie's second day express, which had started from Cleveland a few hours after the New York Express. That second express had pulled out of Erie's Union Depot in the neighborhood of 2 p.m.—carrying passengers including John D. Rockefeller, who planned on catching up to his valise and Christmas gifts in Buffalo within a few hours' time.

At last, Frank Sherman got word that his train's cargo of Dunkirk-bound goods had been fully unloaded, and the one unneeded freight car unhitched from the train's consist. He gave the signal to Charles Carscadin in the cab.[26] Time to press onward, again.

Brakemen John Vanderburg and Gilbert Smith, meanwhile, would have been growing tired. They had been at their work seven hours and thirty minutes, and there was at least another hour and a half to go before dinner and rest. The two brakemen, each with less than a year's experience, rode on the coach platforms two cars apart, working the brake controls for two cars apiece.

The chain brakes were primitive beasts. When they went into action, everyone in the train knew it, due to the bumping and clanking of cars against other cars, because the brakes tended to work at different rates and efficacies—all depending on a single man's muscle. "The brake we use is the ordinary chain brake," said John Desmond, assistant superintendent of the Buffalo and Erie road. "We have none of the…patent brakes on our road. Two brakemen would be the usual number allowed to a train of the size of the New York Express."[27]

Two men to stop four passenger cars usually moving at between twenty-five and thirty miles per hour—a "top speed" of the time, which was usually not exceeded on most railroads, according to one observer—may have been typical, but it wasn't easy.[28] The job of brakemen like Vanderburg and Smith was simple and repetitive, yet grueling. About a mile before any station where a stop was desired, the engineer of a passenger train like the express would blow "one long blast" on his whistle; this put the brakemen on alert that they were needed.[29] Then the engineer would close off the throttle, which would cut the forward-motion energy of the train. "The natural effect of this act," wrote the same observer, "was that the train would drift."[30] This is where brakemen like Vanderburg and Smith sprang into action. Stepping onto the platforms of the cars, the brakeman would scan the landscape for landmarks in order to gauge the distance remaining before the station—and to make a judgment call, on the spot, as to how much braking power would be needed. It wasn't a job for the slow or dull-witted. "Among these factors," the observer noted, "there would be the distance that the train must cover to its proposed stopping point, the grades of the railway to be traversed, and whether they were of the ascending or descending character."[31]

The brakeman then needed to set the hand-brake on his car's platform; if it seemed like the force would not be enough to accomplish his goal in time, he would swing to the adjacent platform and set the brake there as well. If the train seemed to be screeching too quickly to a halt, the brakeman used his foot to kick the ratchets on the platform floor, which would release the brakes a bit. "He might apply and release the brakes a half dozen times in connection with one stop…the train would be alternately plunging forward and slowing up," the observer noted.[32] And that was not all. The engineer at this point also typically got into the mix, by either opening his throttle so that the train dove forward, or "plugging his engine," which was throwing the locomotive into reverse. "Whatever the engineer might do, whether in harmony with the efforts of the hand-brakes or not, serious jerking effects would be communicated to the necks of the passengers," the observer concluded.[33] All in all, stopping a train like the New York Express was a process that was inexact, labor intensive, and dangerous. It could also be, in the hands of a good brakeman, akin to an art.

That afternoon, Vanderburg, twenty-nine, had drawn duty on the rear two passenger cars. The younger and less practiced Smith took the forward two. As usual, when they were between braking sessions, the brakemen were allowed to duck inside the glass-paned doors of the coaches and perch on seats positioned directly next to the potbellied stoves.[34] It served to warm them up—if only temporarily.

Now, as the train groaned forward, off the sidetrack and onto the main line, Vanderburg and Smith were hurrying back to the warmth of the glowing stoves. It was roughly between 2:25 and 2:30 p.m., Sherman would later recall.[35] Ahead lay Silver Creek, where Sherman would get word that the No. 6 freight was being slotted ahead of him on the track to Buffalo. There, wood and water would be loaded onto the train. There also a few passengers— including Dr. Payne, who had realized to his exasperation that the New York Express no longer stopped at Angola, and that he would have to get off and board the next local train to reach his destination—would climb down from the cars and walk away on the platform, the last passengers to leave the train at its final stop.[36]

THE EXPRESS did not linger in Silver Creek. At 2:49 p.m., George P. Ganson, the station's daytime telegraph operator, tapped out a message to his friend J. M. Newton in Angola: the New York was on its way.[37]

In Angola, Newton picked up Ganson's message. He read the letters and numbers over to himself: "O.S. 15 SC. N.Y. Ex. 33 2k."[38] The meaning of the message was simple: "Train report, for all eastward stations along the line, from Silver Creek, the New York Express left this station at 2:49." Newton would have made a mental note to jot down the exact time in his logbook later. First, he had a few tasks to take care of, and they couldn't wait.

He got up from his desk, buttoned himself into his cap and coat, and headed out to the tracks. It was Newton's practice to scan the tracks in both directions before the arrival of any passenger train, whether it was stopping in Angola or not. He knew he had twenty or thirty minutes in which to do it—that was the time it took an express like the New York to travel from Ganson's post to his. Newton now went through his checks, noticing nothing of concern on the track, at the frog juncture, or at the switch. "Mahar told me he closed the switch after the freight train passed," Newton would later say. "I could see from the platform that the switches were all right at that time."[39]

Satisfied, Newton stepped back into his office and closed the door. He bent to his telegraph machine and log book. When the whistle of the inbound express shrilled in the west, Newton barely registered it; nor did the rumbling of the tracks in advance of the train's approach catch his attention. "I can't say whether I heard it whistle on its approach," Newton would later admit. "I am so accustomed to hear whistles that I pay no attention to them."[40]

There was, however, one attentive listener hovering around the station, for James Mahar wanted to hear the express train coming. The switchman wanted to watch it fly over the frog, over the replaced rail, over the creek bridge, and away to Buffalo. He wanted to know everything was fine.

And so, as the minutes ticked down to 3 p.m., then beyond, Mahar hung about outside the freight house, trying not to draw attention to himself, but nonetheless vigilant. For a few minutes at least, until the train had come and gone, he could stand the cold.

ON BOARD the express, railroad employees were busy. In the train's cab, Charles Carscadin pushed the train to thirty miles an hour through the woods and farm fields, even beyond, working steam to earn back time lost earlier in the day. Fireman Newton, a greenhorn on the Buffalo and Erie with two weeks' experience, piled wood from the tender into the engine; only once, about three-quarters of a mile outside Angola, did he take a break to oil some valves. Vanderburg and Smith pulled on their gloves, ready to slow the train while going through the Angola station, even though no stop was planned.

Ahead of them, in the distance, loomed the Big Sister bridge, spare and plain in the afternoon light. They couldn't see much of it from their places on the moving train. To a casual witness observing the structure from nearby, the bridge looked like what it was: a timber and masonry span, old-fashioned, almost quaint, in this age of iron and steel; a structure patched here and there with tin, and everywhere bleached a dirty grayish-brown by winter sleets and summer suns. Technically, the bridge was considered a Howe truss, referring to the angle of its slanted supports. The design had been named for New England architect William Howe, who had begun building such bridges three decades before.

The *New York Times* would later assert that it was "hard to imagine a place where a railway accident would be more certainly fatal."[41] For the Angola bridge was not a simple plank span across a ditch, a glorified culvert, in the fashion of some railroad bridges of the time. No, the Big Sister's creek ravine was surprisingly deep—some fifty feet to the bottom in places—and wide. Wide enough to allow rail travelers to count off the seconds while riding across in a train. The gully was a more abrupt fall to the west than to the east, where there was a generous embankment that made for a less starkly vertical wall. To approach the Big Sister from the west aboard a moving train was to ride along on a horizontal plane until suddenly the land fell away beneath your feet, leaving you suspended in air—a sensation "sufficiently startling," in the words of the *Times*.[42] It was indeed stomach-clenching, on the smoothest of trips.

Below the bridge, which cut across the gorge at a modest angle, a dam for a nearby timber mill created a small pool, frozen over in the months of December and January, its depths hidden beneath a scurf of soot-tinged snow.

Whatever the bridge's aspect, Conductor Sherman had no time to linger upon the scene. In the final minutes before Angola, he was busiest of all. In the twenty minutes that elapsed between Silver Creek and Angola, Sherman walked through all four passenger cars, taking up new tickets and checking over the old ones held by passengers. He started with the coach car nearest the engine and made his way back, row by row, through the other three.

In one of the forward cars, in a smoking section, Benjamin F. Betts no doubt sat looking out of a small circle wiped in the frosty glass window, watching the landscape flash by. He would have showed Sherman his ticket almost automatically. Nearby, Dr. Frederick F. Hoyer, forty-five, a well-known physician—and a neighbor of Betts's, who lived on the same street in the city of Tonawanda—settled into a cushioned seat and pulled out a cigar.[43] He too would have waved his ticket at Sherman, then focused on lighting his smoke. Farther back, in the second-last car, Sherman inspected tickets from William Ross and Josiah P. Hayward, the young men from North East and State Line. He took up the paper of a young fellow by the name of J. W. Kennedy, from Essex County, who carried in one pocket of his clothing a claim tag, No. 4062, which Kennedy hoped would help him find his trunk in the melee that could surround a baggage car at the end of a trip.[44] ("Let us approach the baggage-man with tenderness," one traveler of the day wrote. "Let us tender him a quarter, if he in turn will give quarter to our trunk. He is square-built and broad-shouldered. His vigorous exercise in throwing things has developed his muscles till he projects like a catapult. It is pleasant to watch his playful ways, provided you carry your baggage in your hat.")[45] Sherman then checked the tickets of a party of black-garbed women, their faces surely revealing their tiredness. Frances M. Gale, barely twenty years old, was a new widow; she had just buried her thirty-six-year-old husband, Henry, a doctor, who had died of consumption the week before.[46] Frances was traveling home from Henry's funeral with her small child and her mother, Lydia M. Strong— Dr. Payne's sister-in-law, the forty-seven-year-old wife of a Buffalo jeweler.[47]

Also surrendering their tickets were Simeon and Lizzie Thompson, the Massachusetts siblings, and Randall Butler Graves, forty-five, a hardware store owner who was planning on changing trains in Buffalo to the New York Central's evening express, which would take him into Manhattan so he could pick up his wife and children, who wanted his company for their own train ride from New York City back home to Jackson, Michigan. Sherman checked the tickets of Robert J. Dickson, son of a Lake Erie ship captain, and his friend Frank Walker, the Buffalo jeweler's son. He checked passes of the train's mothers: Christiana Lang and her two children, James and Mary; Emma Fisher and Mary Chadeayne, each of whom had babies in their arms—nine-month-old Minnie and three-year-old Carry.

Moving into the last car of the train, Sherman walked down the long aisle, nodding to people he knew. The three young men from Erie—Towner, Metcalf, and Marten—were likely talking and laughing, making the most of their holiday jaunt. Then there was the little group from rural Pennsylvania: Benjamin Aikin, the Fullers, and Mr. Patterson. Sherman glanced at the passes of the newlywed Kents, Granger and Abbie, and an older couple, the Thomases of Utica, who sat nearby. He checked the ticket of Morgan Kedzie, the eighteen-year-old only son of John Kedzie of Rochester, who was headed home. Sherman also checked the ticket of lawyer Eliakim B. Forbush, fifty-five, who had traveled east from his Cincinnati court appearance with his client, a Silver Creek businessman. Forbush's client had climbed off the train at the last stop. Alone at last, Forbush no doubt turned his thoughts homeward, to Walter, his son and the junior partner in his law firm, and to his wife, Emily.

Last of all, Sherman would have checked over the ticket of Stephen W. Steward, the bank president, who sat in the last car's rearmost seat, his back toward the west.

They were almost to Buffalo. Twenty-one more miles was all. Close enough so that a practiced railman—as Sherman was—could feel the subtle shift in mood inside the cars. People would have seemed restless, but happier. They would have been no longer fixed on the pains and inconveniences of the present; their minds would have shifted, like birds uncaged, to the immediate future.

By the time Angola rose into view in front of the engine, Sherman had his tickets in hand, and was feeling relieved. "I had all my tickets in the entire train collected," he later said.[48] As Sherman gazed around the interior of the car, he would have done the mental arithmetic he had been too busy to do all day. Forty-five people, perhaps, in the last car alone, according to his conservative estimates; about forty or so, he judged, in the second-to-last car.[49] A packed train—but that was to be expected at this time of year.

Sherman decided to remain in the last car of the train until after the express passed through Angola. He walked over to the front end of the car, to where John Vanderburg sat "on the front seat next to the stove."[50] The two men would have nodded at each other and exchanged a word of greeting. Then Vanderburg rose from his seat, for he needed to be near the brake wheel. The brakeman opened the door—the rattle of the coupler and clamor of the wheels would have flooded into the compartment—and passed out onto the front platform of the end car, which shook in the wind and speed like the deck of a ship. Sherman slipped through the door behind Vanderburg, then closed the door, sealing the passengers back into their enclosure of relative quiet.[51] He stood next to Vanderburg on the noisy, vibrating platform deck.

Vanderburg and Sherman could barely hear each other above the din, but they didn't need to talk—their eyes surely said enough. Angola, at last—just ahead. No doubt about it, they would have agreed: today's journey had been a long one. It would be good to be done. Tomorrow was a clean start.

Sherman turned his gaze ahead, to the Angola depot, the storefronts, the creek bridge.

Vanderburg too would have eyed the landscape, picked his landmarks, and moved to the back end of the second-last car in order to operate his braking wheel on the back of that coach.[52] He began to apply the chain brakes to the second-last car, in order to decrease speed—ever so slightly, on an order that may well have been a standing one from Carscadin, the engineer—as they cruised through the village.

The watch on Sherman's vest turned over, to 3:10 p.m.

IN ANGOLA, some residents thought the express was coming in faster than normal—at thirty miles per hour or more. "I thought it was going faster than usual," said one man, the carpenter A. M. Avery, who watched the train pass from the front window of a tin shop that abutted the railroad tracks. "I thought, from the way the engine was running, that it was working steam."[53] Others didn't agree. "I don't think it was running 28 miles an hour," said J. M. Newton, who watched Sherman's express pass from his office window. "I have been on this train when it was said to be running 28 miles an hour and don't believe it was running that fast when it passed me."[54] No matter what its precise speed, the express did not seem to be traveling at anywhere near the cautious twenty miles an hour that Buffalo and Erie officials recommended for express runs passing through bridge crossings like Angola.[55] One passenger on board the train turned to a companion and remarked that the speed seemed a little fast for cutting through a village and crossing a bridge.[56]

On the ground, another person who noticed that the train had not slowed much was Mahar, the switchman. He was still waiting near the freight depot for the express to pass. When the train rushed up, Mahar turned to a friend who was standing nearby with an anxious ejaculation.

"That train's going like Jehovah," he exclaimed.[57]

The two men watched the cars approach them and then roar past; they were enveloped in noise, the smell of smoke, the heat of turning wheels and working metal. As the cars passed, the two men no doubt saw faces pressed against the coach windows, fingers rubbing circles in the glass. They could see, too, the outlines of men standing on the swaying platforms—Smith on the third car from the end of the train, Vanderburg on the second-last car's rear platform.

Mahar's eyes turned to the place on the track off to his right where the frog rail had broken. He fixed his eyes on the place. He willed it to hold.

Then Mahar saw it.

On the rail, between the frog and the switch, where the car wheels now passed in a stream of dull-black metal, the faintest trace of something the switchman's practiced eyes registered as new: a thread-like geyser of dust. Gray in the afternoon light, the column of track dust was nothing you would normally notice, unless you knew it shouldn't be there.

Mahar watched the spray of dust rise, like a wraith, and he felt it in the pit of his stomach: a sudden need to run. He did, as fast as he could, toward the train.

Then there was the noise, one that not only Mahar but everyone heard. The express's whistle, cutting through the icy air. It seemed to last forever.

CHAPTER 7

Breaking

HURTLING toward the Big Sister bridge, passengers in the coach cars didn't see the plume of grit rise into the air behind the rear wheels. Nor did they see James Mahar as he pelted down the track bed, running as fast as he could in the wake of the train.

Mahar's experienced eyes had been the first to see; now, his mind grappled with the meaning of what he had witnessed—a sudden lifting, like a hoist or hitch, to the back of the rear car, which had risen and then dropped, as if snatched up and released by an unseen hand.[1] After that, the plume of gravel and ice, which the Angola switchman thought looked like nothing so much as dust.[2]

It had happened at the section of track Mahar had worried about, the place where the frog connected to the main line, near where the broken rail had been replaced that morning. As the New York Express shot past the freight house, past the railroad's water tank and Cyrus Wilcox's boot shop, Mahar ran on, his mind turning over the image of the rear wheel jerking up, the rooster tail of dirt. Under his boots, frozen soil crunched with each stride.

Then, as the train flew past the hats and dresses in the windows of Mrs. Thompson's millinery store, the glittering pans and basins in the windows of the tin shop—where carpenter A. M. Avery stood silhouetted in the plate-glass window, watching the train stream by—and over the snow-covered Main Street crossing, Mahar's mind fixed upon the most likely explanation.[3]

In a flash, he understood. If he had seen dust rising, something must be digging into the dirt of the roadbed, underneath the rails of the track. And the only thing heavy enough to bite into the wooden ties and the hard-packed earth was a wheel—a wheel that had run off the rails.

Derailment. The word was dreaded by men like James Mahar, practical-minded railroaders whose job was to keep cars rolling down the tracks smoothly and without incident. There was no time, though, for panic. On Mahar ran, his arms pumping, breathing hard. He began to draw stares from those on the sidewalks and in the shop doorways and windows, but he didn't care. The rails stretched away in front of him, receding in his field of vision and drawing together until they met in the neat oblong of the diminishing rear platform of the train.

Mahar picked up speed. John Martin, the tin shop proprietor, who had been loading boxes on the freight platform near the switchman as the express passed, and who had heard Mahar call out that the train was "going like Jehovah," saw his friend take off running—saw the expression on Mahar's face—and began to sprint after him. He, too, realized what was happening. Martin swung his hat in the air above his head like a flag, and hollered words he would later be unable to recall; all he knew was that he was screaming "as loud as I could."[4]

As he ran, Mahar couldn't take his eyes off the back of the train, which seemed to increase speed as it pulled away. His eyesight was not clear: the late-afternoon sky was gray, and he was unsteady as he ran through the snow-drifts. But he was almost certain as he gazed at the platform of the train that he saw two men come out onto the deck and stand there, looking back at him.[5]

As Mahar pursued, the engine roared out onto the bridge, over the first sections of the 160-foot-long span, pulling seven cars in its wake.[6] Behind the engine came the baggage cars, one, two, three of them, the railman counted, all Buffalo and Erie cars, the noise of their wheels changing from muffled to reverberating as they moved out onto the structure. Then the first of the passenger cars, the words "Buffalo and Erie" painted in bright letters on its side, and a second coach car, not a Buffalo and Erie coach, and then the final two passenger cars of the train—the Cleveland & Erie car, No. 21, and the Cleveland and Toledo's No. 21 coach.

The rear truck of the last car was certainly off the rail—Mahar and Martin could now see chunks of wood, rocks, and hunks of dirt spewing up behind the car—but the train was still moving. It headed forward in the winter light, bound by gravity and momentum to the rails beneath its wheels. For a moment, as the engine churned over the span, it looked as if the express would complete its crossing. The train, from locomotive to rear coach—eight thundering pieces of wood and metal, full of some two hundred humans and their plans and dreams, children ranging from babies to adolescents, newlyweds and senior couples and ex-soldiers and journalists and engineers and farmers and shopkeepers and lawyers and teachers—remained for an instant on the track and in motion.

Later, railroad men would walk the track and notice the ties torn to shreds to within twenty-eight feet of the eastern abutment of the bridge.[7] Had the train made it over the bridge, the two rear cars, if they had fallen, would have landed on the embankment near Josiah Southwick's front yard, and the damage may well have been minimal.

Fifty feet in the air, the train clung for one last long moment to its iron path. A careful eye noticed that the rear car hung a little lower than the rest of the carriages; it moved unevenly, jolting up and down. Then the train's rearmost carriage began to tip slowly to the left side.

James Mahar kept his eyes focused on the cars on the bridge, as if by holding them with his gaze he could keep them where they were, on track and in motion. As he gazed, Mahar thought he saw something fluttering off the back of one of the train's platforms, out into the open sky on the side of the bridge—into nothingness.[8]

It was an overcoat, Mahar thought. And then he realized he was wrong. It wasn't an overcoat. It was a man.

CHAPTER 8

Falling

AS THE EXPRESS sped through Angola toward the Big Sister bridge, passengers were subject to a sharp sensation. The jolt coursed through the upholstered seats beneath them, into their travel-weary spines—striking them as "something like an electrical shock," according to one who felt it.[1]

That was their first sign of trouble. Causing it had been the motion of the rear wheels on the rear truck of the last car jumping off the rails: a quick lift, then a drop, the same movement that James Mahar had witnessed from the rail yard. Running after the train, Mahar hadn't paused to look at what had occurred at the site of the derailment.[2] What had happened had been simple but deadly: as the car had run over the frog in the track, 606 feet east of the east end of the depot, the frog's curved iron pieces had struck a wheel on the left-hand side of the back truck—a wheel that had been slightly damaged, or that was attached to an irregular axle—in a way that threw the truck off kilter.[3] The wheel had jarred slightly, and began to shuttle back and forth. With every forward turn of the wheel, the truck was now also moving horizontally.

Even so, the express's wheels might have held the track, except for the fact that on one of its revolutions, some seventeen feet past the frog, the back wheel mounted the rail on the north side of the track. While rising into or falling from this position, or balanced in it, observers later said, the wheel appeared to clip the top of a metal spike that was in the railbed some twenty-one feet to the east of the frog.[4] The New York Express had jumped the track.

The express's back wheels were now dragging along beside the rails, not on them. Covering likely at least forty-four feet each second, the derailed truck chewed up the wooden ties as the wheels bounced along, sending up the burst of dust witnesses had spied. The last car of the train, the Cleveland and Toledo's No. 21 coach, left deep "ridges cut in the wood" as it moved along.[5]

Passengers on the train could see nothing of what was happening on the rails. How strongly they felt the concussion of the derailment depended on where they sat. For those in the forward cars, the shock was not violent. Brakeman Gilbert W. Smith, at his post on one of these coaches, felt a "jerking motion" beneath his boots but did not immediately worry.[6] In the rear cars, however, the shock came as a "fearful jerk," pitching passengers from their seats and causing them to jostle against one another. Isadore Mayer, a New York City man who worked as a traveling agent of the dramatic actress Adelaide Ristori, had what must have seemed like the worst luck, getting caught in one of the train's washrooms during the shock. Mayer was just emerging from the doorway when the jerking of the last car shook him where he stood.[7] The theatrical agent would have gazed around, uncertain as to what was happening. At that moment, Conductor Sherman, standing at the front platform of the rear car, near John Vanderburg's position at the brake on the back end of the second-last car, felt the same jolt and knew at once what must have gone wrong. Sherman turned to the brakeman and clipped out a few quick words: "The hind car is off the track."[8]

Perhaps no passengers on board the express felt more unsettled by the jolt than the mothers traveling with children. Emma Fisher, Christiana Lang, and Mary Chadeayne no doubt reacted much like young Frances Gale, who clutched her child tightly at the first hint of danger. Riding in the second-last car of the train, the Cleveland & Erie's No. 21 coach, the twenty-year-old Buffalo widow felt frightened by the jar and crouched low, holding her baby "as closely as possible" across the front of her black dress.[9] Nearby, her mother, Lydia M. Strong, leapt to her feet and stood in the aisle.[10]

Benjamin F. Betts, meanwhile, who was sitting at least one hundred feet— the length of two coach cars—ahead of the women in the first of the four passenger carriages, knew something was not right, despite his forward position on the train. Betts had been smoking with Dr. Hoyer, his neighbor from Tonawanda. Betts, a railroad-riding veteran, knew what was to be expected on the express run—and what was not. "At the time I felt the jar," he said, "the car I was on was nearly on the creek bridge."[11] Yet Betts couldn't contain his curiosity. He jumped to his feet and began to pick his way through the car toward the forward door.[12] He hoped to see what had happened—or find a crewman he could ask for details.[13] "I was convinced," Betts said, "something was wrong."[14]

PASSENGERS HAD been bruised and shaken. What came next was even more unsettling. The cars of the express began to shudder as they rolled along the track, shaking strongly from their floors to their rooftops.

The rear truck hung off the track to the left side of the train—the northern side, on which lay Lake Erie, Bundy's mill, and Southwick's house. As the rear coach bumped from tie to tie, still traveling at good speed, it jarred the frame of the coach. This movement sent a "trembling motion" forward through the rest of the cars.[15] The noise of rattling boards would have filled passengers' ears; their feet would have slid back and forth as the floors shifted beneath them. Feeling the change in motion, passengers would have started to murmur and exclaim. Some rose to their feet and began gathering their family members and belongings.[16]

The train was steaming forward toward Big Sister bridge, hauling its dead-limbed last coach. Behind engineer Carscadin's back, Charles Newton, the fireman, sweated as he piled wood from the tender into position to be used.[17] In the front of the cab, the engineer's window revealed a striking view: the buildings of Angola, flowing by in a twinkling stream of kerosene lamps and glass shop windows, and then the outline of a Buffalo and Erie railroad sign marked with the single painted word, "Slow." Dusk hadn't yet descended, but one could feel it approaching.

The signpost was all that stood between the onrushing train and the long, gray-brown span. In Buffalo and Erie terms, the sign's message was another term for "danger": crews were supposed to exercise special caution, according to company officials, at such posted places along the track.[18] Carscadin had driven through Angola for fifteen years; he knew the sign referred to the bridge just ahead, which required careful handling. He felt prepared to cross the bridge, as he had hundreds of times before.[19]

Yet as he gazed at the sign—and beyond it, the bridge—Carscadin, who had been insulated from the jolt of the derailment because of his position at the front of the train, had his first signal that something might be wrong with the express. The bell in the cab began to clang and clatter.

That was out of the ordinary. Somewhere in back of him, Carscadin knew, someone in one of the coaches—or a few people—must be pulling on the bell rope, telling him to slow down or stop. Something was amiss; he had no idea what it might be, but his duty was to see to making it right.

The bell continued to jangle. Carscadin looked out in front of him, toward the bridge and the chasm below. Experience had made him a judge of distance; now he could see that it was too late to stop the train before it would begin the Big Sister crossing. They were about to rush out onto the first yards of the span. Carscadin put out his hand and sounded a blast on the train's whistle. He'd give the signal anyway, even though the time in which to stop before the bridge had vanished like so much of the smoke that blew behind his engine, blocking out his rearward field of vision.[20]

Shreeeeeeeeeeeeet. Down with brakes. The bell in his cab clanged ceaselessly, and Carscadin sounded the whistle a second time. Brakes down.[21]

The sounds of working steam, of metal on metal, of crackling fire and the cry of the whistle, echoed off the cab that enclosed Carscadin and Newton. The whistle's shriek bounced off the walls of the ravine ahead of them. The sound sent thirty-three-year-old Cyrus Wilcox running out of the front door of his shop, fearful that the train had somehow driven over his brother walking along the tracks.[22] On the other side of the Big Sister Creek, in the foyer of Josiah Southwick's home, Alanson Wilcox, thirty-eight, heard the whistle and stared in puzzlement at Southwick, who was just bidding him goodbye beneath the half-moon transom of the justice's front door. At the noise, both men froze.[23]

The express wasn't supposed to stop in Angola. But it was stopping.

IN THE BACK of the train, far from where Carscadin blew the whistle, Robert J. Dickson's hands clung to the quivering bell rope. Dickson, twenty-four, had been among the first to rise to his feet as the cars shook, and he had clambered over people and seats to the wall of the Cleveland & Erie coach. As other passengers exclaimed with fear or puzzled over the train's movements, the young Buffalo engineer would have done some quick mental calculations. Dickson knew trains; he knew physics; he knew the dimensions of the Angola bridge. Putting those factors together, he no doubt realized the situation could prove to be extremely serious.

With a leap, Dickson threw himself against the boards of the car's wall and managed to grasp the cord that ran along the ceiling. Bracing himself against the upholstery, Dickson had pulled on the bell rope again and again.[24]

Stop, the bell signaled. *Help.*

As Dickson yanked, he turned to look for his friend, J. Frank Walker. Seconds before, the young men had been sitting together, talking; when Dickson moved toward the rope, Walker had started to follow. Dickson was five years older than Walker, who worked with him in the engineering

Robert J. Dickson, an engineer working for the Buffalo and Erie Railroad, was traveling with a young colleague that Wednesday. He urged J. Frank Walker to jump with him from the moving train. Courtesy of Elizabeth Dickson Sanders.

department of the Buffalo and Erie Railroad. The two Buffalo-bred men had worked on bridges and railroad beds all over western New York. Now Dickson, the well-educated son of a Buffalo lake captain who had been raised in privileged circumstances, surely felt a sense of responsibility toward his less experienced colleague. Already things had gotten away from him when the two men had been separated from their other co-worker, Joseph Stocking Lewis, who had been forced to take a seat elsewhere on the train because of the crowding.[25] Dickson didn't want to lose sight of Walker, too.

During the seconds in which he sounded the alarm, Dickson would have made up his mind: he would risk jumping from the train, if the situation seemed to warrant it. And he would do his best to take Walker with him.

Releasing the rope, Dickson scrambled to the door to the rear platform, and put out his hand to jerk it open. Then he turned back to check on Walker. As he did, he saw that his friend was no longer behind him; the jeweler's son had climbed back to the seats they had been sitting in before the jolt.

Dickson saw the nineteen-year-old take up a position in the aisle next to their seats, and brace himself with his arms on the backs of the chairs.[26] Dickson gestured and called to his friend, but Frank Walker's face was set, or else he was pretending not to hear him. In any case, Walker didn't move.

Dickson would have realized one thing was now certain. Whatever happened, he and his friend would experience events at a distance from one another; they wouldn't be able to stick together to help one another out in the crisis advancing upon them. All around them, other travelers were making similar choices and facing similar realizations. Lydia M. Strong was struggling to stay on her feet in the aisle while her daughter Frances tried to pull her down. John W. Chapman, the Boston attorney and groom-to-be, was choosing to remain in his seat despite the exhortations of his friend, W. T. Caldwell, who wanted to rush forward to escape the danger.

Dickson relented. He had done his best. The time in which to make such entreaties had passed. The engineer turned once more, to face the landscape flashing past the door. He pulled it open and stepped out onto the vibrating platform. It was time to act.

AS THE EXPRESS rushed on, with Dickson balanced on the platform of its Cleveland & Erie coach, passengers experienced a new sensation. The cars had begun to sway. Gently at first, the coaches moved back and forth. Left to right, then back again, like the deck of a ship. But there was something ominous about the sensation: this wasn't the way rail travel, designed as a linear experience, was supposed to feel. The cars' swaying sensation, to men and women who knew the difference between boat and covered wagon journeys and railroad ones, would have felt deeply disorienting.

Almost before they had a chance to register the changed feeling beneath their boot soles, the swaying picked up speed. The cars slammed back and forth, spilling women into the aisles and sending men careering into one another. Children would have cried and tried to bury themselves in the cloaks of mothers who scrabbled and clawed to stay in tilting seats. Boxes and bags would have fallen out of overhead racks and slid from beneath chairs, skittering along the floorboards and striking people who lay prone. In her seat, Frances Gale held tightly to her infant, but Emma Fisher's baby Minnie went flying out of her arms on a violent pitch and could not be found among the shambles of bags and bodies that filled the second-last car. Disorder gave way to chaos as passengers panicked over the tipping sensation.

The rising tide of emotion in the coaches propelled many people into action, and Charles P. Wood was one of them. The Buffalo railroad man began to crawl through the aisle of the Cleveland & Erie coach, trying to make his way toward the end of the train. Wood, who worked as a check agent for the Buffalo and Erie Railroad company, wasn't technically on duty—he had been riding as a deadhead, a railman traveling from one place to another as a passenger—but now he began shouting orders to the passengers around him.

"Keep your seats!" Wood yelled. "Keep your seats! Sit down!"[27]

Some people complied, and tried to find seats; most ignored him. Some of these passengers began to push forward in the cars, in an effort to reach the two frontmost passenger coaches. Frank Sherman found himself being shoved aside by "some six or twelve persons," as he later recalled, who were trying to do just that, as Sherman moved from the rear car into the second-last carriage.[28]

Others in the last two cars, fearful that the swaying would flip the cars onto their sides, encouraged the men and women around them to use their bodies as ballast. These riders threw themselves onto whatever side of the car was rising off the track—first running to one wall, then rushing to its opposite, as the floorboards lifted and sank beneath their feet. "As the car swayed to and fro," one eyewitness said of these passengers, "they would rush to whichever side was uppermost, to prevent its overturning."[29]

Seconds had passed since the frog juncture, and it was apparent the express was now out of control. Sherman pushed his head through a window of the second-last car to see what was happening to the Toledo coach behind him, and caught a fleeting "glimpse of the side of the rear car," which was bent forward at an angle.[30] "The rear car run along a sharp angle," Sherman said, "the end hanging over [the creek gorge]."[31] It was the last look the conductor would get at the train. "All else," he said, was "a blank to me."[32]

This span of seconds—one passenger said the swaying seemed to last half a minute, though that may have been an overstatement—was captured in an illustration that would appear within a few weeks in *Harper's Weekly* magazine.[33] The scene, titled "The Rear Car Jumping from the Track," depicted the period of rocking after the derailment, just at the point when the weight and speed of the cars became too much for the express to hold the track. In the sketch, the cars are shown at the moment in which passengers tried to save the train by hurling themselves back and forth within its walls. The illustration is filled with whiteness, a depiction of the snowiness of the Angola scenery that hints as well at the isolation of the winter landscape. In the *Harper's* illustration, the Big Sister Creek span cuts through the scene on a diagonal; the effect highlights the simplicity of the bridgework, and underlines the vulnerability of the trains that ran upon it. Two swaying train cars, captured at the moment they begin to topple, and a small house fill out the scene. Gazing on the illustration, an observer

This widely circulated image, which appeared in *Harper's Weekly* shortly after the wreck, showed the last car of the New York Express falling from the track as it passed over Big Sister Creek. From *Harper's Weekly* magazine, 1868.

perceives the cars as spheres unto themselves—though no individual passengers are visible—while at the same time feeling the weightlessness and loss of control that passengers on board the cars certainly felt.

In any event, the frantic efforts of passengers to right the swaying cars were futile. The rear coach had begun to fall.

THE ENGINE of the New York Express had churned its way to the middle of the span. The first quarter of the train's four-hundred-foot length balanced in the skyline over the ravine, sharp-edged and dark, like an etching in a children's primer. Smoke poured from the train's top-hatted stack; its whistle had gone silent. In the cab, Carscadin's hand lay motionless on the throttle; Newton's oily rag lay unnoticed on the floor.

The express had traveled 1,230 feet with derailed back wheels.[34] In the first two coaches, passengers were aware that something had gone wrong, but had no idea what. In the two end coaches, however, momentum and time were taking their toll.

The engine's passage vibrated the wooden trusses of the eighteen-foot-wide bridge, sending showers of soot into the white-blanketed creek bed below.[35] Sound from the train filled the ravine, bouncing between the steep cliff face that formed the western wall of the gorge and the less vertical drop of the earthen embankment to the east. Carscadin trained his eyes ahead, to the eastern abutment of the bridge and the land beyond. If the train could cross the remaining eighty feet of bridge and make it to that embankment—regain a measure of connection with solid ground—then any problem with the train could be solved once he brought the express to a stop. It would be close, but it could be done.

The locomotive was quickly on the Buffalo side of Big Sister, a few hundred yards from Josiah and Huldah Southwick's front porch. Another second, two, three, and the rest of the cars would follow. Carscadin's engine climbed the incline of the embankment—Southwick's house had come into view from the cab—and roared forward with its cargo in tow. The three baggage cars were past the bridge. The first two passenger coaches, each fifty feet in length, emblazoned with the names of their railroads, were then on the eastern embankment. All that remained were the final two cars, the Erie and the Toledo coaches, swaying dangerously, the rear one jutting out to the side like a broken limb.[36]

Fractions of a second now. The rear car, tilting to the northern side of the bridge, inclined a degree more precipitously. It was enough. The car, instead of righting itself one more time and holding the track, hesitated for a moment at a forty-five-degree angle—and then, laboriously, with a shriek of tearing metal and the splinter of wooden timbers being ripped apart, toppled.

The rear car dropped off the track. It fell to its left side, crashing through the six feet and six inches of wooden bridgework that extended from the sides of the tracks, and dropping into the empty air below.[37] As it did, a popping sensation shot forward through the rest of the train. In his forward coach, Benjamin F. Betts felt a shudder in the motion of the express, like two pieces of matter pulling apart, or the charged feeling of something that had been bound suddenly being released.[38] The sensation gave Betts "the impression a coupling had broke"; it seemed to him like a feeling of relief or release.[39] Betts was right: the massive iron pin holding the Toledo car to the rest of the train had broken off its link.

The car's back end—the end at which Stephen W. Steward, the bank president, was sitting—fell first. The rear portion began tumbling almost gracefully; it plummeted off the left-hand side of the bridge like a log rolling to one side, or a submerged animal breaching before a dive. Passengers in the front seats of the car pitched into the air like dolls as the body of the car bucked beneath them, propelled upward by the descent of the coach's rear end. One Angolan who witnessed the fall, reaching for the familiar in a metaphor, said the way the Toledo coach rolled off the track reminded him of "a saw log" headed for the mill.[40] Standing in the doorway of Josiah Southwick's home, Alanson Wilcox uttered an "exclamation of horror" as he saw the rear car of the train roll off the bridge.[41] Southwick, standing behind him, missed seeing the end car tip; but from the tone of Wilcox's voice he knew something terrible had happened.[42]

As the body of the coach fell beneath the deck of the bridge, the fall grew rougher. The rear of the car dragged the front end after it; passengers' ears would have been filled with the screech of twisting metal as the bottom of the car dropped out from under them, bending the iron trucks and undercarriage as the car pulled away from the framework of the bridge. They found themselves sliding the fifty-foot length of the car in a tangled heap, toward the coal stove at the back end of the car, the platform, and Steward's seat.

Passengers like Steward, who was crushed beneath this volley of sliding bodies, had the barest fraction of a second to register the new feeling of unfettered downward motion—the weightless lurch in their stomachs—before the car began to revolve. It turned over and over, spinning on its horizontal axis, as it plunged some fifty feet to the snow below. Spinning with the car, passengers inside slammed against the floor, roof, and walls of the coach. Helpless to brace themselves against the momentum, eyewitnesses said, it was all they could do to keep from being pitched forward and crushed together into a heap of humanity as the car whirled toward the bottom of the creek.[43]

Three people were luckier than the rest. Isadore Mayer, the theater agent, remained in the washroom doorway until he felt the lurch of the car going into free fall; then he jumped into the air, caught a bar hanging on the roof of the coach, and held tightly to it with both hands. Mayer managed to avoid the worst of the smashing as the car flipped.[44] And an older couple from Utica, Mr. and Mrs. Amos H. Thomas, also escaped the worst of the fall. Mary Thomas stayed in her seat in the third row despite the revolutions of the coach, while her husband, a coal dealer, stood in the aisle next to her and clung to the seat throughout the plunge.[45]

Then, with a crash that could be heard on the streets of the village above, the rear coach slammed into the floor of the gorge—sending up geysers of splinters and soot that could be seen rising over the walls of the ravine by observers.[46] Grit and soot bellowed from the chasm, though as yet the cars were only smoking from the force of the impact. The car had landed on its roof; it also landed propped against the side of the embankment. The front end of the car tilted unsteadily in an upward direction against the slope, while the rear end was pressed down into the ground, so that the car seemed to be nearly "standing upright" on its end, one eyewitness said, like a crooked chimney.[47]

The car had landed about five feet from the creek's frozen waters.[48] More horrifyingly, it had struck the earth with such force that the height of the coach—about a dozen feet—had been crushed into a wedge of compressed metal and timber that measured, in some places, not more than thirty-six inches high.[49] Passengers were trapped in the dark and shattered interior of the car in positions that were upside-down and sideways; most of them had been intertwined so completely with other victims and pieces of wreckage that they found it impossible to crawl out.[50]

But awful as was their plight at the bottom of Big Sister Creek, encased in a wrecked coach, they had not yet experienced the worst. As the coach spun in the fall, not only people but also possessions and equipment had been thrown about the interior of the car. So too had the heating stoves that held blazing coal fires. Voiding their contents, the stoves spewed coals, ash, and hot embers over plush upholstery and walls slicked with flammable varnish, over suitcases and reading material, and, finally, over the faces and forms of the men, women, and children trapped inside. Coals landed everywhere, and everywhere they found fuel for flame: the voluminous skirts of women like Abbie Kent and Eunice Fuller, the trouser legs of men like John W. Chapman and Granger Kent, Jasper Fuller and Charles Lobdell, the book clasped by J. Alexander Marten, the papers of lawyer Eliakim B. Forbush and banker Stephen W. Steward.

Wherever the white-hot coals landed, they began to smolder. And where they smoldered, they began to burn.

FIFTY FEET ABOVE, passengers on the train's Cleveland & Erie car— some of whom had scrambled through the door mere seconds before the rear car dropped—had less than a moment to feel safe. For the tearing free of the last car had sealed the Erie car's fate. The Toledo car had dropped with such force that, when it broke loose, it pushed the car in front of it off its own equilibrium on the track. The Erie car pitched abruptly toward the right side of the bridge. Coupled with the car's swaying, the force was enough to tip the car farther to the southern side of the span, so it tilted over the void below.

Robert J. Dickson, the Buffalo engineer, who stood framed in the door of the car, would have understood the consequences. He took a last look around the car—where Frank Walker still clung to his seat, terrified—and then turned and lofted himself off the platform and into the air. Dickson would have pushed upward with his legs, seeking to arc himself away from the car, to get as much distance between his body and the abutments as he could. With his overcoat fluttering behind him, Dickson plunged downward alongside the tracks on the right side of the bridge. He crashed through trees and scrub bushes, into the side of the embankment.[51] Loose gravel covered the slope, and Dickson landed in it face down, skidding along the ground, scouring the skin off his face. He came to rest on the side of the slope, blood pouring from his eyes, nose, and mouth.

Several hundred yards away, Josiah Southwick—who had moved out onto his front porch—saw the Erie car tip, and saw the body of at least one man fly out of it. "I saw a man fall on the track off it," Southwick later said.[52] He may have seen Dickson; but it was more likely he saw John Vanderburg, the train's rear brakeman, who had struggled through the second-last car to its front platform, only to be pitched from the rocking train. Vanderburg fell between the rails, but survived.

Now, above the two men, the car they had been riding in held the track for a few seconds more. Then the coach tipped past the point of recovery, and toppled.

The Erie coach broke its coupler pin, then dropped from the bridge on the same side of the span where Dickson lay prostrate—the opposite side from where the Toledo car lay smoldering.[53] Tumbling down the thirty-five- to thirty-seven-degree incline, the Erie car bounced and jolted, sending out sprays of glass shards from its windows, splintering its walls and floorboards, and losing much of its roof.[54]

At one of the more violent jolts, the roof of the car heaved upward and split open like a burst seam. As other men and women aboard the Erie car watched, a single passenger—a young man—went flying into the air and part of the way out of the crack in the roof. He hung suspended there for a moment, until on another jolt the halves of the roof crashed back together. The roof sliced through the man's body like scissors, leaving him "crushed…to a jelly," dead.[55] The man in the roof was Josiah P. Hayward, the station agent. The dream-monk had been right: he had lived six months, and no more.

Lydia M. Strong and her daughter were also thrown about in the descent. Frances Gale hunched into her seat and protected her infant with her arms; her shoulder was dislocated.[56] Mrs. Strong, who remained standing in the aisle, suffered a blow to the head from a piece of debris as the car plunged down; her skull was smashed.[57]

When it came to rest, the Erie car had landed flat on its side on the slanting earth of the eastern incline. It had tumbled thirty-one feet down the slope, and now lay forty-one feet south of the bridge.[58] Inside the car, men and women who had been bruised and bloodied groaned in terror and pain. Around the car lay the debris of the fall: scattered clothing and personal items, overturned stoves, splinters and timbers painted with the car's gay varnish.

The falling was over. What was next was worse.

CHAPTER 9

Horror

———◆———

CRUSHED into three feet of wood and metal, the Toledo car had landed nearly upright against the embankment on the northern side of the bridge. Though the wreckage was nearly flattened, small openings remained at either end—perhaps a dozen inches across.[1] Enough to allow air to circulate, and to provide windows onto the inside of the car. Within, men and women were dying, some were hanging upside down, others were pinioned by the iron frames of the seats, which had torn free and slammed into a heap in the lower end of the car. Passengers lay "over and across each other two deep," some holding out their hands, a few crying and pleading for help.[2] Perhaps they felt the slight stirring of wind, these trapped men and women—the ones who were conscious and whose senses were not blotted out with pain.

The live coals dumped around the car's interior had turned some parts of the wreckage into nursery beds of flame. Clothing, upholstery, wood: here and there, flames licked at the car's contents, and spread. The coach's upright position now made it a chimney in reality as well as appearance. Already a draft of cold air had worked its way through the car from bottom to top, pulling flames in its wake, as it "drew the fire from the rear toward the forward end of the car."[3] Within seconds, flames enveloped the coach. The fire quickly grew fierce, fed by the varnish used to coat most of the car's surface. Isadore Mayer, the theater agent, who was trying to climb out of the wreckage, noted with shock how rapidly the fire spread. "The wreck was all in flames in a moment," Mayer

This illustration of the Angola wreck scene, which appeared in a popular periodical shortly after the catastrophe, branded the site a "slaughter." Though some details of the geography of the scene are inaccurate, the picture gives an idea of the difficulties inherent in reaching the wounded and dead. From *Kelley's Weekly* magazine, January 11, 1868.

said. "Exactly how I crawled out—I do not know. I was one of only three who escaped. I saw an old gentlemen and his wife get out of the wreck. I am sure that not another person escaped. The car was full—not less than fifty persons, I should think, within it."[4] He was right: only two other people, Utica coal dealer Amos H. Thomas and his wife Mary, seemed to have managed to crawl out of the car in these moments.

Row by row, seat by seat, up the flue of the car's interior, flames moved over bodies, bags, and debris. Fumes and smoke filled the space. Men and women who were still conscious felt their throats burn as they drew poisonous breaths that burned the lining of their airways, causing the tissues of their windpipes to swell into what nineteenth-century doctors knew as *oedema:* the body's protective swelling in an attempt to ward off danger.[5] Victims struggled for breath, some suffocating where they hung suspended in the tangle of torsos. The heat was so extreme it exploded guns carried by male passengers in their pockets; one of the bullets ricocheted out through a window.[6]

As passengers in the car struggled to breathe, the heat affected their bodies, inside and out. Temperatures reddened victims' skin and drew moisture out of them; beads of liquid bubbled to the surface of their skin, popped out as blisters, and dripped away. Trapped heat tightened the victims' skin, causing it to split into long tears as trapped liquid and steam forced its way out. Carpenter Zachariah Hubbard, among others, suffered this skin-splitting on the lower half of his body; his legs were "flayed" open from exposure to the heat, while his chest and stomach were "fairly roasted."[7] On top of this, Hubbard's right arm, torn from his body, hung loose from a flap of skin, and he bled profusely from the wound.[8] Hubbard was alive, despite his injuries, as the car burned around him.

The intense heat also fractured passengers' bones and contracted their muscles, particularly in their limbs. This drew forearms and legs into a posture widely recognized by doctors in the era as the "pugilistic" position.[9] This posture, common in people exposed to high temperatures, occurs when the body curls in upon itself; the victim's head is thrown back, the forearms are cocked up and bent in toward the upper body, and the legs are pulled upward into a fetal-like crouch.[10] The position is extravagant pain made tangible; indeed, many members of the public—seeing images of the wreck's victims, or reading about their condition in newspaper listings—would interpret this pose as an expression of unusually grave suffering on the part of the victims in the aftermath of the Angola wreck. Boston attorney and groom-to-be John W. Chapman, when pulled from the remnants of the burned car, would be contorted in this manner, missing the lower half of his face, his forearms burned off up to the elbow joints, his legs incinerated to the knees. It would take some of Chapman's closest friends to try to identify the attorney's remains among the other bodies in the aftermath of the derailment. Benjamin C. Aikin, the fifty-year-old Pennsylvanian from Hydetown, was curled so tightly into the pugilistic pose that it served as protection for his silver spectacles; one of his arms was bent against his body in such a way that it kept the metal frames from melting. Aikin's eyeglasses would be discovered on his body by his wife Zuleann, who would claim his corpse because of them—that, and the scraps of underwear that clung to the lower half of Aikin's torso, which Zuleann would recognize because she had sewn them herself.[11]

As the victims' bodies contorted in the fiery car, they also charred. After their clothing burned away, the surfaces of victims' bodies did: redness turned to blackening, which brought an end to the feeling of pain in their skin, as nerves were destroyed. Arms, legs, and heads—with more insubstantial bones and tissue—burned off entirely. Illustrations of the Angola corpses that appeared in national magazines in the weeks after the wreck would show ranks of twisted, pugilistically posed lumps of charred matter, most without lower legs, arms, or heads. These illustrations of appendage-less torsos were not exaggerations or attempts to shock the public; they were forensically accurate depictions of what the conditions inside the Toledo car had done to its passengers. In some cases, the charring of the victims was so complete that gender was erased. One woman was identified as female only because part of her hoop skirt frame had melted to what remained of her body.[12]

It was a scene of "horrors…piled upon horrors."[13] And it was far from silent. As the fire crackled, sounds of human suffering came from the car. Men and women wept and pleaded to God to be released from their agonies by death; shrieks came from women who saw their husbands consumed by flames before their eyes. Above it all, the "wailing of children…the most soul-piercing and agonizing sound which ever reached mortal ear" flowed from the car—or perhaps not from children. The sound may have been that of grown men and women made incoherent in misery.[14] "The hideous, remorseless flames crackled on; the shrieks died into moans, and moans into silence more terrible," newspapers reported, "as the pall of death drew over the scene."[15]

The audible suffering went on, filling the skies above the Big Sister, for more than five minutes—possibly as long as twenty—before silence descended once more over the snow.[16]

THE CARS that had fallen from the bridge lay, one on either side of the span, around the terrain of the Big Sister Creek ravine. One, the Erie car, was recognizable as a wrecked railway coach lying on its side, with its windows jagged holes, its wooden framework staved in, its roof a gaping hole. The other coach was now a column of fire and smoke; nothing would remain of the car but its iron trucks and wheels, some of the metal frames of the upholstered seats, and "one little fragment" of the car's side.[17] As for the passengers: "Those who were not killed outright," said Isadore Mayer, "were burned to death."[18]

The Toledo coach had fallen close enough to the side of the embankment and eastern abutment of the bridge that one needed to be near the bottom of the bridge work to see it.[19] The Erie car had fallen only partway down the incline, and so lay some twenty feet higher than the other car, a couple of hundred feet away. In the area, the downed cars were not readily visible to each other. Injured passengers in the Erie car had no way of knowing what had happened

This image of the Angola wreck, by J. P. Hoffman, appeared in *Harper's Weekly* shortly after the crash, with the title "The Angola Disaster." It showed the immolation of the end car of the train. Note the bodies on the snow in the foreground. From *Harper's Weekly,* January 1868.

to those people—including some of their friends and relatives—in the coach that had fallen first. From the Erie car, there was no easy way of reaching the other car. Moving from one wrecked coach to the other would have required climbing up and over the bridge deck and then down again on the other side or clambering under the structure around the eastern abutment and piers of the span, over ice-crusted boulders, treacherous snowdrifts, and piles of drift-wood. "The nature of the embankment, together with the ice upon the steep declivity," was dangerous, according to one account of the scene. It "would not admit of immediate assistance even though hundreds of people had been at hand, for no one could go down the bank hurriedly without fear of death."[20]

But circumstances in the Erie car were such that not many of the passengers were in any condition to help others, or even themselves. All over the remains of the coach lay injured passengers. One woman traveler had been completely scalped in the battering she had taken during the fall; the skin of her head and her hair hung behind her, drenched in blood, attached to the back of her skull by a slight web of tissue.[21] Lydia and Ira Babcock, a married couple from Syracuse, had been so bruised by the drop that their bodies were turning black with contusions; Lydia vomited a pool of blood.[22] A male passenger had been struck in the face by wreckage with such violence that his "head was almost cut in two," while not far away another man was bleeding out from the arteries in his leg, which had been shorn off in the crash.[23]

Christiana Lang suffered moderate injuries in the fall of the Erie car; her children James and Mary were shaken up. Other victims lay scattered around in unconscious states, the extent of their injuries unknown. One of these people was Emma Fisher, whose body lay in the shattered car; she had been rendered "insensible" by the fall, and had lost Minnie in the confusion.[24] Pain and panic gripped passengers who were alert enough to realize what had just happened to them. Some men and women swatted at coals from the overturned stoves, in an effort to prevent fire; a few tried to extricate themselves from the Erie's wreck, crying out for aid.[25] "Mother, get well quick! Mother, get well!" wept a little boy to a blood-covered woman so "mangled" he had not recognized her at first as his own relative. "Will my mother get well?"[26] Others cast about them for the bodies of their loved ones, looking for familiar faces amid the debris. "Where is she? Shall I never see her again?" cried a man who had been "stupefied" from shock and was unable to find his wife.[27] Not even those who sat next to their loved ones were guaranteed similar fates. Lizzie Thompson was injured in the fall, but lived. Her brother Simeon had been killed by her side.

Still, in the first moments after the accident, in the fading light of late afternoon that made navigating the scene difficult, some people from the less-damaged Erie car tried to help their fellow travelers. Robert J. Dickson rose to his feet in the snowdrifts at the top of the incline, wiped the blood from his face where the gravel had scoured it, and tried to make his way over the bridge deck to locate Joseph Stocking Lewis, who had been riding in the rear coach at the time of the accident. Brakeman John Vanderburg, who had edged his way down off the bridge work where he had fallen between the rails as the car tipped, followed the Buffalo engineer. At the same time, Conductor Sherman managed to climb out of the end of the Erie car, and limped up the slope to the track bed. Sherman tried to find people to flag down for help.[28] He was in pain, his shoulder bloody and bruised.

Alexander Fisher also tried to help others in the Erie car, especially his sister-in-law. Fisher had been hurt internally, but managed to keep from losing consciousness.[29] After the tumult of the fall stilled, he looked around and could not see baby Minnie in the dimness of the car; he also could see that Emma had been injured badly. Fisher dragged himself through an opening in the car and onto the snow. He crawled up the incline, unsure of his direction, and then pulled himself to his feet. Fisher began to walk through the snow, pushing back the weeds and limbs of bushes that sprang at him from the icy terrain, slowing his progress. He hoped to come to a house where he could raise an alarm.[30] Dazed, Fisher did not head toward the Southwick home on the sparsely populated eastern side of the ravine. He tramped through the snow in the other, more populated direction, where the lights in the windows of a few homes twinkled ahead of him.

By now, the first Angolans were beginning to arrive on the scene. These initial rescuers had followed the spirals of smoke rising from the ravine, the smell of wood burning and the cries that echoed faintly over the snow, to the top of the gorge. They arrived on both sides of the gully, clad in hastily donned winter coats and hats, and tried to glimpse the crash site. Two of the first to arrive were Josiah Southwick and Alanson Wilcox, who had started toward the creek from Southwick's porch immediately after watching the cars fall. "We both ran," said Southwick, simply.[31] Cyrus Wilcox and a few others also ran up, panting for breath, having sprinted from Commercial Street and the railroad tracks to the bridge. Wilcox, a master boot maker and the second of what would become four generations in his family to make shoes for a living, brought along twenty-two-year-old Lucius Blackney, son of grocer Sely Blackney, whose shop abutted Wilcox's, and whom the boot maker had roused with an exclamation—"Some of the coaches are off the bridge! Let us run and see"—as he sped toward the ravine.[32]

As the Angolans gathered at the top of the embankment, some spied Dickson and Sherman and a few other passengers who had been the first to scramble away from the wreckage.

"Are you much hurt?" cried John S. Taggert, an Angola resident and secondary telegraph operator for the Buffalo and Erie Railroad, who found himself face to face with Sherman at the top of the embankment.[33]

"No, not much," replied the conductor.

Sherman ordered Taggert to wire the railroad's main office in Buffalo, to let company officials know what had happened to the New York Express. Train traffic over the Lake Shore route would have to be halted or rerouted for the next few hours, at least, until the damage could be assessed and repairs made. Sherman had no idea what had caused the train to jolt off the track as it passed the depot; there would need to be a thorough investigation of both the rails and the train in the hours ahead. Sherman told Taggert he wanted the superintendent of the Buffalo and Erie company, Robert N. Brown, to personally handle rescue efforts from Buffalo—including rounding up as many city doctors as he could find, to treat what would certainly be a large number of wounded.

"Go back to the station," Sherman rasped out, "and telegraph to Mr. Brown to send up some physicians."[34]

Taggert ran off to do as Sherman had commanded. At the same time, other Angola residents gathered at the top of the ravine. Switchman James Mahar would likely have been arriving on the scene around this time, having spent the first ten or fifteen minutes after the wreck examining the rail along the track where the derailment had occurred, including at the frog juncture.[35] These newly arrived citizens now turned their attention to figuring out ways to get down to the bottom of the gorge.

It was a trickier task than it looked. The degree of the descent was too steep for comfort along much of the bank. No permanent pathways existed between the top of the ravine and the creek bed; whatever animal trails or fishermen's footpaths there might have been were covered over with blankets of snow. Scrub brush and saplings covered the incline, some partially obscured by drifts. Underfoot, rocks shifted precipitously when stepped on, some rolling down into the creek bottom, and showers of loose shale and icy gravel slid away without warning.

On the eastern side of the ravine, some Angola men were able to clamber down the embankment on the southern side of the bridge work, to where the Erie coach lay, by bracing themselves against the ice and holding on to scrub growth for support as they inched along. That coach could be reached, with difficulty. But after several attempts to scale down the incline on the northern side of the bridge to reach the Toledo coach, residents gave up—it was just too slippery and steep, and to climb down unaided would be risking a tumble into the ravine. Frustrated, these villagers stood back and watched thick smoke bellow from the cleft below. The vapors smelled of wood, hot metal, and something else: human flesh. Some rescuers would have turned their faces away, or buried their noses and mouths in their sleeves or scarves so they didn't have to breathe the foul odor. "The smoke from the burning car and inmates arose as high as the bridge, from sixty feet below," one witness described, "and the effluvia from the fire consuming flesh was—unendurable."[36]

Finally, as more residents trudged up to the scene, a few carrying pickaxes and shovels over their shoulders, the rescuers devised a solution. Dozens of Angola men linked arms and formed a human chain, stretching from the top of the gorge to the creek bed below. Holding tightly to one another, hand to hand, the chain of men lowered rescuers, one by one, down into the creek bottom.[37] There, rescuers found themselves faced with the inferno that was consuming what remained of the Toledo car; it glowed orange and white inside the frame of timbers and ironwork that had not yet been burned to ash. Some villagers rushed to the side of this carriage but were unable to approach closer than a dozen feet—the heat radiating from the car pushed them back forcefully. One Angola man heroically tried to edge closer to some of the victims, advancing so near the flames that his own "whiskers and eye-brows [were] burned off," but was finally forced back when overcome with fumes and scorched by the flames.[38] Others who approached close to the Toledo coach in these moments made out what they took to be the outlined shapes of men and women as they were consumed by the fire. Henry Bundy, arriving on the gorge floor after being lowered down by the chain of rescuers, thought he saw the figures of two small children being burned up in the coach as he watched. "I saw them in the flames," the mill owner said. "I am quite positive."[39]

He may have been right; perhaps there were two children in this car, traveling with relatives, and they may have been burned while Bundy looked on. But what Bundy saw may well have been the torsos of men and women who had already been burned into the pugilistic position that would have made them appear small, even child-like, from a distance. "The heart sickens," an account based on eyewitness testimony stated of this scene, "[at] a smouldering mass of half-consumed human beings, of skulls blackened and ghastly, of hands and arms, in one blackened mass of stench, of car wheels and iron work—of death in its most repulsive form."[40]

A few of the local men suggested a bucket brigade to try to put the fires out. No one had thought to bring buckets in any quantity, though, and the creek water was frozen. A few residents began to fling shovelfuls, even fistfuls, of snow onto the wreckage, hoping to tamp down the flames. Cyrus Wilcox, throwing snow onto the burning car, noted with a sickening feeling that the human bodies in the wreckage "seemed to burn much longer than the wood-work of the car."[41] Wilcox counted eight lumps that he recognized as portions of human torsos or limbs in the Toledo car, and twenty skulls.[42] Like others who responded valiantly to the scene—a "goodly" percentage of the citizenry

Henry Bundy, a mill owner in Angola, was among the first residents of the community to respond to the disaster at the bottom of the Big Sister gorge. He later took on the somber job of making coffins for the dead. Courtesy of Chet and Ann Riker.

of Angola at the time—Wilcox and his brother would be unable to blot these images from their memories.[43] "The fearful scenes from which spectators have recoiled in mingled terror and disgust," one newspaper stated of these villagers' diligent efforts at the site, "have all been so painfully real, so simply horrible, that the most sober and accurate statements unrelieved by a single bit of imagination have proved the best and most effective way of telling the story. No magic touch of pencil, though it had been guided by the sombre [*sic*] genius of Dore, could have added horror to the dread reality of the scene."[44]

At this point, some Angolans—accurately judging that the situation with the enflamed car would not permit any more helping of its victims—picked their way under the bridge and climbed upward to the Erie car, to offer aid to men and women who might yet have a chance at survival. Among these rescuers was Alanson Wilcox, who upon arriving at the Erie car spotted a battered body lying partly out of the wreckage. Wilcox pried the figure loose and pulled it onto the snow, to discover that the individual—a middle-aged woman clad in mourning clothes—was still alive. It was a face he recognized: Lydia M. Strong, who had grown up as Lydia Bartholomew in the nearby hamlet of Derby. Mrs. Strong, who was bleeding from her crushed skull, bare-ly registered Wilcox's presence.[45] As Wilcox watched, she died on the snow.

Josiah Southwick also made his way to the Erie car to see if he could help any of its injured passengers. The first person he came upon in the debris was Charles P. Wood, the railroad check agent, whose body lay prone in the smashed car, trapped under one of the car's overturned stoves. Wood, who recognized the Angola justice of the peace as someone he knew, pleaded with Southwick to free him. Southwick was starting to do that, when he saw that the stove was also pinioning a baby—an infant, with no parent by its side.[46] Southwick weighed his choice for a fraction of a second. One of his Quaker ancestors in the Massachusetts Bay Colony, Provided Southwick, had been persecuted for her family's refusal to abandon their religion; the moment had been memorialized by John Greenleaf Whittier in a poem called "Cassandra Southwick," memorized by generations of New England schoolchildren. "*Oh, at that hour the very earth seemed changed beneath my eye,*" the poem ran.[47] Stand-ing beneath the darkening skies of Angola, Josiah Southwick would have felt tested in a similar way. Someone's suffering must be increased in order for both victims, or either of them, to live; it was up to him to decide whose. And time was running short. "I saw the coals of fire from the stove scattered all over the car," Southwick later said, of what he noticed in these brief moments of reflection.[48] There was no assurance that the Erie coach would not turn into the inferno the Toledo car had become.

Southwick grabbed the hot stove. He heaved it up, and shoved it onto the body of Wood. As the railroad agent groaned in pain, Southwick scrambled to the form of the baby, and pulled its soot-covered body free of the wreckage. He jumped clear of the car, found a snowbank, and laid the infant down on it. Then Southwick climbed back to Wood's side.[49] He began to wrestle with the stove to get it off the railroad man—when he suddenly saw another set of hands grasp the stove, and felt its burden lift. John Vanderburg stood beside him, his feet planted in the ruins, helping free Wood from the stove.[50] The twenty-nine-year-old brakeman said nothing, just strained with all his might until the iron weight began to lift. Once Wood was uncovered, Vanderburg ran off without a word, to another part of the car, to pull at another trapped victim.

FRANK LESLIE'S ILLUSTRATED NEWSPAPER

Entered according to the Act of Congress in the year 1867, by FRANK LESLIE, in the Clerk's Office of the District Court for the Southern District of New York.

No. 640—Vol. XXV.]   NEW YORK, JANUARY 4, 1868.   [PRICE 10 CENTS. $4 00 YEARLY. 13 WEEKS $1 00.

End of the Alabama Controversy—A Dead Lock.

THE discussion between the Governments of the United States and Great Britain have come to what may be called "a dead lock." Both got so far as to agree to an arbitration, but diverged again on the question of what should be submitted to arbitration.

Lord Stanley was ready to go to arbitration on the question "Whether in the matters connected with the vessels, out of whose depredations the claims of American citizens have arisen, the course pursued by the British Government and by those who acted upon its authority was such as would involve a moral responsibility on the part of the British Government to make good, either in whole or in part, the losses of American citizens."

Mr. Seward did not object to this, but claimed that "The Government of the United States would deem itself at liberty to insist before the arbiter that the actual proceedings and relations of the British Government, its officers, agents, and subjects toward the United States in regard to the rebellion and the rebels, as they occurred during that rebellion, are among the matters which are connected with the vessels whose depredations are complained of."

The real point of issue is, that Great Britain insists that her conduct in recognizing the rebel States as belligerents shall not be reviewed, or her right to make such recognition be called into question, or the justice or injustice of the act enter as a consideration in the settlement of the claims that may come up for arbitration. This is what Lord Stanley declares in these words: "Arbitration must proceed on the assumption that an actual state of war existed between the Government of the United States and the Confederate States."

That is to say, the United States must admit that the rebel States constituted *de facto* and *de jure* an organized and independent government—a thing impossible. This demand bears date November 16th, and Mr. Seward replied to it December 4th, in an instruction to Mr. Adams, as follows:

"We are now distinctly informed by Lord Stanley's letter that the limited reference of the so-called Alabama claims which Lord Stanley proposes, is tendered upon the condition that the United States shall waive before the arbitration the position they have constantly maintained from the beginning, namely, that the Queen's proclamation of 1861, which accorded belligerent rights to insurgents against the authority of the United States, was not justified on any grounds either of necessity or of moral rights, and therefore was an act of wrongful intervention, a departure from the obligation of existing treaties, and without the sanction of the law of nations. The condition being inadmissible, the proposed limited reference is therefore declined."

The negotiation, therefore, is at an end, and we trust it will not be renewed on our side. Our account with Great Britain remains open, and we shall choose our own time and mode of settlement. Mr. Chandler, of Michigan, proposes to recognize Great Britain and Abyssinia as belligerents, in precisely the same

FRIGHTFUL RAILROAD DISASTER, TWO PASSENGER CARS ON THE LAKE SHORE RAILROAD THROWN DOWN AN EMBANKMENT OF FIFTY FEET, NEAR ANGOLA, N. Y., FORTY-EIGHT PERSONS BURNED TO DEATH.—SEE PAGE 243.

Not far away, Henry Bundy and Cyrus Wilcox were pulling the body of a young woman from the Erie car. The men dragged the form of Lizzie Thompson to a clear spot on the ice, and laid her flat, propping her head on a grimy seat cushion. Bundy would have looked at her doubtfully; he thought she surely must be dead. He had seen the bloody body of her brother, Simeon, in the seat next to her, and guessed correctly that the young Worcester man was no longer alive. Returning to the car to make sure, Bundy found instead the body of J. Frank Walker, Dickson's friend, who had been killed where he stood in the aisle of the train. The Angolan carried Walker's slight form over to Lizzie's side, and laid the nineteen-year-old man down next to the Massachusetts woman on the ice.[51]

In the same vicinity, Angola tinsmith John Martin was hacking away at the ruins of the destroyed car. Martin had come across the form of R. M. Russell, a Tennessean, hanging partway out of the rubble. Russell's body had been compressed into an awkwardly bent position; he was tangled up in some timbers and could not get loose.[52] The Tennessean was not dead, but was hurt about the chest and back. Martin grasped the beams lying across Russell's body and heaved them off. He grabbed Russell and "straightened him out," then helped the man to a place on the snow.[53]

In doing so, Martin thought he spotted something shiny in the wreckage near Russell's body. Going back, Martin saw it again: a faint glimmer in the car's interior. He pulled it out, and saw that it was Russell's gold pocket watch.[54] Martin wiped off the watch, no doubt examining its face to be sure it wasn't cracked. Then he turned and trudged back through the snow to the wounded man. He gently tucked the watch into Russell's pocket.

Nearby, Minnesotan Alexander Fisher had managed to make his way to the top of the landscape, hobbling from the pain of his internal injuries. He limped another four hundred feet or so through the snowy underbrush until he came to a house, not of Southwick but of another village resident. Collapsing from his bleeding, Fisher gasped out news of Emma's injury—and the disappearance of Minnie in the wreckage.[55]

After sending villagers down to the gorge with a description of his sister-in-law and the baby, Fisher had little strength to fight for life. He sank into a low state, murmured a few final words—"With me, all is well," he was heard to say—and died.[56]

MINUTES EARLIER, at the front of the train, Charles Carscadin had throttled down the engine, while Gilbert W. Smith scrambled to cover the remaining sets of brakes. The crew managed to slow the New York Express

to a crawl, then a stop. The locomotive traveled 726 feet from the east abutment of the bridge before it could be halted.[57] Carscadin threw the train into
reverse, as soon as he could, and began backing slowly down the track in the
direction of the bridge.[58]

Some passengers climbed down from the express as it inched back down the
line, and stood clustered in the snow alongside the tracks. A few, among them
Benjamin F. Betts and Dr. Frederick Hoyer, jogged back along the track toward
Big Sister Creek to see what had happened.[59]

Reaching the ravine, at about the same time as the first villagers began to
arrive on the scene, Dr. Hoyer took a moment to assess the situation. As the
first doctor on the scene of the disaster, he knew he would have to take charge
of the treatment of wounded and dying victims until more medical personnel could arrive—from the village, to start with, and then from the nearest
city, likely Buffalo. "I thought it was my duty," Hoyer later said.[60] The doctor
made his way to the place where the splintered Erie car lay, and examined the
victims that had been laid around the car on the snowy hillside. Some were
clearly dead; others were hurting, and crying out for help. Hoyer barely had
time to tend one victim before he was called away to help another.[61]

Betts, meantime, had walked the terrain at the edge of the ravine. He came
across two passengers, a man and a woman, who were trying to make their way
up the embankment and away from the fallen cars. The passengers had been in
the Erie car and were badly shaken. Betts scrambled to the pair, and helped them
away from the gorge. Spotting Southwick's house not far away, Betts took the
victims there and left them with the women of the house. One of the women
was Huldah Southwick, Josiah's wife, whose face would have been gray and
grim as she waited for word of the wreck. Betts told her, as he deposited this first
pair of wounded victims on Huldah's wooden floor, to make room for more.[62]

Hiking away from Southwick's, Betts gazed toward the creek and saw the
smoke bellowing over the top of the gulf.[63] Seeing some metal milking pails
in the farmer's front yard—five of them, from Josiah's dairy operation—Betts
grabbed them and ran through the yard and down to the ravine. He sent the
pails down the human chain of Angolans to the bottom of the creek bed, then
lowered himself down. At the bottom of the gorge, Betts found that the pails
were of no use because of the thick cap of ice on the creek water.[64] He threw
them aside and ran to see if he could free any trapped people.

Approaching the Toledo car, which by this point was beginning to burn
fiercely in the gathering dusk, Betts saw a cluster of men trying to pry loose
the body of one passenger, a man who had landed in a hole under the coach
with wreckage on his leg, which was crushed, his thighbone shattered.[65] The
useless limb was trapping W. C. Patterson in the framework of the burning

car. "His foot was caught between timbers," Betts said, "and they could not draw him out—I slipped down and turned his foot so that he could be drawn out. We then linked hands and drew him out."[66] Betts helped place Patterson on the ice near the car. The Oil Creek man's body was, observers later said, the last to be pulled from the coach before it collapsed upon itself, in a shower of sparks and ash.

Rescuers then moved back, wiping their faces with their sleeves, blinking their eyes in the gritty, soot-filled air. Some moved away from the Toledo car and headed toward the bodies of passengers that had been laid on the ice beneath the bridge, to see if anything could be done for them.

Betts, however, was not the type to give up. Bending over, in the final moments of the inferno in the Toledo car, the wood dealer crawled partway into the lower end of the car, even as it burned above him. He inched past the point at which Patterson had been pinned. In front of him, Betts saw a "heap of human bodies burning."[67] The pile of victims' bodies consisted of four people that Betts could count, three clearly dead, one clinging to life. This one living victim called out to Betts for help, but Betts couldn't reach him or her—he wasn't sure if it was a man or a woman—in time. "I tried to extricate another," he said, of what happened next, "but when I got to him the flames were all about his head—he was lying on his back and it was useless."[68] Betts counted eleven corpses around him in the end of the burning car as he pulled himself forward through the flames.

In these moments, as he gazed at the bodies of the wreck's dead, Betts saw a face he recognized. It was the man Betts had met earlier that day at lunch in Brocton—Stephen W. Steward, the bank president.[69] Steward was buried beneath a mound of corpses, twisted metal and timbers. Somehow, he remained "yet alive."[70] The banker's face was close enough for Betts to see—and want to save. Steward looked into Betts's eyes, and "implored most piteously, with outstretched arms," for Betts to pull him out.[71] Betts tried as hard as he could. But the flames around him grew too intense. He was forced back, the heat in his face and on his skin like a brick wall. "I think everything was done," Betts said, later, "that could be, under the circumstances. And all were saved from the wreck—that it was possible to get out."[72]

Backing away from the collapsing, white-hot interior of the burned car, Betts kept Steward's face in view for as long as he could. Until there was nothing left to see; until the image was seared into his memory.[73]

CHAPTER 10

Rescue

———◆———

IF THERE WAS one thing Angola's new doctor knew how to do, it was battlefield assessment: the sorting of wounded people; the judgment of who would live, with care, and who would die no matter what was done for them. The shifting decks of an army hospital ship, as well as the USS *Burnside,* had been Romaine J. Curtiss's classroom in the art of managing catastrophe. There, amid battle conditions, the intense young Catholic physician had learned to parse injury; to treat shock, dress wounds, and comfort the dying. Now, squinting in the deepening gloom of the Angola evening shortly after his arrival on the scene at Big Sister Creek, Dr. Curtiss would have assessed the number of dead lying at the bottom of the ravine and calculated the chances of survival of some of the worst of the wounded.

One thing he knew immediately. They would need hospitals. Makeshift ones, at least; places to collect those victims who would recover, as well as those who were dying. Robert J. Dickson and the Babcocks, Lydia and Ira; Lizzie Thompson and Emma Fisher; the Lang family; Mrs. Chadeayne and her daughters, Anna and Carry—all had suffered differing fates in the fall of the Erie coach. Carry, the three-year-old, had scratches and "a bruise on the side of her forehead from a man's heel"; her mother Mary had her upper right arm broken, pain in her back, and a head contusion so severe it "caus[ed] both eyes to be black."[1] Anna, thirteen, was the worst of the family, unconscious and in shock, her skull fractured.[2] At first Anna Chadeayne had not even received medical attention from the doctors, she had appeared so close to dead.[3] She would be largely unconscious for three days.[4]

As Romaine Curtiss gazed around the scene of the disaster, he would have carefully weighed his options. Curtiss knew that any temporary hospitals would need to be close by, and that even with proximity it wasn't going to be easy to carry the bodies of injured men and women across the countryside, through the snow and underbrush. Getting victims' bodies to the top of the creek gully would be challenge enough. Many of the most grievously wounded couldn't be transported far—they wouldn't make it alive. The only solution was to make the hospitals out of the homes of the nearest Angola families.

Curtiss would have gestured for the Angolans nearby to gather around him, and began issuing orders. His voice would have carried on the twilight breeze, with the crisp command of an ex-military surgeon. The first thing they would need, he would have told the villagers, would be articles on which to lift up victims' bodies and carry them, by means of the human chain of residents, up the eastern embankment of the creek to the top of the ravine. He would have told the villagers clustered at the bottom of the creek to make stretchers and to get some sleds or sleighs, however rude, for the bodies.

Though his tone was surely confident, Curtiss was scrambling to make up time. He had not been the first villager to respond to the wreck site, for he had apparently not been at home in his house on Main Street overlooking the creek when the express train derailed. The doctor had been, by all accounts, out conducting his routine business, tending to patient calls in the vicinity, when the wreck occurred.[5] Curtiss had quickly heard news of the derailment, however, and had rushed to the creek bottom. Dr. Hoyer, who had been on the express as a passenger, was already on the scene when he arrived. But Curtiss soon took over a good portion of the leadership role in the rescue and recovery effort—a job the other doctor, as a non-Angolan, would surely have been happy to let him handle.[6] If there was anyone in Angola equipped to handle the situation in Big Sister Creek, it was the twenty-seven-year-old ex-army medic. Curtiss was also—of all the medical men who would work to treat the wreck victims—the one most likely to be powerfully affected by the singular sights and sounds of the disaster. The Angola Horror was, for the young doctor, like rushing headlong into his past.

Curtiss had seen this sort of thing—these grievous wounds, this dying in primitive surroundings—before, and not so long ago. After the siege of Vicksburg in the summer of 1863, Curtiss, then a medical cadet in the army, had treated many casualties in his role on board a hospital ship that offered treatment to the wounded.[7] He had worked so hard that he became ill and had to take a break from military service—a pause during which he graduated from medical college in Ohio. After re-enlisting in the navy, Curtiss was made an assistant surgeon on board the *General Burnside,* a two-hundred-ton Union gunboat.[8] On that ship, in late 1864, he saw action while patrolling the Tennessee River. On January 1, 1865, Curtiss jotted down a tally of the men in his sick bays and noted two with gunshot wounds, as well as many others with ulcers, diarrhea, and dysentery.[9] The doctor, who had begun his medical studies while still in his teen years under the tutelage of an Ohio physician, treated his patients with morphine, dressings, and tinctures of chemicals. Many died anyway. Curtiss, whose Roman Catholic faith supported him when it came to coping with these situations—*"judicare vivos, et mortuos,"* he recited in the Credo, of the judgment of "the living and the dead"—nevertheless became so sick from the hard work and distressing conditions aboard the ships he served on that his weight dropped dangerously low for his six-foot frame, to ninety-six pounds. Curtiss started complaining of chronic diarrhea and bowel problems. During his time on the *Burnside,* the eardrum in his right ear was ruptured and damaged, causing him pain and irritation that would trouble him for years.[10] Later in life, he would complain of strange noises—whistles, shrieks, even musical sounds—that would interrupt his hearing in this ear.

No one could have blamed Curtiss for thinking, following the conclusion of the war, that he had seen the worst that human beings could suffer. Nobody could have blamed him for wanting to start his career—and his life—anew, in a small and out-of-the-way place like Angola, where medical needs promised to be simple and routine. Now, in the ravine east of the village, his face lit by the glow of the fires flickering among the ruins of the Toledo car, Curtiss may well have been reconsidering his choices.

Railroad accidents could make for tricky situations for doctors and nurses in the nineteenth century. Train wrecks were often difficult disaster scenes to reach, occurring at or near bridges, gullies, cliffs, blind spots, or other topographical challenges. The Angola wreck had happened on a winter's day, just as daylight was about to fade. Bitter cold arrived with the onset of evening. No hospital or morgue was located within twenty miles of the crash site, and the rudimentary offices of the local doctors provided little in the way of equipment or medicine for treating the victims. Railroads, though becoming more common in average people's daily lives, had not yet figured out how to deal with the devastating scenes of wreckage that their trains could create. Later, for these reasons, newspapers would note in admiring tones how Drs. Curtiss and Hoyer had been able to remain "unremitting in the discharge of the onerous duties which had so suddenly devolved upon them."[11]

Dr. Curtiss was not the only one to notice these problems at the Big Sister site. Citizens working alongside him to help victims on the creek bottom also realized the enormity of their task. Dragging bodies from the cars, these residents soon understood they had reached the limit of what they could do without teams of additional doctors from Buffalo, drugs like ether and chloroform, and proper medical supplies, from warm blankets and clean bandages to tourniquets and surgical equipment. It wasn't easy to watch victims dying for lack of treatment—and that was happening, despite the best efforts of the doctors and citizens. John Martin, the Angola tinsmith, expressed the frustration of tending to the victims in these first hours. "They wanted some medicine," he said, simply. "Nothing else was done after that."[12] It wasn't from lack of trying; there was only so much they could do.

Yet these early hours of response to the tragedy would, in the weeks and months to come, win for Angola's citizenry the praise of newspaper and magazine editors, as well as public officials, in New York State and across the country. The words of newspaper journalists, who typically tended to be sensational in their reporting, seemed almost insufficient and inadequate on this point. "It would be impossible to say too much in praise of the truly humane and self-sacrificing spirit manifested by the good people of Angola," one newspaper stated, in an editorial that reflected the general opinion. "They have given all they had and foregone every comfort to themselves in providing for, nursing and soothing the sufferers; and all this is done so cheerfully, so promptly and in such a truly sympathetic spirit, as to command the warmest gratitude and the highest admiration."[13] These "kind villagers, men and women of Angola," another news correspondent wrote, worked with doctors "untiringly in binding up the wounds, and relieving, as far as medical skill could relieve, the sufferings of the wounded."[14] The Angolans were lauded for being "more than willing to do all in their power to relieve…sufferings," a third newspaper stated.[15] A few people were singled out for special praise, among them Josiah Southwick, Romaine J. Curtiss, and Henry Bundy. Dr. Curtiss, the newspapers noted, expended "untiring and unceasing labors" that warranted particular commendation.[16] "He has remained much of the time night and day," one newspaper noted.[17] Then there was Huldah Southwick—who stayed awake for sixty hours straight to care for the wounded and dying in her own victim-crowded house. Mrs. Southwick "was not the only instance of the kind" among Angola's selfless women, the newspapers glowingly reported.[18]

At Angola, there would never be—as there reportedly were at the scenes of other major railroad wrecks of the century—later reports about the aftermath of the disaster that would tarnish some memories of the actions of those who first responded to the scene. No purported looting or stealing took place, while the train cars lay in splinters on the creek bottom, as was alleged about other wreck scenes; no victims were abused, robbed, or ignored and left to burn when they might still have been rescued—such things came down as legend and lore in the wake of some other shocking Victorian-era train crashes, but not at Angola. No one stole the belongings of the dead, picking through pockets while pretending to mourn. No one carted away the property of the railroad. No one made souvenirs out of the fragments of the coaches, hawking them for profit. No one took violating photographs.

In fact, the only person who would report any sort of foul play after the disaster would be Emma Hurlburt Fisher, the Minnesota mother. Fisher would say at one point after the wreck that as she lay on the ice in the creek bed in a semiconscious state, she "distinctly" felt someone "violently" remove a ring from her hand.[19] Whether that incident happened, or was a product of Fisher's injured brain in the darkened and hectic scene after the crash, no one was ever sure. No one else reported any incident of this kind, throughout the recovery and cleanup process, which stretched on for days. Angolans went so far, in caring for the property of the victims, as to save a thin gold band found in the ashes, so that it might be reunited with its owner. Suspecting that it might have been the wedding ring that lawyer John W. Chapman had intended to give his bride-to-be, the well-publicized Clara Green, on Christmas Day, they would send the ring to Chapman's family members and friends in Boston, only to have the ring returned with their regrets—it was not his.[20]

Indeed, Angolans comported themselves so selflessly in the wake of the wreck that some newspapers that reported on Emma Fisher's complaint felt the need to apologize about casting blame on the village and its people. This was highly unusual, in an age when newspapers were typically quick to point fingers at culprits, and not so quick to correct their mistakes and misapprehensions in print. "Undoubtedly this outrage was not perpetrated by a resident of that place," one newspaper reported, of the Fisher incident, "for language is not strong enough to express the gratitude that seems to pervade the hearts of all that received assistance from the citizens of Angola."[21]

DR. ROMAINE J. CURTISS would have bent low over the bodies of victims, checking their pulses, feeling their limbs and skulls to see where bones might be broken, closing the eyes of the dead. Then he would have directed the Angola men clustered in the area to begin carrying the victims up the sides of the embankment. Curtiss no doubt helped them load the bodies onto makeshift stretchers and litters; he was used to such hands-on work with casualties. The men would have placed the bodies on whatever they could find: sleds, pieces of the roof that had been ripped off the Erie car, tree boughs, and shards of flattened debris. The trip up the eastern incline to the top of the ravine was perilously difficult. Snow made the slope slippery, and rocks and underbrush impeded the men's progress. They would have tried to go carefully, so as to avoid jolts and jars to the bodies, but some couldn't be helped. The victims slipped in and out of consciousness, groaning.

Curtiss scrambled up along with the victims. He would have consulted with Frederick Hoyer, who had been rejected by Frank Sherman when trying to help the injured conductor. According to newspaper reports, Sherman urged Dr. Hoyer to care for the rest of the injured passengers before spending time taking care of him. "For God's sake, let me alone," Sherman reportedly said. "Hurry to the assistance of the passengers who need your aid now more than I do."[22] This story may have been apocryphal—the first half seems like something a distraught Sherman might have said; the second half perhaps more like the extrapolation of a drama-minded news editor—but it hinted at the truth of the Angola rescue effort: the overwhelmed feeling experienced by railroad men and medical personnel at the scene.

Speaking to Hoyer and others at the scene, Curtiss would have outlined his plans. The doctors would split up to treat the victims. Hoyer would go with some of the victims to one village home. Curtiss would handle sorting out the victims at the creek site, and afterward would perform whatever surgical procedures he could in the makeshift hospital houses, given the conditions of the victims.

Curtiss, Hoyer, and others divided the victims into two groups—the most badly hurt, and those with lesser injuries—and then had the Angola stretcher-bearers carry the bodies of the men and women away. The victims were headed for two farmhouses in the near vicinity, as one Buffalo newspaper reported. "Into these the dead, the dying, and wounded were taken," eyewitnesses told another newspaper.[23] One of the homes was the spacious brick residence owned by Josiah and Huldah Southwick.[24] The other was the "little domicil" of one Frank E. Griffith, an Angola husband and father.[25]

Griffith, thirty-two years old and a Civil War veteran, had already lived through tumultuous times. But nothing would have prepared him for opening his front door on a quiet Wednesday evening in winter to behold victims of the train wreck lying spread across the snow in his yard, their blood darkening the white powder, the smell of charred flesh rising into the chill evening air. Griffith must have felt a lurch in his stomach—for this is precisely what he had hoped never to see again.

During the war, Griffith had left home and his wife, Thankful, to sign on as a private in the 116th New York Volunteer Infantry. Serving in Louisiana, where he was wounded in April 1864 at the battle of Pleasant Hill, Griffith wrote this to his spouse back in New York: "Darling, I don't want you to ask me to describe a battle to you nor the field after the battle is over, it is too horrible to think of. I can hear the groans of the poor fellows when there could nothing be done for them, and I cant [*sic*] get it out of my mind."[26] That had been terrible to witness; but at least it had been far away from his own home. Now, the father of two small daughters had something worse to contend with: the sight and sound of railroad victims, spread over his home's wooden floors, the quilts of his family's beds, the hearth in front of his own fire.

But Griffith, if he wavered, never let it show. He took at least ten victims into his home, perhaps more, including Lydia and Ira Babcock of Syracuse, blackened with bruises; a young couple, the Robert Stewarts, from Oneida County, who were shaken but not dangerously injured; and an unknown middle-aged man who appeared to be dying.[27] With Thankful at his side, Griffith began tending the victims, accompanying the doctors as they bound up cuts, braced shattered bones, and pulled out slivers of debris. Perhaps the Griffiths didn't have time to notice the irony in this situation, but that seems unlikely. "Oh Darling," Frank had written to his wife from Baton Rouge, four years before, in 1863, "you little know the horrors and the miseries of a military Hospital—and I pray that you never may know by actual experience."[28]

That wish had been destroyed, along with the stillness of the Angola night. Despite this, the couple bore up under the unexpected trial with kindness and charity. "Mr. Griffith is apparently an humble, hard-working individual," one newspaper correspondent, impressed by the family's attitude, would write. "But he and his family very evidently possess hearts to feel for the misfortunes of others, for they are as kind, attentive, and tender to their maimed and bruised guests as if they were of their own kith and kin."[29]

The worst of the wounded went to Southwick's. The home of the justice of the peace was large enough to accommodate more victims than Griffith's, and so Curtiss and the others at the scene dispatched to the Southwick residence many of the family groups that had been on board the cars, including the two sisters Mary and Maria Sayles, Mrs. Chadeayne and her two daughters, and Christiana Lang and her two children.[30] People were laid out around the first floor of the home and in the upstairs bedrooms, in all sorts of conditions; some estimates later put the number of wounded in the house at twenty, but others suggested higher numbers, and it seems likely there were upward of thirty victims in the Southwick home for a time. One eyewitness to the scene called the environment that of an "army hospital," with rows of victims in the most grievous situations.[31] Josiah Southwick welcomed the victims without a thought for his own property or the toll it would take on his family. "The Quaker principles dominated his life," Southwick's obituary would read, decades afterward, upon his death in Montana, "and served to bring his

This stately brick home in Angola belonged in 1867 to farmer and justice of the peace Josiah Southwick and his wife, Huldah. It is the space that became like an "army hospital," in the words of one observer, following the train wreck. This photograph was taken when the home was owned by a subsequent family. Courtesy of Mark Bouvier.

friends close to him."[32] A quiet man who valued well-being and tranquillity, Southwick did his utmost to offer nothing less to the unfortunate men, women, and children who filled his rooms.

It was a steep challenge. For if the term "army hospital" as a description for the scenes at Southwick's home meant a primitive theater for dressing injuries with a minimum of comfort, the description was not far off. Walking through the rooms of the house, Angolans—many of them women—who attended the victims saw people whose faces and bodies were ravaged in ways that wrung the heart. "In one corner could be seen a woman, insensible, her face bruised and discolored with blood," one newspaper account noted, "and in another a man who had, a few hours previously, started from home in the full enjoyment of health, but now was hovering betwixt life and death."[33] Thirteen-year-old Anna Chadeayne lay in Huldah Southwick's kitchen, convulsing and unconscious.[34] Maria Sayles had a smashed jaw, and her face oozed blood from soot-singed cuts; unable to talk, she gestured and scribbled words on a piece of paper to tell the doctors where her pain was worst.[35] W. C. Patterson of Oil Creek, who had been pulled from the burning car by Benjamin F. Betts and the other rescuers, had received injuries to his head and thigh. But what surely made Huldah and her helpers look away, in pity and dismay, were Patterson's two feet, which had been burned off.[36] "This railroad disaster is accompanied by more horrible circumstances than ever before known in this country," *Frank Leslie's Illustrated Newspaper* would write of these scenes of the wreck's aftermath, "and its results are truly sickening to contemplate."[37]

Some of the victims in these hospital houses engraved themselves on onlookers' memories. In Southwick's home, a young woman who had been a passenger in the Erie car—and who had been badly injured herself—felt moved by pity at the sight of a baby that had been "taken from the breast of its mother," who had supposedly died in the crash.[38] The young woman, despite the fact that her wounds were still being dressed, nursed the slain woman's infant in order to calm and feed the babe.[39] Observers also witnessed the reunion of the married couple who had been separated in the fall of the Erie car; the man who had sobbed for his wife—"Shall I never see her again?"—was informed that his spouse had lived. He had despaired for her life because they had been taken into different homes for medical treatment. "One of the uninjured passengers, discovering the relationship, carried her news of his safety; and took back 'her love' to her husband," *Harper's* magazine would report.[40]

The women of Angola especially distinguished themselves during these hours. Hearing of the accident, many of them hurried to Southwick's and Griffith's from their kitchens and firesides; working together, they cleaned up bodies, soothed victims, boiled water, made piles of bandages, assisted the doctors, and scoured linen cupboards for fresh blankets and sheets. Social conventions and class differences were forgotten as the women worked together to nurse the wounded. Thankful Griffith, a younger and less affluent woman, labored alongside Huldah Southwick, thirty-four, and Henrietta Bennett, thirty-four, the capable spinster daughter of prominent citizen Joseph Bennett—the man who had earlier described the Big Sister as "a *beautiful* flat."[41] In a time in which nearly everyone died at home, not in hospitals, and illnesses were typically tended by female family members rather than doctors, the women of the village had practical abilities that made their presence invaluable.[42] Their household skills—basic first-aid techniques, as well as calming presences—brought comfort to many of the suffering in these early hours. One newspaper account of their actions called them "angels of mercy—kind and true-hearted women," and marveled at the ways in which these women "kindly and tenderly" provided relief for so many.[43] Besides Huldah Southwick, who was singled out for particular praise, at least sixteen women of Angola were listed by name in Buffalo newspapers in appreciation for their efforts on behalf of victims—this, in an era in which proper women almost never saw their names appear in newsprint.[44]

Despite all the townspeople's skill, the victims' sufferings went on. Charles P. Wood moaned in one room of Southwick's home, from his cuts and bruises; in another, the Tennessean R. M. Russell nursed injuries to his breast and back, and seemed to have internal injuries as well.[45] Emma Fisher was out of her head with delirium. One eyewitness, looking into the rooms, said that "in one room…[he] counted sixteen dead bodies," and that "in all the other rooms…were the wounded lying, or walking about distractedly calling for missing friends, or raving in the delirium of pain."[46] Some seemed simply too far gone to last. Anna Chadeayne's skull had, upon examination, proved to be split to its base; she was sinking "very low."[47] Mary Thomas, who had crawled out of the Toledo car with her husband but suffered battering and bruising in the fall, had lost consciousness; when she regained it, she felt a shock at finding herself in "a private house" and not beneath the Big Sister bridge. She fluttered in and out of lucidity, each time returning to alertness with loud assertions that she was "entirely unhurt," and ordering Drs. Curtiss and Hoyer to leave her alone.[48] "It was only some time after the accident," some eyewitnesses related, "that she was convinced she had received injury."[49] Lizzie Thompson kept trying to give an account of her fall in the Erie car, only to find that her mind wandered and would not focus.[50] "I can't remember anything," she lamented, over and over again.[51]

With the victims, into the Southwicks' house went the wreck's detritus. From the piles of ruins, Angolans pulled tokens of personal property: semi-burnt valises, scraps of letters and papers, jewelry that had become separated from owners, including at least six pocket watches and wristwatches, which seemed to have held up better in the fires than other sorts of jewelry. Some of the watches showed the time of the wreck on their stilled faces.[52] They found a gold chain, a pair of iron ice skates, a lady's pin in the shape of a cluster of three leaves, a small trowel, a hatchet, an "old-fashioned tobacco box" decorated with the "Anchor of Hope" design, and numerous rings of keys—some still showing numbers, such as "119" and "300," inscribed on the key tags.[53] "A small gold vest-chain bar has been found in the wreck and is in a good state of preservation," one newspaper noted.[54]

Villagers collected these items, and then didn't know what to do with them. If it seemed heartless to leave them in the rubble, it felt similarly callous to throw the scraps and tatters, the melted hunks of metal, onto the heaps of rubbish being piled up in the creek bed. Memento mori, or remembrances of the dead, were items these men and women would have been familiar with. Touched by war, many of their generation had learned in painful ways what the personal item of a slain loved one could mean—especially when death came suddenly, with no chance to say goodbye. These items—a Bible, a lock of hair, a bullet—could "help to fill the void left by a loved one's departure."[55] They could sometimes be the only thing left behind.

Knowing this, the men and women of Angola could not dispose of, nor ignore, the small and shattered items they found. They had to be stored somewhere, and that somewhere became Josiah Southwick's house.[56]

ZACHARIAH HUBBARD may not have known what was coming, but Romaine Curtiss surely did. The doctor had examined Hubbard at the scene, and would have shaken his head over the Canadian carpenter's body. Fading in and out of consciousness, Hubbard had been hauled to the top of the embankment along with the other victims. Hubbard's legs and feet were burned to ash; his arm had been torn from his torso. Blood was caking around the gaping hole where the limb had been. He was losing his grasp on lucidity.

Curtiss had seen such men during the war. He would have known—as hard as it was—that his job called for him to make difficult decisions in certain cases. He could not expend the time and effort of nurses and doctors, nor the strength of Angola men who would have to haul Hubbard to a hospital house, only to haul him back out again after he died.

Curtiss called to the men who had carried Hubbard's body to the top of the slope. He would have pointed back toward the village, toward the railroad tracks and the station house—directing the Angolans to take Hubbard back to the rail yard. A few of the men hoisted Hubbard onto a litter—he would have been as light as a child, with three of his limbs gone—and carried him down Main Street to Commercial Street. They lifted him across the threshold of the Angola Hotel, which stood next to a handful of other hotels and boardinghouses near the railroad tracks. In the foyer of the building, the men laid Hubbard on the floor.

There, the carpenter suffered "most intensely" for one full hour, then another.[57] Hubbard wept, when he was conscious enough to; he bore his agonies as manfully as he could. Toward the end, Hubbard slipped mostly out of consciousness. But, observers saw, he never stopped murmuring the name of a Canadian community, "St. Catharines." He may have mentioned his wife, Ellen, and children, who waited for him, yet unaware of the train's derailment and the fact that their husband and father was slipping in those final moments from life into death.[58]

When Hubbard gasped a final time and died, it was a matter of a few steps for the Angola men to carry the carpenter's corpse into the village's freight house. That, now, was the place of the wreck's dead.

A FEW BLOCKS away from where the corpses were being laid out, Henry Bundy had other business to attend to. Railroad officials had asked the Angola businessman if his wood mill would make plain wooden boxes to hold the bodies of the dead during their shipment by train to Buffalo.[59]

Bundy knew the delicacy of the task; he would have wanted to handle the job personally. And so, after the worst of the fires on the creek bottom were out, Bundy would have trudged away from the crash site, where parts of the Toledo car still glowed like living coals against the darkness. He would have headed toward his mill, which was situated forty rods to the north of the burned car—some 220 yards—on a gentle bend of the creek, at a place where the Big Sister flowed out from the village toward the farm fields and Lake Erie beyond. Bundy had started the business by making wooden pails and hay rakes for the farmers of the surrounding countryside; his outfit had grown to be one of the biggest milling operations in Erie County.[60]

Inside his mill, Bundy would have run his hands down some new boards, white pine, freshly cut from the woods around Angola, smelling of sap and sunlight. He selected the soundest lengths of wood, then hauled them into his shop and set the planks out onto his tables. Bundy began to plane, to cut, to hammer. He was making coffins.

BY EVENING, those working with the victims in Angola needed a miracle. Something to give them stamina—to help them cope with what had happened in their midst. A large one would in such circumstances have been improbable; they couldn't conceive of it. Angolans got a small miracle instead, and for a moment it seemed nearly enough.

In the seconds after the derailment, Minnie Fisher had been insulated from the worst of the danger. Swaddled in blankets and clasped close to Emma Fisher's chest, the baby had been protected from much of the jarring as the Erie car careered down the track. At some point, however, Minnie seems to have flown out of the arms of her mother.[61]

By nightfall, the worst of the wounded had been removed from the downed cars. Villagers clambering over the debris had a chance to notice other details of the scene—including a large bundle of fabric that some Angolans observed lying on the ground, half buried in dirty snow.[62] The bundle had been "passed over and pushed about" by the rescuers; it had been stepped on and kicked aside. Rescuers had thought it a piece of baggage, or a soiled cushion. Then a tiny voice began to cry. Startled, rescuers paused in their work to listen. A moment of hushed stillness—the first since the cars fell from the track hours before—descended upon the scene. Everyone concentrated on picking up any sound of a human being who might still be alive. It came again, and there was no doubt: a "smothered cry" was coming from the bundle on the ground.[63] Hurrying to lift and unwrap it, the villagers found the bright eyes of an infant blinking back at them.

The baby they discovered may well have been Minnie Fisher. The child's body was unhurt, "without a single scratch."[64] It made tiny fists, and dug them into its eyes as it cried.[65] A ripple of excitement ran through the clusters of rescuers at the sight of the child. The baby's survival was preposterous—but there it was. News of the miracle baby of the New York Express soon spread throughout the village. The story of the baby's rescue flew from person to person. Shortly, it would be picked up by newspaper correspondents down to Angola from the Buffalo dailies, and would flash by telegraph around the country. Within a week, Americans would read of the survival of the baby, and marvel.[66]

The Angola baby's story became a small point of illumination in the aftermath of the Horror. Amid so many heartrending reports about the events at Angola, it gave witnesses—both those on the scene at Big Sister Creek, and those reading newspapers and magazines far away—something hopeful to hold on to.

CHAPTER 11

Recognitions

SOME ANGOLANS now clustered alongside the railroad tracks, waiting for the arrival of two trains. Night had fallen, bringing with it cloudy iron-gray skies and colder temperatures. Snow seemed imminent.

On the eastern side of Big Sister Creek, villagers waited for the Buffalo and Erie's special, a relief train that had headed out from Buffalo's central terminal within the hour packed with people and supplies: city doctors, railroad workers, medical goods, wrecking equipment, mattresses for the injured. As the hands of their pocket watches ticked past five o'clock, residents of the village had grown impatient for the relief train's arrival.

Trying to keep warm, citizens eyed the skies, watching and listening for any sign of the special: a puff of smoke, white against the dull gray-black darkness, the echo of a whistle. Word had spread that some of the railroad company's top officials might be on board the train—if not William Williams, president of the road, then certainly Robert N. Brown, his right-hand man. Anything in the way of expertise and authority would be welcome, the villagers must have felt; in their aching muscles, they knew they had done as much as they could alone.

On the western side of the ravine, near the station house, more villagers stood huddled in the snow, waiting for the incoming Cincinnati express. Because of the wreck, the regular run from Ohio to Buffalo was behind schedule. News had circulated, however, that the Cincinnati had left Dunkirk and was steaming down the line toward Angola. The Cincinnati's consist contained a typical seasonal load of one hundred or more passengers—among them John D. Rockefeller and a reporter for the *Hartford Courant.*

The delay of the Cincinnati express now seemed like a small matter. Angola residents had bigger concerns. The men and women gathered by the tracks no doubt thought about the cleanup of the wrecked train and the disposition of the bodies of wreck victims as they watched and waited for the approaching trains. They would have felt the increasing coldness, the sharpness of the occasional gusts of wind. Near the downed coaches they had felt the heat of the blazing fires; here, at a distance from the wreckage, the frigid air chilled them through. Then, as the sky had promised all day, it began to snow in earnest. Flakes fell from the sky, dotting onto the villagers' woolen overcoats, scarves, and hat brims. Most of the residents stayed where they were; nobody wanted to leave before the trains pulled in.

So they turned their gazes eastward, down the track to where it ran along toward Buffalo—a long straightaway from the village at a forty-five-degree angle to Main Street, then a curve that disappeared into thickets of trees—and also gazed back toward the west, to where the tracks curved to the right and rose up a gentle grade as they headed out of town. Finally the villagers heard it in the distance: the huff of an engine, the clatter of wheels. A Buffalo and Erie Railroad locomotive appeared in the east, followed by several coaches—a short train, hastily assembled to respond to the derailment.[1] As the train slackened speed in order to stop on the eastern side of the gorge, those villagers standing on the eastern side of the creek, farthest from the village along the tracks, could likely see blurs of human faces at the train's windows, men angling for the first glimpse of what had happened in Big Sister ravine.

The relief train rolled to a stop on the eastern side of the bridge. It had to, for the track ahead was blocked by the remaining cars of the New York Express, still halted where Charles Carscadin had left them. Doors snapped open as the special ground to a stop. Even before the cars had stopped moving, men jumped down from the platforms, their arms full of equipment: shovels, pails, pry bars, axes. As the wheels of the train ground and squealed in braking, more men scrambled down. Angolans spotted four or five Buffalo doctors in frock coats, carrying leather bags; police officers wearing the uniform of the Niagara Frontier department; reporters from several Buffalo daily newspapers; and railroad wrecking men, clad in work clothes and heavy boots. Railroad company officials, recognizable in their suits, climbed down as well. Dr. Samuel Wetmore clambered down from the train with the rest. His kindly face well known in western New York, Wetmore had a reputation as one of the city's best doctors.

Villagers greeted the members of the Buffalo group, and then led them toward the ravine. Following the locals, the new arrivals hiked through the snow alongside the tracks, toward the top of the embankment. As they did so, the Buffalo men registered a signifier of the scale of the scene that lay ahead: a singular scent, acrid and cloying—a smell unmistakable to those who had grown up with fire in their homes and barns, their hearths and slaughter yards. It was the smell of burning flesh, observers realized, which "permeated the atmosphere" and "gave convincing evidence that the catastrophe was a heart-rending and awful one."[2] The smell told them more clearly than any words could have what sort of situation they had come upon. Initial estimates sent by telegraph from Angola to Buffalo's central terminal had reported the death toll at three people, then ten, then fifteen, and later twenty.[3] The situation, the arrivals from Buffalo realized, must be worse than the highest number so far reported.

The group hurried through the snow and ice, slipping and stumbling in ruts. As they pushed forward toward the edge of the ravine, the Buffalo men absorbed the sight of the damaged New York Express standing on the main line. The engine and five remaining cars would have to be shifted onto a side-track once the rails had been cleared and checked; but that hadn't happened yet. Shorn of two cars and one hundred feet of its length, the express wore a desolate air. A Cleveland and Toledo coach was now the last car of the train; its rear coupler pin jutted out awkwardly, like a giant safety pin that had been bent and discarded.

From this eastern vantage point, the panorama of Angola, spread out before the newcomers, was deceptively peaceful: the truss bridge and beyond it the village's commercial center, looming "anything but distinct" in the distance; lights shining from Angola's depot and businesses.[4] Angola looked vibrant and serene at this remove, glimmering white and yellow against the darkened backdrop of pine trees. It looked, for a moment, like a pastoral picture post-card of Christmas. Then they reached the edge of the gorge, and looked over. Angolans pointed, described, explained. The Buffalo men nodded and took it all in; then they began to clamber down the slippery slope, holding tightly to each other, the scent of death growing stronger in their nostrils.

AT THE BOTTOM of the gully, work was beginning on the second part of the rescue effort, locating and clearing away the bodies of the dead. Many corpses—likely forty or more—were still trapped within the wreckage of the Toledo car. Some were lying in places where they could be reached; Angolans had been working to loosen those figures and pull them out. Others were so difficult to see in the burned remnants of the coach that rescuers decided to wait until the light of morning to extricate their bodies.[5]

Bodies that were removed were borne by Angola men through the creek bed, up the inclines on either side of the creek, then loaded onto sleds and sleighs and dragged or driven down the streets of the village—Main Street, then right onto Commercial Street—to the freight house. This was a standard wood-frame building, simple in style like the station house it stood near, with wide doors for the loading and unloading of boxes and crates of agricultural products, timber, and other rural goods. The Angola freight building was no different than other freight houses of the period, as plain and utilitarian as most Buffalo and Erie structures of the time, lacking the gingerbread flair of the depots built by the New York West Shore & Buffalo line, or the "pagoda-style" depots that would be built by the Delaware, Lackawanna & Western Railroad in small towns across New York State before the century was out.[6]

In the freight house, the men laid the bodies of the dead on the floor. They placed them in rows as neat as they could manage, trying to keep families together: husbands with wives, parents with children. "Husband, wife and children were laid side by side," one newspaper would report of their efforts.[7] The bodies these Angola rescuers placed in this way included—though as yet these names had not been attached to the victims—the forms of Spartansburg spouses Jasper and Eunice Fuller; Randall Butler Graves; Lizzie's brother Simeon E. Thompson; Buffalo lawyer Eliakim B. Forbush; and station agent Josiah P. Hayward.[8] Frances Gale's mother Lydia M. Strong was also laid in the ranks of bodies, though she had been one of the few already recognized and named.[9]

For victims other than family groups, villagers arranging the bodies did their best to keep the corpses of men and women separate, but that proved an even more difficult task. In more than a few cases, they had to go on guesswork—hazarding judgments about the sexes of the forms they were handling, some of which were so burnt that villagers realized only "surgical examination" would yield knowledge of whether the remains were male or female.[10] Some citizens worried about the remains of babies that may have been in the car that burned—fearing there may have been tiny corpses in the wreckage that were so consumed rescuers were unable to find them. "It is my impression that there were some infants that were so completely burned that we could not gather their remains," said Henry Bundy.[11]

Novelist Thornton Wilder would write, decades later, in a work about the act of sorting out victims in the aftermath of sudden disaster, that the process of making these salvaged forms into recognizable human beings was as much a matter of conjecture as science. "The bodies of the victims were approximately collected and approximately separated from one another," Wilder wrote, "and there was a great searching of hearts."[12] The word *approximately* caught at the truth of the matter; the job of Angolans in the freight house in these hours was a grim, confusing, numbing task. "The sight of those ghastly, bruised and burned bodies," said one observer, "will be recollected for a lifetime."[13]

TO THE WEST, meanwhile, the Cincinnati express chugged toward Angola, carrying passengers simmering with tension. Word had spread on board the train—the second eastbound express of the day between Cleveland and Buffalo—that an accident had happened to the earlier express, somewhere on the tracks near Angola. Some passengers whispered that three or four people might have been seriously injured, even killed—though no one was sure whether to believe that.[14] Sitting on the train as it rolled toward the village, John D. Rockefeller likely speculated about the accident along with the others. The *Hartford Courant's* correspondent, well placed for timely news coverage, would have wondered if he had a story on his hands, or merely a false alarm.[15] There was no way to alert an editor, though. News tips like that needed to be sent by telegraph, and until the train stopped there was nothing even the most enterprising of journalists could do.

As the train neared the station, passengers pressed close to the windows. Nobody wanted to miss seeing the accident, if there was anything to look at. Yet as the Cincinnati slowed to a stop just before the Angola station house, there was no sign of any problem—other than the greater number of people than usual in the rail yard, for a country stop in the middle of December.

Travelers, including Rockefeller and the New England newsman, stepped down from the train's carriages, into the cold air, and headed for the depot and Newton's telegraph office to hear the news. They didn't have to go far. On their way to the station house, passengers turned their eyes toward the freight house, which stood open to the cold air, a humming center of activity. Through the doors of the building, these men and women spied a scene that stopped them in their tracks. "No one expected such a shocking sight," one of the passengers stated, "as met our view."[16] Directly in front of them, they saw Angolans bending over rows of ravaged corpses laid out on the frozen ground inside the freight building: six, eight, ten, a dozen or more—they couldn't tell, at first, how many there were, but the forms spread over the floor of the building were recognizable as the bodies of men and women who had been, like them, passengers traveling eastward just hours before.

Some of the corpses they saw could be recognized as people. The bodies were intact, if battered, with torsos and limbs still semi-clad in woolens and flannels. The Fullers, for instance—though unidentified yet as Jasper and Eunice—had gashes splitting their skulls open, but retained enough of their clothing and appearance to look like individuals who had suffered sudden and traumatic death. Other corpses were recognizable as people more because they were laid out alongside the other victims than because of any identifying marks they bore. An observer would be hard-pressed to guess what these malformed shapes—many with stumps where arms and legs had been—had once been, without the context of the other victims around them. Newcomers from the Cincinnati train surely turned away in shock and dismay from the scene. One of the observers looked long enough to count fourteen corpses, though he was not sure how many were men, how many women, and whether any were children. Many of these victims, the onlooker noted, would never be identified, no matter what rescuers did.[17] There was just not enough to go on.

Among these witnesses reflecting on the devastation of the scene was Rockefeller. The Cleveland oilman, like a few others on the Cincinnati express—a young man named William Green among them—had had the narrowest of escapes from the disaster.[18] Had Rockefeller caught the morning express, he was likely now realizing, he would have been aboard the wrecked train. Green, seventeen years old, claimed that he had also missed the earlier train by failing to board in time at Dunkirk; standing in the station yard, he began to rejoice in his purported good fortune, telling his story to the assembled crowds. Cheers broke out from a number of spectators, who "congratulated" Green on his survival.[19] Rockefeller took the news of his deliverance in a more solemn fashion. And, along with other passengers from the afternoon express, he would have trooped out to the Big Sister span to gaze upon the wreckage of the New York Express.

Looking down from the bridge, these first few outsiders and news reporters to gaze upon the scene surely felt like they were staring into the depths of hell. "Upon the ice below," one newspaper account described, "a large fire had been built from the debris of the wrecked cars."[20] The light from this bonfire—fed by car timbers, upholstery, and detritus—threw enough illumination around the bottom of the ravine that observers on the bridge were able to make out gruesome details of the disaster. They saw the way the burning of the Toledo car had scorched the eastern wall of the ravine; the stone had been blackened by the heat of the flames, and looked charcoal-colored.[21] All that could be seen of the burned car, some observers noted, was the ironwork of the car's frame and a single piece of the wood paneling of the coach that had flopped onto the ice. Tokens of the passengers who had been aboard this last car were scarce. "Here and there could be seen a portion of the scorched wearing apparel of those who had been burned to death while yet alive," one witness stated.[22]

What they saw next was worse. In the "flickering glare" of the bonfire, the observers spotted lump-like objects lying here and there upon the ice of the creek. Discerning more closely, the men and women realized they were looking at corpses—sixteen of them at least—that had not yet been carried to the freight house. The blackened bodies, the witnesses said, evidenced the brutality of their deaths. "All traces of humanity [were] burned out of them," one witness said, to the point that they were "past identification by their nearest friends."[23] What was striking to early eyewitnesses of the scene was the layout of the span and ravine, and the place—so near the eastern side of the bridge—from which the cars had fallen. "The strangest part of the accident," one onlooker said, "is that it should occur at this particular place and in such a manner as to cause the greatest destruction of life. If the train had run ten seconds longer before the cars had left the track they would have rolled over a nearly level ground without probably doing much injury."[24]

As they looked, Rockefeller and the others would have breathed in the smell rising with every gust of hot air from the bottom of the creek: burning wood and fabric, melting glass and heat-seared iron and engine grease, layered over with the stench of flesh. "A sickening scent of burning flesh filled the air," one witness at the scene said.[25] This stink of the wreck filled observers' senses—filled their memories; filled the village itself—with the smell of railroad death.

A devout Baptist who believed that very little happened in the world without being guided by the unseen hand of Providence, Rockefeller would certainly have found himself pondering the lessons he felt must exist in his escape from such a horrible death. For it was clear to him that he had been spared, just as the deaths of the passengers in Big Sister gorge, hard as it was to contemplate, must have been somehow divinely ordained—or, at least, permitted. Thinking along these lines, Rockefeller would have wanted to share the news with the person closest to him: his wife Laura. He walked to the station and got in line at Newton's telegraph office. The instrument had been tied up for the past few hours with messages about the wreck that newspapers would shortly be labeling "the most appalling [train disaster] that ever happened in this country," as well as an "unequalled railroad horror."[26] News bulletins flashed out of the village, but, as one newspaper put it, "owing to the excitement prevailing at Angola…the reports were not always very satisfactory."[27] Nevertheless, a few openings remained for individuals who wanted to send telegrams to their loved ones from the scene. Rockefeller managed to squeeze his way to the front of the line.

John D. Rockefeller sent a telegram to his wife, Laura, from the Angola station on the evening of December 18, 1867, after he had learned of his narrow escape. "I am thankful, thankful thankful," he would tell her later, in a letter mailed after he had reached New York City. Courtesy of the Rockefeller Archive Center.

Scratching his words onto a slip of paper topped by the logo of the Western Union Telegraph Company, Rockefeller composed a short message to his wife, addressing it to their home at 29 Cheshire Street. His message, received in Cleveland at 6:25 p.m., became one of the first dispatches to that city containing news of the wreck.[28] Headed by the word "Angola," Rockefeller's telegram read: "THANK GOD I AM UNHARMED = THE SIX FORTY (640) TRAIN I MISSED HAD BAD ACCIDENT."[29]

His bags had been burned to ash. But Rockefeller—by luck, chance, or the hidden hand of God—had escaped. There must be something, the young Clevelander would have thought, that he was meant to live for.

His telegram sent, Rockefeller would have prepared to climb back on board the Cincinnati Express for the final hour of the train's journey to Buffalo. As he did so, he may have noticed crewmen from the Cincinnati train talking with Buffalo and Erie Railroad officials—or noticed that some parts of the Cincinnati's carriages were being cleared for new boarders. As soon as the track ahead was cleared of the New York Express, as well as the relief train—both would be shifted onto sidings in this period—and the Cincinnati passengers once more loaded onto the later express, it could leave for the east.

By 7:15 p.m., in the village's freight building, which was now guarded by squads of Niagara Frontier Police officers, some of whom had no doubt ridden to town on the relief train, railroad officials were realizing with sinking hearts that they were not going to be able to identify many of the charred bodies without the consultation of the city's coroner—and perhaps not even then.

When they were making identifications, these rail officials saw, it was mostly by luck. One young man's scarred body was matched with his name and hometown not because any one could recognize him, but because during the inferno in the last car his arms and legs had curled in on his torso in the pugilistic pose of the badly burned, trapping against his groin the young man's set of keys and the baggage claim token he had put in his pocket earlier that day.[30] Matching this claim with the trunk he had traveled with, rescuers were able to pinpoint the identity of Morgan Kedzie, eighteen, the only son of a Rochester family, who had been on his way home for Christmas from a trip to Iowa where he had been visiting relatives. Kedzie's set of keys opened the lock on his trunk, railroad workers confirmed, which meant that "there could be no doubt as to the identity of the body," even though "the fire consumed all that could in any manner lead to recognition by friends."[31] But that case was something of a fluke when it came to discovering an identity for one of the victims, and as the evening passed, those working over the corpses laid out in the freight house were beginning to know it.

Meantime, on the railroad tracks at Angola and to the east of the village, maintenance men from the Buffalo and Erie Railroad were walking the length of the track with lanterns and torches, bending down to examine the rails, measuring, and scribbling down figures. The rail at the frog outside the station house, bent and twisted upward for some six to eight feet at the place of derailment like a windblown limb, had been ripped out and replaced; the damaged section had been set aside for inspection at the railroad's car shops in Buffalo. A slew of maintenance men based at Angola—James Mahar, Cornelius Van Elten, and Dennis Graney among them—tested the gauge of the new rail and frog. It was the third rail to occupy its place in the track that day, and they found it to be correct. The men then walked the rest of the line and found no damage to the rails that would make travel dangerous. They made note of deep gouges that had been left in the ties between the frog and the bridge structure by the dragging wheels of the express, and made plans to measure the marks in more detail the next day.

Nearby, at the bottom of Big Sister Creek, workers labored over the remains of some victims, and wrecking crews that had arrived on the Buffalo relief train chopped at fragments of the crushed cars, turning them into kindling to feed the flames of the bonfires that lapped at the bottom of the creek bed.

One Angolan, while walking through the creek bottom, stooped to retrieve an object embedded in the snow. It turned out to be a grimy copy of a book, which, when opened, revealed the inscription of J. Alexander Marten—as well as the $50 Marten had tucked there, earlier in the day in Erie.[32] Marten was dead, his body in the freight house awaiting identification.

BY 7:30 THAT EVENING, twenty miles away in Buffalo, the Reverend John Chase Lord would have been hearing news of the train accident. As pastor of one of Buffalo's largest and most prominent churches, the six-hundred-member Central Presbyterian, Rev. Lord was a well-known figure in Buffalo.[33] Just that morning, he had officiated at another society wedding, leaving his gingerbread-encrusted mansion on Delaware Avenue to travel to the home of the bride's father.[34] Besides the usual rush of weddings timed to the holiday season, Lord also had an ornate church to oversee—located at Genesee and Pearl streets, it had been dedicated in 1852—and preparation to do for his popular winter series of Sabbath lectures on the connections between "sacred" and "profane" history.[35] Nobody, Buffalonians joked, could sleep through Lord's preaching: with his rumpled gray hair rising from a receded hairline, heavy eyebrows, and monumental visage, the stocky Lord even looked the part of the fiery Puritan minister.[36] Some of his congregants hinted that his preaching revealed a strain of New England deep in Lord's soul; after all, he had been born in New Hampshire and educated in the New England states, and though that was many years ago now, the sixty-two-year-old Lord showed flashes of Calvinist rigor often enough to make them wonder. "He felt the spur," said one, of Lord in the pulpit, "and answered to it."[37]

Rev. John Chase Lord, an eloquent speaker whose sermons could call to mind Puritan firebrands, was the pastor of one of Buffalo's biggest and most prominent churches in 1867, Central Presbyterian. To him fell the task of summing up the meaning, and trying to explain, the Angola wreck. Courtesy of Patrick B. Kavanagh.

Now Lord, who had helped the region weather the cholera epidemics of the late 1840s with his preaching, turned his attention to the Angola disaster. He knew he would have to speak about the wreck. Lord was not the type to struggle over fitting a railroad disaster into his Christian worldview, yet finding words with which to address the public about such a tragedy would be a challenging task. As with the cholera epidemic, the scope of the Angola situation would have troubled the minister. He found himself now—as he had then—casting about in his capacious mind for every scrap of Scripture and philosophy that might comfort the grieving and bereft. Lord surely sat down, soon after hearing of the disaster, and put pen to paper.

As Rev. Lord scribbled inside his manse, not far away inside Buffalo's central depot, on Exchange Street, a group of men clustered around the telegraph in the railroad companies' business offices.

Listening to every bit of news that had come over the wire from Angola, the men had caught a name they recognized. It was that of J. Frank Walker, the well-liked son of a man they all knew, businessman Julius Walker. The nineteen-year-old Walker, the listeners knew, had been traveling for work with his friends and colleagues, Joseph S. Lewis and Robert J. Dickson. When word of the accident came, there had been a flicker of concern for the safety of the three, but no one really thought the young men would have been so unlucky as to be on the express, and in one of the fallen cars.

Then they had caught Frank's name. As one, the men clustered about the telegraph instrument turned to stare at a man sitting some distance away. Julius Walker had been waiting on a bench outside their offices for word of his son. He had driven to the offices of the Buffalo and Erie personally, to see what news he could learn about his boy's whereabouts. Now the worried father was waiting outside for this very message.

It came over the telegraph instrument again, and the message was unmistakable. Walker was dead. At the words, the men gathered around the telegraph looked at one another. Though several in the group were hard-bitten newspapermen, none wanted to tell the elder Walker what the report from Angola had said. "All shrank from the task," said one witness, "of announcing the painful news."[38] Finally, an assistant superintendent of the New York Central offices in Buffalo, James Tillinghast, rose to his feet. He went to Walker's side, and bending close to him, told the older man in "a few low-spoken and broken words" that his son was dead.[39] The words changed Julius Walker's face; they changed his life. Those who saw him take the news of his son's death would remember, in later years, just this about the Horror: not the shock of a wrecked train, nor the scale of its death toll, but the look of the wave of pain that ripped through the heart of one man.

SHORTLY BEFORE 8:30 P.M., the engine of the Cincinnati express throbbed on the tracks near Angola. With the cars of the relief train and what was left of the New York Express shunted onto sidetracks, the main line was clear at last, and the later express was ready to pull out. This train held, besides the Cincinnati's group of passengers, many of those who had been on board the earlier express. The severely injured and dead would come later, railroad officials had decided, by a separate train, a grim cargo that newspapers would label the "funeral train."

In his station house, Newton signaled up and down the line that trains could proceed. In Buffalo, railroad officials made an announcement that the Cincinnati run would be arriving within the hour; citizens relayed the word, and before long a large number of people had clustered at the Exchange Street terminal, "among them being many who had, or feared they might have, friends or relatives among the killed or maimed."[40] Hoping against hope, loved ones of those on board the New York Express flocked to the terminal near Buffalo's harbor. Others came just to see what all the excitement was about.

Some had gathered earlier. Julius Walker had hurried from the Mohawk Street address where Frank still lived at home with his parents, to hear what news he could of his son. Sometime between the late afternoon and evening, the friends and family of Robert J. Dickson would have hastened from the lake captain's house on Eagle Street. Emily Forbush and her son Walter would have departed their spacious home on well-to-do Delaware Avenue—or perhaps Emily remained at home, to avoid the painful scene, and Walter went alone. Lydia M. Strong's husband, John, would have made his way from simpler Morgan Street. Family members and friends crowded into the depot, seeking to witness evidence of the tragedy for themselves.

Meanwhile, back on board the Cincinnati train, passengers sat in the flickering glow of potbellied stoves, waiting for the train to pull out of the station, cross the Big Sister, and leave Angola behind. If the thought flashed through their minds—how could it not?—that they would be the first to cross the span since the express had fallen from it a little over five hours earlier, no doubt they squelched it as quickly as possible; it would never do to tempt fate by dwelling on one's proximity to so much machine-mediated death. (Railway passengers of this period often learned this lesson the hard way. Consider the case of one John Melvin, a passenger who like Rockefeller and William Green had apparently had a close call in missing the New York Express on the day of the wreck at Angola, and was heard to boast afterward that he "could not have been born to be killed by a railroad accident." A few months later, in April 1868, Melvin would take a seat on a train that would crash at Port Jervis, and be killed.)[41] If that wasn't enough reminder of what they were following so closely, the greater token of this deliverance rode the train with them, in the form of the wounded.

These men and women, stunned by their ordeal, had been put into seats on the Cincinnati train by railroad officials who wanted to start moving the victims to Buffalo for further medical examination or for connections to trains that would take them home. These were the less injured of the victims, though their injuries were still serious. Robert J. Dickson was among them, his facial skin peeling from where he had skidded through the gravel after jumping from the Erie car.[42] Other wounded people on this train had suffered cuts and sprains, battered bodies and panic attacks, but most could walk on their own, and the railroad wanted to get them to the nearby city. Sherman was loaded onto this train as well. It was better to get him to Buffalo as soon as possible, company officials realized, so that he could begin to recover from his experience—and so that company officials could hear his version of what had happened.[43]

The worst of the wounded, and the dead, would come later. A special train was even then being fitted out with mattresses on the floor to hold the bodies; it would be ready for departure late that night or early the next morning.

Buffalo and Erie Railroad officials likely chose to stagger the flow of injured passengers into Buffalo primarily in order not to overwhelm medical help in the city. A side benefit to this decision was that the railroad would avoid some potentially bad publicity; nothing would affect the public mind more deeply than the image of dozens of bloody and bandaged people stumbling down from a train platform in the wake of an accident. There was likely a third concern on officials' minds, as well. They surely shared the unwillingness, common at the time, to place grievously injured people on board a moving train so soon after a bad jolt—since, as everyone knew, the exigencies of train travel could make poor health worse. (The entire country observed this phenomenon fourteen years later, in 1881, when the stricken President James A. Garfield was transported by train from Washington to the New Jersey seaside in the hopes that it would help him recover from his gunshot wounds; he took a turn for the worse after the railroad trip, and died.)

By 9:30 p.m., the Cincinnati express was pulling into the lamp-lit interior of Buffalo's Exchange Street depot. In that moment, Sherman, in a gesture of puzzling intent—empathy, confidence, defiance—stepped out onto the platform of the car before anyone else could emerge.[44] The bruised and shaken conductor jumped down from the car and straightened up to face the mass of people gathered before him—still in his uniform, which was grimy and bedraggled.

As he did so, an old man rushed past Sherman to the car, which was still rolling to a stop on the track. The gray-haired man threw his body onto the coach, trying to hoist his "aged form" onto the deck of the platform.[45] Superintendent David S. Reynolds of the Niagara Frontier Police, who was standing by the rails to help with the removal of the injured, raced over to the man and dragged him back from where he might have been crushed or run over.

"You'll be killed!" Reynolds warned the agitated man.

"For God's sake, Reynolds!" said the man, his voice charged with emotion. "Let me go! My son was on the train—I want to find him."[46]

Back in Angola, doctors and villagers who were tending the wounded still held back on moving any more of the injured from the temporary hospitals onto train cars that would take them to the city. It didn't happen, finally, until the middle of the night. At that hour, company officials gave the signal to proceed, and residents helped them move all but the worst of the cases to the specially outfitted train. In the still night, bodies were carried on litters out of Josiah Southwick's house and Frank Griffith's, loaded onto sledges and sleighs, and drawn down the quiet streets to the station. Sometime after midnight, the train pulled out of Angola for the east.

Sprawled on mattresses on the floors of the cars, the burned, bandaged bodies rolled with the motion of the train as it rounded the curves east of the village and picked up speed. Guttering wax candles cast a dim glow over faces blue with bruises and scabbed with dried blood. Moans escaped some of those whose broken limbs were beginning to throb along with the clatter of the wheels.

But the ride aboard these cars was quieter than one might have supposed. As the cars rocked toward Buffalo, under the black sky, observers said, almost every one of the injured men and women fell into a deep sleep. They slept so deeply, for a time, that they did not cry or respond to questions; they did not raise their heads for compresses or medicines. Until the train reached Buffalo, early on that Thursday morning, these victims could not be woken by any means.[47]

CHAPTER 12

Reports

———◆———

THURSDAY, DECEMBER 19–FRIDAY, DECEMBER 20, 1867

EARLY THURSDAY MORNING, citizens in Buffalo and Cleveland left their homes to find sullen skies overhead, snow-dusted streets beneath their feet, and early-edition newspapers crammed with columns of dense black type: the first reports of the railroad disaster at Angola.

Men and women snatched up copies of the morning dailies to learn the facts of the accident that had happened the previous afternoon. Newspapers trumpeted the wreck of the New York Express in block headlines studded with exclamations and adjectives: "Appalling Disaster on the Buffalo & Erie Railway!" read one example. "Two Passenger Cars Thrown Down an Embankment Thirty Feet High! Twenty Three Burned to Death! Sickening and Heart-Rending Scenes and Incidents!"[1] News accounts of the crash brimmed with descriptions of the scenes in Big Sister Creek, dwelling on the inferno in the last car, the hunt for survivors, and the efforts of Angolans to aid the injured. The news cast an immediate pall over residents of the two cities and places in between that had been touched by the route of the express—or that had sent men and women to board its cars as passengers. "It seemed as though all felt it sinful to smile," one newspaper observed, of the demeanor of the public.[2] As each new edition thumped onto the streets, residents in these communities scooped up the pages "with avidity," seeking to learn every detail of the tragedy, down to the smallest anecdote. "People developed a morbid curiosity to hear the most minute particulars and sickening details," one newspaper noted.[3] And then, as if by way of explanation, added this: "The curiosity of man follows the scent of blood like a hound."[4]

It wasn't just idle curiosity. People demanded to know who had been killed and who rescued because that was what mattered most to them in reading such accounts. Already, long lists of victims' names—sorted into categories of dead, wounded, and missing—had been published alongside the news reports. These lists were not entirely accurate, but they gave readers something to hold on to. Newspaper editors knew enough by 1867 to know what the public wanted in the face of catastrophe, and that was the ability to quickly locate the name of a spouse, relative, or friend in a mortality list. This had been a lesson of the recent war, which had changed much about the gathering and dissemination of news. These tragedy-hardened editors often printed these lists on the front pages of their newspapers, or on the main news page inside the paper, and the lists were repeated from edition to edition. The lists allowed readers to scan the papers at speed for the names of those they knew, before turning to a full perusal of stories about the railroad wreck. Laura Rockefeller was undoubtedly among those who skimmed the mortality lists that Thursday morning—just to be sure.

Overnight, Angola had become "the Horror," and that was the work of the period's journalists as well. A Buffalo newspaper had been the first to give the derailment that title. In an edition put onto city streets the afternoon after the disaster, the *Buffalo Post* printed as a front-page headline the words "Lake Shore Horror!" in inch-high block letters; below the headline ran a story about the wreck of the express.[5] (The *Cleveland Herald* came close to this mark, with the simple word "Horrible" as its headline for Angola coverage, but missed in its choice of an adjective the pithy concreteness of the *Post*'s noun—which resonated.) The label Horror, succinct and precise, stuck. It also fit into a larger pattern in the century, in which serious railroad wrecks were given dramatic titles such as "Disaster," "Slaughter," "Holocaust," and the like. By the following week, newsmen as far away as Chicago would be using the term to describe what had happened at Angola—that city's *Tribune* titled its front-page coverage "The Railroad Horror."[6] The village of Angola had become overnight a place that everybody knew—or felt they did. "The obscure village of Angola has suddenly become famous," one newspaper stated. "The horrible disaster which occurred...on the Buffalo & Erie Railway, near that place, is the theme of universal comment, and the name of Angola is, and will forever be, associated with the most fearful railway slaughter on record."[7]

Yet death tolls, as printed in these first accounts, were hardly accurate. In some cases, newspaper correspondents—who filtered into Angola and Buffalo over the next two days from locations in New York State and points to the east and west—minced no words in giving assessments of the statuses of various victims. These journalists were not always correct in their estimations—some were careless; others tried to report accurately but found it difficult amid such chaotic conditions—and the result was confusion. In more than a few places, the conditions of injured but living victims were reported to be so bad they could not possibly recover. Portentous descriptors were attached to the conditions of other passengers: *Dangerously. Fatally. Seriously.* Nobody defined what these terms meant for the wounded, as reported in the pages of the news publications—in the formative stage at which journalism stood in 1867, no guidelines or rules of professionalism had been set down to govern the actions of reporters and editors, and associations that promoted ethics and accuracy in reporting were still in the future. Anna Chadeayne, the thirteen-year-old with the head wound, was widely reported to be without hope of survival; she lived. Some newspapers reported that her mother, Mary, died in Angola the day after the wreck; she, too, recovered from her injuries. In one paper, a single terse word—"mortally"— was used to describe the injuries to James and Mary Lang, the children of Christiana Gates Lang; the children were actually less hurt than their mother, and both survived.[8] Mary Lang, ten years old, would be well enough to help nurse her mother back to health in the weeks after the wreck, in Angola and then Vermont. In later generations of the Lang family, a bit of treasured family lore would tell of Mary's reward for her efforts to help her mother recover: a doll.[9]

Haste in putting out news stories, often for multiple daily editions and with little in the way of copyediting or proofreading, led to other inaccuracies in the newspapers that covered the Angola wreck. One of them was the misla-beling of people who had been aboard the train. One family group, comprising a father, mother, and child, was discovered fused together among the burned bodies. Upon the victims' remains were tokens of Roman Catholicism—a crucifix and a "talisman" (possibly a medal of the Immaculate Conception, a doctrine affirmed by the Catholic Church in 1854 and popular as a symbol of devotion among the faithful following the Marian apparitions at Lourdes in 1858)—as well as a blue veil, thimble, and delicate woman's handkerchief re-portedly embroidered with the words "Mary Freeman."[10] Journalists covering the disaster drew conclusions and widely reported the group as the "Freeman family," possibly of Dunkirk, listing them as dead in casualty lists that were sent out over the telegraph to places all over the country.

It took a week for news gatherers to ferret out the truth. The "Freemans" were actually the Irish American O'Donnell family, including Patrick O'Donnell, a worker of "great sobriety and industry" at the Lake Superior Iron Docks in Cleveland, his wife, Bridget, and their son John.[11] The O'Donnells had been traveling to visit friends for Christmas and had nothing to do with anybody named Freeman. The embroidered handkerchief, if it existed at all, must have blown onto the body of Bridget O'Donnell in the train's tumble into the creek—perhaps from the lap of a passenger named Clarissa Freeman, a young lady from Niagara County who was aboard the cars. Newspapers covering the Angola disaster, like those covering other major events of the period, reported first, made corrections later, and didn't apologize for the fact.

Even so, confusion over the conditions and identities of the victims was nothing compared to that displayed over another aspect of the tragedy: the number of dead. Tallies reported by journalists and published in news outlets varied widely in the first forty-eight hours after the wreck, and continued to fluctuate as the week wore on. Some papers reported the death toll at forty; others said fifty. The *Buffalo Commercial Advertiser* set the dead at forty and the wounded at fifty, for a complete casualty list of ninety.[12] The *New York Times* wrote that the total of killed alone must number sixty, and the *Buffalo Post* put the death list at more than that number.[13] Another paper reported confidently that the dead numbered no fewer than eighty-one.[14] The estimates varied so widely that newspapers began to argue with one another, in print, about whose counts were the most accurate—showing their work with columns of mathematical calculations.

After the *New York Tribune* published—as the view of one "who knows whereof he speaks"—the views of a concerned Pittsburgh resident claiming that the dead could not possibly have been fewer than forty from the end car and eighteen from the second car, for a total of fifty-eight, some Buffalo papers responded with scathing criticism.[15] One editorial on the subject in the *Buffalo Evening Courier and Republic* argued that the burning of the bodies, while terrible, had not so completely obliterated the corpses that the rough number of human forms could not be counted. The paper's editorial ran this way:

> All the dead were brought to this city. There were twenty-three un-charred and twenty-one charred bodies, making forty-four in all the actual number of victims, as published in the *Courier* two days after the casualty. It will recommend itself to the common sense of every one, that the timber of a car could not furnish fuel enough to burn a skull or the trunk of a body beyond recognition as such. These portions of the human frame must and did so far retain their semblance that they could each be readily assigned to an individual. Who was the vital owner of their sad testimony of a departed life, will probably never be known in regard to the remains of eighteen persons. But the number of those who perished is certainly fixed at forty-four, despite the arithmetic and knowledge of the *Tribune* correspondent.[16]

Two days later, the same newspaper revised its tally yet again. And the debate in print dragged on.

As Buffalo's seven daily newspapers cranked out stories for every new edition, the task of describing the aftermath of the wreck became taxing, even for the city's most experienced newspaper types. Buffalo newsmen were, in general, a hardy lot. These were men who had experienced the war; they had covered the Erie Canal and the crime and vice that the canal district had inflicted on the city. Now some of these journalists stayed in Angola to update the status of victims; others haunted the places where the burned bodies were kept, seeking to be on hand in the event that a family member or friend made a successful identification of a body. Still others shadowed the coroner, following his every move so as not to miss any development in the investigation and labeling of the corpses. These men were used to scenes that were rough, even disturbing, but they found themselves stretched to the limit by the Horror. Each news-gathering job related to the wreck seemed worse than the last. "No reporter's pen has been found adequate to a description of the event," one newspaper stated. "The bare facts of the disaster, the harrowing incidents, the fearful scenes from which spectators have recoiled in mingled terror and disgust—have all been so painfully real, so simply horrible, that the most sober and accurate statements unrelieved by a single bit of imagination have proved the best and most effective way of telling the story."[17]

Among these journalists was John Harrison Mills, an ambitious young man from Buffalo. Mills, who nursed dreams of becoming a professional artist and newspaper journalist, would within two years be working under Samuel Langhorne Clemens at the *Buffalo Express*. Now, seizing his chance to cover a disaster with national significance unfolding in front of him, Mills filled notebooks with his observations, including drawings and reporting on the scenes related to the wreck. One of his illustrations, "Scene at the Soldiers' Rest, Buffalo, N.Y.," showed the inside of the makeshift morgue for the Angola dead, with burned corpses piled on the tables, and plain wooden coffins with openings for the victims' faces to be glimpsed. Mills's haunting image would appear on the front page of a widely circulated national news magazine, *Frank Leslie's Illustrated Newspaper*, and four more of his illustrations of the scenes of the wreck's aftermath would be published in that magazine. For Mills, and many other young reporters of his generation, a disaster on the scale of the Angola wreck was an exciting opportunity to draw eyes and attention to their work—in a crowded and sensationalistic field, in which it could often be difficult to make a name for oneself or stand out from the crowd. (Most newspaper stories in the late 1860s, as well as editorials, were not bylined, and illustrations sometimes had credit lines but other times did not.) Mills's pictures would become an important visual record of the train wreck, which was not photographed by any of the news reporters at the scene.

By 1867, Mills, a Civil War veteran who had been seriously wounded at the second battle of Bull Run and who had written a book about his regiment's experiences, had already won some degree of fame for a sculpture bust he had made of Abraham Lincoln—in part based on studies he had made of the slain president's body while standing honor guard over Lincoln's casket when the president was laid out for public viewing in Buffalo in 1865.[18] Mills may now have reflected on his wartime experiences while taking in the scenes of the train wreck. Later in life, he would write a prize-winning poem about the battle of Gettysburg that would end on a note not of battlefield glory or bitter defeat, but of the pain and quiet that comes after any great and traumatic event, in a hospital-house type of setting. The poem's conclusion would include these lines, which would seem reminiscent not only of

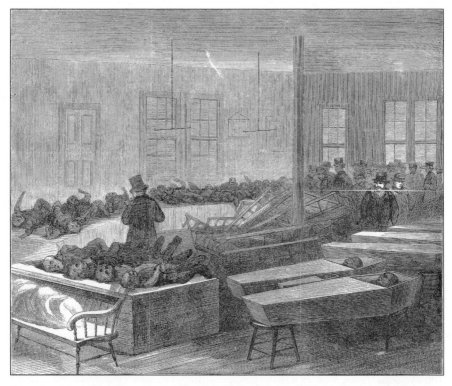

This scene of the makeshift morgue set up inside the Soldiers' Rest in Buffalo in the days after the Angola wreck appeared on the front page of a national news magazine in January 1868. The sketch was by John Harrison Mills, a young Buffalo veteran trying to make a career as a journalist and artist. The image was labeled "Scene at the Soldiers' Rest, Buffalo, N.Y." and noted the "Charred and Unrecognized Remains of the Victims." From *Frank Leslie's Illustrated Newspaper*, January 11, 1868.

Gettysburg but of Angola: "They laid the wounded on the floor, / The little house would hold no more."[19]

Like news of the Civil War two years before, news of the Angola Horror traveled both quickly and shockingly slowly. In the late 1860s, news was moving around the country by telegraphed bulletins, but wire services to create a structure for the organized dissemination of news were still in infancy. Initially, the rapid though less than wholly accurate transmission of information from the wreck site meant that headlines, news reports, and death lists could appear in major newspapers in cities along the train's route—Cleveland, Buffalo, Erie—by the next morning, Thursday, December 19. That they did. "Telegraph operators are seldom ever called upon to 'click' a more serious batch of news over the wires," the *Cleveland Herald* wrote, explaining its use of wire transmissions in its front-page coverage.[20] The telegraph had made possible a transfer of news that—in its best-case applications—was "faster than the swiftest locomotive," making for a country united in a "common, progressive, transnational enterprise as never before."[21] But while this sort of news communication was a technical possibility in 1867, it was not yet a regular practical accomplishment. Though news certainly traveled much faster than it had even a decade before, it was far from instantaneous.

Coverage of news events, including catastrophes like the Angola Horror, was still a parochial occurrence in the United States in the period after the Civil War. Bulletins sent by wire, even when transmitted at regular intervals from the scene of a disaster, were no good without savvy editors in faraway cities to pay attention to them, see their value, and print them in a timely fashion—and then add to their value by assigning local reporters to find hometown angles on the stories. And so, cities along the route of the New York Express printed stories of the Angola crash immediately after it happened. Some of the country's major metropolitan dailies on the East Coast, such as the *Baltimore Sun, New York Times,* and *Boston Herald,* followed suit, printing wire coverage of the wreck on the day after it happened.[22] Newspapers in Wisconsin, where Charles Lobdell had been a journalist in La Crosse and where newsmen were sensitive to his death, also provided immediate, in-depth coverage of the wreck. (Editors in that city blacked the borders of their papers on the day after Lobdell's death was confirmed, and—in an old newspaper tradition— some papers "turned their rules" sideways for a day, shifting the layout of their pages to mourn Lobdell's passing.)[23] After that, news coverage was less immediate—if equally intense. News of the Angola crash flowed outward across the country over the next two weeks in widening arcs, as editors in various cities read the coverage other papers were giving to the wreck, and printed their own lengthy articles and spirited editorial analyses in response.

In Philadelphia, for instance, readers of the *Inquirer* on the morning after the wreck found the barest mention of the disaster—three sentences' worth of summary—in a news roundup on the fourth page of the paper; they had to wait until later in the week for more information.[24] Readers in St. Louis, meantime, waited weeks to read first-day reportage on the wreck in their local papers. The *Chicago Tribune*'s front-page story ran a week and a day after the incident, on December 26, and that was far from atypical. The way news moved in the winter of 1867–1868 was quicker than it had been, but it was far from systematic—or even predictable.

That meant, in turn, the unfolding of a curious phenomenon. Angola remained, because of this pattern of gradually widening impact, a "developing" story in the mind of the public for weeks, if not months, after the wreck occurred. That in its own way became a factor in how the wreck took hold of the public imagination. The way that stories about the disaster washed from one coast to another, then back again, overlapping and echoing the fresh news that was steadily emerging from Buffalo on such topics as coroners' reports, inquest findings, and railroad company payouts, helped to remind people, over and over, of the Horror.

THAT THURSDAY MORNING, in the opalescent glow of daybreak on newly fallen snow, they came: fathers and mothers who had never gone to bed the night before; bleary-eyed husbands and wives; tearful children. The first to arrive, these Buffalonians pushed through the heavy doors on the city's Exchange Street depot and into the frosty interior of Buffalo's central railroad station, home to the Buffalo and Erie, the New York Central, and other rail lines. They pressed close to the tracks—as close as they could; to where the toes of their boots scraped the rails—and settled in to wait.

As the sun crept higher into the sky, other mourners followed. Siblings, classmates, friends. Gray-haired family patriarchs, and old women clutching shawls around their shoulders. Heads were bent, eyes lowered. Children who had been brought along for the significance of the occasion—or because there was nothing else to do with them—darted inquisitive glances this way and that, taking in the scene; no one had the heart to scold them for staring. Women in black cloaks and hats tugged toddlers by the hands; others clasped babies to their chests. Under their feet, as they trudged through the watery morning light to the front doors of the station, the wooden plank walkways that served as the city's sidewalks throbbed with the tread of grief. Their footfalls echoed hollowly, sounding like the drumbeat of war, or the beating of their hearts— hearts that many of them were sure had been broken. Steps away, the city's infamous canal district, the place where sailors and canal-boat men came to let off steam in taverns, gambling houses, and brothels, was just closing its eyes after a long night of rowdiness; the disjunction was palpable. By ten o'clock that morning, two thousand mourners and other witnesses had come.

Three percent of the population of Buffalo, finally, stood assembled inside the Exchange Street station, or just outside its doors, by mid-morning.[25] Most of them had walked distances through the snow to get there. A few had risked driving sleighs or carriages through some of the city's 288 miles of muddy, mostly unpaved streets.[26] No matter how far they had come, these mourners approached the station quietly. They hadn't slept. Much of the city hadn't slept. Together, those who had come to bear witness to the arrival of the Angola corpses in Buffalo stood mutely under the building's great rafters, which arched into the air above them like the folded wings of angels.

They were waiting for the dead. At forty minutes past the hour, Captain John Nicholson of the Niagara Frontier Police cried out the arrival of the Erie Accommodation, which was making its approach to the station.[27] The train, on its way to Buffalo from the west, had stopped in Angola that morning, where it had been loaded with cars containing likely in the range of fifty bodies. This load comprised the remaining victims of the wreck, whom the Buffalo and Erie had decided to ship to Buffalo last, after the less seriously injured people had been transported to the city in two groups the previous evening. The Erie Accommodation carried the victims who had been killed and burned, crushed and badly disfigured. These were corpses in rough condition; among them were the bodies crunched into fetal poses that had so shocked observers on the Cincinnati express the previous day. These were the forms—of John W. Chapman, Charles Lobdell, Elam Porter, and others—that it had also proven hard to identify.

The time for tackling that task—the identification and dissemination of bodies—could no longer be put off. The only place to do it was Buffalo, with its doctors and hospitals, its soldiers' respite homes and morgue facilities. Angola and its people had done all they could. So the Erie Accommodation streamed into the Exchange Street station, straining with extra cars containing the wreck's cargo. Across the street from the main entrance to the station, the Buffalo Soldiers' Rest Home—a tidy building that had been opened three years before by the women of Buffalo's Sanitary Commission and General Aid Society as a way station for military men—had been thrown open in preparation to receive the bodies of the dead.

Captain Nicholson shouted orders to the ranks of officers who stood fanned out along the edge of the press of people, telling them to move the crowd along. Citizens were still trying to push their way into the station, despite the mass of people gathered there. No one had room to move. As with any crowd feeling pent-up emotion, there were likely several moments in which control of the gathering might have slipped away; that it didn't was due to the presence of police, and their grim professionalism in handling the situation.

As Nicholson surveyed the scene, he had reason to be worried. The area around the tracks teemed with people who were too distracted by grief to pay attention. Besides those that had come to view the dead or claim the body of a relative, there were crowds of people trying to maneuver their way to the ticket windows and telegraph office, since William Williams, president of the Buffalo and Erie, had let it be known that free passes would be available to anyone who needed to travel to Angola or Buffalo to retrieve an injured or killed passenger. Williams had also given word that the telegraph instrument might be used by family members and friends of the victims, at the railroad's expense, to send messages back to their homes with news of loved ones. "The railroad telegraph was…placed at the disposal of the relatives and every possible facility was given for obtaining information," one newspaper noted.[28] As a result, both the ticket sellers and telegraph operators in Buffalo and Angola had been overwhelmed by crowds of "frantic" residents looking for help locating loved ones or getting information to or from the scene of the wreck.[29]

The situation had run none too smoothly. In Cleveland, some people complained that private citizens were being given access to the telegraph machines that should have gone toward news transmissions and the most up-to-date casualty lists.[30] The Civil War had been, for many people, the first time in which average Americans had used the telegraph and newspapers for announcements about the deaths and injuries of their family and friends.[31] Now, people turned to these instruments again, to seek—or send—what solace they could, in the aftermath of Angola. "To know that a father, husband or brother was on the train, and be unable to obtain tidings of his safety, or of his being maimed," one newspaper wrote, to describe the emotions of the families left waiting and wondering, "left no chance for hope against the conviction that his shapeless form was smoking in the undistinguishable mass."[32] In cases like this, the only balm at times was information—and that was hard to come by.

One who took advantage of the Buffalo and Erie's offer of telegraph missives was Andrew Fisher, Emma's husband, who had arrived in Angola from the West on the day after the wreck to seek his injured wife among the wounded. At about the same time that Nicholson was trying to restore order inside the Exchange Street station, twenty miles away in Angola, Andrew Fisher was standing in the village's telegraph office, wiring word back home to Owatonna, Minnesota, that his brother Alexander had been killed in the crash and Emma injured badly—but that baby Minnie had been spared.[33]

The hum of panic-laced, whispered conversation; the glint of fear in strangers' eyes as they scuttled past; the press of a crowd eager for the least scrap of news: these were sights, sounds, and feelings they knew well, the men and women who found themselves carried along with so many of their fellow citizens to Buffalo's depot on the day after the Angola disaster. Less than three years before, in a country at war, many of these same people—mothers and fathers, wives and friends—had experienced the flutter of anguish and fear that resulted from hearing news that a loved one was in harm's way, in the danger of battle or lying in a sickbed in a military hospital. Worse yet were the grief and shock that followed word of a death or mortal injury. In a short story called "The Story of an Hour," writer Kate Chopin would turn this idea on its head—depicting a young wife who learns of her husband's death in a railway smash-up and feels liberated rather than bereft—but her use of the formula showed how common the reverse was. People did get bad news very suddenly for much of the Civil War era and afterward. For the Kedzie family in Rochester, news of the Angola wreck came in this way, in a telegram delivered to John Kedzie on Friday morning, two days after the wreck, stating that "the body of his son…was at Buffalo."[34] "The news was sharp," the newspapers stated, "sudden and unexpected, and the shock to the bereaved family can be more easily imagined than described."[35] For Buffalo's populace in the years after the war, as elsewhere around the country, these were scenes engraved on their memories: the sight of civilians crowded around a telegraph operator, or pressing closely upon the railway tracks that would carry home a loved one's corpse. Angola's aftermath called to mind the "railroad junctions crowded with frantic relatives in pursuit of information about loved ones" the war had caused them to witness.[36]

In the midst of this trauma and recollection, their minds sought hope and comfort. Chief among the ideas that consoled these citizens was the thought that perhaps some of the wreck's victims had died peacefully, without suffering any final pain or terror. On the face of it, the chances of this seemed remote. Everyone knew about the charred state of the victims recovered from the Toledo car. Many had also heard or read in newspaper accounts that "surgical examination" was being used by doctors to attach identities to various remains.[37] And yet, despite these facts, myths sprang to life—some as soon as the day after the wreck—about the manner of death inside the last car, and about the condition of the bodies found there. One story, printed in Cleveland newspapers and circulated around the country, described the death of a nameless "babe" that had supposedly been aboard one of the cars. The infant was picked up from the ground by a brakeman, the story went, and then died in a fashion that seemed nearly fairy-tale: "The moment that it discovered that an arm encircled its waist," the newspaper account read, "it nestled up closely to the man, uttered the words 'papa,' 'mamma,' and died without the contraction of a muscle."[38]

The same imaginations that dwelt on the idea of a baby dying happily in the arms of a brakeman also perpetuated another of Angola's myths—that of the unscathed virgin. According to this story, which surfaced soon after the wreck and would be included by 1871 in ballad form in a collection of verse and prose "for railway men and travelers," the body of a young woman was found, seated alone, in the remains of the burned car—wholly untouched by the flames except for some scorching upon her costly bonnet and richly embellished dress.[39] The "rare beauty" of the person of the dead virgin of Angola was preserved even in the chaos and immolation of the wreck, the story went; the conclusion was therefore reached that she likely died from fright rather than from actual injury. Although, perhaps unsurprisingly given the Victorian setting, it was also whispered that the girl may instead have died from terrorized virtue, in response to violations waged upon her person by "some villain, taking advantage of the excitement and confusion," who may have "attempted a nameless crime" during the events at the bottom of Big Sister gorge.

In that case, it went without saying, "she died through fear of a worse fate than death by fire."[40] The closing stanzas of the ballad of the virgin of Angola, pithily called "Dead—and No Name," could not blot out the lingering dread of a death that stripped one's very identity away:

> Years now have passed;
> And her sad history remains yet a mystery,
> Attempts to obtain some clue, were in vain,
> Till hope died at last.

> Dead—and no name!
> Was it some sorrow, the dread of tomorrow,
> Or was there foul play? There is no one to say,
> And no one to blame.[41]

The poetry wasn't perfect, but it was meaningful. Stories like those of the contented babe and the unscathed virgin spread after Angola—and were read and discussed by Victorian-era publics—because they reinforced the cultural trope of the "good death," the *ars moriendi,* that had so permeated the age, despite four years of Civil War. Put simply, train wrecks, like military battles, left behind grieving families and friends who wanted to believe that their loved ones had not suffered as much as they obviously had.

The myths also subtly reinforced the period's prevailing view that the best sort of death was one met at home, surrounded by loved ones, with a peaceful expression upon one's face. That is why, in accounts of the apocryphal Angola babe, newspapers hastened to assure readers that the child's death was so violence-free as to be nearly domestic: "A beautiful smile encircled the lips, after death, so life-like, such as would have been the case had its last sweet words upon earth been uttered in the quiet and happy family circle at home."[42] Death conquered where and when he would, Victorians well knew; but home and hearth offered at least some buffer—even if imaginary—against the darkness.

NOW, STANDING in the middle of the teeming Exchange Street station, gazing upon tension-filled people who were looking for any scrap of comfort they could find—imaginary or not—Nicholson would have known there was nothing to be done but clear the building. If the bodies of the wreck victims were damaged any more, in their transit to the Soldiers' Rest, it would be on his watch and that of the other police officers—and it would be nothing short of desecration. Nicholson was not going to be the man who allowed that to happen. He raised his arms and began to gesture toward the doors, bellowing as loudly as he could.

Nicholson no doubt expected the crowd to grumble at that action, and he wouldn't have been disappointed. Some of the people in the railway station, he would have known, were unhappy with the Buffalo and Erie Railroad Company, now that they had had the time to digest the terrible news of the previous evening. By extension, that feeling applied to other authority figures, including him and the other members of the Niagara Frontier force, the city's one-hundred-strong police department, which had only recently been made a uniformed and badge-adorned outfit by the state legislature.[43] Nicholson and the other officers would have realized that some of these citizens gathered in the station were among those who believed the Angola dead to be, from railroad negligence and carelessness of one sort or another, nothing less than "murdered victims."[44]

There was nothing Nicholson could do about that. He had one problem to handle, for the present, and that was the safe transmission of the corpses. The captain would have waved his arms again, and motioned to his officers to begin pressing the crowd back, toward the Exchange Street doors. At last, with a shuffling of feet, the mass of people began to move.

But they didn't go far. Once outside the station, the crowd halted, then turned. They moved, slowly and quietly, into two long rows. The columns of people lined the path from the doors of the terminal to the arched portico of the Soldiers' Home: the path the victims' bodies would take on their way to the temporary morgue.[45] Above the doors of the classically styled building, the words "Soldiers' Rest" shone in glistening "letters of gold."[46] Beyond, a spacious ward built to accommodate thirty soldiers had been fitted out with bedsteads, mattresses, chairs, washbasins, and spittoons.

As midday approached, the doors of the terminal swung open. Nicholson came out, accompanied by David S. Reynolds, the city's police superintendent. With them, his black coat swinging and his hands clutching the papers and workbag that defined his trade, came the city's coroner, Dr. J. I. Richards. Normally at this time on a weekday morning, Dr. Richards would have been downtown in his office at 148 Main Street, poring over police reports on the stabbing of a harbor delinquent, the drowning of an immigrant in the canal, the burning of an old woman like one Mary Smith, a city resident who had accidentally set fire to her hoopskirts the previous day and been burned alive. Now Richards was handling forty- to fifty-odd corpses—Richards himself wasn't yet sure of the number—and the entire city, maybe the nation, was looking to him. It was not going to be an easy few days, and already Richards's face would have showed the strain.

Last of all came the bodies. In unvarnished pine boxes, yellow and raw-looking in the winter light, the corpses were carried from the terminal out into the street, one by one. Thirty-nine boxes, according to some reporters who looked on; others counted forty-one.[47] As the coffins were carried past, across Exchange Street and through the doors of the Soldiers' Home, the long rows of journalists and civilian observers grew hushed and watchful. "A most respectful silence was preserved," one eyewitness noted.[48] Others observed a different note in the atmosphere. "Death was an almost visible presence," one witness wrote. "His dark wings cast a gloomy shadow over the city."[49]

ROCKEFELLER HAD made his connection in Buffalo to the New York Central train that would drop him in Manhattan early that Thursday morning. He would arrive in New York City in time to shop for clothes to replace the ones that had burned in his bags, and to visit his brother William for a stay that would go "very pleasantly."[50] Rockefeller would tell William's family that the "Christmas presents were burned with the valice [*sic*] and umbrella," but his relatives would not mind the loss. "Our friends appreciate them as though rec[d] and join in expressions of *gratitude* that I did not *remain* in the car with the baggage," Rockefeller wrote to Laura, underlining words for emphasis.[51]

Once settled in New York, Rockefeller would also compose a more detailed account of his trip. "My dear wife," he wrote Laura, in a letter mailed on

Friday, two days after the wreck, "I do (and did when I learned that the first train left) regard the thing as the *Providence of God.*"[52] What had frightened him especially, Rockefeller wrote, was the thought that he could have taken Laura and Bessie with him on the trip, and the entire family could have been killed. "I[t] was *well* that a good work kept you and Bessie at home," Rockefeller wrote. "We certainly should have been in the burned car as it was the only one that went that we could have entered at the time we would have arrived at the station."[53]

Rockefeller signed off with another expression of gratitude. "I am thankful, thankful thankful."[54]

CHAPTER 13

Mourning

ONCE INSIDE the Buffalo Soldiers' Rest Home, the bodies were unboxed and shrouded. Then they were divided. Into one room went twenty-three of the corpses: the bodies of victims who were unburned enough to raise hopes that they might be identified and returned to their families and friends. Attendants placed these forms into open coffins, leaving the shrouding cloths pulled back enough so that the victims' faces might be viewed. The bodies of the Angola dead had been cleaned the barest amount—hardly at all—though no one explained whether this was due to lack of time, an excess of respect, or the superstitious unwillingness to remove traces of their final agonies.

One coffin in this front room, nearest the door, contained the form of an unidentified adult man in working clothes, his face with its full whiskers still slicked with blood, his limbs curled up and distorted into the pugilistic position of exposure to extreme heat.[1] Nearby, another coffin contained the body of attorney Eliakim B. Forbush, his torso badly bruised but his face discernible beneath its crusted-over cuts.[2] Another man, soon to be labeled as shopkeeper Jasper Fuller of Spartansburg, lay in another coffin in this front room, his head bearing a "frightful hole in the centre of his forehead, through which the brains…[had] gushed."[3] Lying in a separate box near Jasper's feet, what was left of his wife, Eunice Fuller, could be seen; the former teacher had had "the left side of her head…literally smashed out of all resemblance to a countenance."[4]

Lizzie Thompson's brother, Simeon, was in this first roomful of victims, as well, as was Frank Walker, Julius Walker's son; both young men were undamaged enough about the head and face to be recognizable. In another corner, Norman Nichols, the Ohioan who had been traveling with his wife, Arila, to look for work, lay battered, having received a hole in his head "almost the counterpart" of Jasper Fuller's, observers noted.[5] And these were the lucky ones. This first group of Angola victims had identities—or, at least, the chance at them.

By Thursday afternoon, the day after the wreck, the twenty-three coffins of these victims had been placed on tables in the front parlor of the Soldiers' Home, a room with spacious dimensions—it was thirty-six feet long, thirty wide—and a decorating scheme that had been picked out, down to the framed engraving on the walls, by the women of Buffalo's General Aid Society.[6] It was a room that had been chosen to make viewings by family members and friends as easy as possible—though that was of course impossible. There was no way to remove the sting of the scene. "A more sickening spectacle than this ghastly array of mutilated and charred humanity," one newspaper correspondent wrote, "mortal eyes never gazed upon."[7] Most agreed with him. John Harrison Mills sketched the scene for *Frank Leslie's Illustrated Newspaper*, focusing his picture, called "Viewing the Remains of the Victims of the Angola Disaster for Identification, at the Soldiers' Rest, Buffalo," tightly on

This illustration by Buffalo artist John Harrison Mills, titled "Viewing the Remains of the Victims of the Angola Disaster for Identification, at the Soldiers' Rest, Buffalo," gave American audiences an idea of the devastating deaths suffered by victims of the wreck after it appeared in January 1868 in a widely circulated news magazine. In his drawing, Mills numbered the corpses so that readers could match them with descriptions that had been publicized in the hopes of identifying the nameless victims. From *Frank Leslie's Illustrated Newspaper*, January 11, 1868.

a long table of charred corpses, many of them limbless or headless. In Mills's drawing, the men and women viewing the bodies, grouped in the background of the scene, bow their heads, avert their eyes, and turn away. One man clutches his hat to his chest at the sight. Another clasps his hands as if in prayer. A woman clasps the hand of her companion for consolation.

As wives, parents, children, and friends slowly filtered into the dim room, where candles and oil-burning lamps threw flickering light on the rows of coffins, gasps and cries could be heard from every corner. In some cases, the gasps came twice: once when visitors' eyes met with what was in the boxes; again when they realized that what they were seeing was not something foreign, but something familiar. Jasper and Eunice Fuller were recognized in this way by their sets of parents, who arrived from Pennsylvania, gazed down at the forms of their children, and claimed the bodies for burial.[8] So, too, John Kedzie spied the body of his only son, Morgan, among the boxes of remains, after rushing to the scene from Rochester, where he had received the telegram telling of his son's death.[9] "Many heart-rending scenes occurred," a Buffalo newspaper noted, "as those in sad quest of dead friends among the unknown bodies, gradually admitted to their minds the full conviction that his or her remains were before them."[10] These visitors to the Soldiers' Rest Home arrived thinking they had already borne the worst, in hearing initial news of the disaster; they left knowing they had been wrong.

Already, within the first two days after the wreck, the smell of decay thickened the air inside the rest home, making it difficult for visitors to breathe. Ladies became weak and asked to be taken outside; gentlemen followed them, holding gloves and handkerchiefs to their noses. Newspaper journalists captured those scenes in their stories; one such illustration would appear in the national press. ("Ghastly Sight at the Dead House," newspaper headlines would read the next day.)[11] All the while, in the back rooms, where the most charred of the bodies had been taken, the tools held by Dr. Richards and his assistants clinked and scraped, as the medical men probed the bodies for clues: tapping teeth, examining arm and leg joints, surveying scraps of skin for scars. It was slow work, but it was the only way to make accurate identifications. One victim, banker Stephen W. Steward, was recognized because doctors noticed an arm he had once fractured and had reset; the break allowed his family members and physician to identify him. Another man, Edward T. Metcalf of Erie, was recognized through a filling in one of his teeth. A third, Metcalf's friend J. Alexander Marten—he who had tucked the $50 inside his book— was attached to a name because part of his pocketbook survived, and in it doctors found a scrap of an old draft notice, which was marked with Marten's name and the date 1864.[12]

Remains like these formed the second group of Horror victims, the ones in the back rooms of the respite home. These were the victims there were fewer hopes for, the ones that had been so burned in the fires that authorities thought it unlikely anyone would be able to attach identities to them. There were upward of twenty people in this category, although the exact count proved difficult to determine. One newspaper reported twenty-one burned corpses, while another correspondent counted twenty-three skulls that were "plainly distinguishable" among the remains.[13] The number was still largely a guess, even by authorities who had laboriously packed what was left of the burned bodies into several large boxes and deposited them in a back-room area on the first floor of the rest home.[14] When all these human remains were packed in, it took seven boxes measuring six feet long by two feet wide to hold the material.[15] As one journalist observer noted, the people filing in to the Soldiers' Rest Home to look for loved ones did not start with these anonymous boxes of remains. They went to the more recognizable bodies in the coffins first, and only with reluctance turned as a last resort to view the cases of charred forms. "The dreadful thought that the object of their love was lying among the blackened fragments of humanity caused a dreariness of the soul which was plainly shown upon their faces," the news correspondent wrote. "Many a sympathetic tear was shed by the spectators."[16]

Dr. Richards moved among these corpses, using scalpels and scissors to cut away traces of fabric clinging to the forms, then digging deeper to find anything that remained in the way of identifying details, starting with clues as to gender. All items of clothing or possessions dislodged from the forms, however minuscule, were labeled and numbered. If identification was impossible now, someday down the road it might not be, and such fragments might make all the difference. "A full record of the bodies has been made…while all relics found upon the persons of the dead or among the *debris* of the burned car, have been carefully marked and preserved, in order to aid, as far as possible, in the future identification of the bodies," one newspaper noted.[17]

In a few cases, doctors got lucky. Scraping away at one burned figure, Dr. Richards found metal eyeglass frames and a metal spectacle case fused to the flesh of the man's breastbone. A few hours later, Zuleann P. Aikin of Hydetown would enter the rest home, see the eyeglasses and their case, and know at once that the body Dr. Richards had removed them from was that of her husband, Benjamin.[18] She claimed his body and took it home to Pennsylvania.

OUTSIDE THE FRONT DOOR of the Soldiers' Rest, trouble was brewing. Word had spread in the streets of Buffalo that the corpses of the Horror victims would be available for public viewing inside the temporary morgue for three days—until the funeral service that had been scheduled for Sunday. The announcement, meant to call forth in prompt fashion families and friends to claim the forty-odd bodies that lay inside the building, accomplished its objective. Anxious relatives queued up outside the doors. But the morgue became a magnet for others now, as well. Hundreds of people without any connection to the wreck gathered along Exchange Street near the building, seeking to gain entrance to the stifling viewing rooms. Warnings did not deter them; nor did pleas for orderliness and manners. A tragedy of national significance had happened in their backyard, and many Buffalonians wanted to see the results directly.

As the crowd grew impatient, some citizens pushed forward and tried to force their way into the building. Exchange Street between the Central railroad station—where workmen could now be heard hammering together the scaffold of a dais for the mass funeral rites—and the Soldiers' Rest Home swarmed with people buzzing with energy and frustration. The area surrounding the morgue was "besieged all day by a crowd of persons, who could not obtain admission, but hung around the charnel-house like vultures hovering over carrion," one newspaper observed in disgust.[19] Finally, when it looked as if the crowd was about to get out of hand—that perhaps weapons stronger than words might be employed to gain entrance to the dead rooms—railroad officials stationed armed guards at all the doors and windows of the building. This move settled things down for a while.

It can be difficult to stop a frenzy built on anxiety, morbid curiosity, and a sense of grand spectacle, however, as railroad officials were now learning. In some ways, that was what the citizenry gathered outside the Soldiers' Rest Home in Buffalo less than a week before Christmas represented. Their emotions were mixed, and stemmed from different sources. Some came just to get close to an event that would surely go down in history. For at least some of the onlookers, though, their feelings had a lot to do with time, and its inverse relationship to the identification of the dead among them who had gone missing. For, with every additional hour that passed, these men and women knew, their chances—or those of the relatives and friends inside the dead house who had legitimate claim to be there—of recognizing people among the victims' remains slipped nearer to impossibility.

They had learned this lesson the hard way, during the late war. Now, those who had known a passenger aboard the New York Express—or knew a family who had—realized that this might be their last chance to retrieve a body to bury, or even to obtain a yes or no answer as to whether that person had died in the wreck or somehow managed to escape. (One Angola passenger, far from the only case of his kind, was mourned by his family as dead—only to resurface in upstate New York later in the week.) By Sunday, any unclaimed bodies would be collected, coffined, and laid to rest. With railway deaths, as with deaths on a field of war, the only chance of claiming a victim was to move quickly and act decisively.

But even some of those who tried this approach found themselves thwarted inside the Buffalo Soldiers' Rest. Two men who came together to the makeshift morgue seeking a lost friend were admitted by the guards and entered the dead rooms in an agony of suspense. One of the men paused before the coffin nearest the door, the one containing a stout, brown-haired man with a whiskered face, whose features had been "convulsed by an agonizing death."[20] The men argued for a while about whether the form could be that of their friend. Finally they struck on a way to settle the debate: they would look at his boots, which would be familiar to both of them. "One of them suggested that the cloth be raised which covered the feet, in order to see the boots he wore," wrote a reporter standing nearby, "when, horrible sight, the limbs were found burned to a cinder, as far as the knees!"[21] Another party of visitors claimed what they hoped to be the remains of their friend, R. F. Gibbs of Galveston, Texas, making their guess based on the size of the remains in the boxes, as Mr. Gibbs was known to be a "very large man."[22] They had nothing else to go on—and a supposed body, even if not a certainty, was better than returning empty-handed.

Those who gave up on finding a body had one remaining option. Many grieving family members and friends were directed by Buffalo and Erie Railroad officials to cross the street, enter the Exchange Street railway station, and ask for the offices of a man named Levi Jerome. Jerome was chief baggage master for the Buffalo and Erie in the central station, and he had been given the task of keeping the collection of items that had been taken by Dr. Richards and other doctors off the victims' bodies.

With these things went many of the items that had been found in the wreckage by Angolans and turned over to the railroad—from J. Alexander Marten's book, still containing his $50, to the inscribed Bible of a young woman named Emma Leonard, to the pink-hued love letters of Samuel Paddock. Standing in Jerome's baggage room, visitors could peer into a small glass-topped case that held six gold men's watches, a ladies' silver watch with a chased-edge case, a delicate golden chain, a tobacco box marked with an "Anchor of Hope" symbol, a heavy Masonic ring marked "C.L. Sept. 28, 1865," which had been on the hand of the newspaper editor Charles Lobdell, and the wedding band, engraved with the inscription "GDK to AFG," which Granger D. Kent had put upon Abbie Gustie's finger the week before.[23] They could also look through a pile of trunks, suitcases, hatboxes, and valises: all baggage that had been left unclaimed by the victims. Finding a loved one's suitcase, or a token like a ring or watch fob, was not nearly enough; but for some families it had to be.

One man who poked through Jerome's case of artifacts, looking for his son's belongings, was surely Julius Walker. Walker had been luckier than most, in that he had been able to recognize and claim his son's body, which had been lying in one of the coffins in the rest home's parlor. But Walker still sought his son's possessions. Some time ago, the prosperous father had given his son one of the best pocket watches in his jewelry shop. Frank had worn the watch since, and had been wearing it on the day of the wreck. But when Julius claimed Frank's body from Dr. Richards, the gold watch had not been attached to it. Dr. Richards, one of the busiest officials in the immediate aftermath of the wreck, would have given the jeweler advice to check baggage claim, before moving off in a fog of foul-smelling air.

In Levi Jerome's rooms, Julius Walker inspected every item, but his son's watch was not there. He would not find it by the start of the public funeral that Sunday afternoon. He wouldn't find it within the thirty days of formal mourning that Frank's friends in a Buffalo baseball club would observe, wearing black armbands in his honor.[24] It would take more than a year, but Julius Walker would finally be handed Frank's gold watch, over the counter in his own jewelry shop, by a man trying to have it repaired, or sell it to him.

He got the watch back. The person suspected as the thief, a young man called Robbins in the newspapers, was sentenced to two years in prison. He was not an Angolan.

THE DAY OF THE FUNERAL dawned gray and troubled. Two days earlier, on Friday evening, December 20, rains had soaked the countryside around Buffalo, leaving cobbled roads slick and sidewalks treacherous.[25] By Sunday morning, change was in the air. Winds off Lake Erie began building by midday, blowing to gusts that snatched hats from men's heads and wrapped ladies' skirts around their legs as they picked their ways through the city's clogged streets. Sleighing, which had been good for the better part of a week, grew doubtful as the air softened. "This queer winter," one newspaper called it.[26] By nightfall, the city would be battered by a gale off the lake, and snow would cover rooftops and avenues.[27] It was a time for sitting "close by the cheerful fire," residents knew, in order to feel "most happy and most secure."[28]

In the face of the wind and weather, men and women left their firesides on Sunday, December 22, three days before Christmas, on the afternoon after the shortest day of the year, and walked or drove to Buffalo's Exchange Street station. It was the only place in the city spacious enough for the crowds that were expected, and was accessible to multitudes streaming in from all directions.[29] Multitudes came. As the clock ticked into the afternoon hours, an estimated 8,000 to 10,000 people gathered beneath the roof of the station and just outside its arched doors—a significant slice of the 74,214 residents of Buffalo, even factoring in visitors from out of town, and a number equal to about two hundred mourners for every one of the roughly fifty or so victims known or assumed to have died in the wreck.[30] J. H. Mills, the young artist, was on hand to capture the scene for *Leslie's*, emphasizing in his drawing the scale of the Buffalo depot, in which the assembled mourners look like small, black-clad dolls. More people lined nearby streets, waiting to catch a glimpse of the funeral cortege that would be leaving the station building after the service for the burial vault at St. Paul's, the prominent Episcopal cathedral a few blocks away. "Had the weather been more favorable," one newspaper correspondent wrote the following day, "the crowd would have been still greater."[31]

These mourners came because they needed to remember loved ones, friends, and neighbors; they needed to witness history—Buffalo's and the nation's. They came to grieve for a shattered rural village, a stunned city, and, in a way, for themselves—for something more than lives had been lost in the railway tragedy. "There is nothing in the railroad annals of this or any other country which furnishes a parallel to the awful catastrophe at Angola," proclaimed one newspaper, capturing the atmosphere of shock and sadness. "The fact that fifty human beings, thrown from a railroad embankment of upwards of fifty feet in height, crushed, mangled and bleeding, were absolutely *burned to death* in the wreck of a single car, is truly appalling."[32]

"There will be suffering of many kinds, for many long years to come," wrote the *New York Times*, "in hundreds of hearts, because of the railway slaughter at Angola."[33] Something here verged on the new and troubling: a celerity and completeness of casualty, and of bodily obliteration, that was strikingly modern in its terrors. The *New York Times's* assessment hinted at what was happening, and what at stake. By the 1860s, railroads had for some years represented the most progressive parts of American culture; they were a feature of the country and its landscape that average citizens wanted to be proud of, wanted to have their lives improved by. Linked to that appeal, however, was clearly a very real danger for the men and women who boarded the trains in ever-increasing numbers. "Slaughter" was a potent word, but one that ably captured the mood of the public in this volatile moment. It was a word that invoked scale of devastation; it was also a term that implied an action or actions on the part of others to bring about disaster. Something or someone is slaughtered by another; slaughters

FUNERAL CEREMONIES OVER THE REMAINS OF THE VICTIMS OF THE ANGOLA RAILROAD DISASTER, IN EXCHANGE STREET DEPOT, BUFFALO, N. Y., SUNDAY, DECEMBER 22ND, 1867.

Scene at the Soldiers' Rest, Buffalo, N. Y.— The Unclaimed Bodies of the Victims of the Angola Railroad Disaster.

Our special artist, Mr. J. H. Mills, sends us the sketches of the Angola disaster, which appear in this paper; and they may be implicitly relied on as correct representations of those terrible after scenes. That on the first page represents the scene in the interior of the "Soldier's Rest," a building erected during the war as a place of refreshment for the soldiers passing through Buffalo, where they could wash themselves and get a good meal without paying for it. Now, being the repository of the unclaimed remains of the burned and blackened bodies taken from the wreck at Angola, as shown last week, it presents a vivid contrast to its first scenes of contented enjoyment as the travel-worn soldier there recruited his energies. Ranged around the walls on the boxes in which the remains were brought in from the cars are nineteen bodies, almost consumed, and of which only three or four have been partly recognized, for in their terrible condition it is almost impossible to be sure of identity. The body wrapped in a sheet, and lying upon one of the benches

INTERIOR OF THE EXCHANGE STREET DEPOT, BUFFALO, ON SUNDAY AFTERNOON, DEC. 22ND, DURING THE FUNERAL CEREMONIES OVER THE REMAINS OF THE VICTIMS.

This scene, by J. H. Mills, depicts the inside of Buffalo's Exchange Street depot during the public funeral for the unnamed victims of the Angola wreck that was held on December 22, 1867. From *Frank Leslie's Illustrated Newspaper*, January 11, 1868.

are not typically random acts of fate or chance. People felt that they, too, were victims of Angola—or, at the very least, that they came close to being victims, or might be next. "It was an awful accident....I am thankful that our friends escaped so well out of such a general slaughter," wrote Daniel Chadeayne, three days after the wreck, in a letter from Angola to friends in Titusville, telling them of the injuries of his family members.[34] Chadeayne's family members were female, which brought to light another disturbing fact of Angola and other major railroad wrecks of the period: they preyed upon women and children, in ways that were shockingly violating as well as public. To have a female relation's name printed in the newspaper, in a listing of victims of a train wreck, was an experience with which people in the period had been until recently utterly unfamiliar. It was deeply unsettling.

At 2 p.m., funeral services began inside the Exchange Street station. First to make his way to the front of the assembly was Captain John Nicholson, who strode from the doors of the station to the south end of the building, clearing a path to where three flat railcars had been pushed into position to form a makeshift platform some one hundred feet long. Close in front of this stage, another car had been positioned as a temporary bier. Both platform and bier had been swathed in garlands of black crepe, a token of mourning. The cars held for the moment nothing but a podium, a melodeon, and rows of empty straight-backed chairs. Behind Nicholson trod a column of thirty-two officers from the Niagara Frontier Police, their badges burnished, who would do duty as honor guard and pallbearers.

Nicholson pushed his way through the throng to the stage, surely gesturing to his officers to form a ring around the platform in order to keep back any onlookers who pressed forward too far.[35] As he did so, Buffalo and Erie Railroad workers proceeded into the station in a line, carrying nineteen pine boxes. The plain coffins gleamed yellow in the flickering lamplight. The railroad men placed the boxes onto the black-draped bier, and stepped back.[36] Simple, unadorned, the coffins contained what had been left of the victims' bodies after three days of public viewing of the remains inside the Soldiers' Rest. They were lidded. After three days in the morgue, and frequent handling, the corpses were deteriorating.

The specificity of the number of wooden boxes had been, in the end, something of a guess. Buffalo and Erie company officials, working with the coroner, had separated the bodies into the number of coffins they felt appropriate, but it was far from a precise count. "Most are filled with human fragments," one account of the boxes ran, "in many cases nothing but skulls, and will never be claimed."[37] Of the boxed bodies on the bier, only one was matched for certain with an identity, the form of Norman Nichols of Ohio. The forty-three-year-old husband and father had been largely unburned in the Toledo car, and his body had been successfully identified by family members in the rest home.[38] But the body of Nichols's wife, Arila York Nichols, twenty-seven, hadn't been found among the rest of the remains. Relatives likely decided to bury Norman in Buffalo with the mass of unknown dead because there was no way to bring Arila's body home with him. At least this way the married couple, who had recently buried a young son back in Ohio, could be together. The Nichols's orphaned daughter, Philinda, would seem to be taken in by one of Arila's relatives.

Inside the Buffalo depot, among the crowd that swelled and pressed toward the nineteen coffins resting on the crepe-covered bier, family members stood clustered into separate spheres of grief. Fresh-faced young men from Buffalo's baseball clubs and the city's scientific association gathered near the coffins in honor of their friend, Joseph Stocking Lewis, the witty twenty-three-year-old Williams College graduate who in photographs looked less a grown man than a cheeky adolescent. Lewis's body was known to be among the burned remains—both Robert J. Dickson and Frank Walker had seen him board the train's last car after the crowding of the express had forced the friends apart, and Lewis had never reemerged—but his corpse had retained no identifying

In this illustration, by J. H. Mills, the bodies of the Angola Horror victims are shown after the funeral service, being deposited into the vault under a Buffalo church. They were later buried in a Buffalo cemetery. From *Frank Leslie's Illustrated Newspaper*, January 11, 1868.

features that enabled his parents to recognize him in the rest home. Now, Lewis's friends stood near his bereaved father and mother, who had rushed to the city from Batavia upon hearing of the wreck, desperate to find any trace of their son. Lewis's friends wore black silk armbands in his memory. His parents had given Lewis's most prized possession—his collapsible scientific microscope—to the Buffalo natural sciences association, as a legacy.

Relatives of Granger and Abbie Kent also surely filed past the row of pine boxes. Two of the boxes, they knew, must hold the remains of the honeymooning pair. The newlyweds' trunks had been located in the Buffalo and Erie's baggage room, but their bodies remained unidentified. Abbie Kent might be one of the boxed forms identifiable as a woman only because some metal pieces of a hoopskirt girding had fused to the charred flesh; or she might be another one of the forms entirely.[39] (Even days after the wreck, newspapers would be correcting initial inaccurate assumptions about the gender of various victims. Zachariah Hubbard's death, for instance, was first reported in Canadian newspapers as that of a woman.)[40] Meantime, family members and classmates of Elam Porter, in town from Vermont and Massachusetts, bowed their heads as they remembered the genial man who had applied himself at Tufts College to Latin prosody, U.S. history, and ancient maps—he was far better at the first course than the latter two—and who was to have married his fiancée, Mary Melcher, on Christmas Day.[41]

Also in the crowd near the bier, Marcus "Brick" Pomeroy and editors from Charles Lobdell's newspaper, the *La Crosse Democrat,* would have looked on, their faces set and somber. Lobdell had never been identified, even after his coworkers spent hours inside the Buffalo morgue, looking for the prospective groom. All that appeared to exist of their friend was his heavy Masonic ring; on it, the initials *C.L.* could just be made out beneath the soot and grime left behind by the heat and flames. Nearby, a large delegation from the city of Rochester, some sixty miles away, represented those who grieved the loss of David J. Cook, a well-known music dealer who had operated businesses in Dunkirk, Fredonia, and Rochester. The latter city's mayor and aldermen were among the party, as well as many businessmen from the city.[42] They had arrived on a special train earlier in the day, and would depart together after the service was over. Cook's widow and his two sons, ages sixteen and twelve, would likely have stood quietly near the coffins.

One side of the bier was surrounded by hundreds of Buffalo's railroad workers. Many of these men—not company executives, but rank-and-file employees who kept the tracks in repair, shoveled coal, and greased down the trains—would have stood, some perhaps uncomfortably, hats doffed and heads bowed. They represented the working class of the railroads that served the city: the Buffalo and Erie, New York Central, and many more. They stood together in solidarity, as the hall filled with civilian mourners. The railroaders' biceps were circled with crepe mourning bands in a sign of respect for the wreck's dead.[43]

As the crowd stood in silence, waiting, the first few clear notes of music sounded. It was an opening hymn, played on the small cabinet organ that had been placed on one end of the platform in order to assist in the singing parts of the program.[44] Members of Buffalo's best choirs—from the First Presbyterian, Washington Street Baptist, and Unitarian churches, plus a few others—filed onto the stage, holding hymnals, lifting their voices in song. A Mr. Bixby led the choir members to their places and took his place at the front of the chorus.

A rustle would have gone through the crowd in the depot; it was the motion of people signing themselves with the cross, raising handkerchiefs to their lips, dabbing at streaming eyes. As the singing continued, a group of black-garbed men mounted the stage, their gray heads reflecting the lamplight, their hands clasping prayer books and Psalters against suits and frock coats. The Reverend Dr. John Chase Lord was among them. Lord's thick eyebrows would have been furrowed, his jowls would have been set in a stoic expression; the mass funerals he had witnessed for Buffalo's cholera dead could not have but been on his mind. Behind the imposing figure of the reverend came a party of Buffalo's foremost clergymen, then the city's Republican mayor, ruddy-cheeked Chandler J. Wells, followed by the members of the city council. Last in the procession of men climbing to the stage came the officers of the Buffalo and Erie Railroad. William Williams, Superintendent Robert N. Brown, and the company's directors, including William G. Fargo, mounted the dais. Fargo's American Express Company had earlier in the day provided wagons, swathed in black crepe garlands and drawn by matching bay horses, for the cortege that would take place when the services were concluded.[45]

As the processional ended, there was a pause. A hush would have descended upon the terminal. An invocation was given. Then the melodeon burst forth in a flood of music, the first bars of an old hymn—a hymn that many of those standing inside the station would have known by heart.

I would not live alway: I ask not to stay—

Across the crowd of people pressed into the depot, men and women would have closed their eyes and lifted their faces to the roof beams. Many of the handbills printed with the first verses of the hymn, which had been circulated among the crowd, would have gone unused and unneeded. Together, the

crowd of grieving citizens sang. The bittersweet words of "I Would Not Live
Alway" rose like crystal slivers into the terminal's cold air:

> Where storm after storm rises dark o'er the way;
> The few lurid mornings that dawn on us here,
> Are enough for life's woes, full enough for its cheer.

The lyrics were taken from the Book of Job, the Bible's meditation on human
suffering, and with the swelling of voices the words of the hymn would have
resounded off the rafters of the depot.

> I would not live alway; no, welcome the tomb,
> Since Jesus hath lain there, I dread not its gloom;
> There, sweet be my rest, till he bid me arise
> To hail him in triumph descending the skies.

Some mourners, despite their sadness, felt the choice of hymn an odd one,
even bordering on inappropriate, "when repeated in services over the charred
bodies of men suddenly and most unwillingly reft of life by a railroad homi-
cide."[46] But others in the crowd surely found comfort in the ancient words of
sorrow, acceptance, and release. In any case, while it lasted, the hymn-singing
united the people collected inside the central depot in a shared sentiment of
loss, so that "the united voices of the thousands who joined in singing it filled
the vast structure with the solemn strains" of the religious melody.[47] Those
in the echoing depot became a single community of grief. It was a powerful
emotion.

Soon after the last notes of the hymn died away, and after a prayer by another minister, the Rev. Dr. Lord stood up to address the crowd.

John Chase Lord would have been primed and ready. His small, intelligent eyes surely read the crowd, and registered the emotional intensity of the
moment. As he stepped forward to the podium, his gray-tipped side whiskers
would have framed a slight frown.

Lord had been working out his speech for days; he would deliver it twice
more inside Central Presbyterian Church before the week was over.[48] This
was a message Lord would have known that he—with his distinguished
Buffalo-bred background, his conservative religious views and unmatch-
able grasp of the historical moment—was uniquely equipped to deliver. In a
career spent working as a man of God in a hardscrabble waterfront city long
on sin and short on repentance, Lord had seen wars, sicknesses, schisms, and

apostasies; he had baptized the children of ruffians and society leaders alike, and said prayers over the bodies of plague victims and politicians. True, some of Lord's political and social views were considered old-fashioned now, in some circles, and even he had begun to realize that. But his opinion of Angola might be just what the people assembled before him needed to hear at such a time in their lives, and that of the nation.

Taking the podium, Lord stood directly behind—and gazed out over—the row of nineteen plain pine coffins. Their lids gleamed palely against the blackness of the crepe. Lord would have waited for the crowd to cease its rustling and grow quiet.

"When," the reverend intoned, his deep voice resonating in the hall, "has such a congregation met—in such a place—for such a purpose?"[49]

Lord let his opening words sink in. Then he continued:

> Here are the mangled and unrecognized dead, the victims of a catastrophe, such as rarely occurs in all the moving accidents by flood, or field, or fire, which are constantly brought to our notice in every day's report. Here are mothers who cannot identify their children—who only know that among this mass of charred and broken bodies are the mortal remains of loved ones whom they shall see no more, until at the Resurrection morning.[50]

Lord paused. He had plenty of time, and by beginning with an appeal to the most sacred of all bonds—that of mothers with their children, now forever broken—he would have known that he had the crowd in the palm of his hand. In front of him, Captain Nicholson and his fellow police officers stood at attention, watching the scene. The hall would have been still, expectant.

Lord would have opened his prayer book, and perhaps gazed down upon it. The words he needed to speak were not printed before him on the page; he no doubt felt them in his heart. The agony of Angola, Lord told the crowd gathered at his feet, was a special agony. It was the agony of not knowing—perhaps for all time—what had happened to the people that had been lost in the train disaster. It was the agony of not knowing why these people—these forty or fifty men, women, and children, and no others—had happened to die, on that running express train, on that workaday Wednesday afternoon.

Lord plunged to the core of what he wanted to say. His attention was on the cosmic mechanics behind the wreck—the reasons that it had happened, and the peculiar plans of Providence it might reveal. "Here in this vast edifice," Lord intoned, "which daily sends its swarming trains over many states, thousands of upturned faces wait to hear what is the meaning of this Providence, and what lessons are taught by this fearful sacrifice of human life."[51]

"Brethren," the minister proclaimed, to the no doubt raptly silent crowd, "this is the hand of God."[52]

Lord watched the crowd take in his words, turn them over carefully. He no doubt empathized with what many of these men and women feared in their secret souls: that they had no real control over the dangers that seemed to swirl everywhere about them—on trains, as in the wars and epidemics they knew intimately—and that they themselves might thus be the next ones to be boxed up, nameless, maybe even forgotten.

"Had the catastrophe been the result of carelessness, or by any fault of human agents, which does not appear to have been the case"—Lord may at these words have glanced quickly at the officers of the Buffalo and Erie Railroad sitting on the stage beside him, as no doubt many others in the crowd did—"still it would have been the act of Him who ordereth all things after the counsel of His own will."

"Trouble does not come forth out of the ground—neither doth affliction spring forth out of the dust, for all are His servants to do His will," Lord declaimed. He knew Buffalo, and he knew human nature. He would thus have known exactly what the people inside the city's central depot needed to hear in this moment: a reinforcement of the thought that had deeply impressed some observers at the wreck site, John D. Rockefeller among them, about the Providential direction that still ruled the world, even in the face of a seemingly random, mechanically induced atrocity that had produced the nineteen coffins in their midst.

"Many of you, have often passed over the same gulf, and you may have thought, as I have done"—Lord surely nodded, here, to the thousands of upturned faces before him—"in passing this dark and drear ravine, what a dangerous point is this!"

"In the same position and in the same danger you and I have been spared, while this doomed company were waited for—of Death."[53]

Lord would have had the crowd in his sway. Through the open doors of the terminal, the huffing of horses and clang of bits and metal-shod hooves in the cold winter air told that Fargo's company wagons had arrived and were waiting outside for the cargo of coffins they would soon carry in procession, flanked by pallbearers, to the vault beneath St. Paul's Cathedral.

"We learn from this broken mass of human bodies," Lord continued, "how great a leveler is Death. The rich and the poor lie here together—the weak and the strong—the child of days and the man of gray hairs."

Inside, all would have been hushed, intent. One could have imagined the same sermon preached inside a seamen's bethel in New Bedford, or delivered from the deck of a Pilgrim-filled ship. Lord leaned forward and delivered his next words with emphasis.

"We have to recognize the hand of God in *this and all* calamities," Lord said. Then he went on: "God is indeed in all events, but here the case was such that we are compelled to mark his hand. Had the wheel broken and the cars been displaced a moment before the casualty actually occurred, the passengers would have been overturned on the other side of the narrow gulf; had it occurred a moment later they would have passed the ravine, and falling in either event upon an even surface, might have escaped without serious injury."

"Let me explain this. Had the coupling of the cars broken sixty seconds before it did, they would have been thrown from the track on the other side of the gulf; had it broken sixty seconds later, it would have been upset on this side of the narrow chasm which engulfed them only because the cars became disconnected at the moment they did, at the very point and at the only place of imminent danger."[54]

The reverend had driven home his point. In order for the two cars of the express train to topple from the track at Angola, at precisely the point at which they would fall into Big Sister Creek, killing dozens of people, then everything in the Angola landscape and in the working of the New York Express had to have come together precisely to produce this instant's worth of time: the single flash of a moment in which the wreck could, and did, occur. Lord was sure of this, and he would have carried the crowd along by his conviction. Angola could only have happened by not being an accident.

Lord would have fixed the crowd before him with his sternest gaze. All he needed to do now was to bring his sermon to an end, and leave his hearers with the conclusion that an Almighty God still controlled the world and all its events. The eye of God saw a single sparrow fall from a nest; surely He had seen fifty people fall to their deaths in Angola.

"Should it be said," the pastor intoned, "it is no more a Divine Providence for this? Yet it seems to me the hand of God may be made manifest, giving to the angel of death *the only moment in many hours, and the only ten rods in many miles,* when such a catastrophe could have occurred!"[55]

Lord closed his remarks on a note of warning, and of exhortation. "Brethren, seeing that no man knows the *time,* the *manner* or the *place* of his death," he urged, "let us come to Jesus, who is the resurrection and the life, that we may be able to say, 'Yea, though I walk through the valley and shadow of death, I will fear no evil, for Thou art with me, Thy rod and Thy staff they comfort me.'"[56]

It didn't matter that Angola's mourners couldn't see the reason for their pain now. They would in time, Rev. Lord surely believed.

But belief in God and a quest for answers were not mutually exclusive responses. And already, within the same city and in other places far away, some were beginning to ask questions about the possible culpability of man, or nature, in the events that had played out at Big Sister Creek.

CHAPTER 14

Judging

LATE DECEMBER 1867–EARLY JANUARY 1868

TWO DAYS AFTER the wreck of the New York Express, on Friday, December 20, Coroner Richards had named six Buffalo men—citizens of good standing, prominent in the community—to an inquest jury. The jurymen were charged with investigating the circumstances of the wreck, including taking testimony from eyewitnesses to the disaster and others involved with the New York Express and Buffalo and Erie Railroad. The purpose of the inquest was to determine, to the extent it could be known, the cause of the accident.

Such coroners' inquests happened routinely in cases of unexplained death, and they varied in thoroughness and skill. But, in the decades before the federal government established the Interstate Commerce Commission in 1901 to investigate railroad accidents, these juries were typically the only way that railroad wrecks were examined in any detail outside the pages of newspapers and popular periodicals.[1] Accident inquests were more familiar to the general public than courtroom trials of individual engineers and conductors on criminal charges following major accidents. Such trials were, in fact, so rare that it sometimes seemed a trainman was more likely to kill himself after being involved in a serious wreck than be found guilty in a court of law.[2] The recommendations made by coroners' juries could be of limited usefulness—especially because no one was forcing the railroads to listen to their findings. They were nonetheless considered important moments of focused public attention. For his part, Dr. Richards no doubt wanted to do his best to extract whatever information he could about the wreck before witnesses' memories became vague or distorted. His job was to bring details into the light. And so, the day after the public funeral inside the Exchange Street depot, the work of the jury examining the facts of the Angola Horror began.

On that Monday morning, December 23, Dr. Richards, along with the six jurors—George D. W. Clinton, C. E. Young, William D. Douglas, H. D. White, S. B. Seward, and C. R. Durkee—entered a courtroom in Buffalo's county courthouse.[3] The mood would have been solemn, the surroundings sobering. As the jurymen took their seats, all eyes would have turned toward a table in the middle of the room, on which lay a six-foot length of iron rail, bent and badly scarred.[4] This was the piece of track rail that had been laid down in Angola on the morning of the disaster, in place of the broken section that had been discovered by switchman James Mahar during his predawn inspection of the track. Now, the iron rail, twisted like an uprooted plant, rested on the table in full view of the jury and members of the press and public assembled in the gallery.

The audience waited, no doubt hushed and expectant. Dozens of reporters from the Buffalo daily newspapers and weekly news journals, notebooks open and pencils ready, filled several rows. Well-dressed company officials of the Buffalo and Erie Railroad, President Williams, Superintendent Brown, and William G. Fargo among them, sat next to roughly clad Angola farmers and shopkeepers in the rows of seats. Family members of the victims would have squeezed into some of the back benches, clutching handkerchiefs and vials of ammonia. Faces in the crowd would have been composed but anxious. Now, everyone surely thought, there would be some answers. Now they would learn whatever facts there were to be known. Christmas was two days off, but inside the courtroom, as snowflakes drifted past the windows and lamps smoked and flickered, nobody smiled.

Dr. Richards had a schedule to maintain, so he called the proceedings promptly to order. Ten witnesses had been summoned for the first day of the hearing. First to mount the stand was perhaps the most well-known among them: Peter Emslie, the chief engineer of the Buffalo and Erie Railroad.[5]

Emslie was the respected Buffalo architect and surveyor for whom two of the victims—Joseph Stocking Lewis and Frank Walker—had been working on the day of their deaths. The chief engineer had traveled to the wreck site at Angola in the days following the disaster to do firsthand measurements, walk the rails, and examine the bridge structure in person; now he was ready to testify to what he had seen.[6] Emslie came prepared with specifics. As he mounted the stand, the railroad official carried under his arm sheaves of penciled notes and posters showing technical drawings and diagrams. Spreading the papers around him, he would have referred to them often as he spoke.

Coroner Richards's first question had to do with general background about the Angola track and bridge. Emslie read off the span's measurements—ones he had made himself, and could swear to. The length of the bridge, he said, measured 160 feet; the distance from the station house to the frog was 606 feet, and the distance from the frog to where the engine had rolled to a stop was 2,504 feet.[7] The height of the Big Sister bridge deck, Emslie said, measured fifty feet above the ice of the creek below.[8] The engineer answered a question from Richards about the overall sturdiness of the Big Sister bridge by defending its soundness and reliability. "I consider the bridge a permanent structure," Emslie said from the witness stand, "and as safe as it can be made."[9] Emslie also testified that he had measured the track gauge at Angola and found it to be the same—a regular four feet, ten inches—along the track as at the frog juncture.

"I have carefully examined the condition of the track since the accident, and found it in proper order," the Buffalo and Erie's chief engineer stated. "I passed over this portion of the road on the morning of the accident twice, and as far as I could see, it was in perfect order."[10] Of course, as everyone in the courtroom knew, Peter Emslie worked for the railroad company; he was in charge of building and repairing these same elements of infrastructure. Audience members—and likely even some jurists—would have expected him to stand behind their worth. Still, Emslie did have some jottings in his over-stuffed notebook that surely cast a chill across the courtroom. Shortly before a midday break in the hearing, Richards pressed Emslie about the marks left behind on the track and bridge after the derailment.

As spectators listened raptly, the engineer checked his notes and replied that the first sign of trouble with the express, in his judgment, could be noticed some seventeen feet past the frog—where the wheels appeared to have mounted the track for the first time as they jumped the rails. By eighty-nine feet past the frog, Emslie went on, the wheels had apparently been dragging on the ties at a distance of one foot and five inches from the rails. By 204 feet beyond the frog, the marks from the thrown wheels were fully four feet from the rails.[11] "The marks of the wheels disappear," Emslie noted at this point, in conclusion, "after striking the east abutment. It must have broken the coupling."[12]

Nine witnesses were still to come, but Dr. Richards and others inside the courtroom in downtown Buffalo surely knew they had just heard some of the most haunting words of the day. Emslie's statements were technical; his terms mathematical. But in their clinical way, the engineer's comments caught at the cold terror of the derailment in a way that some of the more personal accounts struggled to convey.

The remainder of the first afternoon of the hearing was filled with the testimony of Angolans, as well as a few passengers who had been at the scene of the disaster because they had been on the train in one of the forward cars.

These male eyewitnesses—no women would take the stand during the Horror inquest, though they had been on the train and had tended the wounded so tirelessly—tried to find words to describe what had happened. Angolan Charles Kinsley described how he had grabbed an ax as he ran toward the creek after the derailment, and helped pry what he believed were twelve bodies out of the cars. At one point, Kinsley said, the Angolans on the scene had attempted to turn the Toledo car over, to ease the suffering of those crushed inside, "but could not."[13] During his turn on the stand, Josiah Southwick spoke of how he had rushed to the scene with Alanson Wilcox and how he and another man, John Martin, had tried to free the trapped victims. After a while, Southwick said simply, "I then went to my house—the wounded were being taken there."[14] Southwick did not magnify the role that he and his wife Huldah had played in nursing the injured; with characteristic modesty, he didn't mention it at all. John Martin then took the stand to relate events that corroborated Southwick's account, and to name a few people he believed he had seen among the wrecked cars, including J. Frank Walker, R. M. Russell of Tennessee, Mr. and Mrs. Amos and Mary Thomas of Utica, and David Cook of Rochester. "I could see no others," Martin concluded, gravely, "but I could hear them."[15]

A good portion of the first day's testimony was spent on conflicting views about how fast the New York Express had been traveling at the time of the crash. This point of information served from the beginning as a tantalizing difference among eyewitnesses to the disaster. Some, including the Angola grocer Leroy S. Oatman and George Hughes, a Canadian bookseller who had been inside a saloon in the village at the time of the crash, swore that the train was going no faster than normal—in the range of twenty-five to thirty miles per hour at most—when it derailed.[16] One passenger who had raced back from a forward car to help at the scene, Benjamin Brownell of Chautauqua County, agreed, and said the train's speed didn't seem "over fast" to him before the crash.[17] But others averred the express had been traveling much faster than normal as it entered the village the previous Wednesday afternoon at 3:11. Among these witnesses, Charles Kinsley said he knew well the speed of various trains that ran through the village and testified with confidence that the New York Express had been going "unusually fast" that afternoon—perhaps as fast as forty miles per hour.[18]

As interesting as the question of speed was, as a line of inquiry for Coroner Richards's jury, it ultimately—and unsurprisingly, where railroad investigations were concerned—turned into a dead end. Nothing could be proven about the speed of the express at this late stage. Even if the train had been traveling much faster than the twenty miles per hour recommended by the Buffalo and Erie Railroad's rulebook for passage over bridge crossings, the fact remained that speed alone could not have caused the derailment. Another factor had to have been involved.

By Tuesday morning, the second day of testimony, those packed into the cramped, overheated courtroom in Buffalo were ready for the proceedings to take a different tack. It was Christmas Eve. Likely because of the holiday the following day, just four witnesses had been scheduled to appear. At 10 a.m., in the pale light of midmorning, Coroner Richards called the inquest to order, beginning with Simon E. Tifft, a young Angola merchant.

Tifft began his statement by describing how he had hunted for a pail to carry down into the creek gully after he realized the train had derailed.[19] Tifft said that, running alongside the track in the wake of the express, he had seen deep gouges cut in the wood of the ties, stretching from the frog "nearly all the way to the bridge."[20] Tifft then revealed something that surely electrified the crowd in the gallery. On the day after the wreck, he testified, he had inspected the track with care and found what he believed amounted to "one-third of a car wheel" lying broken on the bridge, at the structure's eastern end—a surprising find, given that the wheel had struck the frog well on the western side of the structure.[21] The portions of wheel, he said, lay there in jagged pieces. Tifft had remembered the shattered bits, which he thought would add up to a significant part of a wheel, ever since in vivid detail.

Tifft's words were provocative, and served as a turning point in the Angola inquest. As he uttered them, the atmosphere inside the courtroom would have sharpened like a knife. The attention of the assembly—reporters, jurymen, spectators—had just been drawn to something new: the question of mechanics.

The shift might have been difficult for those sitting inside the Buffalo courtroom to detect, but from this point forward in the inquest, issues of technology and mechanical performance would replace those of speed and timing as the primary foci of the jury inquiry. This was a significant change. Instead of asking about the rate of the train on its approach, witnesses would be asked to tell about what they had seen in the way of irregularity or malfunction in the Angola station's rails, ties, and bridge, as well as in the wheels and trucks of the express's engine and cars. As Simon Tifft excused himself and stepped down from the stand, the atmosphere inside the courtroom would, in a subtle way, have offered a glimpse into a new era that would begin not far in the future, if it hadn't already: a time in which the Victorian preoccupation with how and why things worked would replace the luck-tinged and Calvinistic view that had dominated the public mind for decades. Simon Tifft's words may not have changed the world—they didn't really even change the results of the inquest—but they did offer the barest glimmer of something unexpected: a fully modern age.

Others following Tifft to the stand concurred with his testimony. Dennis Graney, a Buffalo and Erie track maintenance worker at Angola, did not see the broken wheel parts but testified that the broken rail at the frog juncture had been replaced that morning with good-quality materials, and properly gauged, as far as he knew. Graney said that when he inspected the frog rail after the accident, it was twisted and bent upward for a distance of two or three ties. That was the length of iron rail now lying in the courtroom on the table, for all to see. It would have glittered in the lamplight of the courtroom like a living thing.

By the day after Christmas, the third day of testimony, Coroner Richards determined to steer the inquiry further in the direction of mechanical failure. A few of the biggest names in the inquest had yet to testify, and the coroner wanted them to answer questions primarily about the cars' suitability and track conditions. On the morning of December 26, four railroad company men mounted the stand to answer questions about the wheels of the cars, in the wake of Tifft's claims about the broken portions of wheel. J. H. Roach, C. F. Valtz, Lyman Burchard, and James Dougherty worked as wheel inspectors for the Buffalo and Erie Railroad, and had examined the New York Express on December 18 at Erie and Dunkirk. All four swore that in their experience, walking up and down the cars of the express as the train stood in both cities that afternoon, the wheels of the train had appeared, in the words of Valtz, "in perfect order…all sound."[22]

Now, as Richards and the jurymen would have realized, at least three problems were on the table as potential factors in the wreck: the speed of the express; the broken rail section that had been replaced the morning of the wreck; and the broken wheel. On the afternoon of December 26 and the following day, two more issues would be raised that were potentially far more damning. First, John Desmond, assistant superintendent of the Buffalo and Erie road, told the jury that he believed passenger coaches from three separate railroads—the Buffalo and Erie, the Cleveland and Toledo, and one other, likely from the Cleveland & Erie—formed part of the consist of the wrecked train. Under questioning from Richards, Desmond insisted that these public coaches were commonly swapped about on trains between the various railroads, and that the differences in the cars—and in their wheel gauges— were little cause for concern.[23] If a car with a gauge different from four feet, ten inches was running on the Buffalo and Erie's route, Desmond told the assembly, then it was a "compromise car" that was designed to travel in such a manner safely.[24] A compromise car, Desmond explained to the assembly, was a car with wheels built to travel on track with one type of gauge, but made in such a way that it could change its wheel gauge slightly—usually by decreasing roughly an inch or so—to accommodate roads of differing widths. This was a somewhat common situation in a railroading landscape in which many small local lines operated on portions of much longer routes, Desmond told the jury members and audience. "We have no knowledge of the composition of trains west of Erie," Desmond said, in defense of his company's practice. "I am not positive that the Cleveland and Erie coach is a compromise one; the gauge of the Cleveland and Toledo is three-fourths of an inch narrower than the Buffalo and Erie and the Cleveland and Erie....I was under the impression that the Cleveland and Toledo coach had compromise wheels, and did not hear anything to the contrary."[25]

Even more arrestingly, Desmond told the jury that while freight cars with differing wheel gauges had been operating on the Buffalo and Erie Railroad's route for a number of years, to his knowledge the practice of allowing passenger and baggage cars with compromise wheels on the road was actually a more recent occurrence, dating only to the previous spring.[26] Accidents due to compromise wheels had happened on the freight runs, Desmond admitted. "We have had freight trains run off the track," the assistant superintendent said, "on account of the narrow tread of some of the wheels."[27] And yet the railroad company had gone forward with allowing coaches with compromise wheels to be used to carry men, women, and children.

That was clearly the most troubling fact members of the jury had heard so far; but what came next made it more so. After a day's pause in the taking of testimony so that jury members could visit the car shop of the Buffalo and Erie Railroad in Buffalo to examine what was left of the wrecked express—except for the parts that had been burned in the bottom of Big Sister gorge, both by the crash and in villagers' bonfires—the inquest panel reconvened on December 30 for testimony from more railroad authorities. Fitch D. Adams, the master of car repairs for the Buffalo and Erie Railroad and a man with twenty-two years' experience in building railway coaches, testified about his firsthand examination of the wreck site at Angola. Adams told the jury that what he had found was telling: in looking over the trucks of the ruined cars—the carriage-like underbody portions that swiveled, to which the wheels were attached—Adams said he realized that one of the axles, the forward one on the rear truck of the last car, was bent.[28] According to Adams, the bend in the axle was slight. He didn't notice it right away; when he did, he had to verify his hunch with a ruler and wheel gauge. But, Adams said, the bend in the axle seemed like it would have been enough to throw the rear wheels of the end car of the train off-kilter—so that, as Adams explained, the wheels would have wobbled on the track as they rolled along, shuttling from one side to the other and back again. That would have made the wheels vulnerable to anything irregular on or near the track, Adams told the jury. They would have been more liable to jump the track.

"I passed over the axle perhaps 12 times before discovering the bend," Adams testified to the jury. "Our inspectors would not be apt to see it." Still, he said, the bend was frustrating because "the cars are supposed to be in good order when they leave the shop."[29]

After Adams was done, another of the company's master mechanics took the stand to back up Adams's take on the accident. "I discovered no cause for the accident except that the axle was sprung," said William Hart, who had worked on cars for the railroad since 1859.[30]

Now all the possibilities were on the table, and the array was dizzying. Based on the witnesses called by Coroner Richards, the Angola inquest jury had learned of at least a half-dozen factors that could have possibly played into the crash at Big Sister Creek to one degree or another: a bent rear axle; compromise cars with varying wheel gauges; a broken wheel; the broken rail at the frog near the station; the calibration of the frog after the rail was replaced; and the speed of the train. Those factors didn't even include the fact that J. M. Newton's station clock was not working correctly that day, or that Sherman and Carscadin had apparently disregarded standard railroad regulations calling for a slow and cautious twenty miles per hour speed at all bridges.

It was a lot to take into account. In practical terms, what the Angola inquest jury had been asked to consider was a startling accident that had likely been caused by numerous factors in varying degrees, all of which played fatefully into a few seconds' time on the afternoon of December 18, crippling the rear car of an express train just before it crossed a bridge and leaving it vulnerable to derailment. Did the bent axle on the rear truck affect the movement of the rear car? If it had been that way as the moving train crossed through Angola, it seems likely it would have. Was the frog improperly calibrated after the rail was replaced, and did the new rail throw the wheel out of alignment? Both scenarios were possible, and may well have happened. Did the presence of compromise wheels on the last car of the train—a near certainty, given that it was a Cleveland and Toledo coach—cause the wheel to shuttle too far back and forth as it passed over the frog section? It's almost impossible to believe that such a thing did not happen—and that the shuttling action was not further worsened by what may have been a defect in the axle. Would the express have been safer if it had been traveling more slowly? Probably—but it's impossible to tell, given all these other factors, whether Carscadin would have been able to stop the train in time to prevent the cars' fall into the gorge, no matter what its speed.

It was a complicated mess, in short. And, as with seemingly everything related to the Angola disaster, the question of cause was a question of timing. Early railway accidents were more typically the result of one terrible malfunction, like an exploding hotbox or an overheated engine. By the time of Angola, things were getting murkier and more complex. If the Angola Horror had played out a decade or two before, chances are the train would not have been moving as fast as it may have been over a bridge like the Big Sister span; chances also are that the wheels may not have been compromise ones, which were part of the smaller railroads' response to increased competition in the 1860s. A few decades later, better braking systems on passenger trains would have made stopping the express an entirely different affair. Timing at Angola proved—once again—to be everything.

And yet the jury reached a verdict.

After deliberation following the close of a final day of testimony, the six inquest jurymen returned their judgment at 8 p.m. on the last day of 1867, New Year's Eve, inside a closely packed downtown courtroom.[31] The company of the Buffalo and Erie Railroad was found not guilty, in any form or fashion, for the wreck that had killed the fifty or so people at Big Sister Creek in Angola. Jury members also released their opinion as to the cause of the wreck. As reported widely in newspapers shortly thereafter, the jury found that "from some cause which could not be discovered, a car-axle was so bent as to throw the car off the track and down the fateful precipice....The bending of the axle, occurring, perhaps, weeks before the accident, had escaped detection by all the customary expedients of inspection."[32] In other words, the axle was likely the chief culprit, but the Buffalo and Erie Railroad wasn't, because the bend in the axle had been too small a flaw to be identified without an in-depth investigation, and—before the accident—there hadn't been any reason to do such a thing.

The Angola inquest jury's powers had been limited from the start. Working without federal oversight or backup, the most the jury panel probably would have been able to do with a guilty verdict would have been censure the Buffalo and Erie Railroad for allowing the wreck to occur. That didn't happen. Working largely with evidence from expert witnesses who were also the Buffalo and Erie's employees, the jury exonerated the company in total.

But if the verdict was short and simple, the public's reaction to it was not. Growing smarter about rail travel by the month, many citizens knew what the unstated implication of the Angola verdict was—and newspapers were quick to echo and expand upon their concerns. "The most unsatisfactory part of all of this," complained the *Buffalo Patriot and Journal,* shortly after the verdict was handed down, "is the horrid revelation that passengers upon any train are constantly liable to just such a fate as befell those slain at Angola....The same thing might happen at any moment to any train upon any other road in the United States."[33] The newspaper concluded that the situation was "a most uncomfortable thought for those who are obliged to travel."[34]

CHAPTER 15

Debates

———◦———

THE WINTER of 1867–68 was a bad one for railroad accidents. It became known especially for the number of incidents in which people, paying passengers on the railroads, were burned by fires aboard the coach cars in which they rode. Angola was one of the first of the season's train fires, and by far the worst. At about the same time, a pair of young sisters in Ohio lost their lives in a blaze on a railroad car, and that event also garnered national attention.[1] Then, in the months after Coroner Richards's jury concluded its investigation and released a verdict, six more incidents played out around the country in which railroad passenger coaches caught fire during derailments, collisions, or equipment malfunctions, causing injury or death to travelers.[2]

The press took note of the wave of unpleasant reports. "The daily frightful massacres of travelers, and the incessant accidents, make it a very serious thing for any one to leave home even upon the shortest journeys," proclaimed an editorial in *Harper's Weekly*.[3] The events happened all over the country, on the Boston and Providence Railroad in New England, the Erie Railway in Pennsylvania, the Chicago & North Western Railway in the western part of the country, and elsewhere.[4] The occurrences added up to more fiery wrecks than had happened in a single winter season in the country since the start of the war, perhaps longer, and they created a rising tide of concern. "There is…a great and natural excitement throughout the country," the journal *Railway Times* noted in May 1868, surveying the winter season's tallies of crashes and casualties. "What is the cause? Who is to blame? Can it be avoided in future? These are the questions everywhere asked."[5]

Set into that string of events, the Angola wreck—by far the most deadly incident in that noteworthy "smash-up season" on the rails—commanded the attention of both public and press, overshadowing the other incidents and becoming a watchword in the nation for danger lurking on the rails. "The interest felt in the terrible casualty throughout the country is wonderful," marveled one Buffalo newspaper, of the attention focused on the Angola Horror.[6] In many newspapers, at the end of that year, Angola was listed among the worst events of the whole of 1867, and the worst railway calamity within memory. "Our community, like all others, has not yet recovered from the fearful shock of the Angola disaster, the most appalling railroad accident on record," editorialized a newspaper in Titusville, Pennsylvania, in its edition on New Year's Day in 1868.[7]

Angola's grisliness seemed to create an indelible impression. "Laughing misses visiting their friends for Christmas, boys returning from school for the holidays, men hastening from the far West to preside at the festive board just one week from that awful day, men and women complying with the good old fashion of uniting scattered families at the paternal hearth on the day of days, Christmas, were all mangled, maimed, destroyed, burnt, and ground to powder," wrote the editors of *Frank Leslie's Illustrated Newspaper*, of the wreck of the New York Express. "All that is left of the car and its freight, so precious to many homes all over the land, is a mass of blackened and charred remains, in which a separate body can hardly be distinguished."[8] "Angola" was a rhythmic, haunting name—entirely memorable, almost mesmerizing, in the way that "Camp Hill" had been and "Ashtabula" would be. From December 1867 onward, many Americans associated the name Angola with certain specific ideas of railroad disaster: injury stemming from cruel tricks of timing, bad luck, and geography; inescapable death for victims in the most terrible of ways, including being crushed to jelly, trapped in fallen cars, and burned alive; the obliteration of victims' bodies, to the point of namelessness. These associations found printed form in the pages of newspapers and magazines in the winter of 1867–68, and they resonated in the public consciousness, then and afterward, in powerful ways. "It is impossible to convey an idea of the scene in words," wrote *Harper's Weekly*, in a January edition of the periodical that contained three drawings of the wreck, done by two separate artists, one of whom had traveled to the scene.[9]

Those drawings in the pages of *Harper's*, which provided many Americans with their first glimpse of the scenes that had played out in Big Sister ravine—and which remained invaluable long after the wreck, given that no photographs, if any were taken at the scene, survived—served as a window onto the way that the crash was perceived, both at the wreck site and later by the viewing public.

All three *Harper's* scenes depicted the action of the wreck from a middle distance, forsaking the kind of closed-in angles or panoramic vistas of most railroad art of the era—extremes, in other words, along the lines of the close-up of the locomotive in "The Horrors of Travel," or the vast landscape panoramas dotted with steam engines painted by Victorian artists, including George Inness. The effect of this middle-range distance of the Angola images was to formalize the wreck: to render it a discrete historical event, encapsulated, capable of being studied and dissected. It also made observers feel as if they were gazing on the disturbing scene from a vantage point that a regular person might well have had, as an eyewitness in the village at the time of the disaster. This is not a bird's-eye view of tragedy, but a human perspective. The *Harper's* sketches fostered connection with, and empathy for, the Angola crash and its victims. They also had a forensic quality.

Two of the drawings, by artist J. P. Hoffman and engineer Erasmus W. Smith, were similar, showing the aftermath of the fallen cars on either side of the bridge, with clusters of victims' bodies and scrambling rescuers in the foreground and, in the upper distance, rows of stilled train cars outlined against the winter sky. The third picture, by Hoffman, was more of a puzzle. It was also more compelling—even though this third scene did not contain any smudges of burned corpses in the snow, no humans with raised arms pleading for help, as do poignant vignettes in the other two panels. A study of the Big Sister gorge at the moment of the accident, the third scene moved the viewer because it seemed to be in motion itself. To the left of the scene, tones of gray and white suggested farm fields buried beneath piles of snow; to the right, the black shape of the wood-covered truss bridge cut through the scene at a diagonal, disappearing into the distance in the middle of the upper border of the picture—just where an observer's eyes would travel in a movement from bottom to top, right to left. What riveted the attention here was the rear car of the express, which was depicted as having just passed onto the bridge, toward the horizon. The car was portrayed in the act of toppling, falling just past the horizontal toward the north side of the ravine—toward a fence which scars the snow, a single lonely house—and with a great deal of force, as evidenced by the splintering wood in the depiction of the fall, the bending metal. Observers saw the car's clerestory roof as it spun in its descent, and knew from news accounts of the wreck what was happening inside: the maiming of men and woman like the Kents, the Fullers, the Thomases, and the Nichols; the terror of people like Charles Lobdell, John W. Chapman, Elam Porter, Joseph Stocking Lewis, and Isadore Mayer.

These *Harper's* illustrations—and this one scene in particular, which was given prominence over the other two images on the magazine's page—troubled many who studied them. The image of falling captured their attention because it caught the wreck as it was happening; it held the train's coach in suspended animation, forever toppling to its doom, never quite fallen. The effect on viewers of the magazine was potent. This, for them, was "Angola"—the disaster playing out before their eyes.

THE VILLAGE'S NAME was becoming something of a catchall term for railway disaster in general. From the earliest days after the wreck, phrases such as "another Angola" or "a second Angola" were appended to railroad mishaps great and small, ranging from minor derailments and uncouplings to more serious wrecks with high casualty counts, including, in time, the Ashtabula bridge disaster of 1876.[10] "It was a very narrow escape from a second Angola disaster," the *Buffalo Express* newspaper reported, of a railway mishap shortly after the New Year in 1868—except that it wasn't, because the train in question had been pushed off its track by a gale, and no one killed.[11]

The comparisons, clearly, weren't always apt. In 1869, in a crash involving an express train and a freight on the Erie Railroad at a place called Masthope, near Port Jervis in New York, the scene was likened to Angola even though far fewer people were killed and the particulars of the accident—which involved railroad employees who were sleeping aboard their trains at the time of the crash—much different.[12] "We have not heard of anything so lamentable as this in the way of slaughter by the rail since the moment when the country was alarmed by the news of the Angola disaster," one Ohio newspaper reported of the crash.[13] The analogy would persist for decades. Even when it wasn't accurate, the name was used again and again, to summon up railroad horror at its most dire.

But Angola wasn't just a catchphrase; it became a rallying cry. As in France, where it took the murder of a prominent judge, M. Poinsot, inside a railway carriage in December 1860 to focus attention on the need to redesign European railroad compartments for improved safety, in the United States following the Angola disaster the name of the village became a watchword for an increasing public appetite—indeed, a demand—for better and safer railroad transportation.[14] In this period of railway development, sometimes even one or two events—usually crashes or other unfortunate incidents—were enough to focus public opinion on a problem with the railroads, and begin the push for change.[15] At the same time, as the country moved past the Civil War and into a post-war period of change, the public's willingness to see events such as Angola as the simple if mysterious workings of unseen forces was shifting, if not disappearing altogether. Average people were beginning to believe that they should know *why* and *how* things were happening around them—and to them. They were demanding scientific and mechanical explanations for accidents and problems, and they wanted more than explanations. They wanted accountability.

This climate was captured in a letter written to the editors of the *Buffalo Daily Courier* in late December 1867 by a writer signing himself "A Merchant." The writer, presumably a Buffalo citizen, took exception to a statement the newspaper's editors had made after the disaster, calling the derailment an unexplainable act of Providence that might never be solved or understood. "The 'ways of Providence' we are taught to accept as being 'mysterious,'" the letter-writer fumed, in reply to the newspaper, "but they are not mysterious in 'railroading' and 'steam-boating' we suppose, when looked at through the light of science and the rules of mechanic arts....If you, Mr. Editor, and the public treat this awful calamity as one of a class of evils which cannot be remedied and which no human forethought or prudence can prevent, passing it by as a 'nine day's wonder,' we have only to wait supinely with folded hands for others to transpire from like causes upon other roads."[16] The time for mute acceptance of calamities such as Angola had ended, the Buffalo letter-writer insisted—and he was far from a solitary voice. It was time to demand facts and reasons, and then, using these pieces of information, to press for change. Otherwise, the situation was bound to repeat itself, over and over again.

As members of the public vented frustration, journalists picked up on the shift in popular sentiment. Newspapers and magazines, as well as trade periodicals and scientific journals, used the window of opportunity created by a high-profile wreck such as Angola to press forward the causes of safety improvements and innovations. Better oversight of the railroads, including regulation by the federal government when necessary, was called for. Commitments by railroad companies to change their policies and procedures to ensure safer and more reliable travel were demanded. Whereas in 1865 *Harper's* magazine had published the illustration "The Horrors of Travel," showing a scythe-wielding Death aboard a locomotive scattering innocent men and women in his path, many publications ranging from general readership newspapers and magazines to scientific and technical journals in 1867 and 1868 used the Angola tragedy as an opportunity not only to lay out the details of a terrible rail misfortune, but also as a chance to discuss some areas of railway travel badly in need of reform.

The mood among these publications was captured in a news story published in *Frank Leslie's Illustrated Newspaper* in mid-January 1868. This article, about an accident on the Cleveland and Toledo Railroad, drew comparisons to the Angola wreck, and used the word "science" to describe the practice of railroading in the United States—calling for its growth and development. "The frequency of railroad disaster is alarmingly increasing, and calls loudly for a revision of the science of railroading," the newspaper stated. "He who has to risk his life on the cars from necessity has also the right to demand that the journey should be comparatively safe."[17] Such calls for reform, and for better innovation and regulation, clustered thickly in the columns of publications. Within weeks of the crash at Big Sister Creek, in many publications around the country and in Canada, compromise cars were being decried as the culprit for the Angola wreck, and too dangerous for continued use. "It might and should have been prevented," the *Hamilton Times* in Ontario wrote of the crash, printing in its pages an editorial, concerning the gauges at Angola, that had appeared in the *Boston Advertiser* and was circulated throughout the Northeast, including in the *New York Times,* as well as elsewhere in the country. "The compromise…is responsible for the disaster."[18]

In Philadelphia, the *Inquirer* published a technical description of the compromise issue—which many readers were learning about for the first time—and concluded on a note of pessimism. "Of course, under these circumstances," the *Inquirer* stated, "the wonder is that accidents do not occur more frequently."[19] In the pages of *Frank Leslie's Illustrated Newspaper,* nothing less than a call for the members of Congress to enact a uniform gauge for all railroads in the nation was issued. "The pernicious system of running the same car-trucks on rails of different gauge, cannot be too severely reprehended," the magazine argued, "and Congress should take the matter in hand and fix a uniform gauge, to which all railroads carrying the United States mail should be obliged to conform."[20] The magazine noted that pressure was being applied to railroad companies, but that such pressure needed to go further, and extend to the creation of laws to protect the public. "Since the Angola disaster the daily newspapers have teemed with advice to railroad companies; but the matter should not be allowed to rest there," the magazine stated. "Legislation on the subject first, and then to have the law put in operation, is what we require."[21]

SOME OF THE PLEAS for change in the wake of Angola addressed simple problems, even obvious ones, about railroad travel. A few of the criticisms singled out elements of train transportation that were apparent as problems even to novice passengers, or outmoded practices that railways continued to use despite common sense and innovation to the contrary.

On December 23, 1867, one of the first newspapers to editorialize in a thoughtful way about the meaning of the Angola disaster, the *Buffalo Express,* printed an article calling for a basic, easy-to-understand change in standard railway procedure. The *Express* asked railroad companies to begin keeping passenger manifests for all their trains, or at least accurate records of ticket sales.[22] The purpose of this change, the *Express* stated, would be to ensure that never again in the event of a crash would slain passengers be rendered unidentifiable to their families and friends. Rather, families, as well as the general public, would know immediately and with accuracy who had been on board a particular train and who had not. Of course, in suggesting this change, the Buffalo newspaper was likely aiming at an ideal that was impossible to achieve, since the geographic mobility in rail travel, as in other forms of travel such as steamboats, had created problems in fixing the identities of strangers. (You could never be entirely sure that the person next to you on a railcar or steamboat had not lied about who he was.) Yet, in advocating for this change, the Buffalo newspaper channeled the prevailing cultural sense of the value of a "good death," which meant a death that did not go unmarked. "We hold that if it cannot be effected in any other way, a statute should be passed," argued the Buffalo newspaper, "compelling Railroad Companies to keep in each ticket office a register, in which the name of each person purchasing a ticket shall be recorded, setting forth upon what train and in what direction the ticket is to be used—and making it the duty of each conductor collecting fare on the train to take the name of each passenger as paying."[23] The *Buffalo Express* became the first publication to make the case for such legislation in the wake of Angola.

This system, the newspaper concluded, could only be of "great utility," both in the event of accidents and on safe trips by rail, if adopted everywhere.[24] The suggestion was widely acknowledged to be a good one. However, it became buried beneath mountains of coverage devoted to the Angola wreck in the first days after the disaster, and as a result stirred up little in the way of discussion. If the operators of railroad companies wrote any letters to the Buffalo newspaper in defense of their methods, no records of them exist. No such law as the *Express* proposed was introduced, in any event, and the railroads did not appear to make any changes to their practices following the suggestion.

While the *Buffalo Express* was pointing out this problem, other newspapers and magazines around the country focused their attention on another old-fashioned practice, that of railroads' locking the doors of passenger coaches while trains were in motion. In the beginning, as company officials usually explained it, many railroads had done this to prevent overexcited passengers from jumping on or off moving trains. This sort of policy did not appear to have been employed by the Buffalo and Erie Railroad on the New York

Express on the day of the disaster, though some people after the wreck believed that the railroad had indeed locked the doors of the coaches.[25] Still, in the wake of the train's fall, some saw the practice as further endangering their safety during railway trips.

The idea of cars being locked to those inside them was a particularly frightful matter to contemplate during a season such as the winter of 1867–68, in which a spate of accidents saw passengers burned alive or burned after being killed in a crash. "This is a custom which cannot be too severely censured, being unjust to the passengers even in cases where no misfortune affects the trip, and dangerous at all times," reported the *Philadelphia Inquirer,* calling for legislative action on the matter. "There ought to be a law prohibiting the custom of locking the doors of railroad cars when used for traveling, and under the most severe penalties."[26] No such law was immediately passed, but some railroads did change their policies about locking car doors as a result of the public pressure after Angola. One of these roads, the Milwaukee and La Crosse Railroad, used the Angola incident as an impetus to order all conductors on its trains to make sure that no coaches were locked during trips "under any circumstances."[27]

Flaws in hand-braking systems were also discussed, and petitions for improvement in the stopping of railroad cars made to railroad company officers and lawmakers. But railway braking was largely on the back burner as a safety issue during this time. While testifying as part of the Angola inquest, Buffalo and Erie chief engineer Peter Emslie had noted that it took the New York Express 2,504 feet to stop after it derailed at the frog; he noted this without disapproval, as a routine matter.[28] Reaction to this fact from the public, as well as from certain railroaders within the industry, sounded a note of dismay. "Just think of a train running 2,504 feet (and the first 1,100 feet with one car off the track,) before it could be stopped," wrote one letter-writer, who claimed to be a railroad man "of twenty years standing," to the *New York Times.*[29] When asked during the inquest about the brakes the express had been equipped with on the day of the wreck, John Desmond, assistant superintendent of the Buffalo and Erie, replied summarily, "It is the ordinary chain brake."[30] Desmond said the train should have been able to stop within an eighth of a mile if it had been running at twenty-five miles per hour. However, he conceded, "the stoppage…would depend much on the dryness or moisture on the track."[31] In snowy weather or icy conditions, company officials acknowledged, all bets were off.

Besides such general acceptance among railroad companies about the performance of hand brakes, the public found the situation difficult to grasp. Ticket-buying passengers, and even the railroad men who crewed the trains, had a feeling they should complain about the brakes used to stop the trains on which they rode—but they weren't sure exactly how much, or what to ask for in lieu of the hand-crank mechanisms. "Would it not be the plainest dictate of common sense to recognize the dangers that are inseparable from all trains in motion, and then be provided with the best possible antidote, which is the quickest means of stopping the trains when accidents do occur," argued the author of the letter to the *New York Times* in late December 1867, who called himself a long-time railroader. "How much longer must trains be run, and how many more valuable lives is it necessary to sacrifice, before the recognition of this truth becomes universal?"[32] Still, the letter writer had no substantive suggestions on what might be done to make trains stop when needed, quickly and safely. Such a situation might seem far-fetched, until consideration was given to the frames of reference with which these men and women had been raised: farm wagons, stagecoaches, steamboats, canal boats, and river barges. None of these were modes of travel that offered much in the way of useful comparison to trains, especially in light of the challenges—including high and variable speeds, unpredictable track conditions, bad weather, and the shaky integrity of train consists—presented by the railroads. If average travelers of the period focused more on problems on the rails like locked car doors, broken tracks, and inaccurate wheel gauges—things they could see, touch, and measure—they could hardly be blamed. Automatic braking was an abstract concept. Even in displeasure, the public's imagination had its limits.

There were a few exceptions, however. In Schenectady, New York, a twenty-one-year-old mechanic, George Westinghouse Jr., had begun to turn his analytical mind to the problems he observed around him—starting with the railroads.

WHEN IT CAME to one facet of railway travel, the public's ability to visualize—and personalize—disaster ran unchecked. Following Angola and the season's other fiery crashes, the fear of fires on board the cars, and the potential immolation of passengers, became the single most significant target of concern for many members of the public. It didn't matter that for the average passenger the danger of being burned by a coach fire was likely less than that of being pincered between cars held together by link-and-pin couplers or flung from an iron seat by the jolting of a car jumping the track. The public mood that winter fixated on fire, and its ability to spread through a crowded wooden coach, as the source of gravest danger while traveling by rail.

Much of this outrage translated into a focus on warmth and illumination. In the past, systems of heating passenger cars with hot air or "storage" heat,

in which objects like bricks or cannonballs were heated and then stored in
the cars while the trains were in motion, had been tried by some railroad
companies.[33] And, by the mid-1860s, the New York and New Haven Railroad
had outfitted an experimental coach with equipment that provided warmth
to people's feet through hot water circulated in metal pipes under the floorboards.[34] But for the most part, by the winter of 1867–68, few railroads were
trying to heat their passenger cars with any new, or even greatly modified,
warming technologies. The Chicago, Burlington & Quincy Railroad was one
of the few. By 1867, the railroad was using a "stove within a stove" system invented by a Canadian named Henry Jones Ruttan. The device enclosed a wood
or coal stove inside a second stove, which was then positioned on a "water box"
containing five gallons of water, designed to flood the fire in case of an upset
and extinguish any flames.[35]

Most travelers, in any case, still rode on coaches equipped with the familiar
old-fashioned potbellied coal stoves, one or two per car, depending on the railroad and size of the coach, and some even rode aboard cars with the older and
more outmoded wood-fueled stoves. These simple stoves had been an advance
for the railroads, and a source of relief to passengers, when they had first been
installed on railcars in the United States during the 1830s; they had meant
people could travel in cold weather without suffering. Now, three decades later,
they were a source of fear. Reports of the miserable fates of the fifty people
trapped in the New York Express at the bottom of Big Sister ravine had been
vivid, and had circulated to most parts of the country; those images and stories
lingered in people's memories.

For journalists, fire on the cars served as a focus for editorial ire. The public
in turn responded with approval to these calls for change in the way train cars
were heated and lit. "The light is dim but not religious," one passenger had
observed, of the heat and light on board the cars, "with the uncertain glimmer
of candles or the smoky flare of kerosene, which ought to be banished from
every civilized and Christian road."[36] Members of the public felt, moreover,
betrayed by railroad companies that chose to warm and light railcars in the
cheapest possible ways—ways that had the potential to roast hapless passengers alive. Some new hot-water systems for heating cars had been ruled out
by railroad executives because they cost $500 to install, compared with $2 to
$10 for a coal stove.[37] "Where a car in winter time, in which there is a stove,
is overturned, the wood work is sure to catch fire, and if the inmates are without the means of getting the doors open, they must inevitably suffer a horrid death," wrote the *Philadelphia Inquirer.*[38] It seemed to many an imminent
threat. When reports circulated that some roads were taking steps in the wake
of Angola to make their stoves safer—the Boston and Providence Railroad,

for one, was reported to be working to "properly secure" the stoves in its cars to the floorboards—many people felt their worst fears were being confirmed.[39] The railroads must know how dangerous the stoves were, people felt, especially if they were changing the way they installed and fueled the devices after the deaths at Angola.

This sense of being taken advantage of by the railroads manifested itself in written journalism for years, then decades, afterward. Iconography, too, took railroads to task for their treatment of the ticket-buying public. One of the more heartrending of the illustrations that editorialized on the subject of car stoves appeared in the pages of *Harper's* magazine in February 1887. The image, called "The Modern Altar of Sacrifice—the Devouring Car Stove," depicted the interior of a wrecked railroad coach that is being destroyed by fire, in the midst of which stands a coal-burning stove. In the image, the body of a victim—a young female presented as a virginal maiden in a Grecian-style gown and with flowing hair—has been tied to the stove by stout ropes and chain.[40] The message couldn't have been clearer. Railroads and their unsafely heated trains, these stories and illustrations made apparent, were threatening the lives of the most vulnerable of Americans.

Some railroad men and those involved in the industry set themselves the goals of reducing or eliminating the threat. "There ought...to be absolutely no danger" from heating stoves on trains, *Railway Age* exhorted its readers, many of them railroad professionals, in 1881, "and no railway manager should rest satisfied until his cars are supplied with stoves or heaters from which it is absolutely impossible for fire to communicate to the vehicle in case of derailment or overturning."[41]

On Christmas Eve, 1867, the *Baltimore Sun* ran on its front page a two-column editorial on the subject of heating stoves and railway safety. The piece began by describing the number of victims that had been left unidentified by the Angola wreck, and calling for a "formal and searching investigation" of the accident.[42] What was most horrible about Angola, the newspaper continued, was the burning alive of innocent men, women, and children. In eloquent prose, the *Sun* made its case for the lessons taught by the wreck:

> It is often said, with reference to the achievements of steam, that "Peace hath its victories as well as war," but they are not always bloodless victories, and if the battlefields of war are scenes of slaughter on a larger scale, few of them are as horrible, or involve as many helpless victims, as the crushing and burnings inflicted on men, women and children in the last railroad massacre. Nothing can be imagined more awful than these burnings. Surely it cannot be difficult to provide

In the years after the Angola Horror, news publications around the country editorialized about the safety of railroad travel with words and images. In this illustration from the 1880s, titled "The Modern Altar of Sacrifice—the Devouring Car Stove," a helpless young woman is depicted as the victim of the outdated and dangerous technology of American trains. From *Harper's Weekly* magazine, February 19, 1887.

apparatus for such contingencies, or for the extinguishment of fires when they do occur on wrecked railroad trains. It has been suggested that each car be provided with axes, to enable the inmates, in case of fire, to cut their way out—but these axes or other implements should not only be inside but outside, for the use of others; and, again, it may be practicable to heat the cars by some other mode than the present.[43]

The axes may have been a unique touch, but in other ways—particularly in the simply phrased sentiment, "Nothing can be imagined more awful than these burnings"—the *Sun*'s editorial was eloquence itself, reflecting the concerns of many. Shortly afterward, the warnings published in Baltimore were echoed all over the country. One oft-repeated fear about the fires aboard railway cars was the way so many victims were obliterated at once, leaving little chance for escape; such a manner of death struck observers as unusually cruel. "The dead are out of all common proportion to the wounded," the *New York Times* wrote of Angola, capturing this sensibility in a phrase.[44] Fire on the cars was laid at the feet of railroad companies, and change demanded. "We demand at once…the adoption of something like common precautions against the recurrences of such heart-rending outrages," the *Times* stated, about the victims at Angola.[45]

The problem was, of course, that many trains had to travel in cold-weather months and in parts of the country that saw snows and freezing temperatures. How to keep the cars warm and well-lit in such places and seasons? Many opinions on the topics of warmth and illumination circulated in print in the months after Angola. Some people argued that anything would be better than candles and coal; others said they would rather ride with candles than risk kerosene. "Why not return to the old and much safer practice of using candles?" one letter-writer begged the editors of *Railway Times* in February 1868. "It will cost but little more to light the cars, and there will be no violation of the 'rule of safety.'"[46] For providing heat and light, everything from hot air to warm water to coal stoves suspended outside the carriages was suggested. "The Angola disaster has started among the newspapers a discussion as to the best method of warming railroad cars," reported one Wisconsin newspaper. "One paper recommends hot water, another steam, and a third cries out for gas. The last is, for the present, impracticable; and the danger attending the two others is hardly less than that which follows the present use of coal stoves."[47] The best solution, the paper concluded, would be the hanging of a furnace under each passenger coach, "so loosely that, in the event of an accident, it will be brushed off."[48] The opposite solution was suggested in the *Syracuse State League*, which reported to readers that a new "safety stove" featuring a reservoir of water installed beneath the stove in the car floor, and connected to the stove by pipes, seemed to promise the best sort of safety assurances for travelers. "When a car collides, turns over, or runs off the track and drags sufficiently to cause it to lurch one side or the other, the reservoir immediately supplies the pipes with water, and the stove is flooded instanter [*sic*]," the newspaper noted. "This neat and valuable invention can be applied to the stoves now in use on the cars."[49]

As these debates were playing out in popular publications, in scientific and technical journals inventors and mechanics were indeed analyzing the Angola accident and offering suggestions for improvement. In the pages of one, *Scientific American*, a flood of letters about railroading safety appeared in the aftermath of the Angola wreck. "Our exchanges abound in editorial suggestions and the communicated views of correspondents, concerning reforms in railroading," the magazine's editors stated in January 1868. "Space would fail to note all these different plans proposed, some having real merit, and others being the height of absurdity."[50]

Among the stranger suggestions was a plan to make railroad cars with lightweight roofs that were only slightly attached to the bodies of the cars, so the roofs would pop off in case of an accident.[51] Another would-be inventor had the notion that passenger cars—currently "cages of death," in his view—should be manufactured only from glass, so that passengers inside could see everything going on around them, and dash for the exits if they spied danger.[52] F. M. Horning of Corry, Pennsylvania, proposer of the glass cars, said that an additional value to the scheme would be that people riding inside the cars could kick out the windows and escape if the car began toppling down a gorge. "With the sides of glass few would be left in the wreck when it reached the bottom of some declivity, to scorch and burn as at Angola," Horning suggested.[53] Most of the response that poured into *Scientific American* and similar publications called for a new focus on safety improvements that could be easily and universally applied to American railroads. The citizens, along with railroad men and other professionals, who offered their thoughts on the tragedy wrote with the passion of people who frequented the railroads. Angola was mentioned as an example of what the public could expect more of in the future, if improvements were not made. Inventors offered proposals that chiefly centered on heating systems, lighting mechanisms, and wheels. The latter, many urged, should be made as derailment-proof as possible. One correspondent to *Scientific American,* Calvin E. Town, a bookbinder who lived on Clinton Street in Buffalo, wrote to suggest a "double-flanged" wheel as a method of solving the problem of a defective wheel throwing a whole car off the track.[54] Town castigated the plan of heating train cars by hot water, citing the sufferings of the victims at Angola.[55] "Would the flood of scalding water from the broken pipes have been any more merciful to the victims of the Angola holocaust?" Town asked in his letter. "I admit that the bodies would have been recognizable, and perhaps a few might have been saved, but cannot something better be invented?"[56]

Town's letter touched off a debate in the pages of the journal and beyond. A proponent of heating passenger cars with hot water, William C. Baker, an inventor from Maine who had come up with the system Town criticized, defended his mechanism as the best available. "No safer or 'better plan' can be devised," Baker stated.[57] (In one way, Baker did have the last laugh. The Baker stove became one of the most widely recognized railroad stoves of the latter part of the nineteenth century, adopted on enough passenger cars—about seven thousand by 1890, or one-quarter of the country's rolling stock—to make Baker a wealthy man, at least until 1900, when technology shifted to steam heat.)[58] Another correspondent argued that a "safety stove" should be a new goal for the country's inventors, and pursued by all.[59]

The suggestions were so wide-ranging, and so passionately defended, that the editors at *Scientific American* felt it necessary in 1868 to issue a warning that the public's confusion about railroad heating and lighting seemed to be increasing, not decreasing, as a result of the furor. Average citizens were making demands of railroads out of panic—including for wax candles instead of lamps on trains—and some companies were giving in, rather than argue with the public mood. "Passenger cars are not sufficiently illuminated," the *Scientific American* editors chided in an editorial. "The tediousness of a railroad journey is greatly relieved by a cheerfully lighted car....The return to the use of sperm or whale oil, or even worse still, candles, is a retrograde step, which should not be taken until it can be shown that some superior means of illumination, equally safe, is not practicable."[60] In short, the most modern technology aboard the cars—whether in the form of stoves, lamps, or other devices—should have to be proven beyond a doubt to be dangerous and impractical, the magazine's editors felt, before any retrogressive steps should be taken. The past, in railroading, was just too uncomfortable and too unsafe. There could be no going back, without strong reason.

THE DEBATE about safety in the wake of Angola attracted attention internationally. In England, the *Times* of London took note of the controversy stirred up by the wreck. "There have been as many persons killed in a Railway Accident before, but seldom have so many ghastly and appalling incidents been crowded into a catastrophe of the kind as at Angola," the *Times* wrote, in a lengthy report on the disaster.[61] In further analysis, which was reprinted in American newspapers, the *Times* criticized the ways railroad companies in the United States operated passenger trains—including, the paper argued, the companies' cavalier attitude toward wrecks and the safety improvements that might prevent them. Some of this attitude may well have been a bit of national pride on the part of the London newspaper, and a chance to boast of the superiority of English railroads; but there were grains of truth in the claims as well. "Railway accidents are not uncommon in the United States, and when they occur it is seldom that a full and searching inquiry is made into the causes that produce them," the *Times* stated.[62] Of American railway managers, the *Times*'s take was that "when they shut their office doors behind them there is no one to call them to account…thus America is the paradise of Railway Directors, whatever it may be to Railway passengers."[63] One occurrence that might make companies change their ways, the *Times* opined, would be if all passengers in the country who were injured on trains sued or sought monetary damages from the companies that had harmed them. If nothing else would make railroads pay attention, the newspaper posited, money would.

Just as the British paper was making this case, the Buffalo and Erie Railroad was paying out a few initial cash settlements to survivors of the Angola wreck, as well as to families of its victims. One man who was badly injured received $1,000.[64] Also among the first recipients of damages was Ellen McAndrews Hubbard, the widow of Zachariah Hubbard, the Canadian carpenter.

The outspoken Mrs. Hubbard had presented her case directly to the railroad company's top officials, including Williams, the president of the line. She had been persistent, talking to everyone as she traveled from Ontario to the morgue in Buffalo, where she claimed Zachariah's remains, and in the end she had won a monetary award. Ellen Hubbard called the settlement "handsome and liberal," without disclosing the amount, in a letter she wrote to the *Hamilton (Ont.) Spectator* in January 1868. In her letter, Mrs. Hubbard praised the railroad's managers for listening to her.[65] "A disconsolate widow and orphans offer [them]…all they can offer, heartfelt gratitude and thanks," wrote the widow. "May God bless them all."[66] Newspapers estimated that Mrs. Hubbard received $7,000 after her husband was killed. Of that amount, $4,000 was from the railroad company, and the rest from an insurance company that had sold Zachariah a traveler's policy for the trip.[67]

But Ellen Hubbard's case was hardly typical. Company records revealed that the Buffalo and Erie paid out settlements over the Angola incident in neither an orderly nor comprehensive fashion in late 1867 and throughout 1868. Some Angola victims and their families received thousands of dollars. Some got smaller amounts, and some received nothing. Those who let their cases against the railroad drag on too long were the unluckiest, as by 1869 the railroad company disappeared into the Lake Shore and Michigan Southern Railroad, and victims would have been unable to claim further monies.

The lesson of the Angola Horror, to many witnesses, might have been best summed up by the London press. It would have been difficult for some Americans to admit this, given the competition that had long existed between the United States and England over the scale, safety, and quality of railroads. But, some now admitted, maybe what the London newspapers had claimed was true: perhaps citizens in the United States had gotten too careless about what they were willing to endure when it came to the railroads, and now—as at Angola—they were paying a bloody price. The *Times* of London went so far as to tie the dangerousness of the country's railroads to its democratic way of life. This, in particular, would have been hard for American men and women to swallow, given that many of them—whatever their personal concerns about train travel—looked upon the country's ever-expanding railroads as a symbol of the democracy of the nation, and the freedoms conferred upon its citizens. The *Times* argued the opposite view:

> Of course the people have only themselves to thank for all this. If they are ill-used or victimized by Railway or Steamboat Companies, they submit to the wrong as quietly as if it was their portion and inheritance. A train will stop short of its destination, or constantly come in hours behind the appointed time, and no one will complain. Sleeping cars will be charged for when none are in the train, and if the passenger remonstrates he is liable to be insulted. As for incivility from servants on Railways or steamboats, the American people are apt to take it as Republican and an outward sign of freedom. Hence it is that the extremity of discomfort in civilized travelling is to be met with upon the Railroads of the United States.
>
> The burning alive of forty-one men and women may convince the American public that it does not answer to permit Railway Companies to remain completely beyond the reach of law and public opinion.[68]

These words of summation—which placed responsibility on the public to demand better of the railroads—might have contained a bit of superciliousness, but they added fuel to the sentiment on the part of some American citizens that something needed to be done to force the railroads to reform. In the end, people were realizing, laws might be necessary to solve some of the problems. "The only resort appears to be legislation," stated the editors at *Scientific American,* of the issue of safety improvements. "This only has proved effectual in the use of appliances calculated to deprive railroad travel of some of its dangers....Nothing short of legislative enactment will render travel on our railroads free from the constant fear of death or maiming."[69]

CHAPTER 16

Changes

———⋆———

1868–1893

FOUR WEEKS AFTER the Angola Horror, the bodies of its unidentified victims were laid to rest. Graveside services that Monday, January 13, 1868, were brief. The boxes of remains were lowered, one by one, into the ground in Buffalo's Forest Lawn cemetery. Members of the public had not been invited. No grieving crowds pressed around the grave as the coffins disappeared into the muddy earth; no minister offered prayers, no songs were sung, and no press corps of eager reporters hovered nearby. The interment of the wreck's victims was intended to be as efficient and private as the funeral service inside the Exchange Street depot had been orchestrated and public, and that goal was achieved.[1]

In the days leading up to the burial, the nineteen coffins would likely have been stored in a cold vault on the grounds of the cemetery. In Buffalo in the winter, that was common enough practice—bodies were often buried when the soil softened enough for graves to be opened. By mid-January, railroad officials had decided it was time to bury the remains. They ordered the graves dug.

Officials of the Buffalo and Erie Railroad had purchased a triangle-shaped slice of land in the cemetery, a sprawling property located in the city's still largely undeveloped northern section. The plot itself was not far from Forest Lawn's entrance at Linwood and Delavan avenues, and close to the cemetery's sixty-foot-wide driveway, which crossed a wooden bridge before giving out on curving pathways.[2] Modest in size, the plot chosen by the railroad was nonetheless located in a picturesque area of the graveyard. As they dug, workers would have gazed out over rolling slopes, dotted here and there with young trees, bare now in winter—elms and maples, horse chestnuts and lindens—all the way to the wooden fence that circled the property. It was a landscape meant to convey naturalness, serenity, and reflection. "The first impression given," one observer noted about this area of the cemetery, "is that of appropriateness of purpose, and dignity of aspect."[3] No one could deny that the 1,789-square-foot slice of ground selected by the Buffalo and Erie Railroad's officers offered lovely views.

There had been talk that the railroad commissioners planned to erect a "suitable" monument at the site, to indicate for future visitors the place where those slain at Angola lay.[4] Yet no marker or memorial stood on the triangle of ground; no tablet or obelisk indicated, even in a general way, the presence of the wreck's dead. Railroad officials had promised that they had numbered the bodies as they were laid in the mass grave, and created a corresponding list of "relics" that had been found upon the dead and in the debris of the cars.[5] Perhaps, they told the public, some future identification of the victims might be made. But that apparently never happened.

After the soil of Forest Lawn was spread over the top of the grave, no one seems to have come forward to claim a kinship or connection with any of the victims. No one appears to have ever asked for any of the corpses to be removed from the plot and returned to family and friends—nor added a name and identifying details to the cemetery's scant burial record for Lot No. 27, Section 3.

Down through the decades, cemetery files for the Angola Horror grave would include just two names related to the train accident: that of Norman Nichols, who was recognized by his family but buried with his wife—presumably among the unidentified dead—and the other unnamed victims; and that of Joseph Stocking Lewis, whose presence among the charred bodies was taken as fact by those who loved him, but never confirmed. With time, any further information about the other bodies disappeared or was lost, taking with it any chance of preserving their differences. The Horror's victims, united in death, were now banded together for eternity.

AS GRAVEDIGGERS in Buffalo heaped soil over the boxes of the Angola dead, at the other end of New York State a young mechanic living with his parents in Schenectady was thinking about trains. George Westinghouse Jr. was not yet twenty-two years old in early 1868. He was, however, a Civil War veteran, an inventor with multiple patents to his name, and a newly married man. Higher education, which Westinghouse had tried after his stints in the Union cavalry and navy, had not worked out for him; he had left Union

College after one semester. Westinghouse had a restless and analytic mind, a knack for seeing problems and solutions—and a desire to put his ideas into effect without delay. In the winter and spring of 1868, Westinghouse thought about railroad trains, and particularly about the problems with their braking systems.

Despite the fact that the technology for stopping trains had not come very far, braking as a field of exploration for inventors was considered crowded intellectual territory. Early on in his own experiments, Westinghouse met a man who had patented a chain brake, the Ambler brake, which was being tried out by the Chicago, Burlington & Quincy Railroad. The man had assured Westinghouse that "there was no use working upon the brake problem, because he had devised the only feasible plan."[6] Indeed, ever since trains had been set in motion on the nation's rails, people had been looking for better ways to stop them. By the time Westinghouse turned his mind to the problem

George Westinghouse Jr., shown here with his wife, Marguerite, was twenty-one years old and recently married at the time of the Angola wreck. A young mechanic living in Schenectady, New York, Westinghouse had ambitions to devise a brake that would stop railroad trains quickly and reliably. From the collection of George Westinghouse IV.

of train brakes, nearly four decades after the inception of railroad travel in America, "hundreds upon hundreds" of designs for braking systems had been tried and found wanting.[7] Many more ideas had been proposed by inventors, but never turned into models and given proper tests (a process that could be expensive and risky). Even the best schemes for new braking mechanisms still underperformed, especially in poor track conditions, or worked unreliably. While in one test a new steam-braking device cut the distance needed to stop a train, as compared to hand brakes, *Scientific American* noted with dissatisfaction in January 1868 that it still took far too long to stop a running train. "Frequently the danger if ahead is not descried in time to bring the train to a halt before the locomotive has arrived at the point, especially if the track is slippery, the train on a down grade, or running at full speed," the magazine's editors stated.[8]

As a result of the fruitlessness of these efforts, many trainmen had become convinced that hand brakes—the kind that required brakemen to operate them, by climbing on top of and in between the cars—were, despite their well-publicized deficiencies, the only workable option for stopping passenger trains and freights. "You can't stop a heavy train in a moment," one trainman had asserted to Westinghouse, accepting the statement as a law of the roads.[9] Westinghouse had other ideas. He had grown up around his father's business, a factory that made agricultural tools of George Westinghouse Sr.'s design, and had seen the success a timely innovation could bring. The Westinghouse agricultural works was praised for doing "more to advertise Schenectady than even Union College with its educational advantages," and inside its walls George Jr.—the eighth of ten children born to George Sr. and his wife, Emeline—had grown to love tinkering with mechanisms.[10] When he had an engineering problem to fix on, those who knew Westinghouse observed, he focused with single-minded attention.[11]

Westinghouse had already had some success with inventions. In 1866, he had received his first patent on a design for a rotary engine. Even before that, working out ideas while stationed in New York harbor aboard the USS *Muscoota*, George Jr. ran his plans past his father's eye. "I am pleased to think that you stick to your engine. Good or bad there is nothing like holding on," Westinghouse Sr. wrote to his son in 1865. "I hope you will get up something new that will be profitable to you as well as to be creditable to you as an inventor."[12] In another exchange, the elder Westinghouse cautioned his son to guard against illness, especially of the nerves. He warned George Jr. about the expensive nature of the invention process, and urged him to be sure before running trials. "You must be aware that it is quite costly to make experiments and it needs to be well considered before going to expence [*sic*] on it,"

Westinghouse Sr. explained. "You must examine and reexamine…so as to be sure you are right."[13]

It was advice Westinghouse took to heart as he turned his attention to the railroads. And, by 1868, George Jr. had new reasons for seeking success. The previous year, he had met a young woman named Marguerite Erskine Walker while taking a train trip, and in the summer of 1867 the couple had married. Westinghouse in this period patented a railroad car replacer—a device to put train cars back on the rails after a derailment—and a new design for a frog, or track juncture component. He was looking for ways to support his bride and establish a home of his own, and the railroads were in his sights.

George Westinghouse Jr. didn't draw an explicit connection between the Angola Horror and his work that winter on a compressed-air brake for stopping trains. Still, the Angola wreck was on many people's minds that winter season, and in the years afterward; it was part of the average citizen's understanding of recent history. The fact that the wreck happened across the state from Westinghouse's home, at the other end of the Erie Canal from his father's factory, only would have made the Horror more relevant. Moreover, Westinghouse family members, people who avidly read newspapers and traveled on railroads—and who discussed news of the day shared in clippings in the letters they wrote to one another, including about railroad-related subjects—would almost certainly have read and talked over the story headlined "Fearful Accident on the Lake Shore Rail Road," which appeared in the *Schenectady Daily Evening Star and Times* the day after the wreck.[14] "A Car through a Bridge—Another Burned—Sixty Lives Lost—Twenty-Five Burned to Death," the newspaper's headline stated.[15] It was the sort of occurrence Westinghouse himself would have paid special attention to.

Two years earlier, Westinghouse had been personally affected by the aftermath of a less serious railway accident. While a passenger on a train traveling between Schenectady and Troy, he had been delayed because of a crash farther down the track between two freights. The two engines had run into one another in a head-on collision because the trains were too cumbersome to bring to a halt quickly, even though the engineers had seen the danger and tried to stop.[16] The crash threw Westinghouse's journey off schedule, and likely rattled the young man to some degree. The event was entirely unnecessary, the inventor decided.[17] "The loss of time and the inconvenience arising from it suggested that if those trains had had some means of applying brakes to all of the wheels of their trains, the accident in question might have been avoided and the time of my fellow-passengers and myself might have been saved," Westinghouse later said of the occurrence.[18] In the Troy-Schenectady accident, wasted time alone frustrated the young man and spurred his ideas.

Accounts of Angola, and other deadly accidents happening around the same time, would likely have fueled his energies even more.

In the months after Angola, Westinghouse began to make progress in his design for a railroad brake that would work by harnessing compressed air. He had already experimented with a few other models, including chains and steam cylinders. In 1868 he was focused on air power—an idea he had gotten from a magazine story about the digging of a tunnel through Mont Cenis in the Alps. (The younger Westinghouse had been approached in the machine shop of his father's factory by young women selling periodicals. "Induced" by the girls to buy a two-dollar subscription to *Living Age,* Westinghouse read in "a very early number, probably the first one I received," a story about the digging of the Mont Cenis tunnel.)[19] The feat had been accomplished by a machine driven by air, which when compressed was powerful enough to move drills through three thousand feet of pipe. "This account of the use of compressed air," Westinghouse later stated, "instantly indicated that brake apparatus of the kind contemplated for operation by steam could be operated by means of compressed air."[20] Moreover, he thought that this sort of propulsive power might work "upon any length of train."[21] Westinghouse began to experiment with the technology.

Compressed air was not a new concept. As early as the 1840s in England, testing had been done with air appliances for trains.[22] But no one had yet struck on a practicable idea for compressed-air brakes. Westinghouse spent about two years working out the particulars of his invention.[23] The result was his first version of the brake, the so-called "straight" air brake. The young inventor had a sample built in a Pittsburgh machine shop.[24] The earliest Westinghouse brakes were "crude at the start," recalled the first machinists to produce the new brakes. "There was trouble with the pump," one said, as "limestone water clogged the ports."[25] Indeed, those who worked by his side in crafting the first air brakes thought Westinghouse was likely wasting his time. "The men in the shop were very skeptical," recalled one. "Some of us thought he was throwing his money away."[26]

But the air brakes worked—and, in time, impressively so. The brakes stopped trains in distances that seemed breathtaking. Though measurements from some of the earliest trials of the new brake were not noted, it worked in such "unprecedentedly" short distances that orders for the Westinghouse equipment soon poured in.[27] During one early test, in 1869, the brake even prevented a crash. The Steubenville Accommodation train of the Pittsburgh, Cincinnati & St. Louis Railway was emerging from a tunnel near Pittsburgh when crewmen spied a wagon stalled on the track ahead; the brand-new air brakes on the accommodation train were applied by engineer Daniel Tate, and the train screeched to a halt in time to prevent a wreck. "The instantaneous application of the air brakes prevented what might have been a serious accident," said Westinghouse, who was aboard the train at the time.[28]

The air brake's beauty lay in its simplicity. It moved compressed air from the front of the train, through connective hoses and couplings, into each successive car, so that brakes could be applied on cars simultaneously. Because of its continuous action, the brake put the stopping power for an entire consist in the control of the engineer in the cab. Hand-brake technology had assumed the only way to make trains stop faster was to add more brakemen; the air brake made the opposite case, nearly eliminating the need for them.

Westinghouse's apparatus proved a sensation with passengers for this very reason, as engineers were considered far more trustworthy than brakemen.[29] This early brake became safer still when Westinghouse made it an "automatic" air brake: instead of working through an increase in air pressure, the brake worked when air pressure dropped, so that in the event of a derailment or break-in-train, the brakes would be set rather than being shut off. With the innovation of the automatic device the brakes for a train could be applied from the cars themselves, by a person pulling on an emergency cord—a method of stopping the train that "should only be used in cases of emergency," Westinghouse's instructions advised.[30]

Westinghouse received the first patent on his brake on April 13, 1869. His invention was not acclaimed in every quarter from the start—a contingent of competing inventors and cynical railroad men, as well as some newspapers and magazines, argued that the brake was no better than any other, with one claiming it was too expensive and made trains stop with a "jerk."[31] In 1875, Westinghouse wrote to his father that certain men supportive of other braking technologies seemed to be "more bitter against us than ever."[32] But the negativity was isolated. In repeated trials, as well as in practical applications starting with the Pennsylvania and Panhandle railroads and other early adopting lines, the Westinghouse brake proved its clear superiority. Newspaper stories about close calls with railroad mishaps praised the air brake for averting what would have almost certainly been deadly accidents in the past. "It was wonderful that none were killed...the Westinghouse air-brake probably saved an awful slaughter," ran one such newspaper account, in 1872.[33] Railways that installed the Westinghouse brake on their trains boasted of the fact in advertisements, and lured passengers by doing so.

A few months after receiving his first patent, Westinghouse set up the Westinghouse Air-Brake Company, establishing a works on Pittsburgh's Liberty Avenue. The name of the street was propitious as well as symbolic, for Westinghouse's invention had delivered liberty to many—the freedom from fear when traveling by rail.

The air brake became, within the next few years, a standard appliance on passenger trains in the United States. By 1874, 2,281 locomotives and 7,254 cars had been fitted with the straight-air brake.[34] By 1876, railroads operating about 75 percent of the country's passenger car stock—and covering an estimated 85 to 90 percent of passenger miles—would have some form of the Westinghouse brake on their trains.[35] Indeed, the air brake was soon so widely used that it became almost taken for granted. "It is now applied on a very large number of roads in this country," *Railway Times* stated in 1872, "and we have failed to hear of a single case of failure to do all that has been claimed for it."[36]

In a reflection of this changing picture, writers began to use air brakes as plot points in their novels and stories. Tension over the new technology— would it work or wouldn't it?—in these narratives often supplanted an earlier period's fixation with the lack of technology that train travel offered passengers and crew. In some stories, Westinghouse's invention functioned almost as a character in the action. By 1900, in a story called "How McGrath Got an Engine," Buffalo native Frank H. Spearman, the dean of American railroad fiction, would describe a scene in which rails bewhiskered with frost were handled with a liberal application of grit; in this case, "a tankful of sand is better than all the air Westinghouse ever stored."[37] In his story, Spearman made the jamming of a Westinghouse brake the event on which hung the narrative of a heroic young wiper, or track sweeper, Aloysius McGrath, who managed to control a runaway train shooting backward down a mountainside, using just sand, steam, and the work of a dedicated fireman. Such a dramatic episode—which would have been all but unremarkable in the first few decades of American railroading—was by the turn of the century a crisis requiring unique savvy to solve. Spearman's McGrath does the job: "A man that could hold a train from Wind River here on whiskers, with nothing but a tankful of sand and a hobo fireman, wouldn't be likely to fall off the right of way running back," remarks one observer at the end of the story, after the track-sweeper has been promoted to engineer for stopping his train without the use of the air brake, which had "frozen between the first and the second car."[38] "We haven't got half enough men like McGraw."[39]

By this time, the old-style brakeman—that uncouth figure who rode the car tops, grappling with the elements, to apply the hand brakes—had faded from prominence into a state of somewhat shabby anachronism. "Shorn of his usefulness by the air brake, he has been left a victim of evolution, an organ without a purpose," *Harper's Weekly* wrote sympathetically in 1893.[40] Left behind by history—or, at least, moved from the car tops to what were seen as more respectable roles inside the trains—the brakeman changed to some degree into a romanticized figure, a character fast disappearing from the national scene. "Old travelers can never be made fully to believe that this flimsy West-inghouse apparatus," *Harper's* wrote, "can set the brakes like the old-fashioned brakeman."[41] Americans could indulge this nostalgia; they had been riding the rails far more safely for twenty years, thanks to Westinghouse's engineered device.

As for Westinghouse himself, he had learned his lesson as a young man, when his invention of a railroad frog had been copied without his permission.[42] He didn't make the same mistake twice, and became fiercely protective of the air brake. He guarded patent rights, and would not grant licenses to railroads to put together their own air brakes under his imprint.[43] Westinghouse also warded off those he saw as copyright infringers—to the extent that he bought out so-called "vacuum brake" companies in the 1870s when he perceived them as treading too closely to his intellectual territory. The catalog of the Westing-house Air-Brake Company from 1876 contained a preface that rang of the inventor's point of view. "This company desires to so conduct its business that none of its customers shall have cause for complaint, and we believe that care should be taken not to encourage the infringement of our patents by any one," the catalog stated. "It is our intention to adopt all improvements that may tend to perfect the brake, and to purchase those not originated at our own place if necessary for this purpose."[44]

His brake brought Westinghouse wealth and made him a household name. It also gave him the sense of having fixed a wrong. "If some day they say of me," Westinghouse said to an associate, "that with my work I have contributed something to the welfare and happiness of my fellowman, I shall be satisfied."[45]

There was more to come. Congress was about to make his invention not only pervasive, but mandatory.

AFTER ANGOLA, changes to state and federal law took place that made train travel safer for all Americans. The shifts happened slowly, for a variety of reasons.

Most railroads were interested in technology that made it possible for them to operate heavier trains on faster runs with more passengers and, it was hoped, fewer accidents. But many of the companies resisted attempts by the government to regulate their operations or equipment. Adaptations, as the railroads saw it, cost money: a new set of Westinghouse automatic air brakes sold for $300 by 1886 for the locomotive fixtures alone, plus $138 for each passenger car, while a single set of freight car brakes cost $50.[46] As a result, railroad company managers were often hesitant to upgrade older cars with the new technology unless they had to—whether from the force of public pressure or from outside regulation. This was especially true of freight trains. Westinghouse's automatic brake offered better control of the longer freights that had become common during the 1880s and 1890s. In one test, an eyewitness saw a fifty-car train running at twenty miles per hour pull to a stop in an astonishing ninety-eight feet, "surprisingly without shock."[47] Yet by 1893, fewer than 10 percent of the freight cars in the United States were equipped with automatic air brakes, despite the fact that such equipment had become all but standard on passenger trains.[48]

With each new railroad accident, meanwhile, a fresh outcry would arise from the pages of newspapers and periodicals, and fill the halls of the country's governing bodies. ("Look to the past!" urged a New York newspaper after a local train rear-ended the Atlantic Express at Spuyten Duyvil on January 13, 1882, killing seven residents and a New York state senator.)[49] But this pattern of outrage followed by forgetfulness had largely grown tiresome, even to the general public. "When the country was terror-stricken by the details of the railroad tragedy at Angola, when the shocking news came of the sacrifice of life at New Hamburgh, when the world listened with horror at the description of the death scenes at Ashtabula, at each of these calamities there was a loud demand for legislation to prevent their recurrence," the *St. Lawrence Republican*'s editorial stated. "But with the passage of time there came an alleviation of the poignancy of grief, there came a moderation, a forgetfulness in public indignation, there came a mitigation of fear on the part of travelers, and matters fell back into the old 'trust to luck' channels."[50] That was an accurate assessment. In between major railway accidents, the demand by public and press for new laws and greater oversight of the country's railroads died down. Only tragedy seemed to create the pressure needed to push changes along—and only for a time.

Twenty years thus passed between the wreck at Angola's Big Sister Creek and laws that meant meaningful change for the railroads. In 1887, New York State passed a law restricting the ways that coach cars on passenger trains could be heated. The law forbade railroads of more than fifty miles in length operating within the state's borders from heating their passenger cars by means of any type of wood- or coal-burning stoves, whether kept inside the cars or suspended from them.[51] The only type of stoves that could be used on trains carrying people in the state under the new law were specially approved models designed for cooking meals in the dining cars. The hot coals that had covered passengers on board the New York Express as it tumbled into Big Sister Creek were, two decades later, largely a thing of the past.[52]

Other states during the same period established restrictions limiting some of the more egregious elements of train travel. Massachusetts, to take one example, regulated the sort of fluids that could be used to light the lamps on board passenger cars.[53] But these actions were for the most part small-scale and discrete. And in some areas of danger—principally, braking and switching—little that was substantive could be done on the state level. The national railroading landscape had grown to encompass forty-four different kinds of couplers and nine kinds of brakes, which were hard to regulate on any local level because many railroads were interstate lines, or ran mixed train consists with cars borrowed from other railroads.[54]

Thus, calls for governance in these areas on the federal level mounted. New York, Ohio, Massachusetts, Michigan, Iowa, Mississippi, Wisconsin, Nebraska, and Missouri joined a roster of states calling on Congress to pass laws mandating uniform couplers and air brakes for both passenger trains and freights. The push for action by Congress satisfied some of the emotional appeals for such widespread change that had been building ever since the New York Express ran off the bridge in Angola. "Enact a law," one midwestern newspaper had urged Congress, the year after the Angola wreck, "which shall bear uniformly upon all railroads forming through and connecting lines between the states, providing for the safety of passengers and punishing the criminal negligence which has resulted in Angola and Carr's Rock disasters."[55]

Even more touching were pleas to members of Congress and other lawmakers by people whose lives had been affected by the condition of the country's railroads. Many of these cries came from railroad employees and their families. By the early 1890s, thanks to the Westinghouse air brake and other changes, passenger trains were safer than they had been at the time of the Horror. Passenger injuries on American railroads had been reduced to one out of every two hundred thousand people carried, deaths to one out of every 1.7 million.[56] But freight trains remained quite deadly. Death tolls among railroad employees had climbed to striking levels with the increased length and weight of many freight trains, which continued to be largely unequipped with automatic air brakes and uniform couplers. In one year, between the summers of 1888 and 1889, more than two thousand railroad employees were killed on the job, and another twenty thousand injured.[57] By 1890, that number had climbed to 2,451 killed and 22,394 injured.[58] In a report to Congress, the House of Representatives' Committee on Interstate and Foreign Commerce called that total an obscene amount, comparing it to battle casualty totals for Wellington at Waterloo, Meade at Gettysburg, and both sides at the two days' battle of Shiloh. "None of these terrible battles furnished a list of losses equal to the loss in a single year of our railroad men, a loss equal, in fact, to the entire present force of the United States Army," the committee's report stated.[59]

Likening the death toll to another disaster that had gripped the public's attention, the flood at Johnstown, the committee continued:

> The Johnstown disaster filled the imagination with horror and sent a thrill of sympathy throughout the civilized world, but that calamity came in one fell swoop, while fatalities on the railways, involving in the aggregate a far greater sacrifice of human life, have scarcely attracted public attention. Nightly several poor fellows are picked off—in a freight yard, on the rail—often the only vestige that morning reveals being a pool of blood and the dismembered remains of the unfortunate victim. Two lines of a newspaper headed "Brakeman killed" tells the whole story.[60]

In this climate of dissatisfaction and unease, President Benjamin Harrison called upon Congress to act to make railroads in the United States safer for passengers and railroad employees alike. "It is a reproach to our civilization," Harrison stated to legislators, "that any class of American workman should, in the pursuit of a necessary and useful vocation, be subjected to a peril of life and limb as great as that of a soldier in time of war."[61]

In 1893, after lengthy debate, Congress at last passed a federal "Safety Appliances Act," which required both automatic air brakes on all passenger and freight trains in the United States and the use of uniform couplers on the nation's railroads. By the mid-1890s, the era that had been embodied in the Angola Horror had, for the most part, ended. A safer, less anxiety-laden period for the nation's travelers had begun. Of course, many members of the traveling public would carry forward with them into this new era some vestigial concerns held over from the earlier time. And yet many were surely like the Angola Horror survivor who made a cross-country journey by rail fifteen years after the accident and found much changed about the railroads—and her memory of the day of the wreck. "We left Buffalo in the afternoon, traveling on the Lake Shore railroad, and I was on the lookout all the time for that fatal bridge near Angola station where you and I and James came near losing our lives, almost 15 years ago," wrote Mary Lang Swizer to her mother, Christiana Gates Lang of Vermont, after a transcontinental train trip to California in 1882. "But although we passed Angola I could not distinctly point out that spot so eventful in our lives, for all seemed changed."[62]

More than Mary Lang, and her memories of the Horror, had changed in the years since the wreck at Big Sister Creek. Time had carried forward Angola's survivors, as well as the railroads on which they journeyed.

Lost Souls

Anyone else would have said to himself with secret joy: "Within ten minutes myself…!" But it was another thought that visited Brother Juniper: "Why did this happen, to those five?"… And on that instant Brother Juniper made the resolve to inquire into the secret lives of those five persons, that moment falling through the air, and to surprise the reason of their taking off.

THORNTON WILDER,
The Bridge at San Luis Rey

A SIMILAR SETTING, a similar scene. Nine years and eleven days after Angola, the tragedy in Ohio was at once novel and familiar, the way a woodcut of a famous painting suggests the original while muddying one's memory of its details. A high bridge over a shallow stream gone frozen with the onset of winter; the stillness of a snowy December landscape; a falling train. What made Ashtabula different was this: nine years later, people knew what to fear.

And so, when rescuers clambering toward the smoldering debris of a wrecked express train in the Ashtabula river bed on the night of December 29, 1876, heard pistol shots within the burning cars, they immediately assumed that desperate passengers trapped inside were seeking to avoid the flames by killing themselves.

Nearly a decade earlier, at Angola, it had been different. In the late afternoon of December 18, 1867, gunshots were heard inside the passenger coach that had been the last car of the New York Express. Tilted upward against the ravine wall at the bottom of the Big Sister gorge, the car was being consumed by crackling fire when one bullet flew out of the wreckage and pierced the trousers of an Angola man laboring to put out the flames. Onlookers at the scene ascribed the shots to firearms they supposed the victims carried in their clothing, which they imagined had been set off by extreme temperatures in the wreckage.[1] No mention was made of suicide—neither at the scene of the disaster, nor in the months' worth of newspaper coverage afterward. In fact, one Pennsylvania family, reading news accounts of the accident, came forward to claim that their relative, fifty-year-old Benjamin C. Aikin of Hydetown, must have been responsible for the stray shots, because Aikin was known to travel with a loaded pistol in his pocket.

Passengers were savvier by Ashtabula and the wrecks that came after. They were also more jaded. Much had changed since the 1830s, and it was not just the great increases in track mileage of railroads across the countryside. Americans had witnessed dramatic increases in the number of accidents on the railroads, as well as in their deadliness and devastation.[2] Angola had been prominent among these wrecks, and the scenes and stories of the disaster at Big Sister Creek had become ingrained in the public consciousness.

Newspapers and magazines in the post–Civil War period had made Angola a subject of conversation in households across the nation. As average men and women read and thought about the fate of the souls lost aboard the New York Express, they surely put themselves in the places of those husbands and wives, mothers and children, colleagues and friends. They recognized their vulnerability, even as they understood that by the late 1800s they were also seeing enormous advancements in the use and capabilities of science, technology, and engineering to improve all aspects of life. George Westinghouse Jr. and his air brake had been just one example of this sort of forward momentum. Angola's example—captured in news accounts, but also in artwork by J. H. Mills and others, and in poems such as that of the slain virgin of Angola—reminded them that in the brave new world they had entered, filled with expanding opportunities and seemingly limitless modern advantages, some of their most basic needs, such as safety and security, could not be taken for granted. This emerging world was a place that could offer you the thrills and freedom of railroad travel—but it was also a place that could devastate your body so terribly that, like John W. Chapman, your closest friends would struggle to identify your remains. It was a place in which you could be denied the civility and Christian comfort of a proper burial, with a marked grave. Not only that, as Angola showed them, even the most vulnerable classes of citizens—the mothers like Christiana Lang; the babies like Minnie Fisher; the older people like the Thomases of Utica—were at risk.

Angola did not rob Americans of optimism or hope about the experience of traveling by rail. But Angola did, in the context of the other train wrecks of its era, teach men and women to approach the railroads guardedly, with apprehension moderating their pleasure. They could hardly expect to emerge from such experiences unchanged.

And so, at Ashtabula in 1876, Henry A. White, a forty-five-year-old produce dealer who had been dozing in the City of Buffalo sleeper car as the Lake Shore and Michigan Southern's Pacific Express roared over the Ashtabula River bridge, responded to the first jarring motions of the train at 7:15 p.m.

with a surge of fear. White had heard a strange sound—a hollow *chuck,* *chuck, chuck*—and realized that it was a sign that the car he was riding in had derailed.[3] White, like others on board the express who had been conditioned by wrecks including Angola, knew immediately what was in store for him. The resident of Wethersfield, Connecticut, was whirled upside down in his seat, at the same time that he heard the explosive noise of the express—including eleven passenger cars and two locomotives, Socrates and Columbia—crashing off the bridge. The entire train, save Socrates, fell into the ravine, pulling the iron bridge down with it. White felt as if he were dreaming. "It was," he later said, "something like a man's thoughts just before going to sleep."[4] When he realized that he was alive—and that the 186 people, plus children, aboard the train had gone eerily silent—White called out. A man's voice spoke weakly back to him, asking one pointed question.

"Will there be a fire?" the unseen voice whimpered. "Is there going to be a fire?"[5]

Fire and entrapment: this is what passengers had learned to dread. White feared the worst, but he decided to offer the man hope. "There will be no fire," he reassured the stranger.[6] Just then, White saw flames from the corner of his eye. They were advancing, tearing through upholstery and wooden timbers. Though he tried to the last to prevent the trapped man from knowing what was about to come, he could not, in the end, save him.

"I felt badly," White later said, "because I had told him I thought there would not be any."

Angola had been among the events that had taught both men what to fear. It had been the last big railroad wreck of an older era—a time before the new phase ushered in by Westinghouse's brake, improved regulations, and other changes. Angola was the end of things, in many ways, for the period's railroad passengers. But it was also their beginning. Like the sinking of the RMS *Titanic,* the Angola Horror was a transportation disaster that captured the spirit of its age. And that age was one that was passing, even as the disaster played out. Angola and *Titanic* each possessed era-ending qualities that rendered them seemingly indelible in the public mind.

Angola offered lessons, to the multitudes who paid attention to what had happened at Big Sister Creek. That White and his friend couldn't escape a similar fate was, perhaps, one of its grimmest. But changes were coming. In hindsight, Angola was a sadder picture. The accident and its sufferings were all the more horrific because men and women now saw how it could have been prevented.

IN ASHTABULA, visitors can see an elegant obelisk that was erected to the memory of the wreck's dead within a few decades of its occurrence. The slim

A railroad catastrophe similar in some respects to Angola, the Ashtabula Bridge Disaster took place nine years later along Ohio's Lake Erie shore. This monument, in Ashtabula's Chestnut Grove cemetery, commemorates the passengers and crewmen who lost their lives on December 29, 1876. No monument was ever erected to the Angola victims, in either Angola or Buffalo. Photograph by Todd Joseph Pignataro.

granite tower, located in Ashtabula's Chestnut Grove cemetery, is inscribed with names. Flowers are planted in season around the plot—geraniums, begonias—in beds hemmed with railroad ties. The monument that rises into the sky in alternating bands of smooth and rough-cut stone suggests lives unfinished, dreams unfulfilled. The monument's inscription makes special mention of those men and women who were never identified: "To the memory of the unrecognized dead of the Ashtabula Bridge Disaster, whose remains are buried here." Cemetery employees not infrequently see buses of people coming into the cemetery, past a metal sign noting the location of the Bridge Disaster Monument. Even in slow months, a steady trickle of visitors passes by.

For the Angola Horror, nothing like that has ever existed.

In Angola itself, it was in the summer of 2008, after research on this book spurred interest, that a marker was placed at the site of the wreck at Big Sister

The site of the Angola Horror, at Big Sister Creek, in a photograph taken 138 years later, on December 18, 2005. The view of the bridge is looking upstream. The terrain in the foreground is where the second car that fell from the tracks tumbled down the embankment. The bridge has been modified over the years. It is still in use. Photograph by Todd Joseph Pignataro.

Creek to commemorate the spot where the disaster occurred. A small metal sign was installed downstream from the accident site. Officials, local historians and other residents in the village said they would like to do more, in the future, to commemorate the place of the wreck.

In Buffalo's Forest Lawn, the story was much the same. Although the Buffalo and Erie Railroad intended to erect a monument to the unknown dead buried in the mass grave—setting aside $2,000 to do so in the weeks after the wreck—no marker appears ever to have been raised.[7] Part of the reason for that may lie in the fact that, within two years of the accident, the smaller railroad was absorbed into the Lake Shore and Michigan Southern Railway. At some point during the twentieth century, a temporary placard was installed at the burial site, to show visitors where the victims lay. But it fell down or was taken down. Cemetery officials, as well as interested residents of the Buffalo region, at the time of the writing of this book had hopes for a memorial to the unknown victims at some point in the future.

THAT ANGOLA HAPPENED is not surprising. That it was forgotten for so long is.

Just as it occurred at a volatile moment of technological and social change, the wreck took place at a time when public attention was particularly focused on proper forms of death, burial, and remembrance. By 1867, national discourse still revolved around themes connected with the injuries and deaths of three quarters of a million Civil War soldiers. The question of what to do with men killed at Antietam, still in temporary graves, was a topic under debate in the press in the month of the Horror. Citizens also read updates in the newspapers from the federal government about the remediation made to injured veterans. Between the summers of 1866 and 1867, readers learned, 280 wounded soldiers had received artificial legs, 236 got artificial arms, 9 men received hands, 6 men feet, 3 soldiers got artificial eyes, and one veteran had received a "palate."[8] In the spirit of the time, Mark Twain in an 1868 letter jokingly referred to his aversion to both mass and unmarked graves when describing a fall he and a friend took from a carriage. "They buried us both in one grave, but it was too crowded to suit me, because I am not used to sleeping double....I despise to be buried along with another man—it is too sociable. I like to be planted by myself—under a monument."[9]

The Civil War took place in a Christianity-imbued Victorian era in which death was seen as an important last act in one's life—an action as much as a fate, and perhaps even a "glimpse of [one's] future" in eternity.[10] Men and women wanted to die the right way, according to the *ars moriendi*, or art of dying. A "good death," in this view, meant dying at home, surrounded by family, with one's last words recorded and preserved for posterity, the prospect of eternity bright on the horizon. One example from the poems, songs, and works of fiction that figured this idea in the mid-nineteenth-century United States is "A Death Song," a poem published in a women's annual. The verses described the death of a young woman as a painless passage from one breath to the next:

> My spirit plumes her wings for flight,
> I can no longer see the light—
> Kind friends around my pillow stay,
> Nor grieve that I should pass away.[11]

In this same period, hundreds of thousands of men died in circumstances far removed from this ideal, on the battlefields of war and in military hospitals. People like Romaine J. Curtiss and Frank E. Griffith had seen those realities firsthand during the war. Still, those events did not erase the commonly held sense that the sanctity of an individual's last moments should be preserved. Soldiers heading into battle often made arrangements with comrades to be sure news of their fate would reach home.[12] There is something terrible about dying without recognition, bereft of dignity, and being buried in a nameless manner. Americans in the Victorian period, whether in war or in civilian life, realized that—and struggled to care properly for the dead even in the most extreme of circumstances, such as on a battlefield or at the scene of a major accident.

Equally important was the idea of a proper burial, which meant interment with rites and appropriate marking of the grave. Since colonial times, Americans had dealt with the dilemma of how to handle burials in a vast, unsettled land. Formal burials and marked graves were hallmarks of civilization, and it was considered an unsavory and unchristian—and, in many cases, downright unlucky—act to give them up. Andrew Jackson was among those who felt this way. In 1781, when he lost his beloved mother, Elizabeth, Jackson was unable to reclaim her body and give it a proper burial, and was long tormented by the fact. Jackson sought her remains for some time, but was unsuccessful.[13] Nathaniel Hawthorne, recognizing this theme so deeply rooted in the American experience, explored it in an 1832 story, "Roger Malvin's Burial," in which three generations of a New England family are affected by the sin one member commits when he leaves a companion to die alone in the woods, abandoning a solemn vow to return and inter the man's bones beneath the soil. "Return to this wild rock, and lay my bones in the grave," Roger Malvin urges Reuben Bourne, in the story, "and say a prayer over them."[14] But Bourne does not bury or mark the grave of his friend. The omission mars his life, and requires of him an extravagant price—his own son. The cost of an unmarked grave, we are to understand, is the steepest possible.

The significance of these primal passages of human existence in the Victorian period in America—good dying, proper burial—makes the lapse where the Angola Horror is concerned all the more striking. Once its era had ended, the wreck was not remembered. Many of its victims were not named, their grave was not marked. This did not happen by chance, or inexplicably. It happened because individuals and institutions and communities—the railroad, elected officials, average citizens—made choices over the decades not to remember in a public fashion what had happened at Big Sister Creek. There may have been many reasons, even strong ones, for this lack of action. But it meant on the most basic level that the victims of the Angola wreck became over the years invisible, forgotten. The Horror's dead were, in the end, failed by many.

ALMOST AS UNREMEMBERED as the names and fates of the victims at Angola was the story of the wreck—the facts of what happened on December 18, 1867. The narrative of the tragedy, writ both large and small, had been largely lost to history over the decades since it happened. There were several reasons for this lapse.

In Ashtabula, the first book about the train wreck, a detailed account by a local minister, Rev. Stephen D. Peet, that included interviews with eyewitnesses and rescuers, came out just eight weeks after the wreck occurred. This publication kept alive in the public mind the names of the Ohio wreck's victims, in a way that newspaper accounts could not. In Angola, no such book appeared. No firsthand written document captured the immediate emotion of the moment, nor preserved its details. Letters by and about Angola victims are scant; the Chadeayne family's letter, sent by a father worried about his wife and daughters and published in a local newspaper in Pennsylvania, is one of the few that exists. In scholarship and biography, there has been a similar dearth of material. A few mentions of the wreck, in books on American train wrecks, include brief summaries of what happened at Angola. (Even these passing references often get the basic facts of the disaster wrong, adding insult to the injury of failing to consider the wreck more closely.) The wreck is often misattributed to other railroad lines, because the Buffalo and Erie was in existence such a short time and later became part of bigger railroads. In some popular biographies of John D. Rockefeller Sr. and in Rockefeller's own memoirs, the fact that he escaped death on the New York Express receives no treatment at all.

Imagery and artifacts were other factors. In Ashtabula, photographs were taken of the wreck scene shortly after the crash. The Angola site and the scenes afterward in Buffalo were sketched, for a number of newspapers and news periodicals in 1867, by artists including J. H. Mills, but there was no photographic documentation of the wreckage. This fact is somewhat surprising because, by the time Angola occurred, train wrecks had been captured on film for at least a decade. At Ashtabula, a few enterprising souls set up small businesses turning smashed wood and other debris from the wreckage field into souvenirs like canes and walking sticks. At Angola, to the village's credit, nothing appears to have ever been commodified or sold—certainly nothing of this type survives down to the present day to bear witness to the disaster.

Today, the records at the local historical society in Evans contain some information and materials related to the wreck but not much. In many respects, you might never know the Horror had happened in the little village at all. Even longtime residents are sometimes surprised to learn about the tragedy that played out not far from their doors.

This remains a perplexing fact about the Angola Horror. Even in the places where you would expect to learn the most about it—the places where it occurred—the Horror is largely unknown. That has to do with something deeper than a lack of contemporaneous photographs, books, commemorative albums, and souvenirs. It has to do with the way individuals, communities, ultimately a nation, can allow an episode from the past to become forgotten—even when that episode was as close as possible to unbearable. The fact that Angola was gone for so long tells us something, not just of history, but of ourselves.

After the Horror

—◦◉◦—

John D. Rockefeller went on to become one of the richest men in the world.

Charles Lobdell, the newspaper editor, never made it to his Christmas wedding. But his memory lived on in the imaginations of those who knew him—and, perhaps, some who didn't. Six years after the wreck, in 1873, newspapers in the Midwest reported on a "Miss McDermot," a woman billing herself as a spiritualist medium, who supposedly contacted the spirit of Charles Lobdell and two other dead people during her reveries. The so-called medium, it was claimed, brought the former newsman to life in exchanges that were witnessed by numbers of people. In her shows, the performer channeled what were presented as Lobdell's memories of the Angola Horror. One midwestern newspaper described her words during one performance in this way: "Without moving from my seat, I closed my eyes and prayed to God that if I was to die then and there, my death might come speedily; that my home ones would not see me wounded, mangled, and suffering." The newspaper continued: "There was a shriek, a leap of the car, something struck me, as I remember like this (here the medium, with clenched fist, hit her head a stunning blow), and I neither felt or knew more of pain or life."[1] Lobdell's attitude toward the wreck, as presented by the purported medium, was pragmatic. "Well," the woman claiming to channel him said, "you know I always was what you called a fatalist."[2]

Henrietta Bennett and **Dr. Romaine J. Curtiss,** brought together while nursing victims in the early hours after the Horror, fell in love. They got married—but their marriage would not last long. The young woman known as "Etta" took ill and died before the couple's first wedding anniversary. Curtiss moved out of Angola a few years afterward. He would have a long, high-profile, and illustrious career as a railroad surgeon, health commissioner, and writer. Until his death in Illinois in 1900, Curtiss would complain of health problems that may have stemmed from his time in the military—including diarrhea and deafness.[3] When he died, a local newspaper in Joliet, Illinois, would report that Curtiss had waged a battle with addictions near the end of his life, perhaps as a way to control his pain.[4] Curtiss would struggle in particular with nightmares, some of them so terrible they left him pacing the floor at night, afraid to sleep.[5] "And then, when the delirium would seize him," the Joliet newspaper wrote of the doctor's last days, "he would arouse himself, and with his tallow light, wander about the rooms in the dead of night, rehearsing the events of his earlier life."[6]

Christiana Gates Lang recovered from her injuries and finished her journey to Vermont. She later remarried, and still later moved with her children to California. James Lang, twelve at the time of the train wreck, died in his mid-twenties. Mary Lang, Christiana's daughter, married the noted photographer Herve Friend.

Josiah Southwick and his wife, **Huldah,** moved to Montana in 1892. He died just before reaching his eighty-seventh birthday, in 1915. Huldah outlived him.[7]

J. M. Newton died in 1887, at age forty. He is buried in Forest Avenue Cemetery in Angola, not far from Henry Bundy, the Oatmans, the Tiffts, and other citizens of the village from the period of the disaster.

Josiah P. Hayward's remains were buried in the North East cemetery. Like the gravestones of many Angola victims, his makes no mention of the Angola disaster.

Walter H. Forbush, the son of Eliakim B. Forbush and his father's partner in law practice, died while aboard a train that wrecked at New Hamburgh, New York, in 1871.

Artist **John Harrison Mills** became one of Buffalo's most distinguished citizens. After a stint working as a reporter and illustrator under Mark Twain at the

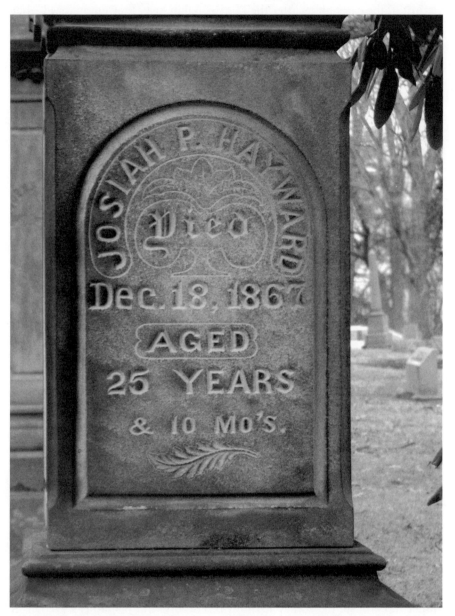

Some of the gravestones of victims of the Angola Horror mention the wreck; some do not. The marker memorializing young station agent Josiah Hayward in North East Cemetery, North East, Pennsylvania, makes no mention of Angola. Hayward died when he was pincered between the closing roof timbers of one car. He left a widow, Anna Shaw Hayward. Photograph by Todd Joseph Pignataro.

Buffalo Express, Mills carved out a business as a portrait painter and sculptor, creating works for many well-connected families on the East Coast. Mills designed a bronze commemorative tablet to the achievements of his Civil War unit, the Twenty-First Regiment New York State Volunteers. He died at age seventy-five—in the town of Evans, not far from Big Sister Creek, while vacationing at a friend's home.

The Buffalo and Erie Railroad became part of the Lake Shore and Michigan Southern Railway a little over two years after the wreck, on August 10, 1869. The Lake Shore and Michigan Southern would go on to become a powerful main line route from Buffalo to Chicago, stretching 540 miles. By 1886, the railroad would manage slightly more than 1 percent of the total rail mileage in the United States, employ 10,400 men on its roads, and move 10,180 passengers a day—3.7 million people a year.[8] The line would enjoy another twenty-nine-year run as a major American railroad, pioneering such iconic trains as the Twentieth Century Limited, before becoming part of an even bigger railroad operation—Cornelius Vanderbilt's New York Central.

Benjamin F. Sherman, before his death in February 1901, concluded a long tenure on the railroads of New York by stepping down from the post of conductor. His last responsibility on the railroad was a job in Buffalo's Exchange Street terminal—the site of the Horror's public funeral. There, Sherman finished his career, in relative obscurity, as a doorman.[9]

Author's Note

SOON AFTER MOVING to the rural areas south of Buffalo in 2002, I began to recall tidbits of lore I had heard as a child, while growing up on the Lake Erie shore in the town of Evans. I had dim recollections of having heard of a tragedy that had played out long ago at one of the creeks in the area. After asking questions of people I encountered, including some who had lived in Angola for a long time, I learned that there had been a train wreck at the railroad crossing over Big Sister Creek. Nobody, beyond that, seemed to know much. Most people who had even an inkling of the event had no idea when it occurred, or to what type of train, or with what result.

A few fortuitous conversations, with local historians, neighbors and friends, sparked my curiosity. Initial trips to the public library in Buffalo—and hours spent in front of microfilm readers, including once with a small troop of friends and neighbors—made me realize that many victims of the wreck had died at the bottom of Big Sister Creek. I learned from these newspaper accounts that some of the victims had been buried in Forest Lawn, a cemetery in Buffalo. Meeting with cemetery employees and historians led to investigations in the cemetery's records that revealed the location of the Horror gravesite, which, like the place in Angola where the wreck had occurred, was unmarked, seemingly forgotten.

Those first discoveries set me on a path of research that would open up avenues of investigation across the state and, indeed, around the country. The Angola Horror became a story that went much deeper and farther than I could have imagined. It became a project of years, not weeks or months. Uncovering a story so long buried—preserved for the most part in antique newspapers and magazines, and never really written about over the decades in any detail— presented numerous challenges and difficulties; the task was never easy, and the responsibility for any errors contained within this volume lies solely, in the end, with me. The Horror rewarded my persistence, however, by proving to be the best kind of story: more gripping and compelling with every twist and turn in the research, full of humanity and heart, and absolutely riveting as a dramatic narrative adventure.

My research was first published in partial form in a lengthy article in *American History* magazine, which appeared in February 2008. From that piece, the concept of this book grew.

From the start, my reasons for wanting to tell the story of the Angola Horror have been simple. I wanted to shed light on a chapter of Angola's history, and the nation's, that I felt had been ignored. I wanted to show why this train wreck, at the time and place it happened, mattered—to people in Angola, of course, but also elsewhere, throughout New York State and in small towns and big cities all over the country. I wanted to bring to light the names and faces, personalities and life stories, of some of the two hundred unfortunate men, women, and children who had climbed aboard the train that fateful day. I wanted, in the only way I knew how, to mark their graves.

UNCOVERING THE STORY of the Angola Horror involved research in well over sixty newspapers and periodicals published across the country and internationally during the 1860s and afterward.

These news accounts, and subsequent editorials calling for changes to American railroading, provided the framework for the book's narrative. Articles and illustrations in major periodicals including *Harper's Weekly, Kelley's Weekly,* and *Frank Leslie's Illustrated Newspaper* further fleshed out the details of the wreck. Material on individual passengers was gleaned from biographical and genealogical research at historical societies, public libraries, and archives, as well as through material from, and conversations with, many surviving descendants and family members.

Railroad company records and documents, material on the Buffalo and Erie Railroad, and state and federal legislation issues were tracked down to archives throughout the country, including the U.S. National Archives and Records Administration in Washington, D.C., and the Western Reserve Historical Society in Cleveland. In 2009, the Rockefeller Archive Center graciously allowed the author to conduct research on John D. Rockefeller Sr.

and his involvement in the Angola Horror in the archive's collections in Sleepy Hollow, New York. David Rockefeller was generous in responding to letters from the author during the early stages of work on this project. In 2010, a grant from the Individual Development Awards Program of the United University Professions organization at the State University of New York at Buffalo made possible research in the National Archives.

Material on George Westinghouse Jr., the Westinghouse family, and Westinghouse's invention of the air brake for railroad trains came from the Westinghouse Archive, located in the Heinz History Center and Historical Society of Western Pennsylvania in Pittsburgh, as well as from the Schenectady County Historical Society in Schenectady, New York. Staff members at both those institutions were indefatigably helpful during the research that went into this project. Family members of George Westinghouse Jr. were also extremely helpful with their time and material during the research, including George Westinghouse IV and John Simpson, who generously shared memories, Westinghouse family lore, unpublished photographs, news clippings, scrapbook items, and other documents with the author. They have been a delight to work with.

Descendants of those men and women directly involved with the wreck of the New York Express contributed in immeasurable ways to the research that went into this book. Family members of Josiah and Huldah Southwick, including direct descendant Diana M. Crippen and her husband, Jerry, helped flesh out the story of the Southwick family. James and Nelda L. Harris shared details of the lives of Christiana Gates Lang and her daughter, Mary Lang Friend, as well as photographs of and information about Mary's keepsake doll; Nelda is a direct descendant of the two women. Wendy K. Bolinger, a descendant of the Fisher family, shared information and valuable textual records about Alex, Andrew, Emma, and Minnie Fisher, including Minnie's diary. Diana Chester Dallosta, a direct descendant of Robert M. Russell, provided letters and other textual material about her family member, as well as an antique photograph of the cavalryman. Wendy Stevens, a relative of train passenger George W. Hayward, contributed thoughts and family history to the project. Ramsey B. McDaniel, a member of Jasper and Eunice Fuller's family, offered family historical records and photographs. Edna Sandell, a relative of Zachariah Hubbard, contributed material from her family's history. Elizabeth Dickson Sanders, a relative of Robert J. Dickson, shared family records, recollections, and a photograph of the engineer.

Other family members of Horror victims and survivors also shared their memories, documents, and photographs. Ann Riker, a descendant of Henry Bundy, and her husband, Chet Riker, allowed the author to use a vintage family photograph of Bundy. Mark Bouvier, who lives in the Angola house where Josiah Southwick lived in 1867, shared his deeds and title paperwork, old photographs of the home, and other material.

Wherever possible, events, actions, quotations, and dialogue in the narrative are taken directly from these sources, both published and unpublished. In some cases, no record of specific sequences of action, emotion, or thought survives, and in such cases the narrative is based upon educated conclusions drawn from research into the time, people, and places.

The village of Angola, which dates to the early 1800s for its first settlements, was not incorporated as a village by the state of New York until July 1873. I chose to describe Angola as a village throughout the text, however, as other language felt circuitous and inaccurate. Though Angola would not be a village in the technical sense for another six years, in 1867 it certainly was a village in population, in its importance as a railroad station in western New York, and in its sense of community.

WITHOUT THE HELP of many people, the story of the Angola Horror would have remained a tantalizing sliver of untold history. I owe all of them deep gratitude.

First on the list is my husband, Todd Joseph Pignataro. It is impossible to explain to anyone who has not written a research-intensive book what such an experience asks of a family. My wish for others is that they could know what it is like to have the kind of unstinting, open-hearted, cheerful support that I have enjoyed as I have worked on this book. T. J. is not only a talented reporter, he is a gifted photographer, and his collection of images that have accompanied the work on this book stand as a history-making record of their own. For years on end, with our young daughters, Mercy and Annabel, he good-humoredly agreed to turn family vacations into train-wreck-themed excursions, and weekend afternoons into chances to ride trains, talk to descendants, and dig through dusty newspapers and boxes of documents. T. J. built a website for the book as I labored to finish it; he created a social-media presence for the Horror project on Twitter and Facebook; he managed and supervised the art program and managed the many digital images that were eventually whittled down to what is included in this volume. He scoured eBay and booksellers for old books, artifacts, maps, and other one-of-a-kind items that made their way into the path of my research. He filled my desk drawer with timely infusions of peanut M&M's, and made me laugh when the work seemed too great. Along the way, he did the most important job: he never let me doubt that the story of the Horror needed to be told, and that I was the one to tell it. This book is his, and our daughters, as much as mine. Mercy and Annabel have lived much of their childhoods knowing this project, and both realize what it means to us as a family and to their hometown. They have been with us on every step of the research—from Ashtabula and Schenectady to Midtown Manhattan and Washington, D.C.—happily and with curiosity and enthusiasm. They will write books of their own, one day.

My father, Michael N. Vogel, the best and most effortless writer I know and a talented historian in his own right, read and offered comments on many drafts of the book over several years. He made the task seem manageable, and offered practical tips on how to put the story together. Most importantly, he encouraged me never to lose the drama and tension of the narrative that was the reason to tell the story in the first place. He's quite a role model, for a writer and daughter. My mother, Stasia Zoladz Vogel, an attorney, did me the greatest favor a child can hope to receive, by giving me an eclectic and inspired—not to mention rigorous—education, as a homeschooler and by founding a private school. She helped in invaluable ways with contractual and other matters, and provided constant encouragement. Rebecca Vogel Kruszka, my sister, has been my best friend and kindred spirit since childhood. She inspires me in countless ways every day, as we raise and educate children together, and her enthusiasm for the book kept me going in frustrating moments. My brother, Alex Vogel, a savvy and wide-ranging reader who cares about history and literature, made it possible for me to conduct a research trip via Amtrak by helping with transportation. My father-in-law and mother-in-law, Paul and Noreen Pignataro, took two trips to Pittsburgh, one in a snowstorm, to make it possible for me to do research and have help with child care. Family members Jason Kruszka, Anne and Jason Ciurzynski, and Jeannine and Tim Sheehan, also supported our family. Kathleen Vogel Mathews, my aunt and a former program coordinator at the Buffalo History Museum, not only supported the project with enthusiasm but also invited me to speak in that venue at an early stage, which helped sharpen the narrative. Other family members helped with time and support when competing work schedules and research agendas led to crazy days for our family. My aunt, Louise Zoladz, a generous and patient help in all we do, was a linchpin of our family life for many of the years that went into this book, giving kindly and without measure of her time, along with that of her husband, Victor Zoladz, to watch the girls, so the author could huddle up—and write. Their help was invaluable, and will never be forgotten.

The best thing about researching an event like the Angola Horror is the people you meet along the way—people who, more often than not, turn into good friends. Special thanks and appreciation in this vein go first and foremost to Edward P. Dibble, native Western New Yorker and talented researcher of

Buffalo's history, whose curiosity, persistence, and common sense (not to mention navigation skills on backwoods country roads) are without peer. Ed's enthusiasm for this project and skill at vetting old census and newspaper records—coupled with his willingness to drive just about anywhere to visit a forgotten grave or nail down a hard-to-find fact—continually revived my spirits, saving my sanity and making the book better in many ways.

Similar thanks go to Mary Soom, a savvy librarian at the University at Buffalo's Amherst campus who specializes in old newspapers and genealogy, and who spent hours doing dogged research into the lives of Christiana Lang and many other victims of the Angola wreck. Mary's hard work and her accessibility—she seems to answer every research question by e-mail within minutes, even while off-duty or on vacation—added immeasurably to the narrative's detail. Among other gems, it was Mary who uncovered the forgotten-about ballad about the "dead virgin" of Angola, and who turned up the tidbit of Mary Lang's prized doll.

Kevin Enser, a retired state trooper and Evans resident who is also a genealogist and history buff, contributed many insights into the lives of Angola residents of the Civil War period, lent the author books, shook family trees and dug up census information, and scouted for descendants who could be interviewed. Kevin also memorably warned the author to avoid writing about trains any more in the future, as she would be "typecast—and never get to do a musical."

When the book began to take shape, the skills of Michael J. McGandy, acquisitions editor at Cornell University Press, made it better in every way. Rarely does an editor blend such capabilities for line-by-line revision with an understanding of the big picture of a historical event. Michael's suggestions about the flow of the story and the themes of the narrative were spot-on, as were his suggestions for shaping individual chapters. From the first, he understood this book and why it was being written. The book would have been a poor shadow of itself without him. Also at Cornell, Sarah E. M. Grossman expertly handled many questions, and senior manuscript editor Karen T. Hwa improved the book with careful editing and guidance as it moved through its final revisions.

Many people have helped this project along, in museum, archive, and library settings, during the past several years. Librarians, archivists, railroad history buffs, and genealogists at the collections and institutions named below have the author's deep gratitude. Their brilliance and passion shines, hopefully, in this narrative. Any faults of the text are the author's own.

At the University at Buffalo libraries, these included Jill Ortner, Anne Bouvier, and the rest of the top-notch staff of the interlibrary loan department; Mike Lavin, in the area of business research; and Linda Lohr, a specialist in medical history. In Schenectady, resident Elizabeth Pieper provided valuable insight and guidance during the research into Westinghouse's early life, and also generously spent time looking up some news clippings for the author. Jean Metcalf provided the same local expertise in Ashtabula County, Ohio, at the Ashtabula County Historical Society; curator of the Jennie Munger Gregory Museum in Geneva-on-the-Lake, Jean also showed the author the sites associated with the wreck of the Ashtabula express, playing tour guide and patient listener to a train wreck fanatic from out of town.

Cynthia Van Ness and other staff members at the Buffalo History Museum were patient, helpful, and perpetually interested in the progress of the Horror project; Cynthia's vast knowledge of the people and places of nineteenth-century Buffalo added depth and color to the story. At the Buffalo & Erie County Public Library, library staff members including Peggy Skotnicki, Amy Pickard, Dawn Peters, Mary Jean Jakubowski, Joy Testa Cinquino, Jeane Lugris, and many others in both the library's regular collections and the Grosvenor Rare Book Collection handled questions about locating materials and citing footnotes with energy and skill. At the Angola branch library of the Buffalo & Erie County system, Mary Truby and other librarians provided access to microfilm copies of the hard-to-find *Angola Record*.

In Washington, D.C., staff members at the National Archives helped uncover research material related to nineteenth-century railroads, congressional reports on transportation, and legislative changes in the period, as well as individual victims' and rescuers' lives. Chris Killillay and Paul Harrison at the National Archives were particularly helpful in understanding the military records of men involved with the Angola wreck, including Dr. Romaine J. Curtiss and Gilbert W. Smith, and David Pfeifer provided overall assistance. Staff at the Historical Society of Western Pennsylvania at the Senator John Heinz History Center in Pittsburgh were also generous with their time and expertise, particularly Robert O. Stakeley, Art Louderback, and Ed Reis, a Westinghouse historian and former director of the Westinghouse museum, all of whom shared Westinghouse research material and family lore with enthusiasm and collegiality.

Ann K. Sindelar in the Western Reserve Historical Society helped untangle footnotes and citations for the Cleveland collection. At the Schenectady County Historical Society, staff members including Katherine Chansky in the Grems-Doolittle Library made investigations into the Westinghouse family enjoyable. Margaret Houghton, an archivist at the Hamilton Public Library in Canada, helped with research into the lives of victims from that area. At the Rockefeller Archive Center in Sleepy Hollow, Nancy Adgent, Kenneth W. Rose, Tom Rosenbaum, and many others provided expert assistance over the span of several years. Nancy was particularly helpful in the final stages of the project, with many questions about citations and footnotes.

Many people from all areas of the country offered their insights, advice, and guidance during this project. The names included here are but a portion of the many men and women who helped this effort along the way; each one of them is owed a deep debt of thanks. Among those who contributed material and support to this project: genealogy researcher Deanna Smith; Nick Zmijewski, collections manager at the Railroad Museum of Pennsylvania in Strasburg, part of the Pennsylvania Historical and Museum Commission, as well as Charles Fox, director of the Railroad Museum of Pennsylvania; Eric Robinson and others at the New-York Historical Society in New York City; Bill Petersen in the archives and local history room of the La Crosse Public Library in Wisconsin; Robyn Christensen, librarian in the Worcester Historical Museum in Massachusetts; Laura Katz Smith in the Dodd Collection at the University of Connecticut; Jacque Roethler in the Special Collections Department at the University of Iowa; staff members at the Syracuse University Library Special Collections Research Center; Ronald Brundage at the Conneaut Railroad Historical Museum in Ohio; John Bromley at the Union Pacific Railroad Museum and Historical Society in Council Bluffs, Iowa; staff librarians at the Joliet Public Library in Illinois; staff librarians and Sarah Greenburg at the Bridgeport public library in Connecticut; librarians at the city public library in Erie, Pennsylvania; librarians at the Utica, New York, public library; and Library and Archives Director Annita Andrick, Alice Henneberry, Tom Greene, and others at the Erie County Historical Society in Erie, Pennsylvania.

In Pennsylvania, the staff of the Meadville Historical Museum was helpful, and the knowledgeable Dick Tefft offered time and effort at both the North East Historical Society and also in Erie, in uncovering the lives of victims from those places. It was with Dick Tefft that we found the graves of Josiah P. Hayward and William H. Ross, and he explained the geography and landscape of the region. Heather Bijeck, collections manager at the Joliet Area Historical Museum in Joliet, Illinois, was instrumental in obtaining information about, and a rare photograph of, Dr. Romaine J. Curtiss.

Closer to home, librarians, archivists, rail fans, and historians throughout upstate New York and its environs gave generously of their time and enthusiasm to aid this project. The author regrets being able to name but some of them. Staff members at Forest Lawn cemetery in Buffalo, including Joseph P. Dispenza, the president of the cemetery, Edward P. Dibble, and Patrick B. Kavanagh, were unfailingly helpful and constructive in their support. Among others helping the project were Michelle Henry, Chautauqua County historian; Vincent P. Martonis, Hanover town historian; John Paul Wolfe,

Sandra Brown, and others at the McClurg Museum in Westfield and the Chautauqua County Historical Society; Marybelle Beigh, Westfield historian; Karen M. Kamery, Town of Portland historian, and the Town of Portland Historical Museum; Nancy Brown, curator of the Barker Museum in Fredonia, and Doug Shepard, an associate of the Barker Museum, for help with victim research. Local railroad aficionados including members of the Western New York Railway Historical Society and the Arcade & Attica Railroad in Arcade, New York, also offered feedback and educational materials and experiences to the author, including up-close examinations of the ways that train engines and braking systems work. Kavanagh, a researcher and tour guide at Forest Lawn, also shared his extensive knowledge of Rev. John C. Lord and other figures of mid-nineteenth-century Buffalo, as well as a rare text about the reverend.

In Angola and Evans, many residents have helped this project along with generous spirits and welcoming attitudes during the several years of its gestation. Not everyone who helped can be mentioned, but the author is thankful for all of their contributions. Karen and Mike Kennelly and their sons, Justin and Brandon, who live in Dr. Curtiss's former home, allowed access to their home for research purposes; Karen also handled the technical side of a presentation on the Horror made by the author at the New Angola Theatre, which was opened for the occasion by the Claddagh Commission. Mark Bouvier, owner of the former home of Josiah and Huldah Southwick at the time of this research, graciously opened his doors and brought out his deeds and title paperwork to help shed light on the Southwick family's time in the home. Cheryl Delano, William Haberer, Gifford Swyers, and other members of the Evans Historical Society were unfailingly kind and helpful. Timothy and Fran Dybdahl, along with Jim and Patty Pingitore and Jean and Tony Galfo, have made living in the area an ongoing pleasure; Tim and Fran also have provided old maps, newspapers, and other documents over the years to the author. Others who offered support, advice, and good ideas to this project included Kevin Siepel, Caryl Youngers, and Pete Mirando (author of what may be the first and only folk song about the Angola wreck). Angolan Marge Frawley, and her husband Howard "Hub" Frawley, the mayor of Angola, provided much neighborly support and enthusiasm for the book. Hub helped spearhead in 2008 the installation of the first signage to mark the place of the wreck site, the metal historical marker to the victims that now stands near the crash site. Joan Houston, an active Angola and Evans historian, and her husband William G. Houston, a longtime village board and school official, offered their encouragement and insight. Lake View resident and businessman Rob Nagel provided early insights on John D. Rockefeller, by pointing out a reference in a book he was reading; Rob has always been an enthusiastic supporter of a potential memorial or marker in both Angola and Forest Lawn.

Several members of the expert medical staff at the medical examiner's office in Erie County, New York, took time out of their busy schedules to meet with the author to discuss the effects of the Angola Horror on the bodies of its victims, and studied illustrations of the wreck and its aftermath in order to provide insight into the tragedy during the course of the research for this book. Former Erie County Commissioner of Health Dr. Anthony J. Billittier IV also provided support and guidance. Their commentary was invaluable in framing those chapters of the narrative, and these doctors and coroners have the author's deep gratitude. Lieutenant Michael Kaska of the Buffalo Police Department provided helpful insights into understanding the role and history of the Niagara Frontier police force, a predecessor of the Buffalo Police Department.

Before this book got under way, Robert Daly at the University at Buffalo, Martin Berger at the University of California at Santa Cruz, and John Gatta at Sewanee: the University of the South, took time out of their busy schedules to write letters of support for the project. Each of these three scholars has been an example of scholarship, intellectual curiosity, and personal generosity to the author for many years now—since dissertation days—and all have her deep gratitude for their ongoing mentoring and support.

The editors at *American History* magazine published a lengthy piece on the train wreck by the author in 2008, greatly helping the subject matter become a book. When the book was in its proposal stage, two anonymous outside readers offered Cornell their thoughts on the feasibility of the project and made excellent suggestions for reading and research avenues. These two, along with Amy Richter, a railroad historian who served as an outside reader in the final stages of the book's preparation along with one anonymous reader, are owed a debt of gratitude for their many savvy suggestions for concrete ways to make the book better. I am humbled by their kindness to a newcomer to the field.

Finally, *The Buffalo News* kindly allowed the author to take a six-month book leave to pursue research intensively in microfilm collections and out-of-town archives, and the University at Buffalo extended a sabbatical from teaching and advising duties for the period in which the book was in its final stages. Colleagues from both workplaces were perpetually interested in and supportive of this project, and have the author's deep indebtedness. Without such support, especially in the newsroom, this project would have taken many more years to finish.

During the course of this research, there were losses. Cheryl Delano, a longtime historian in Evans and Angola, and Ken Rose, who served as associate director of the Research and Education program at the Rockefeller Archive Center, both encouraged and aided this project in its infancy. Both passed away during the work toward its completion, and both will be missed.

Notes

PROLOGUE

1. Griswold, *Train Wreck!* 58.

2. *Times* of London, Jan. 11, 1868, p. 9.

3. J. David Hacker, "A Census-Based Count of the Civil War Dead," *Civil War History* 57, no. 4 (2011): 311.

4. Stover, *Life and Decline of the American Railroad*, 40.

5. Schivelbusch, *Railway Journey*, 131–34.

6. Smith, *Romance and Humor of the Road*, 215–16. This collection includes the poem "Dead—and No Name," about a supposed unidentified and unknown young female victim of the Angola wreck.

7. Daniel Chadeayne's letter was published in the *Titusville (Pa.) Morning Herald,* Dec. 24, 1867, p. 3.

8. Keith, *Fever Season*, 8–9.

9. Schivelbusch, *Railway Journey*, 131–34.

10. Aldrich, *Death Rode the Rails*, 91.

11. Ibid., 14.

12. The development of the automatic coupler and the time frame of the replacement of the link-and-pin coupler are described in Aldrich, *Death Rode the Rails*, 27–28.

13. Recollections of Harry French, originally published in *Railroadman* by Chauncey Del French, excerpted in Reinhardt, *Workin' on the Railroad*, 274.

14. *Harper's Weekly*, Sept. 23, 1865, p. 593. The idea of the locomotive as a vehicle for Death itself had been planted somewhat earlier. As early as 1843, Nathaniel Hawthorne had used the railroad and the conflicting emotional responses it elicited as the central metaphor for death and the soul's journey toward eternity in his story "The Celestial Rail-road." In Hawthorne's story, the railroad was a negative force, seeking to draw the human being away from what was good and secure. Hawthorne thus described trainmen as minions of Beelzebub, and called the engine, rather than a "laudable contrivance," a "mechanical demon" that would sooner "hurry us to the infernal regions." See Hawthorne, "Celestial Rail-road," in *Selected Tales and Sketches*, 319–20.

15. *Harper's Weekly*, Sept. 23, 1865, pp. 593, 600.

16. Whitman, "To a Locomotive in Winter," *Leaves of Grass*, 375.

17. Alcott, *Behind a Mask*, 92.

18. *Buffalo Daily Post*, Dec. 23, 1867, p. 2.

19. Reed, *Train Wrecks*, 28–29.

20. Shaw, *Down Brakes*, 377–78.

21. Griswold, *Train Wreck!* 28, 60, 95. Griswold's book, which presented capsule histories of the worst rail wrecks of the nineteenth and twentieth centuries, remains one of the more accurate of such compilations. Griswold cited the death toll for the 1856 wreck at Camp Hill, Pennsylvania, as sixty dead and sixty injured, and reported a toll of eighty-two killed and more than one hundred injured for the 1887 wreck at Chatsworth, Illinois. Of Ashtabula, a tricky wreck for which to gauge casualties, Griswold estimated that "at least 80 persons died…the figure was never more than approximate, and generally thought to be low."

1. TROUBLED SLEEP

1. An account of Josiah P. Hayward's dream appeared in news coverage of the Angola Horror in many newspapers around the country; here, material is taken from the version "Strange Dream and Its Fulfillment," which appeared in the *Nunda (N.Y.) Weekly News*, Feb. 8, 1868, p. 1.

2. These and all quotes for Hayward here are from the *Nunda (N.Y.) Weekly News*, Feb. 8, 1868, p. 1.

3. Ibid.

4. Ibid. Hayward's frequent return to the dream in conversation is noted in the newspaper article.

5. For the rush of American men in this period to employment in the railroads, see Burton, *Age of Lincoln*, 327.

6. The estimate of one-tenth of the adult population working in jobs on or connected to the American railroads is given in *Lake Shore and Michigan Southern Railway System*, 22.

7. For this commentary on the winter season of death and disaster, see the item headlined "Horrors!" in the "Our New York Letter" column in the *Boston Herald*, Dec. 21, 1867, p. 2.

8. Taylor, *Transportation Revolution*, 74, 85.

9. *Scientific American*, "Candles for Cars—the Kerosene Scare," March 7, 1868, p. 153.

10. Ibid.

11. Freeman, *Railways and the Victorian Imagination*, 13.

12. Ibid.

13. Locomotive names are from a locomotive roster (one page) of the Buffalo and Erie Railroad and the Buffalo & State Line Railroad, in the collection of the Railroad Museum of Pennsylvania in Strasburg, Pennsylvania Historical and Museum Commission.

14. Twain, *Innocents Abroad*, as quoted in Goodman, *Writing the Rails*, 43.

15. Ives, *Meteorological Observations at Buffalo*, vol. 2, *1858–1903*, month of December 1867.

16. For William Ives's remark about sleighing weather, see ibid.

17. "Melange" column, *Hamilton (Ont.) Evening Times*, Dec. 20, 1867, p. 2.

18. In its December 1867 issue, *Godey's Lady's Book* had suggested some of these items as gifts; see pp. 486 and 546.

19. For death tolls in the Civil War, see J. David Hacker, "A Census-Based Count of the Civil War Dead," *Civil War History* 57, no. 4 (2011): 311.

20. Whitman, "When Lilacs Last in the Dooryard Bloom'd," in *Leaves of Grass*, 270.

21. For the omnipresence of reading material on trains in this period, see Schivelbusch, *Railway Journey*, 66.

22. This editorial on Christmas in 1867 appeared in *Godey's Lady's Book*, December 1867, p. 543.

23. *Baltimore Sun*, Dec. 25, 1867, p. 2.

24. O'Malley, *Keeping Watch*, 65, 121. A railroad standard time regulating time all over the United States would not be adopted until 1883.

25. Buffalo clocks described, ibid., 82.

26. The story of J. Frank Walker's watch, and its subsequent fate, was described in the *New York Herald*, June 2, 1869, p. 15.

27. Quote about the "finny tribes" left flummoxed by the Niagara River occurrence is from the *St. Lawrence Republican and Ogdensburgh (N.Y.) Weekly Journal*, Dec. 31, 1867, p. 1.

28. Story about the Niagara River seiche of 1867 from the *Philadelphia Inquirer,* Dec. 20, 1867, p. 4.

29. Vogel, *Echoes in the Mist,* 54–55.

30. The earthquake was recounted in newspapers including the *Jamestown (N.Y.) Journal,* Dec. 27, 1867, and received coverage as far away as Philadelphia. Canadian reports of an earthquake on Dec. 18, 1867, were included in a piece called "Severe Shock of an Earthquake" in the *Hamilton (Ont.) Evening Times,* Dec. 18, 1867, p. 2.

31. *Buffalo Evening Post,* Dec. 20, 1867, p. 2.

32. *St. Lawrence Republican and Ogdensburgh (N.Y.) Weekly Journal,* Dec. 24, 1867, p. 4.

33. Length of the New York Express train on December 18, 1867, from the testimony of Fitch D. Adams during inquest proceedings; see *Buffalo Express,* Dec. 31, 1867, p. 2.

34. "The Nation Mourns: Buffalo and Erie Rail Road Special Time Table for Funeral Train Conveying the Remains of the Late President Abraham Lincoln, from Buffalo to Erie, Thursday, April 27, 1865," commemorative timetable, printed in 1865, from the collection of Vincent P. Martonis, Gerry, NY. With permission of Vincent Martonis. See also "Lincoln Funeral Train," in Hubbard, *Encyclopedia of North American Railroading,* 184.

35. "The Nation Mourns: Buffalo and Erie Rail Road Special Time Table for Funeral Train."

36. James Husted Diary, 1861, p. 1, Special Collections Research Center, Syracuse University Library, Syracuse, NY.

37. "Benjamin F. Sherman," *Buffalo Sunday Times,* Feb. 24, 1901, p. 19. See also the obituary for Sherman in the *Buffalo Express,* Feb. 21, 1901, p. 7, in which he is called one of the most familiar and well-known railroad men of the era.

38. Commentary about the windows on railroad passenger coaches of the late 1860s may be found in "Crystal Coaches for Railways," a letter published in *Scientific American,* Sept. 17, 1870, p. 180.

39. For the inscription on the gold wedding band worn by Mrs. Kent, see the *New York Times,* Dec. 29, 1867, p. 5.

40. For a news item about the trip of Morgan Kedzie, see the *Rochester (N.Y.) Evening Express,* Dec. 20, 1867, p. 1.

41. Lewis, Joseph Stocking, Report of the Class of 'Sixty-Four, 1865 Report, in *Alumni Notes, Class of 1864–65 Report,* compiled by F. G. Smedley, '64, secretary, p. 8. Williams College Archives and Special Collections, Williamstown, Mass. With permission of Williams College.

2. ANGOLA AT DAWN

1. Inquest testimony of J. M. Newton, *Buffalo Daily Courier,* Dec. 27, 1867, p. 3.

2. *Angola's History,* 9. See also Delano, *Evans and Angola,* 43.

3. *Angola's History,* 7.

4. Figures for the production of steel rails in the United States in the period may be found in the Lake Shore and Michigan Southern Railway Company's 1900 publication *Lake Shore and Michigan Southern Railway System and Representative Employees,* 19–20. For the assessment of Bessemer steel rails as a significant invention of the age, see "Bessemer Steel," in the *American Railroad Journal,* a reprint of an account originally in the *Albany Evening Journal,* May 18, 1867, 481.

5. Aldrich, *Death Rode the Rails,* 20. See also p. 31 for information on the timing of the introduction in the United States of steel rails, which Aldrich writes "remained experimental until about 1870."

6. Inquest testimony of James Mahar, *Buffalo Daily Courier,* Dec. 31, 1867, p. 8.

7. See "Trial Trip Was between Buffalo and Dunkirk Just after the Civil War—Last Ten Miles Made in 13 Minutes," in the *Buffalo Times,* June 9, 1907, n.p.

8. Aldrich, *Death Rode the Rails,* 54.

9. For information on youthful railroad employees, see ibid., 87–88. As for Newton, his father, J. R. Newton, a Freemason of high standing in Angola, would play a small role in the Ashtabula train wreck in 1876 when he ensured that the body of one victim, Boyd L. Russell, received transport on the railroad through Angola back to Russell's hometown of Auburn. See the *Auburn (N.Y.) Daily Bulletin,* Jan. 3, 1877, page unmarked.

10. Inquest testimony of J. M. Newton, *Buffalo Daily Courier,* Dec. 27, 1867, p. 3.

11. Material on the first settlers in the town of Evans may be found in Morrison, *Erie County, N.Y.*

12. Obituary for pioneer Evans settler Whiting Cash, in the *Buffalo Express,* Dec. 18, 1867, p. 1.

13. *Fredonia (N.Y.) Censor,* Dec. 25, 1867.

14. Buffalo History Museum Archives, Mss. W-5, Joseph Bennett, *Reminiscences and Diary,* pp. 37, 40–41.

15. Ibid.

16. Ibid.

17. Beauchamp, *Aboriginal Place Names of New York,* 268.

18. Item about Angola being "crowded with summer visitors—or, 'campers' as they are called," was printed in the *Angola Record,* July 3, 1879, p. 3.

19. *Angola's History,* 7.

20. Advertisement for Oatman's general store, in the first month's worth of editions of the *Angola Record,* May 29, 1879, p. 3.

21. Freeman, *Railways and the Victorian Imagination,* 78–79.

22. Schivelbusch, *Railway Journey,* 98.

23. O'Malley, *Keeping Watch,* 61.

24. *Angola's History,* 7.

25. For Romaine J. Curtiss's account of his military experiences in the Union army and navy, see his obituary, which includes biographical material provided by the doctor himself, in the *Joliet (Ill.) Daily Republican,* Nov. 20, 1900, p. 6.

26. See letter by Dr. Romaine J. Curtiss, "Voice of the People" column, *Chicago Tribune,* July 14, 1899, p. 10.

27. For Dr. Romaine J. Curtiss's experiences with procedures in which women's uteruses were manipulated and cervixes incised in order to ease gynecological complaints, see Romaine J. Curtiss, MD, "Thirteen cases of sterility and dysmenorrhoea, caused by abnormalities of the uterus," *Medical & Surgical Reporter* (Philadelphia), July 3, 1875, pp. 1–4. For descriptions in Curtiss's own words of his manipulations of female patients, using shock and other techniques to restore fertility and gynecological health, see Romaine J. Curtiss, MD, "Nervous Shock as a Therapeutical Agent," *Saint Louis Medical and Surgical Journal* 42, no. 2 (February 1882): 119–247.

28. Bryson, *At Home,* 301.

29. For a sample of Dr. Romaine J. Curtiss's views on germs and hygiene theory, see the *Chicago Tribune,* July 14, 1899, p. 10. For his beliefs and arguments about the deleterious effects of Chicago sewage in the waterways of the Midwest, see Romaine J. Curtiss, MD, "Chicago Sewage and Its Sanitary Relations to the Public," *Saint Louis Medical and Surgical Journal* 40, no. 5 (May 1881): 611–17; as well as Romaine J. Curtiss, MD, "The Hygiene of Nature or the Relation of Immunity from Disease to Natural Selection," *Annals of Hygiene* 1 (July 1884): 313–17. In his article "Cholera and Chicago Sanitation," *Saint Louis Medical and Surgical Journal* 49 (September 1885): 146–50, Curtiss grows strident about the issue, writing this: "People who drink their own sewage are always to be pitied. It is one of the saddest of all social phenomena when a free citizen, of a free country, is so situated that his cup of cold water, even if it is a charitable cup, is tainted with the giver's excrement."

30. For Romaine J. Curtiss's public letter to Andrew Carnegie, see "A Thousand Years of Life," *Chicago Tribune,* July 14, 1899, p. 10.

31. Ibid.

32. For the description of Curtiss's mind as "one of the most brilliant…in the west," see the *Joliet (Ill.) Daily Republican,* Nov. 20, 1900, p. 6.

33. Romaine J. Curtiss, MD, "Ethical Myopia," *Saint Louis Medical and Surgical Journal* 46 (March 1884): 238–45.

34. For this anecdote, recalled by Curtiss a few years later, see Romaine J. Curtiss, MD, "The Ideal Medical Education," in the *New England Medical Monthly* 4 (1884): 404–11.

35. Romaine J. Curtiss, MD, "Medical Empiricism, Homoeopathy and Codes," *Saint Louis Medical and Surgical Journal* 45 (July 1883): 18–27.

36. Inquest testimony of James Mahar, *Buffalo Daily Courier,* Dec. 31, 1867, p. 8.

3. GETTING UNDER WAY

1. Expenditures on shoe repair and other household expenses by John D. Rockefeller and the Rockefeller family, in the fall and winter of 1867–68, as noted in John D. Rockefeller Sr.'s Ledger B, p. 107, Series F—Financial, Record Group 1—John D. Rockefeller Papers (hereafter JDR Papers), Rockefeller Family Archives, Rockefeller Archive Center, Sleepy Hollow, N.Y. (hereafter RAC).

2. Rockefeller, *Random Reminiscences,* 49. This book is based on interviews that Rockefeller gave to the magazine *World's Work* for a series of articles beginning in 1908.

3. Stover, *Life and Decline,* 36.

4. Costs and details of the Rockefellers' honeymoon tour, as noted in John D. Rockefeller Sr.'s Ledger B, p. 50, Series F—Financial, Record Group 1—JDR Papers, Rockefeller Family Archives, RAC.

5. Costs and details of the trip by the Rockefeller family to New York City in July 1867, Ledger B, p. 139, Series F—Financial, Record Group 1—JDR Papers, Rockefeller Family Archives, RAC.

6. Rockefeller, *Random Reminiscences,* 52.

7. Hawke, *John D.*, 54–58.

8. Goulder, *John D. Rockefeller,* 82.

9. For figures on the earnings of average workers during this period in U.S. history, see U.S. Bureau of the Census, *Statistical History of the United States,* 165.

10. Costs of the Rockefellers' 1867 Christmas gifts, as outlined in Ledger B, p. 139, Series F—Financial, Record Group 1—JDR Papers, Rockefeller Family Archives, RAC.

11. For the cost of John D. Rockefeller's 1867 train trip, Erie-to-Buffalo portion, see *Annual Report of the State Engineer,* 236.

12. Background about the clothing and underclothing of women and men in the 1860s may be found in Severa, *Dressed for the Photographer,* 185–212.

13. The traditional Victorian-era mourning period of two and a half years for women who had lost a spouse or child is noted in Faust, *This Republic of Suffering,* 147–49.

14. Weather data for the period may be found in Ives, *Meteorological Observations at Buffalo,* vol. 2, *1858–1903,* month of December 1867.

15. News of the boats frozen in on the Erie Canal and their cargoes reported in the *Boston Herald,* Dec. 19, 1867, p. 4.

16. *Buffalo Express,* Dec. 18, 1867, p. 1.

17. *Hamilton (Ont.) Evening Times,* Dec. 26, 1867, p. 3.

18. Details about Elam Porter's intended may be found in "Sequel to the Angola Disaster," in *Vermont Chronicle,* Feb. 8, 1868, p. 2.

19. Information about Elam Porter's class at Tufts College was provided by the institution. For Porter's transcripts, see Matriculation Book, Tufts College, ca. 1854–75, Artifact Collection, ca. 2500 BC–, box 36, Digital Collections and Archives, Tufts University, as well as Matriculation Book, Tufts College, ca. 1862–69, Artifact Collection, ca. 2500 BC–, box 37, Digital Collections and Archives, Tufts University. The quote by Porter comes from a sermon delivered about him on December 29, 1867, in Stoughton, Mass., by Rev. A. St. John Chambre. The sermon, called "In Memoriam of Elam Porter, Esq.," is located in the New-York Historical Society in Manhattan. See p. 7.

20. Lobdell's father is cited as the earliest printer to make a living at the trade in the state in the *Bridgeport (Conn.) Daily Standard,* March 24, 1882.

21. Edward W. Green's crime is recognized as the first bank robbery by a U.S. citizen by Bryan Burrough in *Public Enemies: America's Greatest Crime Wave and the Birth of the FBI, 1933–34* (New York: Penguin Press, 2004), 15. Others qualify it as the country's first bank murder and robbery excluding military actions. In *Wanted! Wanted Posters of the Old West and Stories behind the Crimes,* by Barbara Fifer and Martin Kidston, Green's crime is called the "first armed bank robbery" in the nation (Helena, MT: Farcountry Press, 2004), 6.

22. Clara Green's letter begging for clemency for her husband was printed in the *Boston Daily Advertiser,* June 11, 1864, p. 1. For more on her state of "agony" upon her husband's arrest, see the *Lowell (Mass.) Daily Citizen & News,* Feb. 8, 1864, p. 1.

23. For information on the Chapman-Green engagement, see the *Vermont Chronicle,* Feb. 8, 1868, p. 2.

24. Alexander E. Fisher's wedding plans were described in the *Potsdam (N.Y.) Courier and Freeman,* Jan. 2, 1868, p. 3.

25. *Thomas' Buffalo City Directory for 1867* (Buffalo: Thomas, Howard & Johnson, 1867), advertisement for "Forbush Patent Agency," p. 142.

26. Story from Cleveland about misplaced and lost baggage, as reprinted in the *Utica Morning Herald,* Jan. 1, 1868, p. 1.

27. The essay on too-late-to-the-train passengers may be found in Taylor, *World on Wheels,* 110. If amusing to onlookers, these tardy passengers were not so funny to the railroads, for passengers who ran after trains and tried to jump aboard them were not just silly—they were dangerous. "Many who sprinted did not make it," wrote one recent historian, Mark Aldrich, who noted that American railroads were much more open to this sort of danger since they left stations unfenced, used cars with doors and platforms at each end, and allowed passengers to buy tickets from the conductor—meaning a passenger late to the station could sprint after a departing train without impediment. In the early 1850s, Aldrich calculated, more rail passengers in the United States died trying to jump on or off cars—or falling from them—than from collisions and derailments put together. See Aldrich, *Death Rode the Rails,* 19.

28. The "I've Got Your Trunk" illustration is in Taylor, *World on Wheels,* 110.

29. The *Cleveland Herald* first printed a story on John D. Rockefeller's narrow miss of the New York Express in the aftermath of the wreck, on Dec. 20, 1867, p. 4. A version of this story was picked up and run, under the headline "Providential," in the *Buffalo Evening Courier & Republic,* Dec. 23, 1867, p. 3. The stories include differing details, so there may have been another wire story circulating about Rockefeller that the Buffalo paper used in preparing its report.

4. EN ROUTE

1. Measurements of the Ashtabula bridge and its date of opening are taken from Rev. Stephen D. Peet's 1877 book, *The Ashtabula Disaster,* 13–15. In coverage of the bridge disaster in the *Ashtabula News,* Jan. 3, 1877, p. 1, a few facts differ slightly: the span of the bridge is put at 155 feet and its year of construction 1864.

2. Peet, *Ashtabula Disaster,* 14.

3. The bridge as Amasa Stone's "crowning achievement" is taken from Charles A. Burnham, "The Ashtabula Horror," in Corts, *Bliss and Tragedy,* 91–92, 111.

4. An explanation of how the Ashtabula bridge was considered an "experimental" structure may be found in Darrell E. Hamilton's essay "Almost the Perfect Disaster," in Corts, *Bliss and Tragedy,* 1. This assessment is backed up by Peet, *Ashtabula Disaster,* 16–17. The cost of the bridge is reported in the essay "In Search of the Story," by David G. Tobias, in Corts, *Bliss and Tragedy,* 134.

5. For the changes in weaponry during the Civil War, including the development of the long-range, breech-loading rifle, see Faust, *This Republic of Suffering,* 39–42.

6. Details about Amasa Stone's death from "A Millionaire's Suicide; Lamentable Death of Amasa Stone, of Cleveland," in the *New York Times,* May 12, 1883, p. 1. Commentary about Stone becoming a "harassed and tragic figure" in his later years comes from Goulder, *John D. Rockefeller,* 159.

7. Advertisement for the Owatonna Marble Works, *Owatonna (Minn.) Journal,* Jan. 23, 1868, p. 5.

8. For context on the expectations and restrictions affecting women riding the rails as passengers in this period, see Richter, *Home on the Rails,* 6–7. Among other themes, Richter notes this: "When women boarded railroad cars, they entered cultural conversations about social difference, racial dominance, and order."

9. For the moons and tides of March 1867, see *The (Old) Farmer's Almanack, Calculated on a New and Improved Plan, for the Year of Our Lord 1867* (Boston: Brewer & Tileston, 1867), 10–11.

10. Diary of Minnie Fisher, in the possession of the Fisher family, p. 1. Courtesy of Wendy Bolinger and the Fisher family.

11. Biographical details about Christiana Gates Lang, including information about the death of Robert Lang and her decision to move west, may be found in the *Vermont Chronicle,* Jan. 25, 1868.

12. A description of the death of Annie Lang may be found in the article on Christiana Gates Lang in the *Vermont Chronicle,* Jan. 25, 1868.

13. The omnipresence of tobacco spit on American railcars can be found in accounts of passenger car conditions of the period, including Mencken, *Railroad Passenger Car,* 14–15.

14. This assessment of the cleanliness of railroad coaches was made by Alfred Bunn in *Old England and New England* (London, 1850), and is excerpted in Mencken, *Railroad Passenger Car,* 115–17.

15. This popular joke about tobacco on trains in the Civil War period was published in the *Owatonna (Minn.) Register,* Dec. 18, 1867, p. 3.

16. Average rates of speed for express and non-express passenger trains, with and without stops, as operated by the Buffalo and Erie Railroad in 1867, may be found in the New York State engineer's report for that year: see *Annual Report of the State Engineer,* 236.

17. Martin and Hirst, *Mark Twain in Buffalo,* 27.

18. *Godey's Lady's Book,* December 1867, pp. 553–54.

19. Mencken, *Railroad Passenger Car,* 43.

20. Charles Richard Weld, *A Vacation Tour in the United States and Canada* (London, 1855), excerpted in Mencken, *Railroad Passenger Car,* 118–22.

21. For contemporary passengers' accounts of the delicacy involved in picking seats near the car stove, see Mencken, *Railroad Passenger Car,* 106–8.

22. The "pestiferous decoction" of spat tobacco all over American trains is described by Alexander Mackay's *The Western World; or, Travels in the United States in 1846–47 (London, 1850),* excerpted in Mencken, *Railroad Passenger Car,* 104–11.

23. From an editorial, "The Tragedy of Travel," in *Harper's Weekly,* Jan. 11, 1868, p. 18.

24. The change from flat or arched roofs to raised clerestory roofs is described in detail in White, *American Railroad Passenger Car,* part 1, 26–30.

25. That the Buffalo and Erie Railroad's train that day offered clerestory roofs can be concluded from the eyewitness testimony of Angola resident Alanson Wilcox before the inquest jury, as quoted in the *Buffalo Daily Courier* of Dec. 28, 1867, p. 8. Wilcox testified about the "raised deck" on the cars, through which he saw people try to crawl.

26. "Lighting Cars," letter to *Railway Times* magazine, signed "Shawmut," published in *Railway Times* on Feb. 1, 1868, p. 39.

27. Mencken, *Railroad Passenger Car,* 23.

28. This account of an 1880 trip, by C. B. Berry, is excerpted in Mencken, *Railroad Passenger Car,* 173–74.

29. Ibid.

30. This hot-water heating system in use on some American railcars on a trial basis in the winter of 1867–68 is described in a letter from the inventor, W. C. Baker, titled "Heating Cars," in *Railway Times,* Feb. 22, 1868, p. 58.

31. From an editorial, "Heating Railway Cars," in *Railway Times,* Jan. 11, 1868, p. 14.

32. From F. Barham Zincke, *Last Winter in the United States* (London, 1868), excerpted in Mencken, *Railroad Passenger Car,* 143–44.

5. DELAYS

1. The words Conductor Benjamin F. Sherman would have used to call passengers to the New York Express may be gleaned from contemporary accounts, including the "Conductor's Gossip" section of Stephe R. Smith's 1871 book, *Romance and Humor of the Road,* p. 62. "All aboard" was a phrase in common use at this time.

2. The tardiness of the express's departure from Erie was detailed by multiple railroad officials during the official inquest into the wreck. The testimony of John Desmond, assistant superintendent of the Buffalo and Erie Railroad, on this matter may be found in the *Buffalo Daily Courier,* Dec. 27, 1867, p. 3.

3. For Benjamin F. Sherman's reputation for "personal humor" in the execution of his duties as a conductor, see his obituary in the *Buffalo Express,* Feb. 21, 1901, p. 7.

4. For rules for the conductors of passenger trains during this period, see Lake Shore and Michigan Southern Railway Co., *Rules and Regulations*, p. 18.

5. See Benjamin F. Sherman's obituary in the *Buffalo Express*, Feb. 21, 1901, p. 7.

6. Details of the ladies' parlor waiting room in Erie's 1866 Union Depot, as well as about the matron employed by the railroads to help female travelers, can be found in the *Erie Business Directory for 1867–68, Comprising a List of All Residents and an Historical Sketch of the Place, together with Statistical and General Information, and the Advertisements of the Most Prominent Business Houses of Erie* (Erie, Pa.: Lynn & Co., 1867), 30–32. In the collection of the Erie County Historical Society, Erie, Pa.

7. Details on the plans and movements of Norman and Arila Nichols may be found in the *Daily Cleveland Herald*, Feb. 7, 1868, p. 2.

8. Worcester resident Simeon E. Thompson's death was noted in the *Boston Herald* of Dec. 21, 1867, p. 2. The travel plans and backgrounds of the Thompson siblings, Simeon D. and Lizzie E., come from the *Worcester Evening Gazette*, December 20, 1867. See also the *Buffalo Daily Courier* for material on Simeon Thompson from Boston newspapers, including Dec. 24, 1867, p. 4.

9. For the nickname "car knockers" for men with this job, see Hubbard, *Railroad Avenue*, 336.

10. Inspectors' checks of the wheels and axles in the moments before the departure of the New York Express from Erie may be found in the inquest testimony, including that in the *Buffalo Daily Courier*, Dec. 28, 1867, p. 8.

11. For use of the terms "captain" and "skipper" for railroad conductors starting with the Civil War period, see Hubbard, *Railroad Avenue*, 336.

12. Wilder, *By the Shores of Silver Lake*, 17.

13. Taylor, *World on Wheels*, 67.

14. *Buffalo Express*, Feb. 21, 1901, p. 7.

15. Material on the role and conduct of conductors is taken from Lake Shore and Michigan Southern Railway Co., *Rules and Regulations*, 16. This example of a conductors' rulebook from the post–Civil War period is in the collection of the Western Reserve Historical Society in Cleveland. It is a good guide to what rules and regulations Benjamin F. Sherman would have been operating under on December 18, 1867; conductors' materials of the Buffalo and Erie Railroad do not appear to survive. The Lake Shore and Michigan Southern was the road that the Buffalo and Erie Railroad was absorbed into by 1881.

16. "Order of Railway Conductors," in Hubbard, *Encyclopedia of North American Railroading*, 245.

17. The three are referred to as among Erie's "most promising" young men in the *Erie (Pa.) Observer* of Dec. 26, 1867.

18. See enrollment rolls of Erie's First Presbyterian Church for the 1860s, in the collection of the Erie County Historical Society. Courtesy of the Erie County Historical Society, Erie, Pa.

19. The name of J. Alexander Marten is given as "Martin" in some contemporary newspaper accounts, as well as in some census records of the period. However, church registers in Erie give the spelling of his last name as "Marten." Since the church members likely knew Marten personally, the author decided to take their spelling of his surname as the most accurate version obtainable. (Newspaper accounts and census reports in the nineteenth century often contained misspellings, as names were often spelled phonetically or were transcribed by takers with uncertain spelling abilities.) In many cases of such uncertainty, the final answer as to a person's name is generally available on a tombstone. However, Marten had no tombstone in the Erie city cemetery that could be located during the research for this book.

20. For Marten traveling to visit his sick mother, see the *Erie (Pa.) Observer* of Dec. 26, 1867. Marten's book and money are noted in the *Crawford (Pa.) Democrat*, Dec. 28, 1867, p. 1.

21. Details of the construction, cost, and interior fittings of Erie's 1866 Union Depot are described in the *Erie Business Directory for 1867–68*, 30–32. The cost of the building had been split by the two railroads feeding the site, the Buffalo and Erie and Cleveland & Erie lines.

22. This quote about the imitation sandstone used for Erie's 1866 Union Depot may be found in the *Erie Business Directory for 1867–68*, 30–31.

23. Claims about Erie's 1866 Union Depot rivaling the depots that were being built in the American West may be found in the *Erie Business Directory for 1867–68*, 30–31.

24. Stover, *American Railroads*, 88–89.

25. For details on the gauge-width wars and the resultant inconveniences for passengers traveling in New York and Pennsylvania, see Lake Shore and Michigan Southern Railway Co., *Lake Shore and Michigan Southern Railway System and Representative Employees*, 56.

26. For details on the course of the Erie Gauge War, see Kent, "Erie War of the Gauges," 253–75. For reference to the conflict as the "Peanut War," see 254–55.

27. For the comment about the region's gauge problem as a "fish-bone" in the gullet, see Leland, "History of the Lake Shore and Michigan Southern Railway," 351.

28. Hubbard, *Encyclopedia of North American Railroading*, 112–13.

29. Kent, "Erie War of the Gauges," 261–62.

30. Horace Greeley's experience in Erie and his reflections on it in the *New York Tribune* can be found in Kent, "Erie War of the Gauges," 261–62.

31. Details of the Erie Railroad War may be found in Hubbard, *Encyclopedia of North American Railroading*, 112–13. The date of the first successful run at the newly installed gauge width in February 1854 is from Leland, "History of the Lake Shore and Michigan Southern Railway," 351.

32. The *Buffalo Courier*'s account of the merger was reprinted in the *Railway Times* periodical shortly afterward: see "Buffalo and Erie Railway," *Railway Times*, July 20, 1867, p. 230.

33. Ibid.

34. In practical terms, the combination of these two railroads into one longer line didn't cause much upheaval in the way the lines operated; they had been under a united management system for almost fourteen years before the merger.

35. Lake Shore and Michigan Southern Railway Co., *Lake Shore and Michigan Southern Railway System and Representative Employees*, 56.

36. Dunn, *History of Railroads in Western New York*, 46–47.

37. Details about this "teasing and drumming" for seed money for the fledgling Buffalo & State Line road may be found in Leland, "History of the Lake Shore and Michigan Southern Railway," 349. Leland notes that most people who gave money to start the line marked it down in their ledger books as a loss; but, he purports, "no more profitable 68 miles of road was ever constructed in the world than was this."

38. For the official gauge of the Buffalo & State Line Railroad, as well as the gauge of the New York Central, see Poor, *Manual of the Railroads of the United States, for 1868–69*, 35–38, 241; as well as Ashcroft, *Railway Directory for 1867*, 31, 142–43.

39. For the earnings of the railroads in their first years, see Lake Shore and Michigan Southern Railway Co., *Lake Shore and Michigan Southern Railway System and Representative Employees*, 57.

40. For payment to Samuel Bevier of Silver Creek for his heifers, see the cash book of the Buffalo & State Line Railroad from November 1856, vol. 4, reel 1, p. 16; for payment to a local farmer for the sixteen slain sheep, see cash book of the Buffalo & State Line Railroad from October 1857, vol. 5, reel 1, p. 111. Both are in the collection of the New York State Library, Albany.

41. For ledger accounts of the payment of a $500 settlement to "Senior Devino" and his troupe, see the cash book of the Buffalo & State Line Railroad from July 21, 1865, vol. 10, reel 4, no page number, in the collection of the New York State Library, Albany.

42. "Steam Boiler Explosions," *Railway Times*, June 2, 1860, p. 212.

43. Ibid.

44. The incident badly damaged the Vulcan and killed a fireman employed by the Buffalo & State Line, F. J. Matteson. Two years later, the railroad made a $75 payment to Matteson's widow. At the time, it didn't have to; as John Fabian Witt showed in his study of workplace injuries in nineteenth-century America, in this period before workman's insurance or compensation, American companies were under no obligation to pay any amount to surviving family members of injured or killed workers. In fact, common law of the era, Witt wrote, "generally required an injured employee to prove that an injury was caused by the employer's negligence." For the case of Mrs. F. J. Matteson and the "gratuity" paid to her in 1858, see the cash book of the Buffalo & State Line Railroad from October 1858, vol. 5, reel 1, p. 221, in the collection of the New York State Library. Also see Witt, *Accidental Republic*, 3.

45. "Steam Boiler Explosions," *Railway Times*, June 2, 1860, p. 212.

46. Aldrich, *Death Rode the Rails*, 91.

47. Information on the careers of Benjamin F. Sherman and his crew members in the *New York Times*, Dec. 30, 1867, p. 1. Sherman's assessment of Charles Carscadin, ibid.

48. John H. White, "George Westinghouse," in Frey, *Railroads in the Nineteenth Century*, 430–36.

49. Newspapers of the day contain some discrepancies regarding the identity of Gilbert W. Smith, the train's forward brakeman. Some newspapers gave a different hometown for Smith. However, the consensus of more reliable Buffalo papers, including the *Buffalo Daily Courier* and *Buffalo Patriot and Journal*, was that Smith was from Irving; coverage in the *New York Times* also called him an Irving resident. Thus the research for this book concluded that this Gilbert W. Smith was the train brakeman. Information on Gilbert W. Smith's military service, physical appearance, and occupations are taken from Smith's Civil War military records and pension applications, National Archives and Records Administration, Washington, D.C., Record Group 94, Records of the Adjutant General's Office, 1780s–1917, Entry 519 Compiled Military Service Records.

50. Lonn, *Desertion during the Civil War*, 150–51.

51. This statement, signed by Smith, was part of his civil court proceedings in Chautauqua County over the charge of desertion. It is in Smith's Civil War military records and pension applications, National Archives and Records Administration, Washington, D.C., Record Group 94, Records of the Adjutant General's Office, 1780s–1917, Entry 519 Compiled Military Service Records.

52. Licht, *Working for the Railroad*, 191.

53. The car composition of the New York Express train between Erie and Angola was detailed by various officers of the Buffalo and Erie Railroad during the official inquest into the crash. Railroad officials' and crew members' accounts include some discrepancies about the makeup of the train. But most if not all agreed that the last two cars of the train that day were not Buffalo and Erie coaches. In this narrative, the testimony of Benjamin F. Sherman as to the consist of the train on Dec. 18, 1867, is used as likely the most reliable and accurate account, as Sherman was the conductor charged with overseeing the operation and makeup of the express train that day. Sherman stated in court testimony that the train's last three cars belonged to the Cleveland and Toledo and Cleveland and Erie railroads, and that the Erie car was between the two Toledo cars on the back end of the train. The second-class coach belonged to the Buffalo and Erie Railroad, according to Sherman's testimony in court. The three baggage cars still on the train at Angola were all Buffalo and Erie cars, Sherman also testified. For Benjamin F. Sherman's testimony about the train's composition, see inquest testimony printed in the *Buffalo Daily Courier*, Dec. 28, 1867, p. 8. For John Desmond's testimony on this point, see the *Buffalo Daily Courier*, Dec. 27, 1867, p. 3.

54. Car interchange during this period is discussed in Aldrich, *Death Rode the Rails*, 65.

55. Benjamin F. Sherman made this statement during the official inquest into the causes of the accident; his comment may be found in the *Buffalo Daily Courier*, Dec. 28, 1867, p. 8.

56. The noteworthy low temperature was recorded at Mayville on Thursday, December 19, 1867, and noted in the *Fredonia (N.Y.) Censor* of Dec. 25, 1867.

6. APPROACH

1. Benjamin F. Betts's account of his trip on the New York Express on Dec. 18, 1867, can be found in inquest testimony, including that published in the *Buffalo Daily Courier*, Dec. 27, 1867, p. 3.

2. The plight of Mary Chadeayne, the wife of Daniel Chadeayne, and her daughters Anna and Carry is recounted in the *Titusville Morning Herald*, Dec. 24, 1867, p. 3.

3. The selection of the "Salem Cross Roads" name in 1834, by a settler pulling the title from a hat, is described in Kurtz, *Brocton and Portland*, 27.

4. Statistics on the town of Portland in this period may be found in J. H. French's *Gazetteer of New York State* (1860), Chautauqua County section, p. 217. This document drew on the quinquennial New York State census of 1855, among other sources.

5. George Mortimer Pullman's roots in Brocton, as well as his accomplishments in 1867, including incorporating the Pullman Palace Car Company and unveiling the hotel car "The President," are described in Husband, *Story of the Pullman*, 24–25, 47–52.

6. The story of the formation of the name "Brocton" is recounted in various sources, including Kurtz, *Brocton and Portland*, 27.

7. Railroad service to Brocton in 1910 is outlined in an advertisement card reproduced in Kurtz, *Brocton and Portland,* 37.

8. Reports of stranded passengers in Brocton being treated to dinner parties and sleigh rides can be found in local newspapers, including the *Fredonia (N.Y.) Censor* of Jan. 29, 1868.

9. The movements of Benjamin C. Aikin and W. C. Patterson from Hydetown to Brocton on Dec. 18, 1867, were traced in local papers, including the *Titusville (Pa.) Morning Herald,* Dec. 24, 1867, p. 3.

10. Detail on the Oil Creek Railroad and Buffalo, Corry and Pittsburg [*sic*] Railroad from Poor, *Manual of the Railroads of the United States, for 1868–69,* 273–74, 370. In many newspaper accounts of the disaster, including in some obituaries, Steward is described as president of the Oil Creek Railroad. However, Poor's manual does not show Steward as an officer of the Oil Creek Railroad in that year, nor does the other major railway directory used in 1867, *Ashcroft's Railway Directory for 1867.* Newspapers of the day may well have gotten the name of the Oil Creek road confused with that of the Buffalo and Oil Creek Cross-Cut, which was folded during this period into the Buffalo, Corry and Pittsburg Railroad. But, in any case, Steward was a director of that railroad line in 1867, and not the line's president. He had good company, however, as William G. Fargo of Buffalo, former mayor of the city and a founder of the American Express Company, was both president of the Buffalo, Corry and Pittsburg road and one of its directors in 1867.

11. The meeting of Benjamin Betts and banker Stephen W. Steward in Brocton while waiting for the train is described by Betts in his inquest testimony, *Buffalo Daily Courier,* Dec. 27, 1867, p. 3.

12. Stephen W. Steward's choice of the last seat in the last car is recounted in the *Titusville (Pa.) Morning Herald,* Dec. 24, 1867, p. 3.

13. That the last coach car of the New York Express on Dec. 18, 1867, was a Cleveland and Toledo Railroad car, and that the second-last car was a Cleveland & Erie coach being used by the Buffalo and Erie, was confirmed during inquest proceedings by the assistant superintendent of the Buffalo and Erie Railroad, John Desmond. His testimony to this point may be found in the *Buffalo Daily Courier,* Dec. 27, 1867, p. 3. That both cars shared the same number—No. 21—was noted in Desmond's inquest testimony published in the *Buffalo Patriot and Journal,* Jan. 1, 1868, p. 1.

14. Details about Benjamin F. Betts's family and his residence, a wood-frame structure, valued at $400, in Tonawanda, N.Y., were found in the 1865 New York State census population schedules for the town of Tonawanda. This record is available on census microfilm 591 in the Grosvenor Room of the Buffalo and Erie County Public Library, Buffalo, N.Y.

15. The order for Freight No. 6 on Dec. 18, 1867, is described in official inquest testimony. See the *Buffalo Daily Courier,* Dec. 27, 1867, p. 3. Among other details, John Desmond testified at the inquest into the accident that both of the end cars of the train were number 21 cars.

16. For Emslie's movements that morning, see the official inquest testimony of Peter Emslie, as reported in the *Buffalo Express,* Dec. 24, 1867, p. 4.

17. The development of block signaling as a technique for making railroad schedules safer is outlined in Stover, *American Railroads,* 147. Stover points out that the transition to such signaling was hardly uniform or immediate; by 1921, only 16 percent of U.S. railroads—thirty-nine thousand miles—were equipped with the technology. Ibid., 183.

18. The telegraphic prank was reported in papers including the *Chicago Tribune,* March 10, 1867, p. 3.

19. James Mahar's actions shortly after 2 p.m. on Dec. 18, 1867, and his assessment of the frog and rail after the passage of the No. 6 eastbound freight, were part of official inquest testimony after the disaster. See the *Buffalo Daily Courier,* Dec. 31, 1867, p. 8.

20. *Buffalo Daily Courier,* Dec. 31, 1867, p. 8.

21. Josiah Southwick's milk production is noted in the "Domestic Animals" chapter of *Report of the Commissioner of Patents for the Year 1854: Agriculture,* U.S. House of Representatives, 33rd Cong., 2d Sess. (Washington, D.C.: A. O. P. Nicholson, printer, 1855), p. 21.

22. Special thanks to Mark Bouvier, an Angola resident, owner of the Southwick home in 2009, for an interview and his permission to examine deed and title paperwork for the property. Mark Bouvier, interview, 154 Mill Street, Aug. 10, 2009. Quoted with permission.

23. Thanks to Diana Crippen for biographical material about the Southwick family. Diana Crippen, interview, July 26, 2009. Quoted with permission.

24. The trip of Dr. Orin C. Payne is recounted in the *Fredonia (N.Y.) Censor,* Dec. 25, 1867, in the obituary for his sister-in-law, Mrs. Lydia M. Strong of Buffalo.

25. For the Buffalo and Erie Railroad's schedule of arrivals and departures in Dunkirk, see the railroad's official timetable printed in the *Fredonia (N.Y.) Censor,* Dec. 25, 1867.

26. Information about the final two stops of the New York Express, at Dunkirk and Silver Creek, may be found in various newspaper reports about the official inquest, including the testimonies of Benjamin F. Sherman, John S. Vanderburg, Gilbert W. Smith, and others on the train crew, as reported in the Buffalo daily papers during the week of the inquest. See, for example, the testimony of Sherman reported in the *Buffalo Daily Courier* of Dec. 28, 1867.

27. Testimony of John Desmond, assistant superintendent of the Buffalo and Erie Railroad, in the *Buffalo Daily Courier,* Dec. 27, 1867, p. 3.

28. For an eyewitness observer's account of the work of train brakemen using hand brakes on railroad trains in 1867, see the commentary of George S. Davison, past president of the American Society of Civil Engineers and Engineers' Society of Western Pennsylvania, as collected in *Anecdotes and Reminiscences of George Westinghouse, 1846–1914, Contributed by His Former Associates: A Collateral Project with the "George Westinghouse Commemoration" of the American Society of Mechanical Engineers, December 1936.* See p. 2 in the G. S. Davison section. By the Westinghouse Air-Brake Co., Westinghouse Electric & Manufacturing Co., and American Society of Mechanical Engineers, collected and edited by Dr. Charles F. Scott. Pittsburgh: Westinghouse Air Brake Co., 1939. In the collection of the Library and Archives Division, Historical Society of Western Pennsylvania, Pittsburgh, in the Heinz History Center.

29. George S. Davison account, in *Anecdotes and Reminiscences of George Westinghouse,* p. 2 in the G. S. Davison section.

30. Ibid.

31. Ibid.

32. Ibid., pp. 2–3 in the G. S. Davison section.

33. Ibid., p. 3 in the G. S. Davison section.

34. That the brakemen of the Buffalo and Erie Railroad were allowed to sit inside between braking efforts is made clear in inquest testimony of Conductor Benjamin F. Sherman. See, for example, the *Buffalo Daily Courier* of Dec. 28, 1867, p. 8.

35. Testimony of Sherman reported in the *Buffalo Daily Courier* of Dec. 28, 1867.

36. For Dr. Orin C. Payne's disembarking the train at Silver Creek, see the obituary for Lydia M. Strong in the *Fredonia (N.Y.) Censor,* Dec. 25, 1867.

37. The testimony of George P. Ganson, telegraph operator in Silver Creek, may be found in the *Buffalo Daily Courier,* Dec. 27, 1867, p. 3.

38. The exact text of the telegram George P. Ganson sent J. M. Newton and other agents along the line that day can be found in inquest testimony in the *Buffalo Daily Courier,* Dec. 27, 1867, p. 3.

39. Inquest testimony of J. M. Newton, in the *Buffalo Daily Courier,* Dec. 27, 1867, p. 3.

40. Ibid.

41. "The Disaster at Angola," *New York Times,* Dec. 24, 1867, p. 1.

42. Ibid.

43. Dr. Frederick F. Hoyer's lighting of a cigar in the moments before the wreck is noted in the *Buffalo Express,* Dec. 21, 1867, p. 4.

44. For J. W. Kennedy's baggage claim number, see the *Buffalo Express,* Dec. 20, 1867, p. 2.

45. From Taylor, *World on Wheels,* 62.

46. The burial of Dr. Henry Gale is noted in an obituary published in the *Jamestown (N.Y.) Journal,* Dec. 20, 1867, p. 2.

47. Lydia M. Strong's relationship to Mrs. Frances M. Gale and her child is outlined in an obituary for Mrs. Strong in the *Fredonia (N.Y.) Censor,* Dec. 25, 1867, as is their reason for traveling on the express.

48. Conductor Benjamin F. Sherman spoke of his final round of ticket-taking on board the New York Express during the official inquest. See the *Buffalo Daily Courier* of Dec. 28, 1867, p. 8.

49. Conductor Sherman's assessment of the number of passengers on board each of the last two cars of the New York Express may well have been low, given the total number of victims, dead and wounded, after the accident. He may not have counted babies and children, among other factors. But

he was not alone; it was common for conductors and train crew to underestimate passenger loads after accidents, in this early era of railroading. For Benjamin F. Sherman's recollection of the numbers in these cars, see his testimony in the *Buffalo Daily Courier* of Dec. 28, 1867, p. 8.

50. Ibid.

51. For the movements of Vanderburg and Sherman out of the last car in these moments, see the inquest testimony of Vanderburg in the *Buffalo Daily Courier* of Dec. 28, 1867, p. 8.

52. For Vanderburg's operation of the brake on the second-last coach, see his testimony in the *Buffalo Daily Courier* of Dec. 28, 1867, p. 8.

53. Testimony of Angola resident A. M. Avery, in the *Buffalo Patriot and Journal*, Jan. 1, 1868, p. 1.

54. Testimony of J. M. Newton about the speed of the New York Express, in the *Buffalo Daily Courier*, Dec. 27, 1867, p. 3.

55. Testimony of John Desmond, assistant superintendent of the Buffalo and Erie road, in the *Buffalo Daily Courier*, Dec. 27, 1867, p. 3.

56. *Buffalo Patriot and Journal*, Jan. 1, 1868, p. 1.

57. Words and actions of James Mahar from testimony before the inquest jury, as reported in the *Buffalo Daily Courier*, Dec. 31, 1867, p. 8.

7. BREAKING

1. James Mahar's observations at the time of the derailment are described in his inquest testimony, as published in the *Buffalo Daily Courier*, Dec. 31, 1867, p. 8.

2. Switchman James Mahar testified before the coroner's jury on Monday morning, December 30, 1867. His testimony was covered by many newspapers, among them the *Buffalo Daily Courier*, on Dec. 31, 1867, p. 8.

3. The viewpoint of A. M. Avery from the tin shop window was part of testimony published in the *Buffalo Daily Courier*, Dec. 25, 1867, p. 8.

4. Testimony of John Martin, *Buffalo Daily Courier*, Dec. 24, 1867, p. 8.

5. James Mahar asserted that he saw these two male figures on the back platform of the train in inquest testimony, including that published in the *Buffalo Daily Courier*, on Dec. 31, 1867, p. 8.

6. The bridge was soon dubbed the "Bridge of Death" by some newspapers, including the *New York World;* a piece from this newspaper making this statement was reprinted in the *Buffalo Patriot and Journal*, Jan. 1, 1868. For the measurement of the bridge from end to end, see the testimony of Peter Emslie, chief engineer of the Buffalo and Erie Railroad, *Erie (Pa.) Dispatch*, Dec. 24, 1867, p. 1.

7. The digging of the rear truck of the train into the rails to within twenty-eight feet of the easternmost abutment of the truss bridge was described by Western New York railroad officials in inquest testimony and published in newspapers including the *Buffalo Patriot and Journal*, Jan. 1, 1868, p. 1.

8. Mahar described the figure he thought he saw falling from one of the train's platforms in inquest testimony published in the *Buffalo Daily Courier*, Dec. 31, 1867, p. 8.

8. FALLING

1. The likening of the initial jolt to an "electrical shock" may be found in the inquest testimony of Benjamin F. Betts as reported in the *Buffalo Daily Courier*, Dec. 27, 1867, p. 3.

2. See the testimony of Cornelius Van Elten, foreman for the Buffalo and Erie Railroad based at Angola, on the condition of the track after the accident, in the *Buffalo Express*, Dec. 28, 1867, p. 4.

3. The distance between the Angola depot and the frog in the track was measured and testified to by Peter Emslie, chief engineer of the Buffalo and Erie road, in inquest proceedings. See the *Buffalo Daily Courier*, Dec. 24, 1867, p. 8.

4. Testimony of Peter Emslie, chief engineer of the Buffalo and Erie Railroad, *Erie (Pa.) Dispatch*, Dec. 24, 1867, p. 1.

5. Eyewitness account in the *Pittsfield (Mass.) Sun*, Dec. 26, 1867, p. 2.

6. Gilbert W. Smith's reaction to the "jerking motion" is described in the *Buffalo Express,* Dec. 28, 1867, p. 4.

7. Isadore Mayer's location during the derailment is described by Mayer in a personal statement given to the *Buffalo Post,* Dec. 19, 1867, p. 1.

8. Conductor Sherman's words to John Vanderburg upon the derailment may be found in Vanderburg's inquest testimony, as reported in the *Buffalo Express,* Dec. 28, 1867, p. 4. Sherman's description of the "jar" is found in his own inquest testimony, as reported in the *Buffalo Daily Courier,* Dec. 28, 1867, p. 8.

9. The actions of Frances M. Gale and Lydia M. Strong in the final moments of the New York Express's journey may be found detailed in the *Fredonia (N.Y.) Censor,* Dec. 25, 1867, p. 1.

10. Lydia M. Strong's actions at the time of the derailment are described in the *Fredonia (N.Y.) Censor,* Dec. 25, 1867, p. 1. Information on her belongings in 1867 may be found in her estate papers, on file in the Erie County Surrogate's Court, Buffalo.

11. Benjamin F. Betts's response to the first jolt felt on board the train cars is included in inquest testimony, including that in the *Buffalo Patriot and Journal,* Jan. 1, 1868, p. 1.

12. *Buffalo Daily Courier,* Dec. 27, 1867, p. 3.

13. Betts's move toward the coach's forward door is found in inquest testimony in the *Buffalo Daily Courier,* Dec. 27, 1867, p. 3.

14. Betts's statement on something being "wrong" with the train is included in testimony in the *Buffalo Daily Courier,* Dec. 27, 1867, p. 3.

15. Betts testimony, *Buffalo Patriot and Journal,* Jan. 1, 1868, p. 1.

16. The fact of passengers getting to their feet in the cars in these moments was testified to by Benjamin Brownell, a passenger on the train, in the *Buffalo Daily Courier,* Dec. 24, 1867, p. 8.

17. Charles Newton testimony, *Buffalo Express,* Dec. 28, 1867, p. 4.

18. The meaning of the "slow" sign posted before the Big Sister Creek bridge at Angola, and other signs along the Buffalo and Erie Railroad's route, was described by Assistant Superintendent John Desmond in inquest testimony, in the *Buffalo Patriot and Journal,* Jan. 1, 1868, p. 1.

19. Testimony of Charles Carscadin, engineer on the New York Express, as reported in the *Buffalo Morning Express,* Dec. 24, 1867, p. 4.

20. That Carscadin couldn't easily see behind him is found in testimony in the *Buffalo Morning Express,* Dec. 24, 1867, p. 4.

21. The fact that Carscadin sounded his whistle twice during these moments may be found in his testimony included in the *Buffalo Morning Express,* Dec. 24, 1867, p. 4. Angolans and others heard various versions of the train's final whistle: some remembered hearing one blast, some two, and a few none.

22. Cyrus Wilcox reported that this is what he thought when he heard the first whistle blast; see his testimony, *Buffalo Daily Courier,* Dec. 28, 1867, p. 8.

23. Testimony of Angola resident Alanson Wilcox before the coroner's jury in the Angola inquest, *Buffalo Daily Courier,* Dec. 28, 1867, p. 8.

24. Robert J. Dickson's heroics with the bell rope are described in various newspaper accounts, including the *Buffalo Morning Express,* Dec. 24, 1867, p. 4.

25. The position of Robert J. Dickson and J. Frank Walker aboard the second-last car is detailed in the *Buffalo Express,* Dec. 20, 1867, p. 4, and in the *Buffalo Post,* Dec. 19, 1867, p. 1.

26. *Buffalo Post,* Dec. 19, 1867, p. 1.

27. For the words of Charles P. Wood, see the *Buffalo Daily Courier,* Dec. 28, 1867, p. 8.

28. Testimony of Benjamin F. Sherman, *Buffalo Daily Courier,* Dec. 28, 1867, p. 8.

29. From an eyewitness account of Mr. and Mrs. Amos H. Thomas of Utica, given to the *Utica Herald* shortly after the wreck, and published in the *Utica Morning Herald* on Dec. 23, 1867, p. 8.

30. Testimony of Benjamin F. Sherman, *Buffalo Daily Courier,* Dec. 28, 1867, p. 8.

31. Ibid.

32. Ibid.

33. This illustration of the derailment of the Angola train, by artist J. P. Hoffman, appeared in *Harper's Weekly* magazine on Jan. 11, 1868, p. 20. The estimate that the train swayed badly for thirty seconds was included in the eyewitness testimony of Amos H. Thomas and Mary Thomas of Utica, passengers on the train, as reprinted in the *Buffalo Daily Courier* of Dec. 25, 1867, p. 8.

34. Peter Emslie, chief engineer of the Buffalo and Erie road, testified to this distance in inquest proceedings. See the *Buffalo Daily Courier,* Dec. 24, 1867, p. 8.

35. Testimony of Peter Emslie, chief engineer of the Buffalo and Erie Railroad, *Erie (Pa.) Dispatch,* Dec. 24, 1867, p. 1.

36. Eyewitness account of Alanson Wilcox, in the *Buffalo Daily Courier,* Dec. 28, 1867, p. 8.

37. Testimony of Peter Emslie, chief engineer of the Buffalo and Erie Railroad, *Erie (Pa.) Dispatch,* Dec. 24, 1867, p. 1.

38. Testimony of Benjamin F. Betts, *Buffalo Daily Courier,* Dec. 27, 1867, p. 3.

39. Ibid.

40. Testimony of John Martin, Angola resident, in inquest proceedings, as reported in the *Buffalo Daily Courier,* Dec. 24, 1867, p. 8.

41. Testimony of Josiah Southwick before the coroner's jury in the Angola inquest, *Buffalo Daily Courier,* Dec. 24, 1867, p. 8.

42. Ibid.

43. Statement of Isadore Mayer to the *Buffalo Post,* reported Dec. 19, 1867, p. 1.

44. Isadore Mayer, as reported in the *Buffalo Post,* Dec. 19, 1867, p. 1.

45. Eyewitness account of Mr. and Mrs. Amos H. Thomas of Utica, as given to the *Utica Herald* shortly after the wreck, and published in the *Utica Morning Herald* on Dec. 23, 1867, p. 8. Their account was also reprinted in the *Buffalo Daily Courier,* Dec. 25, 1867, p. 8.

46. Cyrus Wilcox testimony, *Buffalo Patriot and Journal,* Jan. 1, 1868, p. 1.

47. Eyewitness account of an Albany resident who visited the site of the wreck on the evening of December 18, 1867, as reported in the *Pittsfield (Mass.) Sun,* Dec. 26, 1867, p. 2.

48. Testimony of A. M. Avery, *Buffalo Patriot and Journal,* Jan. 1, 1868, p. 1.

49. Eyewitness testimony about the crushing of the car to less than three feet between roof and floor, as given by Cyrus Wilcox, one of the first Angolans on the scene of the wreck, and reported in the *Buffalo Patriot and Journal,* Jan. 1, 1868, p. 1.

50. Cyrus Wilcox testimony, *Buffalo Patriot and Journal,* Jan. 1, 1868, p. 1.

51. *Crawford (Pa.) Democrat,* Dec. 28, 1867, p. 2.

52. Testimony of Josiah Southwick before the coroner's jury in the Angola inquest, *Buffalo Daily Courier,* Dec. 24, 1867, p. 8.

53. Eyewitness testimony of Alanson Wilcox on the derailment and fall of the second-last car of the train, as published in the *Buffalo Daily Courier,* Dec. 28, 1867, p. 8.

54. For the degree of the incline on this part of the Big Sister topography, see the testimony of Peter Emslie, chief engineer of the Buffalo and Erie Railroad, *Erie (Pa.) Dispatch,* Dec. 24, 1867, p. 1. For details of the car's fall, see the *Pittsfield (Mass.) Sun,* Dec. 26, 1867, p. 2.

55. An account of Josiah P. Hayward's grisly death can be found in the *Fredonia (N.Y.) Censor,* Dec. 25, 1867. Some newspapers in the wake of the wreck reported that a passenger named Kennedy had been the one killed in this terrible manner; that may have been error or confusion, or it could also have been the case that more than one passenger was ejected and crushed in this way. The *Fredonia Censor* account seems to be accurate in several respects in ways that other newspapers were not.

56. A description of Frances M. Gale's experience may be found in the obituary for her mother, in the *Fredonia (N.Y.) Censor,* Dec. 25, 1867.

57. An account of the conditions of Lydia M. Strong's death may be found in the obituary "Mrs. J. M. Strong," in the *Fredonia (N.Y.) Censor,* Dec. 25, 1867.

58. Testimony of Peter Emslie, chief engineer of the Buffalo and Erie Railroad, *Erie (Pa.) Dispatch,* Dec. 24, 1867, p. 1.

9. HORROR

1. Cyrus Wilcox testimony, *Buffalo Daily Courier,* Dec. 28, 1867, p. 8.

2. Ibid.

3. Ibid.

4. The eyewitness testimony of New York City theatrical agent Isadore Mayer was reported widely in newspapers around the nation after the wreck, including in the *Buffalo Post,* Dec. 19, 1867, p. 1, as well as in the *Erie (Pa.) Observer,* Dec. 26, 1867, page unavailable.

5. Information on what would have happened to the human bodies aboard the New York Express in the immediate aftermath of the wreck, including in the fire which consumed the Toledo car, was provided by the medical and forensics staff of the Erie County (N.Y.) Medical Examiner's Office, Buffalo.

6. *Buffalo Post,* Dec. 19, 1867, p. 1.

7. *Cleveland Herald,* Dec. 20, 1867, p. 4. Some material was reprinted from wreck coverage by the Buffalo papers, including the *Express.*

8. *Crawford (Pa.) Democrat,* Dec. 28, 1867, p. 1.

9. See "Viewing the Remains of the Victims of the Angola Disaster for Identification, at the Soldiers' Rest, Buffalo," a scene of bodies inside the Soldiers' Rest Home in Buffalo, by J. Harrison Mills, published in *Frank Leslie's Illustrated Newspaper,* Jan. 11, 1868, p. 265, for examples of this type of pugilistic pose and extreme charring.

10. Background provided by the medical and forensics staff of the Erie County (N.Y.) Medical Examiner's Office, Buffalo.

11. *Semi-Weekly Wisconsin,* Jan. 25, 1868, p. 4.

12. See the lists of corpses and injured victims, and descriptions of their conditions, as printed in papers around New York State, including the *St. Lawrence Republican and Ogdensburgh Weekly Journal,* Jan. 21, 1868, p. 1.

13. "The Tragedy of Travel," *Harper's Weekly,* January 11, 1868, p. 18.

14. *Crawford (Pa.) Democrat,* Dec. 28, 1867, p. 1.

15. *Erie (Pa.) Observer,* Dec. 26, 1867, page unavailable.

16. Estimates of the duration of the screams of the dying at more than fifteen minutes, and even twenty minutes, as reported in various papers, including the *Cleveland Herald,* Dec. 20, 1867, p. 4; the *Erie (Pa.) Observer,* Dec. 26, 1867, page unavailable; and the *Owatonna (Minn.) Register,* Dec. 25, 1867, p. 1, the latter report based on interviews with a passenger who had been on board the forward part of the train, as well as family members of the Fishers—Alexander, Emma, and Minnie—who were on the train.

17. *Erie (Pa.) Observer,* Dec. 26, 1867, page unavailable.

18. Testimony of Isadore Mayer, in the *Erie (Pa.) Observer,* Dec. 26, 1867, page unavailable.

19. Testimony of Peter Emslie, chief engineer of the Buffalo and Erie Railroad, *Erie (Pa.) Dispatch,* Dec. 24, 1867, p. 1.

20. *Crawford (Pa.) Democrat,* Dec. 28, 1867, p. 1.

21. Ibid.

22. Report on the condition of Mrs. Lydia Babcock, in the *Utica Weekly Herald,* Dec. 24, 1867, p. 8.

23. *Crawford (Pa.) Democrat,* Dec. 28, 1867, p. 1.

24. Account of the Fisher family group in the fall of the second-last car, in the *Utica Morning Herald,* Dec. 23, 1867, p. 8. Description of Emma Fisher as "insensible" after the wreck, *Owatonna (Minn.) Journal,* Jan. 23, 1868, p. 4.

25. *Erie (Pa.) Observer,* Dec. 26, 1867, page unknown.

26. *Harper's Weekly,* January 11, 1868, pp. 19–20.

27. Ibid., p. 20.

28. *Crawford (Pa.) Democrat,* Dec. 28, 1867, p. 1.

29. Account of the aftermath of the derailment for Alexander Fisher, Emma Hurlburt Fisher, and Minnie Fisher, as described by Emma's husband Andrew Fisher to various Minnesota newspapers, including the *Owatonna (Minn.) Journal,* Jan. 23, 1868, p. 4.

30. *Owatonna (Minn.) Journal,* Jan. 23, 1868, p. 4.

31. Testimony of Josiah Southwick before the coroner's jury in the Angola inquest, *Buffalo Daily Courier,* Dec. 24, 1867, p. 8.

32. The quote of Wilcox to Blackney comes from Wilcox's inquest testimony, *Buffalo Daily Courier,* Dec. 28, 1867, p. 8.

33. Testimony of John S. Taggert, *Buffalo Daily Courier,* Dec. 24, 1867, p. 8.

34. Ibid.

35. Testimony of James Mahar as to his actions immediately after the wreck, in the *Buffalo Express,* Dec. 31, 1867, p. 2.

36. Testimony of an eyewitness in the *Pittsfield (Mass.) Sun,* Dec. 26, 1867, p. 2.

37. *Crawford (Pa.) Democrat,* Dec. 28, 1867, p. 1.

38. *Pittsfield (Mass.) Sun,* Dec. 26, 1867, p. 2.

39. Angola resident and mill owner Henry Bundy, as quoted in the *Buffalo Evening Courier and Republic,* Jan. 2, 1868, p. 4.

40. *Pittsfield (Mass.) Sun,* Dec. 26, 1867, p. 2.

41. Cyrus Wilcox inquest testimony, *Buffalo Daily Courier,* Dec. 28, 1867, p. 8.

42. Ibid.

43. Assessment of the "goodly" number of Angola citizens working on the wreckage in the *Buffalo Patriot and Journal,* Dec. 25, 1867, p. 1.

44. *Buffalo Patriot and Journal,* Jan. 1, 1868, p. 1.

45. Testimony of Angola resident Alanson Wilcox before the coroner's jury in the Angola inquest, *Buffalo Daily Courier,* Dec. 28, 1867, p. 8.

46. Testimony of Josiah Southwick before the coroner's jury in the Angola inquest, *Buffalo Daily Courier,* Dec. 24, 1867, p. 8.

47. Details of the ancestry of Josiah and Huldah Southwick are found in the family documents and records preserved by the family of Diana and Jerry Crippen; Diana Crippen is a direct descendant of the Southwick couple. Used with permission of the Crippen and Southwick families.

48. Testimony of Josiah Southwick before the coroner's jury in the Angola inquest, *Buffalo Daily Courier,* Dec. 24, 1867, p. 8.

49. Chain of events by which Josiah Southwick rescued the baby and the check agent, as described in the *Buffalo Daily Courier,* Dec. 24, 1867, p. 8.

50. Actions of John Vanderburg upon reaching the bottom of the gorge, as described by Vanderburg in the *Buffalo Daily Courier,* Dec. 28, 1867, p. 8.

51. Henry Bundy, as quoted in the *Buffalo Evening Courier and Republic,* Jan. 2, 1868, p. 4.

52. For the rescue of Tennessean R. M. Russell, see the testimony of Angola resident John Martin, *Buffalo Daily Courier,* Dec. 24, 1867, p. 8. The R. M. Russell rescued from the Angola wreckage, reportedly from Trenton, may have been Robert Milton Russell, a Tennessean from that part of the state who had fought during the Civil War for the Confederacy, including under General Nathan Bedford Forrest. An 1848 graduate of West Point, Russell had won distinction during the war for his bravery and leadership abilities. He had recruited a volunteer infantry regiment from his home county in Tennessee in 1861; later, though injured in battle, at least once seriously, he had risen from the ranks of the cavalry to be named a colonel under Forrest. Russell's service had included fighting at Fort Pillow and at battles including Paducah and Harrisburg. After the war, Russell had heard reports that officers like himself might suffer penalties for their service under Forrest, a widely reviled figure in the North. "If it should prove to be true you will probably hear from me from Mexico or Canada after a while," Russell had written in 1866 to his brother John Russell. "Although my conscience is perfectly clear of having done any wrong yet I think this would be the best course for me to pursue as to go before a Military commission is the same thing as to go to the gallows, all cases being prejudged." Information about Robert Milton Russell's service in the Civil War can be found in *Tennesseans in the Civil War,* part 2, 97–99, 198–200. The letter of Robert M. Russell to John Cowan Russell, dated Feb. 12, 1866, is in the collection of Russell's family, including Diana Dallosta. With permission of Diana Chester Dallosta and the Chester and Craner families.

53. Ibid.

54. John Martin's discovery of R. M. Russell's watch, and his return of this item, are described in the *Buffalo Daily Courier,* Dec. 24, 1867, p. 8.

55. Statement of Andrew Fisher, brother of Alexander Fisher, about his brother's last hours, as given to the *Owatonna (Minn.) Journal,* Jan. 23, 1868, p. 4.

56. Death of Alexander Fisher, as described by Angola pastor Rev. Charles R. Strong in a sermon reprinted in Fisher's hometown newspaper, the *Owatonna (Minn.) Journal,* Jan. 23, 1868, p. 3.

57. Testimony of Peter Emslie, chief engineer of the Buffalo and Erie Railroad, *Erie (Pa.) Dispatch,* Dec. 24, 1867, p. 1.

58. *Buffalo Daily Courier,* Dec. 28, 1867, p. 8.

59. Testimony of Benjamin F. Betts, *Buffalo Patriot and Journal,* Jan. 1, 1868, p. 1.

60. Testimony of Dr. Frederick F. Hoyer, *Buffalo Evening Courier and Republic,* Jan. 2, 1868, p. 2.

61. The fact that "two physicians" were aboard the train and thus ended up being the first doctors to treat the seriously wounded is mentioned in the *Buffalo Daily Courier,* Dec. 25, 1867, p. 8. The newspaper does not mention Dr. Frederick F. Hoyer by name in this account, but he was aboard the express and detailed his work on the wreckage in subsequent inquest testimony. The other doctor may have been Dr. Orin C. Payne, who reportedly got off at Silver Creek but may later have arrived in Angola and worked on the victims at the scene; it may have been a misstatement about Dr. Curtiss; or, there may have been a third doctor who was, like Hoyer, on board the train. For Dr. Payne getting off the train at Silver Creek, see the *Fredonia (N.Y.) Censor,* Dec. 25, 1867, in the obituary for his sister-in-law, Mrs. Lydia M. Strong of Buffalo.

62. Benjamin F. Betts, *Buffalo Patriot and Journal,* Jan. 1, 1868, p. 1.

63. Testimony of Benjamin F. Betts, *Buffalo Daily Courier,* Dec. 27, 1867, p. 3.

64. Ibid.

65. Testimony of John Martin, *Buffalo Daily Courier,* Dec. 24, 1867, p. 8.

66. Testimony of Benjamin F. Betts, *Buffalo Daily Courier,* Dec. 27, 1867, p. 3.

67. Ibid.

68. Ibid.

69. Benjamin F. Betts's view of Stephen W. Steward is mentioned in inquest testimony in various papers, including the *Buffalo Daily Courier,* Dec. 27, 1867, p. 3, and the *Buffalo Patriot and Journal,* Jan. 1, 1868, p. 1. The story of his encounter with Steward in the burning car was picked up by the *New York Times.*

70. *Buffalo Courier and Republic,* Dec. 20, 1867, p. 3.

71. Ibid.

72. *Buffalo Patriot and Journal,* Jan. 1, 1868, p. 1.

73. *Buffalo Daily Courier,* Dec. 27, 1867, p. 3.

10. RESCUE

1. A report on the condition of the Chadeayne family after the accident was made in a letter from Daniel Chadeayne, father of the family, from Angola on Dec. 21, 1867, to a Titusville resident, and reprinted in the *Titusville (Pa.) Morning Herald,* Dec. 24, 1867, p. 3.

2. Ibid.

3. Ibid.

4. Ibid.

5. Interestingly, if Dr. Curtiss had been at home at the time of the derailment, almost no one in the village would have had a better view of the devastation. In fact, Curtiss might have beaten Dr. Hoyer in a race to the creek bed. Curtiss's home and medical practice shared space in a structure on Main street in the village, just up the street from Henry Bundy's mill. The wreck happened practically in his front yard.

6. In newspaper accounts following the wreck, Dr. Curtiss's leadership role in taking care of the wounded on-site in the village would be noted. See, for example, the column titled "Angola" in the *Buffalo Express,* Dec. 24, 1867, p. 4. In that column, Curtiss is described as having the "patients in charge" in Angola.

7. Basic information on Dr. Romaine J. Curtiss's military service may be found in the *Genealogical and Biographical Record of Will County, Illinois, Containing Biographies of Well-Known Citizens of the Past and Present* (Chicago: Biographical Publishing Co., 1900), 545–47. For more detailed descriptions of his service, see Curtiss's file in the U.S. government archives: National Archives and Records Administration, Washington, D.C., Record Group 15, Records of the Bureau of Veteran Affairs, Pension Application Case File (Widow's Certificate #523979).

8. Romaine J. Curtiss's military experiences are detailed in his obituary in the *Joliet (Ill.) Daily Republican,* Nov. 20, 1900, p. 6, which contains biographical material provided by the doctor himself.

9. Romaine J. Curtiss's shipboard experiences are described in the government files on his Civil War service: National Archives and Records Administration, Washington, D.C., Record Group

15, Records of the Bureau of Veteran Affairs, Pension Application Case File (Widow's Certificate #523979). Also, there is a record of his service on board the USS *General Burnside:* National Archives and Records Administration, Washington, D.C., Copy of Medical Journal for the USS *General Burnside,* Record Group 52, Records of the Bureau of Medicine and Surgery, Entry A1 (22) (Medical Journals of Ships, 1813–1910).

10. For Curtiss's health and the aftereffects of the war on his person, see the National Archives and Records Administration, Washington, D.C., Record Group 15, Records of the Bureau of Veteran Affairs, Pension Application Case File (Widow's Certificate #523979).

11. For this praise of Dr. Curtiss and Dr. Hoyer, see the *Buffalo Express,* Dec. 23, 1867, p. 4.

12. *Buffalo Daily Courier,* Dec. 24, 1867, p. 8.

13. *Buffalo Commercial Advertiser,* Dec. 19, 1867, p. 3.

14. *Buffalo Patriot and Journal,* Dec. 25, 1867, p. 1.

15. *Buffalo Express,* Dec. 24, 1867, p. 4.

16. Ibid.

17. Ibid.

18. *Buffalo Express,* Dec. 23, 1867, p. 4.

19. Statement of Emma Hurlburt Fisher, as reported in the *Buffalo Evening Courier and Republic,* Jan. 14, 1868, p. 3.

20. *Erie (Pa.) Morning Daily Dispatch,* Dec. 25, 1867, p. 1.

21. *Buffalo Evening Courier and Republic,* Jan. 14, 1868, p. 3.

22. *Buffalo Patriot and Journal,* Dec. 25, 1867, p. 1.

23. Testimony of eyewitness observers, as reported in the *Pittsfield (Mass.) Sun,* Dec. 26, 1867, p. 2.

24. *Buffalo Commercial Advertiser,* Dec. 19, 1867, p. 3.

25. Ibid.

26. Frank E. Griffith, letter to Thankful Myers Griffith, April 13, 1864, from Grand Encore on the Red River, Louisiana, as reprinted in *The Griffith Letters: The Story of Frank Griffith and the 116th New York Volunteer Infantry in the Civil War,* ed. Joan Metzger (Berwyn Heights, Md.: Heritage Books, 2004), xi.

27. The presence of the Babcocks in Griffith's home was noted in the *Buffalo Commercial Advertiser,* Dec. 19, 1867, p. 3. For descriptions of the Babcocks, Stewarts, and others who were treated in the home of Frank and Thankful Griffith, see the *Buffalo Courier and Republic,* Dec. 19, 1867, p. 3.

28. Frank E. Griffith, letter to Thankful Myers Griffith, April 5, 1863, from Camp Banks, Baton Rouge, La., as reprinted in Metzger, *Griffith Letters,* 50.

29. *Buffalo Commercial Advertiser,* Dec. 19, 1867, p. 3.

30. Ibid.

31. *Buffalo Courier and Republic,* Dec. 19, 1867, p. 3.

32. *Ravalli (Mont.) Republican,* July 16, 1915, p. 1.

33. *Buffalo Courier and Republic,* Dec. 19, 1867, p. 3.

34. *Buffalo Courier and Republic,* Dec. 20, 1867, p. 3.

35. Ibid.

36. Ibid.

37. See "Frightful Railroad Disaster in New York State," in *Frank Leslie's Illustrated Newspaper,* Jan. 4, 1868, p. 243.

38. *Harper's Weekly,* Jan. 11, 1868, p. 19.

39. Ibid., 19–20.

40. Ibid., 20.

41. Buffalo History Museum Archives, Mss. W-5, Joseph Bennett, *Reminiscences and Diary,* 37, 40–41.

42. Faust, *This Republic of Suffering,* 9–10.

43. *Buffalo Courier and Republic,* Dec. 19, 1867, p. 3.

44. For the mention of sixteen women of Angola, by name, for their work on behalf of the wreck victims, see the *Buffalo Express,* Dec. 23, 1867, p. 4.

45. *Buffalo Commercial Advertiser,* Dec. 19, 1867, p. 3. For mention of internal injuries, see *Buffalo Courier and Republic,* Dec. 19, 1867, p. 3.

46. *Pittsfield (Mass.) Sun,* Dec. 26, 1867, p. 2.

47. *Buffalo Commercial Advertiser,* Dec. 19, 1867, p. 3.

48. *Buffalo Daily Courier,* Dec. 25, 1867, p. 8.

49. Ibid.

50. *Buffalo Courier and Republic,* Dec. 20, 1867, p. 3.

51. Words of Lizzie Thompson in the *Buffalo Courier and Republic,* Dec. 20, 1867, p. 3.

52. Description of some of the watches and other items found among the wreckage, in the *Buffalo Courier and Republic,* Dec. 21, 1867, p. 3.

53. This list of items recovered from the scene directly after the wreck was printed in the *Buffalo Patriot and Journal,* Jan. 1, 1868, p. 1.

54. *Erie (Pa.) Morning Daily Dispatch,* Dec. 25, 1867, p. 1.

55. Faust, *This Republic of Suffering,* 29.

56. The items placed at Josiah Southwick's house are referenced in coverage in the *Buffalo Express,* Dec. 25, 1867, p. 2. For accounts showing that some items remained at Southwick's for at least a week, see the *Erie (Pa.) Morning Daily Dispatch,* Dec. 25, 1867, p. 1.

57. Length of time Zachariah Hubbard suffered, in the *Buffalo Express,* Dec. 21, 1867, p. 4.

58. Placement of Zachariah Hubbard in the Angola Hotel, and his last words, as reported in the *Buffalo Commercial Advertiser,* Dec. 19, 1867, p. 3. This account was picked up by the *New York Times* and reprinted in their issue of Dec. 21, 1867, p. 1.

59. Henry Bundy described making "cases for the killed" at the request of officials of the Buffalo and Erie Railroad immediately after the accident, in his later testimony to the inquest jury, as reported in newspapers including the *Buffalo Evening Courier and Republic,* Jan. 2, 1868, p. 4.

60. For a history of Henry Bundy's businesses, see *Angola's History,* 9. See also Delano, *Evans and Angola,* 43.

61. For accounts of Minnie Fisher's separation from her mother and recovery, see the *Buffalo Daily Courier,* Dec. 25, 1867, p. 8. Descriptions of the baby found in the wreckage of the Erie car fit Minnie Fisher, although she was not named in news reports; the descriptions of the family group she was traveling with also fit the Fisher family.

62. Ibid.

63. Ibid.

64. Ibid.

65. Ibid.

66. See, for instance, the *Baltimore Sun,* Dec. 27, 1867, p. 1.

11. RECOGNITIONS

1. For the length of the relief train, see the *Buffalo Post,* Dec. 19, 1867, p. 1.

2. *Buffalo Courier and Republic,* Dec. 19, 1867, p. 3.

3. Ibid.

4. Ibid.

5. Ibid.

6. Dunn, *History of Railroads in Western New York,* 140–41. Dunn's work describes the gingerbread-adorned structures of the West Shore line, another western New York railroad, and sets them out as different from most other freight and station houses of the period; he also describes the general uniformity of railroad structures at the time, within individual companies. No photographs or sketches of the Angola railroad freight house in 1867 seem to have survived.

7. *Pittsfield (Mass.) Sun,* Dec. 26, 1867, p. 2.

8. Names of the first victims to be laid in the Angola freight house for review, as noted by an eyewitness in the *Buffalo Courier and Republic,* Dec. 19, 1867, p. 3.

9. Ibid.

10. Ibid.

11. *Buffalo Evening Courier and Republic,* Jan. 2, 1868, p. 4.

12. Wilder, *Bridge at San Luis Rey,* 4.

13. *Buffalo Courier and Republic,* Dec. 20, 1867, p. 3.

14. *Philadelphia Inquirer,* Dec. 25, 1867, p. 3.

15. For the fact that the *Hartford Courant* reporter—who goes unnamed—was aboard this train, see the *Philadelphia Inquirer,* Dec. 25, 1867, p. 3.

16. Ibid.

17. Ibid.

18. For an account of the supposed deliverance of young William Green, see the *Buffalo Post,* Dec. 19, 1867, p. 1. For John D. Rockefeller's experience that day, see the *Cleveland Herald,* Dec. 20, 1867, p. 4.

19. *Buffalo Post,* Dec. 19, 1867, p. 1.

20. *Philadelphia Inquirer,* Dec. 25, 1867, p. 3.

21. *Buffalo Courier and Republic,* Dec. 20, 1867, p. 3.

22. Ibid.

23. *Philadelphia Inquirer,* Dec. 25, 1867, p. 3.

24. *Boston Herald,* Dec. 24, 1867, p. 4.

25. *Philadelphia Inquirer,* Dec. 25, 1867, p. 3.

26. *Pittsfield (Mass.) Sun,* Dec. 26, 1867, p. 2.

27. *Buffalo Post,* Dec. 19, 1867, p. 1.

28. That John D. Rockefeller's telegram from Angola was one of the first to announce the wreck in that Ohio city was reported in the *Cleveland Herald,* Dec. 19, 1867, p. 1.

29. John D. Rockefeller's telegram to Laura Rockefeller, sent on December 18, 1867, from Angola and received in Cleveland at 6:25 p.m., contains this message. John D. Rockefeller to Laura Spelman Rockefeller (telegram), December 18, 1867, folder 270, box 36, Correspondence—Office, Record Group 1—JDR Papers, Rockefeller Family Archives, RAC.

30. The account of Morgan Kedzie's recognition among the victims was reported in the *New York Times,* Dec. 25, 1867, p. 5. Material in this story had been reprinted from the Rochester newspapers.

31. *New York Times,* Dec. 25, 1867, p. 5.

32. *Titusville (Pa.) Morning Herald,* Dec. 20, 1867, p. 3.

33. Information on the stature of Rev. John Chase Lord in Buffalo of this era may be found in Gerber, *Making of an American Pluralism,* 33. A bust of Rev. Lord, incidentally, adorns the reading area of the library and archive of the Buffalo History Museum in Buffalo.

34. A wedding announcement for the couple married that day by Rev. John Chase Lord may be found in the *Buffalo Express,* Dec. 21, 1867, p. 1.

35. Rev. Charles Wood, "Biographical Sketch," in *Memoir of John C. Lord, D.D.* (Buffalo: Courier Co., 1878), 33.

36. Ibid., 16.

37. Ibid., 13.

38. This account of the sad announcement of J. Frank Walker's death to his father was reported in the *Buffalo Post,* Dec. 19, 1867, p. 1. Other Buffalo papers also carried accounts of this moment.

39. *Buffalo Post,* Dec. 19, 1867, p. 1.

40. *New York Times,* Dec. 21, 1867, p. 1.

41. Port Jervis railroad wreck victim John Melvin's connection to the earlier Angola wreck was recounted in the *Titusville (Pa.) Herald,* April 20, 1868, p. 1.

42. *Chicago Tribune,* Dec. 26, 1867, p. 1.

43. Ibid.

44. Ibid.

45. Ibid.

46. Ibid.

47. *Pittsfield (Mass.) Sun,* Dec. 26, 1867, p. 2.

12. REPORTS

1. Buffalo *Commercial Advertiser,* Dec. 19, 1867, p. 3.

2. *Buffalo Courier and Republic,* Dec. 20, 1867, p. 3.

3. Ibid.

4. Ibid.

5. *Buffalo Post*, Dec. 19, 1867, p. 1.

6. *Chicago Tribune*, Dec. 26, 1867, p. 1.

7. *Buffalo Patriot and Journal*, Jan. 1, 1868, p. 1.

8. *Buffalo Post*, Dec. 19, 1867, p. 1.

9. The story of Mary Lang's reward of a doll after the Angola train wreck, as a memento and also to thank her for her work caring for her injured mother, was passed down for generations through descendants of the Lang and Friend families, including Nelda Harris. Nelda, the granddaughter of Mary Lang Friend, passed on the story of the doll to the author during research for this book.

10. *New York Times*, Dec. 22, 1867, p. 5.

11. *New York Times*, Dec. 29, 1867, p. 5.

12. *Buffalo Commercial Advertiser*, Dec. 19, 1867, p. 3.

13. *New York Times*, Dec. 20, 1867, p. 4.

14. *Vermont Chronicle*, Jan. 4, 1868, p. 4.

15. Letter and editorial comment from the *New York Tribune*, as reprinted in the *Buffalo Evening Courier and Republic*, Jan. 11, 1868, p. 3.

16. *Buffalo Evening Courier and Republic*, Jan. 11, 1868, p. 3.

17. *Buffalo Patriot and Journal*, Jan. 1, 1868, p. 1.

18. *Buffalo Express*, Nov. 6, 1916, page unavailable.

19. *Buffalo News*, July 21, 1906, page unavailable.

20. *Cleveland Herald*, Dec. 19, 1867, p. 1.

21. Burton, *Age of Lincoln*, 332.

22. *Baltimore Sun*, Dec. 19, 1867, p. 1, and *Boston Herald*, Dec. 19, 1867, p. 2. The *Sun* used wire reports from Buffalo, sent in two dispatches, for its front-page coverage; the *Herald* offered slightly more information, also wired from Buffalo.

23. For a note about the "turned rules" at Lobdell's passing, see the *Buffalo Patriot and Journal*, Jan. 1, 1868, p. 1.

24. *Philadelphia Inquirer*, Dec. 19, 1867, p. 4.

25. Crowd estimate from the *Buffalo Patriot and Journal*, Dec. 25, 1867, p. 1. Buffalo population tallies taken from J. H. French, *Erie County, N.Y.: History, Statistics, Etc., from the State Gazetteer of 1860*, compiled by Wayne E. Morrison, p. 17.

26. Ibid., 6.

27. For the role of Captain Nicholson of the Buffalo police during this event, see the *Buffalo Patriot and Journal*, Dec. 25, 1867, p. 1.

28. *Buffalo Post*, Dec. 19, 1867, p. 1.

29. *Chicago Tribune*, Dec. 26, 1867, p. 1.

30. *Cleveland Herald*, Dec. 19, 1867, p. 1.

31. See Faust, *This Republic of Suffering*, 126.

32. *Chicago Tribune*, Dec. 26, 1867, p. 1.

33. Andrew Fisher's use of the telegraph to transmit this sad news made news of its own back in Minnesota. See the *Rochester (Minn.) Federal Union* for an item about his telegraph transmission, Jan. 11, 1868, p. 3.

34. *Rochester (N.Y.) Evening Express*, Dec. 20, 1867, p. 1.

35. Ibid.

36. See Faust, *This Republic of Suffering*, 127.

37. *Buffalo Courier and Republic*, Dec. 20, 1867, p. 3.

38. *Rochester (Minn.) Federal Union*, Jan. 4, 1868, p. 3.

39. For the poem "Dead—and No Name" and a brief description of its genesis, see Smith, *Romance and Humor of the Road*, 215–16. The ten-stanza poem is accompanied by an introduction that gets some particulars of the Angola wreck wrong (such as the conductor's name) but is worth reading for its brilliant window into Victorian thinking on mortality and gender.

40. Ibid., quotes p. 215.

41. Ibid., 216.

42. *Rochester (Minn.) Federal Union,* Jan. 4, 1868, p. 3.

43. For a history of the early years of the Buffalo police, see http://www.bpdthenandnow.com/historypage01.html. Authors of the page on the earliest years of the force are Cindy Diem and Michael Kaska.

44. *New York Times,* Dec. 20, 1867, p. 4.

45. *Buffalo Patriot and Journal,* Dec. 25, 1867, p. 1.

46. A description of the Soldiers' Rest Home is given in coverage of the grand opening of the new facility in Buffalo during the summer of 1864; see the *Buffalo Daily Courier,* June 8, 1864, p. 3.

47. *Buffalo Patriot and Journal,* Dec. 25, 1867, p. 1.

48. Ibid.

49. *Buffalo Courier and Republic,* Dec. 20, 1867, p. 3.

50. Rockefeller's activities after arriving in New York City on December 19, 1867, including his shopping trip and visit to William and Mira Rockefeller, are outlined in his letter to Laura of December 20, 1867. John D. Rockefeller to Laura Spelman Rockefeller, December 20, 1867, folder 270, box 36, Correspondence—Office, Record Group 1—JDR Papers, Rockefeller Family Archives, RAC.

51. Ibid.

52. Ibid.

53. Ibid.

54. Ibid.

13. MOURNING

1. For descriptions of individual bodies among the group of victims, see newspaper coverage in the Buffalo daily newspapers in the days after the wreck, including the *Buffalo Courier and Republic,* Dec. 20, 1867, p. 3.

2. Ibid.

3. Ibid.

4. Ibid.

5. Ibid.

6. The facility is described in the *Buffalo Daily Courier,* June 8, 1864, p. 3.

7. *Buffalo Courier and Republic,* Dec. 20, 1867, p. 3.

8. For the recognition of the Fullers by their families, see the *Titusville (Pa.) Morning Herald,* Dec. 21, 1867, p. 2.

9. For the recognition of Morgan Kedzie by his family, see the *Rochester (N.Y.) Evening Express,* Dec. 20, 1867, p. 1.

10. *Buffalo Courier and Republic,* Dec. 20, 1867, p. 3.

11. Ibid.

12. For the identification of these three men, see the *Buffalo Express,* Dec. 21, 1867, p. 4.

13. *Syracuse Daily Standard,* Dec. 21, 1867, p. 2.

14. For the disposition of these bodies, see coverage in the *Buffalo Courier and Republic,* Dec. 20, 1867, p. 3.

15. *Syracuse Daily Standard,* Dec. 21, 1867, p. 2.

16. For this tendency of the family members and other mourners, see the *Buffalo Express,* Dec. 21, 1867, p. 4.

17. *Semi-Weekly Wisconsin,* Jan. 25, 1868, p. 4. The italics are the paper's.

18. Ibid.

19. For a description of the scene around the temporary morgue, see the *Buffalo Courier and Republic,* Dec. 20, 1867, p. 3.

20. Ibid.

21. Ibid.

22. For the comment on R. F. Gibbs, see the *Titusville (Pa.) Morning Herald,* Dec. 30, 1867, p. 3.

23. For the Masonic ring belonging to Charles Lobdell, see the *Buffalo Express,* Dec. 21, 1867, p. 4; for a description of the Kents' rings, see the *New York Times,* Dec. 29, 1867, p. 5. For a description of the glass-topped viewing box, see the *Titusville (Pa.) Morning Herald,* Dec. 30, 1867, p. 3.

24. *Buffalo Express,* Dec. 21, 1867, p. 4.

25. See weather information in a report about the monthly Teachers Association meeting, held Friday, Dec. 20, 1867, in the town of Eden, as reported in the *Buffalo Express,* Dec. 30, 1867, p. 4.

26. *Buffalo Express,* Dec. 30, 1867, p. 4.

27. Ives, *Meteorological observations at Buffalo,* December 1867.

28. *Buffalo Express,* Dec. 30, 1867, p. 4.

29. *Titusville (Pa.) Morning Herald,* Dec. 25, 1867, p. 3.

30. *Buffalo Express,* Dec. 23, 1867, p. 4. Buffalo population tallies taken from Morrison, *Erie County, N.Y.,* 17.

31. *Boston Herald,* Dec. 23, 1867, p. 2.

32. *Titusville (Pa.) Morning Herald,* Dec. 20, 1867, p. 3.

33. *New York Times,* Dec. 20, 1867, p. 4.

34. *Titusville (Pa.) Morning Herald,* Dec. 24, 1867, p. 3.

35. *Buffalo Express,* Dec. 23, 1867, p. 4.

36. In at least one published illustration of the scene, the coffins are depicted as flanking the podium on either side. Descriptions of the scene state that the bier was created out of a railcar.

37. *Buffalo Express,* Dec. 30, 1867, p. 4.

38. Ibid.

39. Ibid.

40. *Hamilton (Ont.) Evening Times,* Dec. 23, 1867, p. 1.

41. For Elam Porter's transcripts, see Matriculation Book, Tufts College, ca. 1854–75, Artifact Collection, ca. 2500 BC—, box 36, Digital Collections and Archives, Tufts University, as well as Matriculation Book, Tufts College, ca. 1862–69, Artifact Collection, ca. 2500 BC—, box 37, Digital Collections and Archives, Tufts University.

42. *Fredonia (N.Y.) Censor,* Dec. 25, 1867, p. 2.

43. *Buffalo Express,* Dec. 23, 1867, p. 4.

44. *Boston Herald,* Dec. 23, 1867, p. 2.

45. *Buffalo Express,* Dec. 23, 1867, p. 4. For the detail of the bay horses, see the *Erie (Pa.) Daily Dispatch,* morning edition, Dec. 23, 1867, p. 1.

46. *Hamilton (Ont.) Evening Times,* Dec. 26, 1867, p. 2.

47. *Buffalo Express,* Dec. 23, 1867, p. 4.

48. For a note about Rev. John C. Lord's sermons that week, see the *Buffalo Express,* Dec. 23, 1867, p. 4.

49. The text of Rev. John Chase Lord's address was widely reported by, and reprinted in, several Buffalo newspapers. For one example, see the *Buffalo Express,* Dec. 23, 1867, p. 4. Quotes from Lord's address in this chapter are from that edition of the paper unless otherwise noted.

50. *Buffalo Express,* Dec. 23, 1867, p. 4.

51. Ibid.

52. Ibid.

53. Ibid.

54. Ibid.

55. Ibid. Italics that of the newspaper.

56. Ibid. Italics that of the newspaper. The small inaccuracy in Rev. Lord's quotation from the Bible—"valley and shadow" for "valley of the shadow" of death—may well have been an error in transcription by a *Buffalo Express* newspaper reporter or editor, and not a mistake by the minister.

14. JUDGING

1. See Shaw, *Down Brakes,* 15, 20.

2. Ibid., 446–54.

3. See coverage of the first day of the official Angola Horror inquest in Buffalo's many daily newspapers, including the *Buffalo Express,* Dec. 24, 1867, p. 4.

4. For the presence of the length of twisted rail in the courtroom for the inquest, ibid.

5. For the number of witnesses testifying on the first day of the inquest, and their names, ibid.

6. Ibid.

7. Ibid.

8. Ibid.

9. For engineer Peter Emslie's testimony on this point, ibid.

10. Ibid.

11. Ibid.

12. Ibid.

13. For Charles Kinsley's testimony, ibid.

14. For Josiah Southwick's testimony, ibid.

15. For John Martin's testimony, ibid.

16. For the testimony of both men, ibid.

17. For Benjamin Brownell's testimony, ibid.

18. For Kinsley's testimony, ibid.

19. *Buffalo Express,* Dec. 25, 1867, p. 4.

20. Ibid.

21. Ibid.

22. For C. F. Valtz's testimony and that of the other wheel inspectors, see the *Buffalo Express,* Dec. 27, 1867, p. 4.

23. Inquest testimony of John Desmond, ibid.

24. Ibid.

25. Ibid.

26. Inquest testimony of John Desmond, *Buffalo Patriot and Journal,* Jan. 1, 1868, p. 1.

27. Inquest testimony of John Desmond, ibid.

28. Inquest testimony of Fitch D. Adams, *Buffalo Express,* Dec. 31, 1867, p. 2.

29. Ibid.

30. Testimony of William Hart, *Buffalo Express,* Dec. 31, 1867, p. 2.

31. For an account of the last day of testimony and the verdict in the Angola inquest, see the *Buffalo Evening Courier and Republic,* Jan. 2, 1868, p. 4.

32. *Buffalo Patriot and Journal,* Jan. 8, 1868, p. 1.

33. Ibid.

34. Ibid.

15. DEBATES

1. See the editorial "The Tragedy of Travel" in *Harper's Weekly,* Jan. 11, 1868, p. 18. The magazine called the death of the Ohio sisters and the Angola disaster the two worst railroad incidents in memory.

2. See the article "Burning of Passenger Cars and Its Cause," in the periodical *Railway Times,* May 2, 1868, p. 143.

3. *Harper's Weekly,* Jan. 11, 1868, p. 18.

4. *Railway Times,* May 2, 1868, p. 143.

5. Ibid.

6. *Buffalo Daily Courier,* Dec. 28, 1867, p. 8.

7. See the story "The Old Year" in the *Titusville (Pa.) Herald,* Jan. 1, 1868, p. 1.

8. *Frank Leslie's Illustrated Newspaper,* Jan. 4, 1868, p. 243.

9. *Harper's Weekly,* Jan. 11, 1868, p. 19.

10. See, among other instances, the story "Another Angola Disaster" in the *Petersburg (Va.) Index,* March 7, 1868, p. 2.

11. *Buffalo Express,* Jan. 4, 1868, p. 1.

12. See coverage of the Masthope wreck in the *New York Herald,* July 16, 1869, p. 4.

13. See the story "Frightful Railroad Accident: Slaughter on the Rail" in the *Ohio Democrat*, July 23, 1869, p. 2.

14. For the M. Poinsot murder case discussed in the context of changes to European railway compartment design, see Schivelbusch, *Railway Journey*, 84–86.

15. Ibid.

16. *Buffalo Daily Courier*, Dec. 25, 1867, p. 4.

17. *Frank Leslie's Illustrated Newspaper*, Jan. 11, 1868, p. 269.

18. *Hamilton (Ont.) Evening Times*, Dec. 26, 1867, p. 4.

19. *Philadelphia Inquirer*, Dec. 27, 1867, p. 4.

20. *Frank Leslie's Illustrated Newspaper*, Jan. 11, 1868, p. 269.

21. Ibid.

22. *Buffalo Express*, Dec. 23, 1867, p. 4.

23. Ibid.

24. Ibid.

25. Some newspapers did report that the Buffalo and Erie Railroad had locked the doors of the New York Express while it was in motion. One of these papers was the *Times* of London, Jan. 11, 1868, p. 9.

26. *Philadelphia Inquirer*, Dec. 20, 1867, p. 4.

27. See the news item about this railroad in the *Owatonna (Minn.) Journal*, Jan. 9, 1868, p. 3.

28. *Buffalo Express*, Dec. 24, 1867, p. 4.

29. "The Angola Sacrifice," letter to the editor of the *New York Times*, from "Another Railroad Man of Twenty Years Standing," in the *New York Times*, Dec. 27, 1867, p. 8.

30. *Buffalo Patriot and Journal*, Jan. 1, 1868, p. 1.

31. Ibid.

32. "The Angola Sacrifice," letter to the editor of the *New York Times*, from "Another Railroad Man of Twenty Years Standing," in the *New York Times*, Dec. 27, 1867, p. 8.

33. White, *American Railroad Passenger Car*, part 2, 380.

34. See the lead editorial, "Railroad Accidents—Is There a Remedy?" in *Scientific American*, Jan. 11, 1868, p. 25. The magazine's editors called the development a promising one.

35. See "Burning Cars," an explanation of the Ruttan system by its inventor, in the *American Railroad Journal*, Feb. 8, 1868, p. 145.

36. Taylor, *World on Wheels*, 154.

37. White, *American Railroad Passenger Car*, part 2, 387.

38. *Philadelphia Inquirer*, Dec. 20, 1867, p. 4.

39. See the news item about this railroad's stoves in the *Owatonna (Minn.) Journal*, Jan. 30, 1868, p. 2.

40. "The Modern Altar of Sacrifice—the Devouring Car Stove," *Harper's Weekly*, Feb. 19, 1887, p. 129.

41. "Chief Causes of Railway Accidents," in *Railway Age*, Jan. 27, 1881, p. 44.

42. *Baltimore Sun*, Dec. 24, 1867, p. 1.

43. Ibid.

44. *New York Times*, Dec. 20, 1867, p. 4.

45. Ibid.

46. "Lighting Cars," letter to the editor by "Shawmut," in *Railway Times*, Feb. 1, 1868, p. 39.

47. See the *Semi-Weekly Wisconsin*, Dec. 28, 1867, p. 3.

48. Ibid.

49. *Syracuse State League*, Feb. 22, 1868, p. 4.

50. *Scientific American*, Jan. 18, 1868, p. 38.

51. Ibid.

52. Letter of F. M. Horning of Corry, Pa., to *Scientific American*, Sept. 17, 1870, p. 180.

53. Ibid.

54. Letter of Calvin E. Town of Buffalo to *Scientific American*, Jan. 25, 1868, p. 52.

55. Ibid.

56. Ibid.

57. Letter of W. C. Baker to *Scientific American,* Feb. 22, 1868, p. 116.

58. White, *American Railroad Passenger Car,* part 2, 386–89.

59. *Scientific American,* Feb. 22, 1868, p. 116.

60. See the editorial "Candles for Cars—the Kerosene Scare," in *Scientific American,* March 7, 1868, p. 153. The magazine suggested that railroad companies use kerosene and other oils first tested to be safe at a "commercial fire test" temperature of 110 degrees.

61. *Times* (London), Jan. 11, 1868, p. 9.

62. Ibid.

63. Ibid.

64. *Buffalo Evening Courier and Republic,* Jan. 3, 1868, p. 3.

65. Ellen Hubbard's letter was reprinted in some of the Buffalo newspapers; see the *Buffalo Evening Courier and Republic,* Jan. 8, 1868, p. 3.

66. *Buffalo Evening Courier and Republic,* Jan. 8, 1868, p. 3.

67. *Buffalo Evening Courier and Republic,* Jan. 6, 1868, p. 2.

68. *Times* (London), Jan. 11, 1868, p. 9.

69. *Scientific American,* Jan. 11, 1868, p. 25.

16. CHANGES

1. *Buffalo Express,* Jan. 13, 1868, p. 2.

2. *Forest Lawn: Its History, Dedications, Progress, Regulations, Names of Lot Holders, Etc.* (Buffalo: Thomas, Howard and Johnson, 1867), 16–17.

3. Ibid.

4. *Semi-Weekly Wisconsin,* Jan. 25, 1868, page unavailable.

5. Ibid.

6. Presidential address, "The Conception, Introduction and Development of the Air Brake," given by George Westinghouse Jr. at the annual meeting of the American Society of Mechanical Engineers, New York, Dec. 6, 1910 (New York: American Society of Mechanical Engineers, 1910). Included in Leigh, Westinghouse, Turner, and Vial, *Air Brake Papers 2,* p. 5.

7. Aldrich, *Death Rode the Rails,* 29.

8. Lead editorial, "Railroad Accidents—Is There a Remedy?" *Scientific American,* Jan. 11, 1868, p. 25.

9. *George Westinghouse, 1846–1914* (Wilmerding, Pa.: George Westinghouse Museum Foundation, n.d.), 4.

10. *Schenectady Reflector,* July 18, 1878, p. 4. In the collection of the Grems-Doolittle Library, Schenectady County Historical Society, Schenectady, N.Y.

11. Reminiscence of G. Pantaleoni, who knew Westinghouse for more than thirty years at his various companies. "He really at heart never had his mind off his work," Pantaleoni said. See his reminiscence of the inventor, as collected in *Anecdotes and Reminiscences of George Westinghouse, 1846–1914, Contributed by His Former Associates: A Collateral Project with the "George Westinghouse Commemoration" of the American Society of Mechanical Engineers, December 1936,* by the Westinghouse Air-Brake Co., Westinghouse Electric & Manufacturing Co., and American Society of Mechanical Engineers, collected and edited by Dr. Charles F. Scott (Pittsburgh: Westinghouse Air Brake Co., 1939), 4–5 in Pantaleoni section. In the collection of the Library and Archives Division, Historical Society of Western Pennsylvania, in the Heinz History Center, Pittsburgh.

12. See George Westinghouse Sr. to George Westinghouse Jr., letter of March 8, 1865, in the collection of the Library and Archives Division, Historical Society of Western Pennsylvania, in the Heinz History Center, Pittsburgh.

13. See George Westinghouse Sr. to George Westinghouse Jr., letter of January 12, 1865, in the collection of the Library and Archives Division, Historical Society of Western Pennsylvania, in the Heinz History Center, Pittsburgh.

14. One example of this type of activity can be found in a letter from George Westinghouse Sr. to one of his sons in 1873: "I enclose an item from the *Union* in regard to Tillinghast Supt of R.R.s," the

father wrote. See George Westinghouse Sr. letter of March 9, 1873, in the collection of the Library and Archives Division, Historical Society of Western Pennsylvania, in the Heinz History Center, Pittsburgh.

15. *Schenectady Daily Evening Star and Times,* Dec. 19, 1867, p. 2.

16. "Conception, Introduction and Development of the Air Brake," in Leigh, Westinghouse, Turner, and Vial, *Air Brake Papers 2,* p. 4.

17. Ibid.

18. Ibid.

19. Ibid., 6. For the title and cost of the magazine subscription Westinghouse purchased, see *George Westinghouse, 1846–1914,* 8.

20. "Conception, Introduction and Development of the Air Brake," in Leigh, Westinghouse, Turner, and Vial, *Air Brake Papers 2,* p. 6.

21. Ibid.

22. Aldrich, *Death Rode the Rails,* 29.

23. "Conception, Introduction and Development of the Air Brake," in Leigh, Westinghouse, Turner, and Vial, *Air Brake Papers 2,* p. 6.

24. Ibid., 7.

25. Reminiscence of John Millhiser, first machinist to produce the air brake for Westinghouse's Pittsburgh brake works, as collected in *Anecdotes and Reminiscences of George Westinghouse,* p. 1 in the Millhiser section.

26. Reminiscence of Thomas Campbell, as collected in *Anecdotes and Reminiscences of George Westinghouse,* p. 1 in Campbell section.

27. Prout, *Life of George Westinghouse,* 30–31.

28. "Conception, Introduction and Development of the Air Brake," in Leigh, Westinghouse, Turner, and Vial, *Air Brake Papers 2,* p. 7.

29. Usselman, *Regulating Railroad Innovation,* 131.

30. Westinghouse Air-Brake Co. official catalog for the year 1886, p. 69. In the collection of the Library and Archives Division, Historical Society of Western Pennsylvania, in the Heinz History Center, Pittsburgh.

31. "The Westinghouse Air-Brake," *Railway Times,* July 20, 1872, p. 231.

32. See George Westinghouse Jr. to George Westinghouse Sr., letter on Westinghouse Air-Brake Co. letterhead, dated Sept. 14, 1875, in the collection of the Grems-Doolittle Library, Schenectady County Historical Society, Schenectady, N.Y.

33. *Schenectady Daily Union,* March 9, 1872, page unknown. From the collection of the Grems-Doolittle Library, Schenectady County Historical Society, Schenectady, N.Y.

34. Prout, *Life of George Westinghouse,* 31.

35. Aldrich, *Death Rode the Rails,* 30.

36. "Westinghouse Air-Brake," *Railway Times,* July 20, 1872, p. 231.

37. Frank H. Spearman, "The Wiper's Story: How McGrath Got an Engine," in Spearman, *Held for Orders,* 43.

38. Ibid., 61–62.

39. Ibid., 62.

40. "An Instance of Degeneration," from *Harper's Weekly,* July 15, 1893, in Reinhardt, *Workin' on the Railroad,* 105–6.

41. Ibid., 105.

42. Usselman, *Regulating Railroad Innovation,* 134.

43. Ibid., 133.

44. Company catalog for 1876, Westinghouse Air-Brake Co., Liberty Avenue between 24th and 25th Streets, Pittsburgh, preface, pp. 1, 9. In the collection of the Library and Archives Division, Historical Society of Western Pennsylvania, in the Heinz History Center, Pittsburgh.

45. Reminiscence of H. H. Heinrichs, as collected in *Anecdotes and Reminiscences of George Westinghouse,* p. 2 in Heinrichs section.

46. Catalog for the year 1886, Westinghouse Air-Brake Co., p. 14. In the collection of the Library and Archives Division, Historical Society of Western Pennsylvania, in the Heinz History Center, Pittsburgh.

47. "George Westinghouse Commemoration: A Forum Presenting the Career and Achievements of George Westinghouse on the 90th Anniversary of His Birth," held by the American Society of Mechanical Engineers, Dec. 1, 1936, p. 16. In the collection of the Grems-Doolittle Library, Schenectady County Historical Society, Schenectady, N.Y.

48. Usselman, *Regulating Railroad Innovation,* 277.

49. See editorial "Governor Cornell's Special Message," in the *St. Lawrence Republican* (St. Lawrence County, N.Y.), Jan. 25, 1882, page unknown.

50. Ibid.

51. See "Car-Heating Act," New York State Laws 1887, Chapter 616.

52. Although some railroads did violate the law and continue to use their coal- and wood-fired stoves at times; see lawsuits against certain of these roads, including an 1891 case involving the New York, New Haven and Hartford Railroad, in *People v. Clark et al.,* Court of Oyer and Terminer, New York County, May 1891, in New York Supplement, vol. 14, p. 642.

53. See "Lighting Cars with Kerosene," *American Railroad Journal,* June 27, 1868, p. 605.

54. House of Representatives report, no. 1678, June 27, 1892, "Safety of Railway Employes and the Traveling Public," by the Committee on Interstate and Foreign Commerce, House of Representatives, 52nd Congress, p. 4. From the collection of the National Archives, Washington, D.C.

55. See editorial "Congressional Regulation of Railroads," in the *Dubuque (Iowa) Daily Herald,* June 26, 1868, p. 2.

56. House of Representatives report, no. 1678, June 27, 1892, "Safety of Railway Employes and the Traveling Public," p. 7.

57. Ibid., 1.

58. Ibid., 7.

59. Ibid.

60. Ibid., 7–8.

61. Ibid., 2.

62. See "Letter from California," a letter written by Mrs. Mary Lang Swizer, in Los Angeles, to her mother Christiana Gates Lang, in Ryegate, Vt., April 1882, reprinted in the *St. Johnsbury (Vt.) Caledonian,* June 16, 1882, p. 1.

EPILOGUE

1. For a reference to the explosion of guns carried in the pockets of male passengers at Angola, see the *Titusville (Pa.) Morning Herald,* Dec. 24, 1867, p. 3.

2. Aldrich, *Death Rode the Rails,* 38. Aldrich pinpoints the year in which this change toward more frequent and deadlier American railroad wrecks occurred as 1853.

3. Henry A. White's first-person account of his experiences in the Ashtabula Bridge Disaster of December 29, 1876, can be found in the *Ashtabula (Ohio) News* of Jan. 10, 1877, pp. 1–3.

4. Ibid.

5. Ibid.

6. Ibid.

7. Records of the Buffalo and Erie Railroad, including a note about the money set aside for a monument to the Angola Horror victims, are in the collection of the Penn Central Transportation Co., box 76, in the Bentley Historical Library at the University of Michigan. With permission of the library.

8. *Scientific American,* Jan. 18, 1868, p. 41.

9. Martin and Hirst, *Mark Twain in Buffalo,* 39.

10. Faust, *This Republic of Suffering,* 8.

11. Park Moody, "A Death Song," in *The Ladies' Wreath: An Illustrated Annual* (New York: Martyn & Miller, 1851), 356.

12. Faust, *This Republic of Suffering,* 14.

13. Meacham, *American Lion,* 13.

14. Hawthorne, "Roger Malvin's Burial," 58.

POSTSCRIPT

1. "Spiritualism Examined: Strange Interview with a Medium Controlled by Dr. Smith, Charles Lobdell, and Fanny Wheeler of Mobile," published in the Chicago-based newspaper *Pomeroy's Democrat,* April 5, 1873, p. 4.

2. Ibid.

3. For information on Dr. Romaine J. Curtiss's long-running health problems, see his file in the National Archives and Records Administration, Washington, D.C., Record Group 15, Records of the Bureau of Veteran Affairs, Pension Application Case File (Widow's Certificate #523979).

4. For evidence of Dr. Curtiss's struggle with addictions, see "Aged Joliet Physician and His Woes," *Chicago Tribune,* April 26, 1900, p. 5. For claims about Curtiss's use of substances to "deaden the pain and ease his mind," see the *Joliet (Ill.) Daily Republican,* Nov. 20, 1900, p. 6.

5. *Joliet (Ill.) Daily Republican,* Nov. 20, 1900, p. 6.

6. *Joliet (Ill.) Daily Republican,* Nov. 20, 1900, p. 6.

7. *Ravalli (Mont.) Republican,* July 16, 1915, p. 1.

8. Statistics detailing the extent of the Lake Shore and Michigan Southern Railway Co. operations in 1886 may be found in Leland, "History of the Lake Shore and Michigan Southern Railway," 341.

9. Obituary for Benjamin F. Sherman, *Buffalo Express,* Feb. 21, 1901, p. 7.

Bibliography

NEWSPAPERS AND PERIODICALS

Below is a selected list of some of the newspapers and periodicals used in the preparation of this book. The endnotes to each chapter have bibliographic citations for materials used.

Albany Evening Journal
American Railroad Journal
Angola (N.Y.) Record
Ashtabula (Ohio) News
Baltimore Sun
Batavia (N.Y.) Spirit of the Times
Boston Herald
Buffalo Commercial Advertiser
Buffalo Courier & Republic
Buffalo Daily Courier
Buffalo Evening Courier & Republic
Buffalo Express
Buffalo Patriot and Journal
Buffalo Post
Buffalo Times
Chicago Tribune
Cleveland Herald
Cleveland Plain Dealer
Clyde (N.Y.) Times
Crawford (Pa.) Democrat
Erie (Pa.) Daily Dispatch

Erie (Pa.) Observer
Erie (Pa.) Weekly Observer
Frank Leslie's Illustrated News
Fredonia (N.Y.) Censor
Godey's Lady's Book and Magazine
Hamilton (Ont.) Evening Times
Hamilton (Ont.) Spectator
Harper's Weekly
Ithaca Journal
Jamestown (N.Y.) Journal
Joliet (Ill.) Daily Republican
Kelley's Monthly
La Crosse (Wis.) Democrat
La Crosse (Wis.) Republican
Louisville Daily Journal
Milwaukee Daily News
New Orleans Picayune
New York Daily Tribune
New York Times
Ohio Democrat
Owatonna (Minn.) Journal

Owatonna (Minn.) Register
Philadelphia Inquirer
Pittsfield (Mass.) Sun
Potsdam (N.Y.) Courier & Freeman
Railroad and Engineering Journal
Railway Age
Railway Times
Rochester (N.Y.) Evening Express
Rochester (Minn.) Federal-Union
Rochester (Minn.) Post
Rome (N.Y.) Roman Citizen
Scientific American

Springville (N.Y.) Journal
Syracuse Courier & Union
Syracuse Daily Standard
Syracuse Journal
Syracuse State League
Times (London, U.K.)
Titusville (Pa.) Morning Herald
Utica Morning Herald
Utica Observer
Utica Weekly Herald
Vermont Chronicle

ARCHIVES USED OR VISITED

Below is a selected list of some of the archives, collections, and libraries used in the preparation of this book. The endnotes to each chapter have bibliographic citations for materials used.

Angola Public Library, Angola, N.Y.

Arcade & Attica Railroad, Arcade, N.Y.

Ashtabula County Historical Society and Jennie Munger Gregory Memorial Museum, Geneva-on-the-Lake, Ohio

Buffalo History Museum, Buffalo, N.Y.

Chautauqua County Historical Society, Westfield, N.Y.

City of Tonawanda Historical Society, Tonawanda, N.Y.

Conneaut Railroad Historical Museum, Conneaut, Ohio

Darwin R. Barker Library and Museum, Fredonia, N.Y.

Erie City Cemetery, Erie, Pa.

Erie County Historical Society, Erie, Pa.

Erie County Surrogate's Court, Buffalo, N.Y.

Evans Historical Society and museum, Town of Evans, N.Y.

Fenton History Museum, Jamestown, N.Y.

Forest Lawn cemetery, Buffalo, N.Y.

Grosvenor Rare Books Collection, and general collections, Buffalo and Erie County Public Library, Buffalo, N.Y.

Hanover Historical Center, Silver Creek, N.Y.

Heinz History Center and Historical Society of Western Pennsylvania, Pittsburgh, Pa.

James Prendergast Library, Jamestown, N.Y.

Joliet Area Historical Museum, Joliet, Ill.

Meadville County Court and Surrogate's Court, Meadville, Pa.

Penn Central Transportation Company collection, Bentley Historical Library, University of Michigan, Ann Arbor, Mich.

Railroad Museum of Pennsylvania, Pennsylvania Historical and Museum Commission, Strasburg, Pa.

Rockefeller Archive Center, Sleepy Hollow, N.Y.

Schenectady County Historical Society, Schenectady, N.Y.
State University of New York at Buffalo libraries, Buffalo, N.Y.
Syracuse University Library Special Collections Research Center, Syracuse, N.Y.
Town of Portland Historical Museum, Brocton, N.Y.
Tufts University, Digital Collections and Archives, Medford, Mass.
Union Pacific Railroad Museum and Archive, Council Bluffs, Iowa
University of Iowa, Iowa City, Iowa
U.S. National Archives and Records Administration, Washington, D.C.
Western New York Railway Historical Society, Buffalo, N.Y.
Western Reserve Historical Society, Cleveland, Ohio
Williams College Archives and Special Collections, Williamstown, Mass.

PRIMARY SOURCES

Adams, Charles Francis, Jr. *Railroads: Their Origins and Problems.* New York: G. P. Putnam's Sons, 1878.

Alcott, Louisa May. *Behind a Mask: The Unknown Thrillers of Louisa May Alcott.* Edited and with an introduction by Madeleine Stern. New York: William Morrow, 1975.

Angola's History: 1873–1973. Compiled in commemoration of the centennial of the Village of Angola, N.Y. Angola, N.Y., 1973.

Annual Report of the State Engineer and Surveyor of the State of New York, and of the Tabulations and Deductions from the Reports of the Rail Road Corporations for the Year Ending September 30th, 1868. Albany: Argus Co., 1869.

Anonymous. *The Life, Character, and Career of Edward W. Green, Postmaster of Malden, the Murderer of Frank E. Converse.* Boston: Benjamin B. Russell, 1864.

Ashcroft, John. *Ashcroft's Railway Directory for 1867, Containing an Official List of the Officers and Directors of the Railroads in the United States and Canadas, together with Their Financial Condition and Amount of Rolling Stock.* New York: D. Van Nostrand, 1867.

Bennett, Joseph. *Reminiscences and Diary.* Mss. W-5. Buffalo History Museum Archives, Buffalo.

Bryant, Benjamin F. *Memoirs of La Crosse County from Earliest Historical Times Down to the Present with Special Chapters on Various Subjects, Including Each of the Different Towns, and a Genealogical and Biographical Record of Representative Families in the County, Prepared from Data Obtained from Original Sources of Information.* Madison, Wis.: Western Historical Association, 1907.

"Candles for Cars—the Kerosene Scare." *Scientific American,* March 7, 1868, p. 153.

Chambre, Rev. A. St. John. *In Memoriam of Elam Porter, Esq., of Cincinnati, Ohio, Killed at Angola, New York, December 18th, 1867.* Boston: William Bense, 1868.

Chopin, Kate. *Complete Novels and Stories.* Edited by Sandra M. Gilbert. New York: Library of America, 2002.

Dickens, Charles. "Mugby Junction." In *Our Mutual Friend, with "Mugby Junction" and "George Silverman's Explanation."* Part 2. New York: P. F. Collier & Son, 1911.

Galton, Sir Douglas Stratt. *The Effect of Brakes upon Railway Trains.* Pittsburgh: Westinghouse Air-Brake Co., 1894.

Giacometti, Paolo. *Elizabeth, Queen of England, an Historical Play in Five Acts.* Translated by Thomas Williams. New York: Edward O. Jenkins, 1866.

Godey's Lady's Book, December 1867.

Griffith, Frank Elnathan. *The Griffith Letters: The Story of Frank Griffith and the 116th New York Volunteer Infantry in the Civil War.* Westminster, Md.: Heritage Books, 2004.

Harper's New Monthly Magazine. Vol. 36. December 1867–May 1868. New York: Harper & Brothers, 1868.

Harper's Weekly, January 4, 1868. New York.

Harper's Weekly, January 11, 1868. New York.

Hawthorne, Nathaniel. "The Celestial Rail-road." In *Selected Tales and Sketches.* Introduction by Michael J. Colacurcio. New York: Viking Penguin, 1987.

——."Roger Malvin's Burial." In *Selected Tales and Sketches.* Introduction by Michael J. Colacurcio. New York: Viking Penguin, 1987.

Howells, William Dean. *Their Wedding Journey, with an Additional Chapter on Niagara Revisited.* Boston: Houghton Mifflin, 1913.

Ives, William. *Meteorological Observations at Buffalo: 1851–1854, 1858–1903.* Manuscript. Buffalo, N.Y., unnumbered pages. Month of December 1867. Grosvenor Rare Book Collection of the Buffalo and Erie County Public Library, Buffalo.

Kurtz, Edward T., Sr. *Brocton and Portland.* Charleston, S.C.: Arcadia Publishing, 2007.

Kelley's Weekly, January 11, 1868. New York.

Lake Shore and Michigan Southern Railway Co. *Lake Shore and Michigan Southern Railway System and Representative Employees.* Buffalo: Biographical Publishing Co., 1900.

——. *Rules and Regulations for the Government of the Employes of the Lake Shore and Michigan Southern Railway Company.* Cleveland: J. B. Savage, 1881. In the collection of the Western Reserve Historical Society, Cleveland.

Leigh, Edward B., George Westinghouse, W. V. Turner, and F. K. Vial. *Air Brake Papers 2* [S.l.: s.n.] 1906.

Leland, C[yrus] P. "History of the Lake Shore and Michigan Southern Railway." *Journal of the Association of Engineering Societies* 6, no. 9 (Sept. 1887): 340–53. From a paper delivered to the Civil Engineers' Club of Cleveland, May 10, 1887, now in the collection of the Western Reserve Historical Society, Cleveland.

Lonn, Ella. *Desertion during the Civil War.* New York: Century Co., 1928.

Memoir of John C. Lord, D.D.: Pastor of the Central Presbyterian Church for Thirty-Eight Years. Compiled by Order of the Church Session. Buffalo: Courier Co., 1878.

Morrison, Wayne E., Sr. *Erie County, N.Y.: 1860; History, Statistics, Etc.* Compiled from *The State Gazetteer of 1860,* by J. H. French. Ovid, N.Y.: W. E. Morrison & Co., 1986. A copy of this 1860 volume may be found in the Grosvenor Rare Book Collection of the Buffalo and Erie County Public Library, Buffalo.

Peet, Rev. Stephen D. *The Ashtabula Disaster.* Chicago: J. S. Goodman-Louis Lloyd & Co., 1877.

Peterson's Magazine, 1867. Philadelphia.

Poor, Henry V. *Manual of the Railroads of the United States, for 1868–69, Showing Their Mileage, Stocks, Bonds, Cost, Earnings, Expenses, and Organizations; with a Sketch of Their Rise, Progress and Influence; Etc.* New York: H. V. & H. W. Poor, 1868.

Porter, Horace. "Railway Passenger Travel: 1825–1880." Originally published in *Scribner's* magazine, Sept. 1888. Reprinted by *Americana Review,* 1962.

Ravenstein, E. G. "The Laws of Migration." *Journal of the Statistical Society of London* 48, no. 2 (June 1885): 167–235.

Ristori, Adelaide. *Studies and Memoirs: An Autobiography*. Boston: Roberts Brothers, 1888.

Rockefeller, John D. *Random Reminiscences of Men and Events*. Tarrytown, N.Y.: Sleepy Hollow Press and Rockefeller Archive Center, 1984.

Severance, Frank H., ed. *The Picture Book of Earlier Buffalo*. Buffalo: Buffalo Historical Society, 1912.

Smith, Stephe R. *Romance and Humor of the Road: A Book for Railway Men and Travelers*. Chicago: Horton & Leonard, Railroad Printers, 1871.

Spearman, Frank H. *Held for Orders: Stories of Railroad Life*. New York: McClure, Phillips & Co., 1900.

Tarbell, Ida M. *The History of the Standard Oil Company*. New York: Macmillan Co., 1904.

Taylor, Benjamin F. *The World on Wheels and Other Sketches*. Chicago: S. C. Griggs & Co., 1874.

Thoreau, Henry David. *Walden*. New York: Barnes & Noble, 1993.

U.S. Bureau of the Census. *The Statistical History of the United States from Colonial Times to the Present*. Introduction by Ben J. Wattenberg. New York: Basic Books, 1976.

U.S. Department of Commerce. *Historical Statistics of the United States, 1789–1945: A Supplement to the Statistical Abstract of the United States*. Washington, D.C.: U.S. Department of Commerce, 1949.

Watkins, J. Elfreth. *The Development of the American Rail and Track, as Illustrated by the Collection in the U.S. National Museum*. Report of the National Museum, 1889.

Webb, Thomas Smith. *The Freemason's Monitor; or, Illustrations of Masonry*. Providence: Henry Cushing and Thomas S. Webb, 1805.

Welch, Samuel M. *Home History: Recollections of Buffalo during the Decade from 1830 to 1840, or Fifty Years Since*. Buffalo: Peter Paul & Bro., 1891.

Whitman, Walt. "When Lilacs Last in the Dooryard Bloom'd." In *Leaves of Grass: The 1892 Edition*. Introduction by Justin Kaplan. New York: Bantam Books, 1983.

——. "To a Locomotive in Winter." In *Leaves of Grass: The 1892 Edition*. Introduction by Justin Kaplan. New York: Bantam Books, 1983.

Wilder, Laura Ingalls. *By the Shores of Silver Lake*. 1939. In *Laura Ingalls Wilder: The Little House Books*, vol. 2. Edited by Caroline Fraser. New York: Library of America, 2012.

Wilder, Thornton. *The Bridge of San Luis Rey*. 1927. New York: HarperCollins Perennial Classics, 1986.

SECONDARY SOURCES

Aldrich, Mark. *Death Rode the Rails: American Railroad Accidents and Safety, 1828–1965*. Baltimore: Johns Hopkins University Press, 2006.

Bangsberg, Harry F. "Mark M. Pomeroy: Copperhead Editor—a Study in Transition." Unpublished graduate school paper, State University of Iowa, 1953.

Billings, John S. "An 1893 View of the American Fertility Decline." *Population and Development Review* 2 (June 1976): 279–82.

Blum, Stella, ed. *Victorian Fashions and Costumes from Harper's Bazar, 1867–1898*. New York: Dover Publications, 1974.

Bryson, Bill. *At Home: A Short History of Private Life*. New York: Doubleday, 2010.

Burns, Grant. *The Railroad in American Fiction: An Annotated Bibliography*. Jefferson, N.C.: McFarland & Co., 2005.

Burton, Orville Vernon. *The Age of Lincoln*. New York: Hill & Wang, 2007.

Capfield, Steven. *It Took a Village: The Lynching of Edward Green for the Murder of Frank Converse*. Boston: Capfield's Press, 2007.

Chernow, Ron. *Titan: The Life of John D. Rockefeller, Sr*. New York: Random House, 1998.

Corts, Thomas E., ed. *Bliss and Tragedy: The Ashtabula Railway-Bridge Accident of 1876 and the Loss of P. P. Bliss*. 2003. Reprint, with a new preface, Birmingham, Ala.: Samford University Press, 2008.

Cottrell, W. Fred. *The Railroader*. Dubuque, Iowa: Wm. C. Brown Reprint Library, 1971. First published by Stanford University Press, 1940.

Dalrymple, Priscilla Harris. *American Victorian Costume in Early Photographs*. New York: Dover Publications, 1991.

Daly, Nicholas. "Blood on the Tracks: Sensation Drama, the Railway, and the Dark Face of Modernity." *Victorian Studies* 42, no. 1 (Oct. 1, 1998): 47–76.

——. *Literature, Technology, and Modernity, 1860–2000*. Cambridge: Cambridge University Press, 2004.

——. "Railway Novels: Sensation Fiction and the Modernization of the Senses." *ELH* 66, no. 2 (1999): 461–87.

Dando-Collins, Stephen. *Tycoon's War: How Cornelius Vanderbilt Invaded a Country to Overthrow America's Most Famous Military Adventurer*. New York: Da Capo, 2008.

DeHaan, John D. *Kirk's Fire Investigation*. 5th ed. Englewood Cliffs, N.J.: Prentice Hall, 2002.

Delano, Cheryl. *Evans and Angola*. Charleston, S.C.: Arcadia Publishing, 2009.

Dickens, Laurie C. *Wreck on the Wabash: The 1901 Railroad Disaster in Lenawee County, Michigan*. Blissfield, Mich.: Made for Ewe Press, 2001.

Donovan, Frank P., Jr. *The Railroad in Literature: A Brief Survey of Railroad Fiction, Poetry, Songs, Biography, Essays, Travel and Drama in the English Language, Particularly Emphasizing Its Place in American Literature*. Boston: Railway & Locomotive Historical Society, 1940.

Dunn, Rev. Edward T., S.J. *A History of Railroads in Western New York*. Buffalo: Heritage Press, 1996.

Edson, William D. *Railroad Names: A Directory of Common Carrier Railroads Operating in the United States, 1826–1982*. Potomac, Md.: Compiled and published by William D. Edson, 1984.

Faust, Drew Gilpin. *This Republic of Suffering: Death and the American Civil War*. New York: Alfred A. Knopf, 2008.

Freeman, Michael. *Railways and the Victorian Imagination*. New Haven, Conn.: Yale University Press, 1999.

Frey, Robert L., ed. *Railroads in the Nineteenth Century*. Encyclopedia of American Business History and Biography. New York: Bruccoli Clark Layman and Facts on File, 1988.

Gerber, David A. *The Making of an American Pluralism: Buffalo, New York, 1825–1860*. Urbana: University of Illinois Press, 1989.

Goodman, Edward C., ed. *Writing the Rails*. New York: Black Dog & Leventhal, 2001.

Gordon, Sarah H. *Passage to Union: How the Railroads Transformed American Life, 1829–1929.* Chicago: Ivan R. Dee, 1996.

Goulder, Grace. *John D. Rockefeller: The Cleveland Years.* Cleveland: Western Reserve Historical Society, 1972.

Griswold, Wesley S. *Train Wreck!* Brattleboro, Vt.: Stephen Greene Press, 1969.

Hacker, J. David, "A Census-Based Count of the Civil War Dead," *Civil War History* 57, no. 4 (2011): 311.

Haine, Edgar A. *Railroad Wrecks.* New York: Cornwall Books, 1994.

Harris, Kristina, ed. *Victorian Fashion in America.* Mineola, N.Y.: Dover Publications, 2002.

Harter, Jim. *American Railroads of the Nineteenth Century: A Pictorial History in Victorian Wood Engravings.* Lubbock: Texas Tech University Press, 1998.

Hawke, David Freeman. *John D.: The Founding Father of the Rockefellers.* New York: Harper & Row, 1980.

Heaton, Ronald E. *Masonic Membership of the Founding Fathers.* Washington, D.C.: Masonic Service Association, 1965.

Horrocks, Christopher. *George Westinghouse, the Man.* Wilmerding, Pa.: Westinghouse Veteran Employees' Association, 1914.

Hubbard, Freeman H. *Encyclopedia of North American Railroading: 150 Years of Railroading in the United States and Canada.* New York: McGraw-Hill, 1981.

——. *Railroad Avenue: Great Stories and Legends of American Railroading.* New York: McGraw-Hill, 1945.

Hurst, Jack. *Nathan Bedford Forrest: A Biography.* New York: Vintage Books / Random House, 1994.

Husband, Joseph. *The Story of the Pullman Car.* New York: Arno Press, 1972.

Jacob, Margaret C. *The Origins of Freemasonry: Facts and Fictions.* Philadelphia: University of Pennsylvania Press, 2006.

Keith, Jeanette. *Fever Season: The Story of a Terrifying Epidemic and the People Who Saved a City.* New York: Bloomsbury Press, 2012.

Kent, Donald H. "The Erie War of the Gauges," *Pennsylvania History* 15, no. 4 (October 1948): 253–75. This originated as a paper read before the annual meeting of the Pennsylvania Historical Association in 1947.

Kern, Stephen. *The Culture of Time and Space, 1880–1918.* Cambridge, Mass.: Harvard University Press, 1983, 2003.

Kirby, Lynne. *Parallel Tracks: The Railroad and Silent Cinema.* Durham, N.C.: Duke University Press, 1997.

Klein, Herbert S. *A Population History of the United States.* New York: Cambridge University Press, 2004.

Leupp, Francis Ellington. *George Westinghouse: His Life and Achievements.* London: John Murray, 1919.

Licht, Walter. *Working for the Railroad: The Organization of Work in the Nineteenth Century.* Princeton, N.J.: Princeton University Press, 1983.

Maddox, Kenneth W. "The Railroad in the Eastern Landscape: 1850–1900." In *The Railroad in the American Landscape, 1850–1950.* Wellesley, Mass.: Wellesley College Museum, 1981.

Martin, Albro. *Railroads Triumphant: The Growth, Rejection, and Rebirth of a Vital American Force.* New York: Oxford University Press, 1992.

Martin, Patrick E., and Robert Hirst. *Mark Twain in Buffalo,* William S. Hein & Co., 2010.

Marx, Leo. *The Machine in the Garden: Technology and the Pastoral Ideal in America.* New York: Oxford University Press, 1964.

——. "The Railroad in the American Landscape." Introduction to *The Railroad in the American Landscape, 1850–1950.* Wellesley, Mass.: Wellesley College Museum, 1981.

Mencken, August. *The Railroad Passenger Car: An Illustrated History of the First Hundred Years with Accounts by Contemporary Passengers.* Baltimore: Johns Hopkins University Press, 1957.

O'Malley, Michael. *Keeping Watch: A History of American Time.* New York: Viking, 1990.

Pfeiffer, David A., comp. *Records Relating to North American Railroads: Reference Information Paper No. 91.* Washington, D.C.: National Archives and Records Administration, 2004.

Prout, Henry G. *A Life of George Westinghouse.* New York: American Society of Mechanical Engineers, 1921.

Reed, Robert C. *Train Wrecks: A Pictorial History of Accidents on the Main Line.* New York: Bonanza Books, 1968.

Reinhardt, Richard, ed. *Workin' on the Railroad: Reminiscences from the Age of Steam.* Palo Alto, Calif.: American West Publishing Co., 1970.

Reis, Ed. "A Man for His People." *Mechanical Engineering* 130 (October 2008): 32–35.

Renehan, Edward J., Jr. *Commodore: The Life of Cornelius Vanderbilt.* New York: Basic Books, 2007.

Richardson, Reed C. *The Locomotive Engineer: 1863–1963.* Ann Arbor: University of Michigan Bureau of Industrial Relations, 1963.

Richter, Amy G. *Home on the Rails: Women, the Railroad, and the Rise of Public Domesticity.* Chapel Hill: University of North Carolina Press, 2005.

Ritzau, Hans Joachim. *Schatten der Eisenbahngeschichete: Ein Vergleich britischer, US- und deutscher Bahnen.* Pürgen: Ritzau, Verlag Zeit und Eisenbahn, 1987.

Schantz, Mark S. *Awaiting the Heavenly Country: The Civil War and America's Culture of Death.* Ithaca, N.Y.: Cornell University Press, 2008.

Schapiro, Morton Owen. *Filling Up America: An Economic-Demographic Model of Population Growth and Distribution in the Nineteenth-Century United States.* Greenwich, Conn.: Jai Press, 1986.

Schivelbusch, Wolfgang. *The Culture of Defeat: On National Trauma, Mourning, and Recovery.* New York: Metropolitan Books, 2003. (English translation; first published in German, 2001.)

——. *The Railway Journey: Trains and Travel in the 19th Century.* 1977. Translation from the German by Anselm Hollo. New York: Urizen Books, 1979.

Severa, Joan L. *Dressed for the Photographer: Ordinary Americans and Fashion, 1840–1900.* Kent, Ohio: Kent State University Press, 1995.

Shaw, Robert B. *Down Brakes: A History of Railroad Accidents, Safety Precautions and Operating Practices in the United States of America.* London: P. R. Macmillan, 1961.

Simmons, Jack. *The Victorian Railway.* London: Thames & Hudson, 1991.

Steadman, Jennifer Bernhardt. *Traveling Economies: American Women's Travel Writing.* Columbus: Ohio State University Press, 2007.

Stiles, T. J. *The First Tycoon: The Epic Life of Cornelius Vanderbilt.* New York: Alfred A. Knopf, 2009.

Stout, Harry S. *Upon the Altar of the Nation: A Moral History of the Civil War.* New York: Viking, 2006.

Stover, John F. *American Railroads.* 2nd ed. Chicago: University of Chicago Press, 1997.

——. *The Life and Decline of the American Railroad.* New York: Oxford University Press, 1970.

——. *The Routledge Historical Atlas of the American Railroads.* New York: Routledge, 1999.

Tabbert, Mark A. *American Freemasons: Three Centuries of Building Communities.* New York: NYU Press, 2005.

Taeuber, Conrad, and Irene B. Taeuber. *The Changing Population of the United States.* New York: John Wiley & Sons, 1958.

Taylor, George Rogers. *The Transportation Revolution: 1815–1860.* New York: Rinehart and Co., 1951.

Tennesseans in the Civil War: A Military History of Confederate and Union Units with Available Rosters of Personnel, in Two Parts. Part 2. Nashville, Tenn.: Civil War Centennial Commission, 1965.

Thompson, Warren S., and P. K. Whelpton. *Population Trends in the United States.* New York: McGraw-Hill, 1933.

Usselman, Steven W. *Regulating Railroad Innovation: Business, Technology, and Politics in America, 1840–1920.* New York: Cambridge University Press, 2002.

Vinovskis, Maris A., ed. *Studies in American Historical Demography.* New York: Academic Press, 1979.

Vogel, Michael N. *Echoes in the Mist: An Illustrated History of the Niagara Falls Area.* Chatsworth, Calif.: Windsor Publications, 1991.

Vogel, Michael N., Edward J. Patton, and Paul F. Redding. *America's Crossroads: Buffalo's Canal Street / Dante Place, the Making of a City.* Buffalo: Western New York Heritage Press, 1993. Reprint, Derby, N.Y.: Acorn Books, 2009.

Volo, Dorothy Denneen, and James M. Volo. *Daily Life in Civil War America.* Westport, Conn.: Greenwood Press, 1998.

Walther, Susan Danly, curator. *The Railroad in the American Landscape: 1850–1950.* Catalog of exhibition at the Wellesley College Museum, 1981. Meriden, Conn.: Meriden Gravure Co., 1981.

——. "The Railroad in the Industrial Landscape: 1900–1950." In *The Railroad in the American Landscape, 1850–1950.* Wellesley, Mass.: Wellesley College Museum, 1981.

——. "The Railroad in the Western Landscape: 1865–1900." In *The Railroad in the American Landscape, 1850–1950.* Wellesley, Mass.: Wellesley College Museum, 1981.

Ward, James A. *Railroads and the Character of America, 1820–1887.* Knoxville: University of Tennessee Press, 1986.

Wells, Robert V. *Revolutions in Americans' Lives: A Demographic Perspective on the History of Americans, Their Families, and Their Society.* Westport, Conn.: Greenwood Press, 1982.

White, John H. *The American Railroad Passenger Car.* Parts 1 and 2. Baltimore: Johns Hopkins University Press, 1978.

White, Paul, and Robert Woods, eds. *The Geographical Impact of Migration.* New York: Longman, 1980.

Witt, John Fabian. *The Accidental Republic: Crippled Workingmen, Destitute Widows, and the Remaking of American Law.* Cambridge, Mass.: Harvard University Press, 2004.

Index

Page numbers in *italics* indicate figures.